B.R. Ambedkar
The Quest for Justice

Editorial Advisory Board

Anand Teltumbde
Annapurna Waughray
G. Haragopal
Kalpana Kannabiran
Laurence R. Simon
Meena Dhanda
Moses Seenarine
Rochana Bajpai
S. Japhet
Sukhadeo Thorat
Suraj Yengde
Valerian Rodrigues

B.R. Ambedkar
The Quest for Justice

VOLUME I
Political Justice

Edited by
Aakash Singh Rathore

Oxford University Press is a department of the University of Oxford.
It furthers the University's objective of excellence in research, scholarship,
and education by publishing worldwide. Oxford is a registered trademark of
Oxford University Press in the UK and in certain other countries.

Published in India by
Oxford University Press
22 Workspace, 2nd Floor, 1/22 Asaf Ali Road, New Delhi 110 002, India

© Oxford University Press 2021

The moral rights of the authors have been asserted.

First Edition published in 2021

All rights reserved. No part of this publication may be reproduced, stored in
a retrieval system, or transmitted, in any form or by any means, without the
prior permission in writing of Oxford University Press, or as expressly permitted
by law, by licence, or under terms agreed with the appropriate reprographics
rights organization. Enquiries concerning reproduction outside the scope of the
above should be sent to the Rights Department, Oxford University Press, at the
address above.

You must not circulate this work in any other form
and you must impose this same condition on any acquirer.

ISBN-13 (print edition): 978-0-19-012682-7
ISBN-10 (print edition): 0-19-012682-5

ISBN-13 (eBook): 978-0-19-099188-3
ISBN-10 (eBook): 0-19-099188-7

Typeset in Trump Mediaeval LT Std 10/13
by Tranistics Data Technologies, Kolkata 700 091
Printed in India by Rakmo Press, New Delhi 110 020

Contents

Foreword by Shashi Tharoor	vii
Preface by S. Japhet	xiii
List of Abbreviations	xxi
Introduction by Aakash Singh Rathore	xxiii

1. The Intellectual and Political Legacy of B.R. Ambedkar — 1
   BHIKHU PAREKH

2. B.R. Ambedkar and Antonio Gramsci: Justice for the Excluded, Education for Democracy — 31
   COSIMO ZENE

3. Ambedkar and Democracy: Critical Reflections — 76
   ANAND TELTUMBDE

4. Repairing Complex Historical Injustice — 109
   NEERA CHANDHOKE

5. Dr Ambedkar and the Trio of Principles: Liberty, Equality, and Fraternity — 131
   PRADEEP GOKHALE

6. Discrimination, Colonial Injustice, and the Good Society — 148
   VIDHU VERMA

7. Communication, Justice, and Reconstruction: Ambedkar as an Indian Pragmatist — 175
   SCOTT STROUD

8. Of Castes and Crowds: B.R. Ambedkar's Anti-colonial
   Endosmosis 196
   J. DANIEL ELAM

9. A Constellation of Ideas: Revisiting Ambedkar and Gandhi 219
   PUSHPARAJ DESHPANDE

10. Self-Respect as a Primary Political Ideal: Ambedkar's
    Challenge to Political Theory 243
    SHAUNNA RODRIGUES

Index 270

Editor and Contributors 281

Foreword

It is difficult today to imagine the scale of what Dr Babasaheb Bhimji Rao Ambedkar accomplished. To be born into an 'untouchable' family in 1891, and that too as the fourteenth and last child of a poor Mahar subedar in an Army cantonment, would normally have guaranteed a life of neglect, poverty, and discrimination. Not only did Ambedkar rise above the circumstances of his birth, he achieved a level of success that would have been spectacular even for a child of privilege. One of the first untouchables ever to enter an Indian college, he became a professor (at the prestigious Sydenham College, Mumbai, India) and a principal (of no less an institution than Mumbai's Government Law College, India). One of the earliest Indian students in USA, he earned multiple doctorates in economics, politics, and law from Columbia University, USA, and the University of London, UK. An heir to millennia of discrimination, he was admitted to the bar in London and became 'India's James Madison' as the chair of the Drafting Committee of the Constitution. Born to illiterate parents, he wrote a remarkable number of books, whose content and range testify to an eclectic mind and a sharp, if provocative, intellect. An insignificant infant scrabbling in the dust of Mhow (now Dr. Ambedkar Nagar) in 1891 became the first law minister of a free India, in the most impressive cabinet ever assembled in New Delhi. When he died, aged only 65, he had accumulated a set of distinctions few have matched since—only one remained. In belated recognition of that omission, he was conferred posthumously in 1990 the highest award his country has to offer—the Bharat Ratna.

Dr Ambedkar was a 'self-made man' in the profoundest sense of the term. Even his name was his own creation, for he was born a Sakpal, but decided to take a name based on his village (Ambavade), as Maharashtrian Brahmins did. (And he married a Brahmin.) He was born a Hindu Mahar, but died a Buddhist, converting with hundreds of thousands of his followers at a public ceremony months before his death. He wore Western suits in rejection of the traditional trappings of a society that had for so long enslaved his people, and raged against the injustice of social discrimination. The mealy mouthed platitudes of the well-meaning were not for him: He was prepared to call a spade a bloody shovel, and do so in print. It was an attitude that Indian society was not prepared for, but at a time when Indians were fighting for their freedom from foreign rule, it was both appropriate and necessary that Indians should fight equally against domestic oppression.

Dr Ambedkar rejected what he saw as the patronizing indulgence of the Gandhian approach to untouchability. The Mahatma called them 'Harijans': children of God. Arrant nonsense, said Ambedkar—are we all not children of God? He used, instead, Marathi and Hindi words for the 'excluded' (*Bahishkrit*), the 'oppressed' (*Dalit*), and the 'silent'. He publicly burned the Manusmriti, the ancient lawbook of the caste Hindus. He was an equal-opportunity offender, condemning caste consciousness in the Muslim community with as much vehemence as he savaged the Hindus. Dr Ambedkar was an enemy of cant and superstition, an iconoclast who had contempt for traditions that he felt deserved no sanctity.

It was not easy. As a nationalist, he was sensitive to the charge that he was dividing Indians at a time when they needed to be united against the British. When he demanded separate electorates for his people, Mahatma Gandhi undertook a fast unto death until an unconvinced Ambedkar, fearing mass reprisals if the Mahatma died, caved in. Gandhi, who abhorred untouchability, believed that the answer lay in the social awakening of caste Hindus rather than in building walls of separation. Ambedkar, who lived with the daily reality of caste discrimination, was not convinced that the entrenched practices of traditional Hinduism could ever disappear. In the end, he opted out of the religion altogether, embracing the ethics of equality that Buddhism embodied.

Buddhism also inspired his faith in democracy, which infused his role as the father of the Indian Constitution. Whereas some saw Ambedkar, with his three-piece suit and formal English, as a Westernized exponent of occidental constitutional systems, he was inspired far more by the democratic practices of ancient India, in particular the Buddhist sanghas.

Dr Ambedkar saw in the institutions of Indian democracy that he was helping to create the best guarantee for the future development and welfare of his own people, the oppressed and marginalized of India. He fought hard to introduce into the Constitution fundamental protections and guarantees of civil liberties for individual citizens. Ambedkar also convinced the Constituent Assembly that it was not enough to abolish untouchability: What was needed to undo millennia of discrimination and exploitation was a system of affirmative action to uplift the oppressed, including reservations of jobs in the civil services, schools, and universities.

One of the aims of the Indian Constitution is to secure justice for all its citizens. The Preamble identifies three essential components of justice—social, economic, and political. The three are interrelated; they are of the same fundamental substance, but manifest themselves in different distinct forms without a prescribed hierarchy. One may view this as a constitutional trinity. Otto Kirchheimer, the jurist and advocate of the philosophical tradition of the Frankfurt School, Germany, saw 'political justice' as obtaining political power through the use of legal institutions. However, the Indian constitutional understanding of political justice is much wider in scope, as it is the embodiment of principles regarding the rights of the people, especially in relation to a democratic form of government and participation in political affairs.[1]

Dr Ambedkar, as one of the principal makers of modern India and one of the leading icons for the oppressed and impoverished sections of society, played a seminal role in the development of political justice through his emphasis on constitutional ethos and rights in his role as an advocate for liberties and freedom during the British Raj, and later in his position as chairman of the Drafting Committee of the Constitution. Dr Ambedkar is one of the few Indian leaders who participated in all the deliberations

---

[1] *Raghunathrao Ganpatrao and Ors* vs *Union of India*, 1993 AIR 1267.

to provide a constitutional framework for India, right from the Southborough Committee till the Cabinet Mission Plan. In 1928, when many countries were still unsure of granting universal adult franchise, Dr Ambedkar made a strong case in favour of it before the Simon Commission. For him, the right to vote was fundamental to all citizens, not merely to the landed and educated classes. He stressed the importance of allowing impoverished sections of society to participate in political affairs in order for them to use political power for social empowerment. He furthered this principle with the incorporation of reservations for the Scheduled Castes (SCs) and Scheduled Tribes (STs) in the legislature and public services and in the Constitution of India, thereby providing them an opportunity to break from the shackles of centuries of exploitation.

Dr Ambedkar shared the profound conviction that political democracy cannot exist in the absence of a social democracy. He viewed social democracy as 'a way of life which recognizes liberty, equality and fraternity as the principles of life. These principles of liberty, equality and fraternity are not to be treated as separate items in a trinity. They form a union of trinity in the sense that to divorce one from the other is to defeat the very purpose of democracy.'[2] Therefore, the development of a social democracy is a sine qua non for the realization of the constitutional trinity, and especially for political justice.

In his address to the Constituent Assembly on 4 November 1948, he advocated the need to diffuse 'constitutional morality', a term which has been made fashionable of late by our Supreme Court. The term 'constitutional morality' was defined by Grote, the Greek historian, as

> a paramount reverence for the forms of the constitution, enforcing obedience to authority and acting under and within these forms, yet combined with the habit of open speech, of action subject only to definite legal control, and unrestrained censure of those very authorities as to all their public acts combined, too, with a perfect confidence in the bosom of every citizen amidst the bitterness of party contest that the forms of the constitution will not be less sacred in the eyes of his opponents than his own.[3]

---

[2] Constituent Assembly Debates, Vol. XI, 25 November 1949.
[3] Constituent Assembly Debates, Vol. VII, 4 November 1948.

According to Dr Ambedkar, constitutional morality can only be realized through an administration that is in sync with the spirit of the Constitution and through the cultivation of constitutional values among the masses, by defeating the forces of feudalism, casteism, bigotry, and parochialism. By adhering to constitutional authorities, revolutionary and extra-judicial methods need to be discarded, as they represent the 'grammar of anarchy' in the eyes of Dr Ambedkar. In order to further the goals of the Constitution, India requires strong and credible institutions to maintain checks and balances, not power centralized around one figure. The strengthening of institutions is essential to prevent the creation of an authoritative regime, one which feeds off Bhakti or hero-worship, which Dr Ambedkar strongly warned against in his last address to the Constituent Assembly. In an age of growing centralization of power, it is important to revisit Dr Ambedkar's advice.

One of the most powerful institutions created by the Constitution is the judiciary. Constitutional morality has been invoked by the judiciary to strike down laws that violate fundamental rights, such as the criminalization of same-sex relations through Section 377 of the IPC or laws that treat women as the chattel of men. The judiciary plays an important role in furthering political justice through the cultivation of constitutional morality and by acting as a vanguard of fundamental rights. Dr Ambedkar and other framers of the Constitution provided the stewardship for the creation of a robust fundamental rights chapter in Part III of the Constitution. One of the most important features of the fundamental rights chapter in the Constitution of India is Article 32, which allows any citizen to approach the Supreme Court of India to enforce his or her right. This was described by Ambedkar as the heart and soul of the Constitution, and has gone a long way in holding the instrumentalities of the State accountable and in remedying gross violations of fundamental rights.

Dr Ambedkar had warned us of the consequences of allowing forces that do not believe in the ideals of the Constitution forming the administration. He said that irrespective of the positive features of the Constitution, it may turn out to be ineffective if the people entrusted to enforce it are those who do not believe in it. In an atmosphere of growing contempt towards cherished values and foundational principles of the Constitution, such as secularism, freedom of expression, equality, and so on, Dr Ambedkar's writings and body of thought are extremely relevant to our times. We all have a fundamental duty to uphold the constitutional ethos of our country, which Dr Ambedkar tirelessly struggled for.

I commend the scholars and academics for this useful study on the works and ideology of Dr Ambedkar and his quest for justice. I hope this collection of essays will encourage others to engage with Ambedkar's ideas and fight for the principles he stood for.

As a political leader, Dr Ambedkar was better at articulating powerful ideas than in creating the structures to see them through. However, the Constitution of which he was the principal author remains the best instrument for pursuing his ideas. The leader and spokesman of a community left his greatest gift to all communities—a legacy that belongs to all of us, and one of which we are yet to prove ourselves wholly worthy.

Shashi Tharoor
Member of Parliament, Lok Sabha,
Thiruvananthapuram, Kerala, India

Preface

This book forms part of a five-volume publication entitled *B.R. Ambedkar: The Quest for Justice,* an ambitious project that originated during the B.R. Ambedkar International Conference, 'Quest for Equity', held at Bengaluru, India, in July 2017, with some 350 speakers and thousands of participants. That conference took place keeping in view that the values of social, political, and economic justice that were so vigorously championed by Dr Ambedkar are now under attack at several levels: constitutional norms and public institutions created to fight against dominance and subservience have proved inadequate or have been subverted; norms and policy often merely pay lip service to egalitarian considerations; and the rise of social intolerance and exclusion tends to effectively whittle down and even sabotage an inclusive conception of polity and citizenship. The complexity of the social, political, and economic environment in which the value of social justice has to be envisaged too has undergone significant changes: we understand social inequality and diversity to be layered and multidimensional; and the State has to reckon with several competing centres of religious, communal, and cultural allegiances. Despite these serious challenges, new sites for social and political assertions have re-emerged, renewing the call for justice. These five volumes are very much part of that engagement.

Social activism in India today is inspired by Dr B.R. Ambedkar's insightful lifework analysing complex social and political challenges and proposing daring and radical policy measures in response. His approach to critical intellectual and policy challenges may inspire similar interventions elsewhere in the world, particularly throughout the Global South. Thus, in the light of the conference, this five-volume collection emerged as an invitation to scholars and policymakers to substantially rethink current political, social, legal, economic, gender, racial, religious, and cultural paradigms motivated by Dr B.R. Ambedkar's imaginative and creative work.

The project has succeeded in encouraging a wide interdisciplinary engagement among academics, scholars, activists, and policymakers on each of these themes, which are treated across the five volumes. This is apparent from a review of their tables of contents:

B.R. Ambedkar: The Quest for Justice
(in five volumes)
Volume I: *Political Justice*

1. Bhikhu Parekh *The Intellectual and Political Legacy of B.R. Ambedkar*
2. Cosimo Zene *B.R. Ambedkar and Antonio Gramsci: Justice for the Excluded, Education for Democracy*
3. Anand Teltumbde *Ambedkar and Democracy: Critical Reflections*
4. Neera Chandhoke *Repairing Complex Historical Injustice*
5. Pradeep Gokhale *Dr Ambedkar and the Trio of Principles: Liberty, Equality, and Fraternity*
6. Vidhu Verma *Discrimination, Colonial Injustice, and the Good Society*
7. Scott Stroud *Communication, Justice, and Reconstruction: Ambedkar as an Indian Pragmatist*
8. J. Daniel Elam *Of Castes and Crowds: B.R. Ambedkar's Anti-colonial Endosmosis*
9. Pushparaj Deshpande *A Constellation of Ideas: Revisiting Ambedkar and Gandhi*
10. Shaunna Rodrigues *Self-Respect as a Primary Political Ideal: Ambedkar's Challenge to Political Theory*

Volume II: *Social Justice*

1. Martin Fuchs *Ambedkar's Theory of the Social: The Universal Condition of Recognition*
2. James Manor *B.R. Ambedkar: Visionary and Realist*
3. G.C. Pal *Caste and Delivery of Social Justice: Revisiting Ambedkar*
4. Meena Dhanda *'Made to Think and Forced to Feel': The Power of Counter-Ritual*
5. David N. Gellner, Krishna P. Adhikari, and Arjun Bahadur B.K. *Dalits in Search of Inclusion: Comparing Nepal with India*
6. Navyug Gill *Ambedkar, Labour, and the Political Economy of Dalit Conversion in Colonial Panjab*
7. Shailaja Menon *The Fractured Society of the Republic*
8. Karen Gabriel and Prem Kumar Vijayan *Whose State Is It Anyway? Reservation, Representation, Caste, and Power*
9. Jagannatham Begari *Reclaiming Social Justice and Deepening Democracy*
10. Suraj Yengde *Ambedkar's Internationalization of Social Justice*
11. Karthik Raja Karuppusamy *Foregrounding Social Justice in Indian Historiography: Interrogating the Poona Pact*
12. Ajay Verma *Ambedkar and the Metaphysics of Social Justice*

Volume III: *Legal and Economic Justice*

Part One: *Legal Justice*

1. Upendra Baxi *Lawless Law, Living Death, and the Insurgent Moral Reason of Babasaheb Ambedkar*
2. R. Sudarshan *B.R. Ambedkar's Exemplary Adherence to Constitutional Morality*
3. Arvind Narrain *Radical Constitutionalism: Towards an Ambedkarite Jurisprudence*
4. Antje Linkenbach *B.R. Ambedkar's Imaginations of Justice*
5. Umakant *The Significance of Rights and Rule of Law under the Indian Constitutional Framework*
6. Anupama Rao *B.R. Ambedkar and Indian Democracy*

Part Two: Economic Justice

7. Vijay Gudavarthy *Development through Informalization and Circulation of Labour: The Emerging Anatomy of an Uncivil Society*
8. Joseph Tharamangalam *India's Paradox of 'Hunger Amidst Plenty' Has a Name: Caste-Based Discrimination and Exclusion*
9. Aseem Prakash *Dalits Enter the Indian Markets as Owners of Capital: Adverse Inclusion, Social Networks, and Civil Society*
10. Pritam Singh *Ambedkar's Economic Methodology for Social Justice: The Centrality of Dalits*
11. Jawed Alam Khan *Economic Justice: Policy and Public Investment for Pasmanda Muslims*

Volume IV: *Gender and Racial Justice*

Part One: Gender Justice

1. Sanghmitra S. Acharya *Double Disadvantage of Sanitation Workers and Government Responses*
2. Mushtaq Ahmad Malla *The Shame of India: Stigma and Shame among Dalit Women in Rural Agricultural Relations*
3. Rajesh Raushan *Gender Equality and Women's Empowerment: Ambedkar in Contemporary Context*
4. Sunaina Arya *Ambedkar as a Feminist Philosopher*
5. Mala Mukherjee *Ambedkar on Women's Empowerment and the Status of Dalit Women in Karnataka*
6. Komal Rajak and N. Sukumar *Constructing a New Female Subjectivity: Ambedkar's Perspective*

Part Two: Racial Justice

7. Moses Seenarine *Organic Resistance: The Relevance of Ambedkar, Du Bois, and Garvey to Diaspora, Caste, Race, and Women's Liberation*
8. Goolam Vahed and Ashwin Desai *Racelessness and Ambedkar's Idea of Annihilation: Post-apartheid South Africa*

9. Kevin Brown and Lalit Khandare *Common Struggles? Why There Has Not Been More Cooperation between African-Americans and Dalits*
10. Goolam Vahed *Can Ambedkar Speak to Africa? Colour, Caste, and Class Struggles in Contemporary South Africa*

Volume V: *Religious and Cultural Justice*

Part One: *Religious Justice*

1. Laurence R. Simon *Searching for a Theology of Liberation in India*
2. Kanchana Mahadevan *Ambedkar's Critical Hermeneutics of Religion*
3. Debora Spini *Civil Religion, Uncivil Society: A Reflection on Baba Sahib Dr B.R. Ambedkar's Conception of a 'Religion for Civil Society'*
4. Priyanka Jha *The Gaze on Justice: A Genealogy from Anagarika Dharmapala to B.R. Ambedkar*
5. Bansidhar Deep *B.R. Ambedkar's Philosophy of Religion*
6. Matthew H. Baxter *Two Concepts of Conversion at Meenakshipuram: Seeing through Ambedkar's Buddhism and Being Seen in EVR's Islam*

Part Two: *Cultural Justice*

7. Pramod K. Nayar *Marginality, Suffering, Justice: Questions of Dalit Dignity in Cultural Texts*
8. Y. Srinivasa Rao *Asura: Myth into Cultural Reality*
9. John Clammer *Cultural Rights in the Context of Ambedkarite Social Justice*
10. Raju Sakthivel *Education in a Hierarchical Culture*
11. Jadumani Mahanand *Ambedkar in/and Academic Space*

Despite the wide range of themes spread across these five volumes, the collection as a whole is oriented towards articulable specific aims and objectives. These aims and objectives are inspired by and fully consistent with the life and legacy of Dr Ambedkar, a man who was, on the one hand, a scholar of indubitable genius, and on the other hand, a dynamic agent of social and political action.

1. *B.R. Ambedkar: The Quest for Justice* seeks to explore the multifaceted idea of justice in dialogue with Ambedkar's *opus* for a society that encompasses manifold social inequalities, deep diversities, exclusion, and marginality.
2. In dialogue with Ambedkar's writings, the contributions to the collection aim in an overall way to suggest constitutional, institutional, and policy responses to the concerns of justice, and to reformulate the conceptual and policy linkages between social justice and other related norms and concerns.
3. Through high-level scholarship, this collection aims to help identify modes of thought and agency and social and political practices inimical to the pursuit of justice, and to delineate social and political agency and modes of action conducive to the furtherance of justice in line with Dr Ambedkar's own writings and mission.

Thus, in sum, Dr Ambedkar's conception of justice and his life's work shaping the idea of India offer this collection the vantage points for sustained reflection on concerns of justice and its relation to other human values. This is particularly relevant, indeed urgent, in our day, not only in India but also throughout the world.

As convener of the organizing committee of the Dr B.R. Ambedkar International Conference, 'Quest for Equity', held at Bengaluru, India, in July 2017, where many of the chapters included in this volume were originally presented, I would like to gratefully acknowledge the people and institutions that made the conference a success and helped to make these volumes possible.

First and foremost, I must acknowledge the Government of Karnataka with Chief Minister Siddaramaiah at the helm, which hosted and funded the conference. Many put in extraordinary time and effort: Dr H.C. Mahadevappa, convenor and hon'ble minister for Public Works Department (PWD); H. Anjaneya, hon'ble minister for Social Welfare Department; Dr G. Parameshwara, hon'ble minister for home affairs; Shri T.B. Jayachandra, hon'ble minister for law and minor irrigation; Shri R. Roshan Baig, hon'ble minister for infrastructure development and information; Shri Basavaraj Rayareddy, hon'ble minister for higher education; Shrimati Umashree, hon'ble minister for women and child welfare development; Priyank M. Kharge, publicity convener and hon'ble minister for information technology and biotechnology; Krishna Byre Gowda, logistics convener and hon'ble minister for agriculture;

and Captain Manivannan, secretary, Social Welfare Department. Thanks also to Dr M.C. Srinivasa, joint director, Social Welfare Department, and Dr H. Nataraj, secretary, State Safai Karmachari Commission, both nodal officers attached to Captain Manivannan, for taking care of the logistics of the conference organization. I would also like to thank Dr Nagalakshmi and Mehroz Khan, who were coordinators for the conference; Shri Srinivasulu, managing director, Ambedkar Development Corporation, attached to Krishna Byre Gowda; and Dr Nandan Kumar, officer on special duty to Priyank Kharge. I must also thank Luthfulla Atheeq, principal secretary to the chief minister; Shri Venkataiah, special advisor to Social Welfare Department; M.V. Savithri, commissioner, Social Welfare Department; and numerous other officials and staff of the Social Welfare Department, who worked so diligently.

Special thanks are due to the Scheduled Castes Department team of the All India Congress Committee: Shri K. Raju, head of the Congress President's Office, for his ideation and immense political support, and Pushparaj Deshpande, in-charge of the Quest for Equity website and other logistical support. I cannot fail to mention Oum, Navil, Deepika, and the rest of the Phase I team, who worked tirelessly.

I would like to express my profound thanks to the members of the various committees, specially members of the academic committee, Professors Sukhadeo Thorat, Valerian Rodrigues, G. Haragopal, Aakash Singh Rathore, and Dr Rochana Bajpai, Sudhir Krishnaswamy, S.G. Siddaramaiah, K. Marulasiddappa, Siddalingaiah, L. Hanumanthaiah, Mallika Ganti, and K.B. Siddaiah. Special thanks are also due to the editorial advisory board for their invaluable advice and assistance throughout, including those members from the academic committee mentioned earlier, as well as Dr Suraj Yengde and Professors Anand Teltumbde, Kalpana Kannabiran, Lawrence R. Simon, and Meena Dhanda. My heartful thanks to Professor Aakash Singh Rathore for taking the responsibility of editing these volumes.

Of course, I cannot fail to mention the support of Shabin John and Chandrashekar for their office and logistics support and Dr Ramkhok Raikhan for research assistance to the editor.

S. Japhet
Professor and Vice Chancellor,
Bengaluru Central University, India

Abbreviations

AFSPA	Armed Forces Special Powers Act
BJP	Bharatiya Janata Party
CWC	Congress Working Committee
ESMA	Essential Services Maintenance Act
INC	Indian National Congress
IPC	Indian Penal Code
JNU	Jawaharlal Nehru University
MACOCA	Maharashtra Control of Organised Crime Act
MISA	Maintenance of Internal Security Act
MLA	Member of Legislative Assembly
NCERT	National Council of Educational Research and Training
NNC	Naga National Council
NSA	National Security Act
OBC	Other Backward Class
PCI	Partito Comunista Italiano (Italian Communist Party)
POTA	Prevention of Terrorist Act
RBI	Reserve Bank of India
RSS	Rashtriya Swayamsevak Sangh
RTC	Round Table Conference
SC	Scheduled Caste
SCF	Scheduled Caste Federation
SPAF	Special Powers of Armed Forces
SPN	*Selections from the Prison Notebooks*
ST	Scheduled Tribe
TADA	Terrorism and Disruptive Activities (Prevention) Act

Introduction

AAKASH SINGH RATHORE

Political Justice[1]

Justice is a complex and multi-faceted concept, and none of its components or constituent aspects are necessarily exclusive of all of the others. If we distinguish political justice from social, legal, economic, or gender justice, it is only for the sake of focus and spotlight, and not any sort of essentialist claim. Political justice is not axenic, but, it does evoke a general range of broadly definable concerns. For example, some questions central to political justice include:

1. What are the basic political rights of individuals or of communities?
2. What is the proper role of government or the State?
3. What are the basic principles of democracy?
4. Why are all citizens equal and in what ways should that equality be manifest?
5. When is political power legitimate or illegitimate, and what duties do those enjoying power have?
6. Should some political communities be superior to others?

Ambedkar addressed each of these and related questions of political justice throughout his work. Just a few of the most salient of

---

[1] Much of the material in this and the following four brief sections has appeared, slightly modified, in Chapter 1 of Rathore (2020).

these texts include his early 'Evidence before the Southborough Committee' (1919); his speech at the Round Table Conference (1930); *Annihilation of Caste* (1936); *What Congress and Gandhi Have Done to the Untouchables* (1945); *States and Minorities: What Are Their Rights and How to Secure Them in the Constitution of Free India* (1947); *Thoughts on Linguistic States* (1955); and the lecture titled 'Buddha and Karl Marx' (1956).

Ambedkar was deeply committed to democratic modes of resolving social and political disagreements. He understood democracy to be a political association of equal and free citizens defining itself in the indefinite future. He was committed to designing democratic institutions for postcolonial India as a politician, lawyer, and of course as the chairperson of the Drafting Committee.

Living Justice

Dr Ambedkar's life offers unique vantage points for sustained reflection on concerns of justice and its relation to other human values. His story perfectly depicts an irrepressible spirit on a lifelong, contagiously inspiring quest for justice. Ironically, however, Dr Ambedkar's comprehensive life story actually remains untold in the English language. Whereas Marathi biographies have been more complete, textured, and nuanced, for Anglophone readers, there have till date been only two main approaches to telling Ambedkar's life story. The first approach has been reverential if not hagiographic.[2] For those readers already sympathetic to Ambedkar and what he stood for, accounts such as these are wonderful and worthwhile. However, for those many readers resistant to various aspects of the Ambedkarite movement, hagiographic biographies fail to provide a neutral and objective foundation for this readership to comfortably stand on, and indeed no hook at all for bringing them into the varied fold of sympathizers.

The second approach has been the polar opposite of the first: callous character assassination.[3] The appeal of the second approach is utterly baffling to anyone who is properly informed about the life of Ambedkar, and indeed the second approach actually feeds upon

---

[2] For example, Omvedt (2008).
[3] For example, Shourie (2012).

and is fuelled by the absence of widespread information about him. What we require, then, is a vivid life portrait of this foremost persona of the twentieth century, a personality-driven narrative covering his birth to death, along with salient aspects of his contemporary legacy, in order to reveal his bold and inspiring story. Unfortunately, no such thing can even be remotely approximated here. Here we can, at most, signal just a very few select events from Ambedkar's profoundly consequential life. Ambedkar's life is an inspirational one, which often seemed to unfold as a series of trials and struggles; it is a tale of his remarkable tenacity and talent that led, in nearly all cases, to his eventual triumph. In this way, Ambedkar's story is exemplary, a testament of the quest for justice.

It is interesting to note at the outset that in many ways the world was both ready, and not ready, for the arrival of Ambedkar. He had his predecessors, nineteenth-century social reformers such as Mahadev Govind Ranade, Pandita Ramabai, and Jotirao Phule, and in this respect the world was ready for him. However, Ambedkar profoundly intensified, radicalized, and widened their critiques, channelling social action into other domains, disrupting them: political, juridical, economic, historiographical, sociological, religious—for all this, the world was clearly not ready for him. In some certain respects, it remains unready for him even today.

From Young Bhim to Dr Ambedkar

Sometime around 1935, Ambedkar wrote about thirty pages of an unfinished autobiography, now known as *Waiting for a Visa*. It consists of a series of brief stories about the profound discrimination and humiliation that he was forced to suffer throughout his childhood and as a young adult. Several of these motifs (for example, inability to find drinking water, exclusion from school) would eventually transform into major issues that the mature Ambedkar would address structurally and nationally.

There were also some signs of things to come during his school years, 1900–8, when Ambedkar graduated from Elphinstone School to Elphinstone College. Noteworthy was young Bhim's defiance of his casteist college teacher, who had told him that Mahars (the untouchable caste to which Ambedkar belonged) had no business seeking higher education. Within fifteen years from that early confrontation, Ambedkar would emerge as the most highly educated Indian in pre-Independence history, eventually earning advanced degrees from Columbia University, USA, and the London School of Economics and Political Science, UK.

It is worth pausing for a moment to speak about Ambedkar's years at Columbia University because of how central they turned out to be for his intellectual trajectory. In 1930, reflecting on his time spent in New York City, Ambedkar wrote, 'The best friends I have had in my life were some of my classmates at Columbia and my great professors, John Dewey, James Shotwell, Edwin Seligman and James Harvey Robinson.'[4] Among these great professors, the most lasting influence was certainly that of the pragmatist philosopher John Dewey.[5]

Decades after his period of study in New York, having attained international notice for his work on the Constitution of India, Ambedkar was invited by Columbia University in June 1952 to receive an honorary doctorate. He was particularly looking forward to meeting his former professor John Dewey. As chance would have it, Dewey died on 2 June 1952, while Ambedkar was transiting through Rome on his way to New York. As Ambedkar wrote in a poignant letter to his wife Savita, 'I am so sorry. I owe all my intellectual life to him. He was a wonderful man.'[6]

After Ambedkar had returned to India from his studies at Columbia University and London School of Economics and Political Science, in 1917, Ambedkar began working in the service of Baroda State to repay the scholarship he had received for studying abroad. Due to caste prejudice, he was unable to find a bed to sleep on. He finally posed as a Parsi in order to be given access to a rat-infested attic room. But even this he had to flee after a violent encounter with an armed Parsi mob who discovered his deception. He left Baroda (now Vadodra) immediately and returned to Bombay (now Mumbai).

Back in Bombay, Ambedkar joined the faculty of Sydenham College, Mumbai, India, as a professor of political economy. Despite academic credentials far exceeding all the other faculty members, Ambedkar suffered constant humiliation and was

---

[4] I rely here on the work of Scott Stroud and his source, *Columbia Alumni News*, 19 December 1930, p. 12.

[5] Zelliot (2013: 69).

[6] Rattu (1997: 35).

asked not to use the same utensils as the rest of the faculty members. In 1919, Ambedkar gave evidence before the Southborough Committee regarding franchise. Through doing so, he attracted the attention of the prince of Kolhapur, Chattrapati Shahu Maharaj, who offered him financial assistance. Ambedkar was thus able to launch his fortnightly magazine *Mook Nayak*, and began organizing large-scale conferences, such as the All India Depressed Classes Conference in Nagpur.

With money saved from his salary and assistance from Shahu Maharaj, Ambedkar was finally able to return to London in 1920 to earn his MSc and DSc (economics), as well as his law degree. He also had a stint in Germany (Bonn and Berlin) learning Sanskrit, as he knew that this would be impossible for him in India.

After completion of his formal education, Ambedkar returned once again to Bombay, where he sought to start a legal practice but did not have the money to pay the registration fee of the Bombay High Court. His friend Naval Bhatena loaned him the required 500 rupees, and thus Ambedkar launched his legal practice. He took on some noteworthy cases, often hopeless cases where he championed the underdog, and this brought him into early conflict with some prominent and powerful people, including Bal Gangadhar Tilak.

Dr Ambedkar was also inextricably connected with the Reserve Bank of India (RBI). The RBI was created on the basis of guidelines Ambedkar had presented in 1925 to the 'Royal Commission on Indian Currency and Finance' and under the influence of his definitive book *The Problem of the Rupee—Its Problems and Its Solution* (1923).

With the cooperation of Gandhian satyagrahi P.N. Rajbhoj and others, Ambedkar launched a series of satyagrahas, including the monumental march to Mahad (1927) to drink water from the public well, and several important temple-entry campaigns (for example, Kalaram Temple satyagraha). Ambedkar was shocked to realize that, far from receiving the support he was promised from the Congress party, various Congress members actually sabotaged these satyagrahas. In another related landmark event in 1927, Ambedkar publicly burned the Manusmriti. He also launched the newspaper *Bahishkrut Bharat*, where the word 'Dalit' began to gain prominence.

In 1927, Ambedkar was appointed as member of the Legislative Assembly of Bombay Province for a term of five years (it was renewed in 1932 for another five years). In this capacity, he submitted a statement before the Simon Commission on 29 May 1928, noteworthy because it departed radically from all other submissions by pontificating on the nature of constitutional democracy and, within that framework, raising attention to the plight of untouchables. Thus launched the era of his large-scale political prominence.

Ambedkar's strong performance representing the depressed classes at the 1930 Round Table Conference (RTC) in London catapulted him onto the national (and indeed international) stage. The second RTC in 1931 inaugurated the lifelong feud between Gandhi and Ambedkar. The Communal Award that Ambedkar had fought so hard for at the RTC was granted in 1932, providing for a scheme of separate electorates for the untouchables. Gandhi resorted to a fast unto death against the Award, which placed Ambedkar in an impossible predicament. Blackmailed into it, Ambedkar signed a pact with Gandhi in 1932, with terms quite disagreeable to Ambedkar. Ambedkar thus characterized Gandhi not as a Mahatma but as a wild and dangerous opponent, famously quipping about this period that Gandhi 'showed me his fangs'.

From Dr Ambedkar to Babasaheb

In 1936, Ambedkar wrote a long speech titled 'Annihilation of Caste' to address a Lahore-based organization for social reforms, but the organization objected to certain passages of his text. Ambedkar published the controversial speech as a booklet, and it attracted attention from all corners, also adding further fuel to the long-standing debate with Gandhi regarding the casteist nature of Hinduism.

In August 1936, Ambedkar founded the Independent Labour Party, a party based not on caste but on class. He joined hands with the Left and attempted to apprise Marxists about their shared interests. Ambedkar was a champion of labour rights at a time when the concept of workers' rights did not exist. In India, much before other nations even started thinking about instituting just and fair conditions for workers, Ambedkar successfully led the struggle for reducing working hours from twelve to eight hours in 1942. He also vehemently (and successfully) protested against the 'Black Bill', which the colonial government was using to suppress workers' strikes. His commitment to labour rights remained visible through Article 19 (c) of the Indian Constitution, which guarantees the fundamental right to form associations or unions.

In November 1939, Ambedkar's Independent Labour Party floated a bill on 'birth control'. Ambedkar argued that 'population policy' was necessary for the eradication of poverty. The bill was regarded as scandalous, however, because it spoke explicitly about issues of sexuality and contraception, and received no support from any single party other than Ambedkar's own.

Around that period, in 1937, the cry of 'Jai Bhim!' was heard for the first time. It was coined by a member of the Legislative Assembly (MLA) of the Independent Labour Party from Kamptee (Nagpur), Babu L.N. Hardas. The expression remains a mainstay salutation amongst the former Mahar community specifically and can be heard upon the lips of Ambedkarites globally.

From Babasaheb to Bodhisatta Ambedkar

Throughout 1946–7, Dr Ambedkar was responsible for establishing the Central Water Irrigation and Navigation Commission. He also played an important role in the establishment of the Damodar Valley project, Hirakud project, and Sone river project. As a child, he was constantly denied drinking water. In Baroda, the office peons refused to give him water. As a faculty member at Sydenham College in Bombay, he was asked not to drink the water meant for the faculty. He was arrested for drinking water at a Mahad public tank well. After all this, in 1947, he acquired the authority and mechanisms to begin to ensure water for everyone. Dr Ambedkar is, in some respects, the father of the democratization of water— a concept and concern that will persist well into the twenty-first century and beyond.

In August 1947, Ambedkar joined the Nehru Cabinet as law minister. He had hoped to be given the portfolio for development so he could pursue massive projects in electricity, transportation, health, and so on to improve the quality of life for millions of destitute people. Nevertheless, he accepted the law ministry portfolio, thereby launching his uneasy tenure in the Union Cabinet, from which he resigned in protest after four years of service.

On the personal front, Ambedkar had several health problems by the late 1940s, his loneliness exacerbating them further. In 1948, he married Dr Sharada Kabir (thereafter known as Dr Savita Ambedkar), a physician, who also happened to be Brahmin. Many members of his community were displeased, and indeed the conspiracy theories surrounding his late, inter-caste marriage continue to proliferate to this day. However, Ambedkar was reported to have taken comfort in the fact that Gandhi would have been proud of his decision.

As law minister, Ambedkar spearheaded the introduction of the Hindu Code Bill, giving rights of inheritance and property ownership to women. Both he and Nehru believed it was a 'vital step in the introduction of true democracy in India, and would remove the practices and the logic that underpinned the caste system'.[7] Yet, all disperse factions from the right united to defeat the bill, as well as to vilify and attack Ambedkar personally. When Nehru himself withdrew support from the bill due to political expediency, Ambedkar resigned from the Cabinet.

Ambedkar was one of the most prominent voices of the empowerment of women. As far back as his very first academic paper (1916), Ambedkar specifically addressed the position of women in India. In his later work, Ambedkar posited a thesis that women traditionally enjoyed a high status in ancient India, but reactionary developments—well represented through the patriarchy of the Manusmriti—led to systematic decline in their stature. Thus, women in India were accorded no rights to education, property, or divorce, and were eckoned as property.

In January 1952, Ambedkar was defeated in his bid for member of Parliament by N.S. Kajrolkar of the Congress. It appears that the latter may have enlisted the support of V. Savarkar and the Hindu Mahasabha for ensuring Ambedkar's defeat. Shortly before his death, Ambedkar sketched the constitution for a new national party, the Republican Party of India. Though it made a promising start, soon after his death, it split into a number of factions, and remains heavily splintered today.

During the final decade of his life, Ambedkar was hard at work on a manuscript that would eventually prove to be one of his most controversial posthumous publications, 'Riddles in Hinduism'.

---

[7] Newbigin (2013: 162–96).

Although people often take this work as nothing more than a motivated attack on Hinduism, what they fail to understand is that Ambedkar turned his razor-sharp rationalism to Buddhism just as much as he did to Hinduism. Ambedkar's monumental 'The Buddha and His Dhamma' stands testament to his relentless demand that religion be rational and promote values of unity rather than division.

Around 1948, Ambedkar had turned to Buddhism as personal faith as well as an ideology that offered an alternative to Hinduism. On 14 October 1956, he formally converted to Buddhism, alongside hundreds of thousands of his followers. In doing so, he finally fulfilled the vow he had made publicly at Yeola in 1935 that although he was born a Hindu, he would not die a Hindu. To the Navayana, or new, Buddhists, now numbering in the millions, Ambedkar was nothing less than a Bodhisatta, leading all towards the path of liberation.

In a touching anecdote, the head of the Western Buddhist Order, Sangharakshita, described his final encounter with Dr Ambedkar, shortly before the latter's death. He described Ambedkar as very ill, and unable to speak clearly—a shocking change from his usual booming voice. Ambedkar was repeating something impassionedly but inaudibly to Sangharakshita. Sangharakshita placed his ear to Ambedkar's lips to be able to hear what he was saying. Ambedkar's last words to the monk to whom he had entrusted the Buddhist education of the hundreds of thousands of new converts: 'There is still so much to be done ... So much to be done'.[8]

Essaying Justice

This life sketch, as incomplete as it is, nevertheless serves to reveal something of the character, tenacity, and temperament of B.R. Ambedkar. Ambedkar interpreted the formal notion of 'securing justice' to mean the real struggle for *removing* social, political, and economic inequalities. And indeed, that was how Ambedkar's life was spent, from an early age at school right until death: fighting to secure justice for the people of India, which is to say, to deploy every means available to him to remove social, political, and economic inequalities, especially for minorities and depressed classes.

---

[8] Sangharakshita (1986: 20).

In this brief introduction, we chose to detour from a conceptual history of the concept of justice in general, or political justice in particular, and to turn instead to Ambedkar's lived experiences. Ambedkar's life was a life lived justly. Beyond simply tracing the concept, the abstract idea of justice, we see in Ambedkar a concrete embodiment of the true meaning of that word.

In the present volume, each of the contributors directly takes up issues of central relevance to exploring the nature and destiny of political justice, either as such or specifically in terms of their interpretation of Dr Ambedkar's own position. In the first chapter, Bhikhu Parekh ('The Intellectual and Political Legacy of B.R. Ambedkar') attempts to elucidate, re-examine, and 'question the questions', as he puts it, that Dr Ambedkar himself had asked. In a wide-ranging discussion covering the Poona Pact, the issue of conversion, and several important enduring political ideas of Dr Ambedkar, Parekh concludes his chapter with some points of concern. For example, he queries whether Ambedkar properly gauged the need for society to alter its mentality in order to be in a position to successfully operationalize the radical egalitarian values laid out in the Constitution. Echoing, in a sense, the final remark of Shashi Tharoor in 'Foreword', Parekh also wonders whether we Indians are capable of raising our consciousness to the level demanded by Ambedkar's Constitution.

The second chapter, by Cosimo Zene ('B.R. Ambedkar and Antonio Gramsci: Justice for the Excluded, Education for Democracy'), fruitfully and critically compares Ambedkar and Gramsci, rightly viewing them as two major political intellectuals and activists of the twentieth century. According to Zene, despite being neglected by both academia and mainstream politics, the political philosophies of both Ambedkar and Gramsci keep returning well into the twenty-first century to awaken our conscience and to prompt us to reflect on current issues affecting our troubled democracies. The author nevertheless remains attuned to their differences, which he judges to be mostly dictated by their diverse social and cultural backgrounds. But he aims to show that Ambedkar and Gramsci share numerous common traits regarding political theory and praxis. Above all, Zene hones in on their convictions that no one should be excluded from active participation in the democratic process of nation building—a situation that relies upon education in order to be realized.

In the third chapter, Anand Teltumbde ('Ambedkar and Democracy: Critical Reflections') narrows in on Ambedkar's vision of democracy, which he regards as the distillate of his philosophy as a whole. Each section of the chapter focuses in on a different aspect of democracy. Overall, Teltumbde posits that democracy, for Ambedkar, was a form and a method of government whereby revolutionary social changes may be brought about without bloodshed. He argues, however, that the march of India over the last several decades has not followed the path that Ambedkar laid ahead for us. What hope lies ahead for the future?

Neera Chandhoke, in the fourth chapter ('Repairing Complex Historical Injustice'), takes the reader through a clear and precise reconsideration of how we ought to think about the problem of reparation within the framework of redistributive justice. There are three elements to this: the right to material goods through redistribution; the right to voice; and the right to recognition. Efforts at repairing complex forms of historical injustice, specifically untouchability, have produced unanticipated outcomes. Although economic deprivation has been attended to somewhat, and while Dalits have wrested the right to voice from elites, the community is still denied recognition. It is difficult, if not impossible, to repair every manifestation of complex historical injustice. This is particularly true of recognition or the lack thereof. Developing partial autonomy from other forms of injustice, denial of recognition relentlessly pushes historical injustice into the present and perhaps also into the foreseeable future. Chandhoke conceptualizes the issue as being fundamentally grounded in equality. She argues that if equality is compromised, the project of redistributive justice has borne inadequate results. Till date, the right to recognition has not been realized. In order for this right to be recognized, social movements that speak the language of equality for their own particular constituencies have to come together and support the idea of building a political consensus on what is due to all human beings, what should be done for them, and what should not be done to them.

The next chapter takes up the concept of equality within Ambedkar's own work. Pradeep Gokhale ('Dr Ambedkar and the Trio of Principles: Liberty, Equality, and Fraternity') catalogues the most significant treatments of these principles within Ambedkar's writings and attempts to pin down the exact scope of their meaning for his political thought overall. Ambedkar's earliest major reference to the three principles (liberty, equality, and fraternity) can be found in 'Annihilation of Caste', where he refers to them as foundations of an ideal society. However, Ambedkar does not refer to Buddhism in this context but the French Revolution. While discussing equality as one of the principles, Ambedkar admits that it had been the most contentious part of the slogan of the French Revolution. Thus, at this stage Ambedkar was treating these principles as occasioned by the French Revolution. Even at a later stage, when he wrote 'The Hindu Social Order: Its Essential Principles', Ambedkar discusses the principles in the context of the French Revolution. Thus, even here he does not refer to Buddhism as the source of these principles.

Gokhale reasons, then, that when Dr Ambedkar says that he has derived his philosophy, which was enshrined in the three principles, from the teachings of the Buddha, his statement is not to be taken literally; instead, it should be interpreted in the context of the would-be Buddhist phase in which he was making this statement. Gokhale's chapter aims to show that though Ambedkar originally accepted these socio-political principles from the context of the French Revolution, he gradually reinterpreted them as religious principles. Thus, when Ambedkar came to the conclusion that Buddhism was the ideal religion, he re-appropriated them as principles rooted in the Buddha's message. According to Gokhale, this underlines the need to understand Dr Ambedkar's thought, not as a static or constant viewpoint, but as a dynamic flow of thought.

Neither, then, ought we to understand his political philosophy as perfectionist. So argues Vidhu Verma in a chapter ('Discrimination, Colonial Injustice, and the Good Society') that analyses the debates around Ambedkar's political theory, with a focus on his theory of action through conversion to Buddhism. Tying together elements from the previous two chapters, Verma also explores Ambedkar's critique of caste within the paradigm of modernity based on the three principles of liberty, equality, and fraternity, and his adherence to the principle of historical injustice. According to Verma's reading, Ambedkar's concept of justice carries an unwavering commitment to difference within marginalized groups, yet it equally rejects radical cultural essentialisms which refuse to engage in ideals of exchange across a plurality of subject positions. The author argues that Ambedkar's original reading of nationalism heralded the Dalit collective as the only group capable of addressing the social justice question in a postcolonial liberal polity.

The next chapter begins a fresh line of enquiry. Scott Stroud ('Communication, Justice, and Reconstruction: Ambedkar as an Indian Pragmatist') details the connection between Ambedkar, the contours and leanings of his political thought, with one of his most influential teachers at Columbia University, the American pragmatist John Dewey. By documenting the courses that Ambedkar took with Dewey, as well as the many books of Dewey's that he owned and annotated, Stroud identifies themes and structures in Ambedkar's later work that serve as a unique application of pragmatism to the Indian context of caste oppression. Stroud shows that John Dewey inspired Ambedkar with an everyday notion of democracy, as well as with the importance of ethics as a reflective morality.

The eighth chapter continues along this motif. In it, J. Daniel Elam ('Of Castes and Crowds: B.R. Ambedkar's Anti-colonial Endosmosis') argues that in addition to being one of the leading political thinkers of the twentieth century, B.R. Ambedkar was also a sociologist at an early moment when sociology was, to quote his colleague W.E.B. Du Bois, 'hesitant'. That is, sociology had yet to fully develop its own social scientific protocols necessary for disciplinary autonomy, and therefore revelled in a heady blend of empiricism, psychology, anthropology, vitalism, political theory, pragmatism, and metaphysics. Elam, then, traces the theoretical lineaments of a curious term found scattered throughout Ambedkar's writings (especially important in 'Annihilation of Caste') tracing its circuitous path through early twentieth-century pragmatism, social psychology, and proto-empiricism that form the basis for the sociology that Ambedkar was to inherit, adapt, and, most crucially, render politically potent in colonial and postcolonial India. That term was 'endosmosis', which was borrowed from biology by John Dewey, William James, and Henri Bergson for use in philosophy, political theory, and psychology across the transatlantic world.

From Ambedkar and Dewey, we move along to another frequent 'other' of Ambedkar's, M.K. Gandhi. In the ninth chapter, Pushparaj Deshpande ('A Constellation of Ideas: Revisiting Ambedkar and Gandhi') takes up the Ambedkar–Gandhi debate in an innovative way. In recognizing the significant areas of divergence between

Ambedkar and Gandhi, the author avoids a rote narration of the incidents in which the two giants engaged, and instead focuses on four themes: their different views and strategies on caste; untouchability; the urban/rural; and actualizing social transformation. Deshpande shows that Gandhi's views on at least two of these four issues (that is, on caste and on how to eradicate untouchability) undergo an evolution, and eventually mirror those of Ambedkar's. The author then argues that on one issue (that is, on how to actualize a social transformation), Gandhi's blueprint may have been more effective. Finally, Deshpande posits that on the issue of rural vs. urban, the arguments of both Ambedkar and Gandhi need to be viewed complementarily for a nuanced understanding. The author concludes that it is through the interplay of their very differences that we can re-conceptualize the political culture of India and find strategies to holistically address caste inequities and discrimination.

The tenth and final chapter continues to examine the work of Ambedkar alongside or in juxtaposition to others, and also looks back at an issue of central focus of the fourth chapter. Shaunna Rodrigues ('Self-Respect as a Primary Political Ideal: Ambedkar's Challenge to Political Theory') tests Ambedkar's notion of self-respect against dominant liberal accounts of the concept. Despite being given pride of place as 'the most important primary good' for a democratic polity by contemporary political theorists like John Rawls, when self-respect is used in a political argument, it tends to be used in a thin and positivist manner. That is, merely as the capacity of people to have a sense of justice and their own conception of the good. The thick, substantive form that examines self-respect as a counter to ideas like servility or shame is skimmed over. The author asks: Can an argument that attempts to orient a political community towards self-respect ignore the counter-concepts in opposition to which self-respect is defined? Rodrigues attempts to answer this question by looking at the Rawlsian formulation of self-respect closely and then comparing it with that of Ambedkar. In the process of doing so, she develops a framework for examining the concept of self-respect through Ambedkar's writings: first, by broadening the range of counter-concepts to self-respect to capture what emerges when persons are not recognized as being 'human' or having the typical qualities of a humanistic conception of the self, such as having a capacity for a conception of the good; and second, by developing a conception of self-respect that employs the ideas of recognition, communication and political emotion, self-mastery, and public presence as its nodal points. According to Rodrigues, Ambedkar deploys this framework against a far wider range of conceptions of the good and political emotions than contemporary liberal theorists. In doing so, she concludes, Ambedkar provides us with a positive, substantive, and more workable political ideal of self-respect, making him one of the most profound theorists of self-respect in the world.

Each of these ten contributions précised here lays a single foundation stone towards erecting the pillar of political justice. This volume on political justice, in turn, serves as a unit of support for the broader edifice formed by the five volumes taken together. This broader edifice of research and scholarship may seem imposing from the academic point of view. However, when viewed from the more panoramic perspective of Dr Ambedkar's lifelong quest for justice, it may rightly be seen as itself only a single foundation stone towards colossal goals. These are goals we have as a legacy of Dr Ambedkar's exemplarity. They will only be achieved by accumulating the momentum of critical masses enlightened and thundering forward. Speaking on behalf of the participants in this particular project, I think we can take some satisfaction in the small part that we are playing through what we have achieved. The intersection and synergy between Dr Ambedkar's own profound and prolific writings with the most current scholarship and intellectual insights on offer here is a crucial step in the right direction. It is, as logicians say, necessary but insufficient. Again, as Ambedkar put it, there is still so much to be done.

References

Newbigin, E. 2013. 'B.R. Ambedkar's Code Bill: Caste, Marriage and Postcolonial Indian Citizenship'. In *The Hindu Family and the Emergence of Modern India: Law, Citizenship and Community*, Cambridge Studies in Indian History and Society, pp. 162–96. Cambridge: Cambridge University Press.

Omvedt, Gail. 2008. *Ambedkar: Towards an Enlightened India*. New Delhi: Penguin.

Rathore, Aakash Singh. 2020. *Ambedkar's Preamble: A Secret History of the Constitution of India*. New Delhi: Penguin.

Rattu, Nanak Chand. 1997. *Last Few Years of Dr. Ambedkar*. New Delhi: Amrit Publishing House.
Sangharakshita. 1986. *Ambedkar and Buddhism*. London: Windhorse Publications.
Shourie, Arun. 2012. *Worshipping False Gods*. New Delhi: Harper Collins.
Zelliot, Eleanor. 2013. *Ambedkar's World*. New Delhi: Navayana.

1

The Intellectual and Political Legacy of B.R. Ambedkar

BHIKHU PAREKH

The reputation of Ambedkar, one of the truly creative thinkers of twentieth-century India, has oscillated between uncritical demonization and virtual deification. Thanks to the causes for which he fought and the manner in which he did so, he was quite underrated and even maligned during his lifetime. Gandhi did not seek him out until August 1931, nearly sixteen years after Ambedkar had been in public life, and, in his first interview, had a highly patronizing attitude towards Ambedkar. He even mistook him for a Brahmin and discovered his real identity only during the Second Round Table Conference! Pandit Nehru did not meet him until as late as October 1939 and did not think much of him. M.R. Jaykar thought that he was a 'destructive' force bent on creating what Jaykar called 'Maharistan', a separate land for the Mahars along the lines of Pakistan. Subhas Chandra Bose expressed a widely held view when he observed that 'Ambedkar had had his leadership thrust upon him by the benign British government because his services were necessary to embarrass the nationalist leaders.'[1] Some other leaders of the independence movement such as C. Rajagopalachari and K. Santhanam were even more unkind in their assessment of him. Even today, many see him as a one-eyed man who could not

---

[1] Keer (1990: 196).

look beyond the interests of Dalits and allowed his great talents to be misdirected, even distorted, by his hatred of Hindu society and even its most well-meaning leaders. Some resent that, like Jinnah, he was a political free rider who acquired power without making the obligatory sacrifices for the independence of the country, such as getting beaten up by the police and going to prison.

The pendulum has swung to the other extreme 1980s onwards. Largely as a result of a better historical perspective offered by the passage of time, continuing atrocities against Dalits even after over seventy years of Independence, and the growing intellectual and political visibility of the Other Backward Classes (OBCs) and the Scheduled Castes (SCs), he is now almost deified in some circles. Some Dalit spokesmen compare him to the Buddha and Prophet Mohammed and find even the mildest criticism of him intolerable, as was evident during the recent silly controversy over a sixty-year-old cartoon in a National Council of Educational Research and Training (NCERT) textbook. Across many states of India, his statues, portraits, posters bearing his image, and schools and parks named after him have proliferated. His finely framed photos in an immaculate Western attire are lovingly garlanded and placed in prominent places. While most other leaders' statues and photos appear in traditional dresses, Ambedkar's modern outfit is suggestive of the Dalit view of him and their place in the Indian society. Also, he is generally presented as carrying a copy of the Indian Constitution, implying that he is its sole author and that it is an instrument of Dalit liberation. In some parts of India, there are competitions to build taller statues of him. All this is perfectly understandable and, within limits, even proper. It is one way in which the long-suppressed communities express their pride in the achievements of someone who did so much for them for so long at such a high personal price. It also fosters a sense of collective solidarity among them and strengthens their resolve to fight for a better life.

While the adoration of Ambedkar is understandable, it has its dangers. It turns him into a Dalit hero and diminishes his stature as a great national and international thinker and leader. It is striking that as his life was coming to an end, another great minority leader—Martin Luther King Jr—was emerging in USA. Although both had similar concerns and did much for their communities, Ambedkar was, in some respects, a deeper thinker and had a greater impact on his community and country than Martin Luther King Jr had on his. Yet, while King enjoys an iconic global status and is much admired and even revered the world over by those fighting for minority rights, Ambedkar sadly remains a local and rather dated figure, partly because of India's comparatively low political and intellectual visibility in the world, and partly because of the tendency to reduce him one-dimensionally to a spokesman for the Dalit community. Even as no one thinks of Nehru as a Brahmin leader and Gandhi as a Bania, there is no reason to think of Ambedkar as a Dalit leader. To suggest that his intellectual and political identity is defined or exhausted by his caste is to reflect the very casteism he vigorously attacked.

The best and fairest way to respond to Ambedkar is neither to marginalize nor to deify him, neither to de-historicize him nor to reduce him one-dimensionally to Gandhi's sparring partner, but rather to judge him in his own terms and context and interrogate his ideas and actions. We need to elucidate, re-examine, and even question the questions he asked, challenge what is dubious in his answers, and build on his profound insights. Such an approach shows that we consider him big enough to be worthy of a critical engagement and relevant to our concerns. This is how Gandhi, Nehru, and others are being currently reassessed, this is also how Ambedkar himself interpreted the Buddha seeing him as *margadata* (guide) rather than *mokshadata* (saviour), and that is how I shall approach him in this chapter.

Untouchability

Although Ambedkar's intellectual interests covered a wide range, including religion, philosophy, political theory, sociology, social psychology, history, and economics, the practice of untouchability in all its tragic complexity was one of their major unifying themes. It was also the prism through which he looked at Hindu society, and brought to it the insights derived from his personal experiences and various disciplinary perspectives. For Ambedkar, untouchability was a product of the uniquely Hindu form of inequality as embodied in the caste system. He examined the structure of the caste system, the way in which it differed from other kinds of inequality, how it was sustained for centuries, and how it shaped the Hindu self-consciousness. He asked whether untouchability was adventitious or integral to the caste system and how it originated, was maintained, and could be ended. He also asked the related question of why caste Hindus had not felt ashamed of or even embarrassed by it and continued it for centuries without significant opposition. He thought that this was so because Hindus took it to be self-evident or part of the natural order of things, and asked why they held such a view.

While inequality, be it social, political or economic, was to be found in all societies, caste system represented its historically unique form. For Ambedkar, it had six distinguishing features.[2] First, it was based on birth, was articulated into neatly demarcated and self-contained groups, and followed their members until their death. Second, self-contained castes were not distinct social groups like classes and tribes, but embedded in and formed part of a wider social whole which graded and related them in a hierarchical manner. Third, the ideas of purity and pollution lay at the centre of caste hierarchy. Hierarchy itself was common to many unequal societies, but one involving purity and pollution was unique to the Hindus. Higher castes felt defiled and their social standing was lowered in their own and others' eyes when they mixed with the lower castes, especially in culturally significant areas such as commensuality and marriage. Castes were like 'closed corporations', had no meaningful contacts with each other, shared no common experiences, and remained rigid and inflexible.

Fourth, each caste had a name which '[gave] it fixity, continuity and individuality'.[3] It was unambiguously bounded, internally homogeneous, and had public marks of identification. It was even carried over into the surnames of its members, who could not hide it and hope to pass as someone else. All this made caste inequality easy to enforce, difficult to escape, and highly oppressive.

---

[2] Ambedkar (1917; 1979–96: 22–96). This essay was written as an address to a meeting of the Jat-Pat-Todak Mandal, a body created under the auspices of the Arya Samaj to reform Hindu society. When the organizers saw his draft, they postponed the meeting! Ambedkar published his address as a brochure. In this chapter, I use the terms 'untouchables' and 'Dalits' interchangeably and risk historical anachronism in the interest of fidelity to political rhetoric.

[3] Rodrigues (2002: 97–8).

Fifth, inequality in Hindu society was minutely graded. This inequality did not come across as the stark hostility between two or more unequal and sharply separated groups facing each other as in a feudal or modern bourgeois society, but was rather an elaborate and a carefully delineated hierarchy based on 'an ascending scale of reverence and a descending scale of contempt'.[4] Every caste had some castes that were superior and others that were inferior to it. Even Dalits had their own internal hierarchy, in which people at the lower rungs were rendered untouchable. Since the contours of inequality were blurred, it did not appear stark and unbearable as it did in a slave-owning or racially or class-divided society. Every caste could live with its inferior status and the contempt it entailed because it found compensating satisfaction in enjoying and exercising its superiority over others. Such a minutely graded system made it exceedingly difficult for the oppressed groups to unite, let alone take a holistic view of and mount a challenge to the entire social order.

Finally, according to Ambedkar, the caste profoundly shaped the Hindu's identity or sense of himself. He defined himself in terms of his place in the hierarchy and could not relate to others without viewing them as superior or inferior to him. If he ever sought to establish some kind of equality with them, he did so by seeing them as superior in some and inferior in some other real or imaginary respects. The consciousness of hierarchy had struck such deep roots in the Hindu psyche, argued Ambedkar, that it was incapable of entertaining the closely related ideas of unique individuals sharing a common humanity. Since Hindu inequality was not just a matter of social but also personal identity, it had a social and a psychological basis and required the resources of both sociology and social psychology to understand and undermine its continuing hold.

For Ambedkar, inequality in this exceedingly complex form was the organizing principle of Hindu society. As he put it in moments of despair, 'Hindu, thy name is inequality.'[5] To be a Hindu was to belong to a particular caste and that involved getting caught up in a system of inequality. One could not escape the system of inequality without escaping the caste, and one could do the latter only by

---

[4] Moon (1979–96, Volume 2: 506).
[5] Moon (1979–96, Volume 1: 23–4; Volume 3: 105).

ceasing to be a Hindu. In some of his writings, Ambedkar thought that the caste system could be eradicated within the Hindu framework.[6] In others, he argued the opposite: Since the Hindu society was structured in terms of the caste system, to destroy the latter was to put an end to the Hindu society itself. It would create a new society, but that would not be Hindu.

Ambedkar's extreme view made sense only if one accepted his identification of the Hindu society with the caste system and defined a Hindu in exclusively social terms. There are no good reasons to do either. Several Hindu thinkers over the centuries thought that the caste system was a historical excrescence, a product of invasion and migration or imposed by the Brahmins, and not central to their society. They rejected it without ceasing to be Hindus in their own or even others' eyes. And if castes were to disappear one day, Hindus would not cease to be Hindus. One can define the Hindu, as many have done, in civilizational, religious, or cultural rather than social terms, as one who subscribes to a particular view of man and the world or to a particular moral and religious tradition rather than as someone belonging to a particular kind of social order. A Hindu could then reject the caste system without ceasing to be one as is the case with millions of them today.

In Ambedkar's view, the practice of untouchability was an inevitable product of the caste system. The latter involved hierarchy, and the untouchables occupied its lowest rung. The caste system involved purity and pollution, and the untouchables represented the most impure group whose contact brought the highest degree of pollution. In these and other ways, untouchability was the concentrated expression of the spirit informing the caste system. The two were inseparable, and untouchability could not be abolished without abolishing the caste system and radically restructuring the very basis of the Hindu social order.

Ambedkar traced the origins of untouchability to between 200 and 600 CE. He rejected the widely held view that it was pre-Aryan,

---

[6] In a joint memorandum submitted to the Round Table Conference's Minorities Committee, Ambedkar said that the untouchables should be called 'non-caste Hindus', 'Protestant Hindus', or 'non-conformist Hindus'. See Keer (1990: 189). In his evidence to the Simon Commission in 1928, he said, 'It does not matter whether I call myself a Hindu or a non-Hindu as long as I am outside the pale of Hinduism' (Keer 1990: 118).

and explained its origin in terms of the Brahmanic struggle for domination. When different groups of Indo-Aryans came to India, they settled down in villages. As new ones arrived and fought for land, those defeated were pushed outside their villages and segregated and subordinated. Many of these 'broken men' converted to Buddhism. The dominant Brahmanic groups who felt threatened by and fought against Buddhism sought to bring the 'broken men' within their fold. When they resisted, the Brahmins devised ways of humiliating and degrading them by placing them beyond the pale of normal social intercourse and declaring them untouchable. The latter ate meat including beef. Although the Brahmins used to do the same, they became vegetarians and made it a mark of purity and status. Over time, eating meat, especially beef, became the strongest taboo, and those engaged in it came to be seen as the lowest of the lowly or the untouchables.[7] As to why the 'broken' men did not give up beef, Ambedkar argued that they were extremely poor and survived on dead cows whom no one else would eat. Like other Hindu practices, the ban on beef was a case of using culture to legitimize domination. The real motive behind the practice of untouchability was political: to subdue the 'broken men', eliminate potential competitors for resources, and to declare a war on the Buddhists.

Ambedkar explained the continued existence of untouchability for nearly two millennia in terms of three interacting factors, the ideological, the economic, and the political. Untouchability was justified as a just dessert for deeds done in the previous life, and its victims were conditioned into thinking that their social position was their own fault. Caste Hindus also wielded enormous economic power, which they used to exploit and keep the untouchables in degrading and dehumanizing conditions. As Ambedkar put it, untouchability was a 'gold mine' for caste Hindus.[8] It provided cheap and abundant labour to do the dirty work and protected upper castes from competition by limiting the supply of talented people. The Brahmin 'enslaves the mind and the Bania enslaves the body',[9] and their deadly alliance throughout history crippled and crushed their victims. Finally, caste Hindus controlled the institutions of

---

[7] Ambedkar (1948: 146–7). See also Ambedkar (1946).
[8] Ambedkar (1945: 196). See Moon (1979–96, Volume 9: 216–17n192).
[9] Ambedkar (1945: 196).

government and enforced their will by imposing the most horrendous forms of punishment for even the smallest deviations from caste norms.

Ambedkar asked why caste Hindus never protested against or even felt embarrassed by the practice of untouchability. In his view several factors played a part. Like the untouchables, caste Hindus shared the dominant ideological justification of untouchability in terms of the doctrine of karma. 'Hindus observe caste not because they are inhuman or wrong-headed. They observe caste because they are deeply religious.'[10] Furthermore, their hierarchical sense of identity let them to create a system in which one can be 'somebody' only if others are 'nobodies', the lowest of whom were the untouchables. Another extremely important factor had to do with the absence of what Ambedkar called 'public conscience', that is, 'conscience which becomes agitated at every wrong, no matter who is the sufferer' and 'leads an individual to join the struggle to remove that wrong'.[11] Public conscience was the product of what Ambedkar called 'fellow feeling', 'fraternity', a sense of concern for fellow human beings in general and for the members of one's society in particular. Thanks to the caste system, which fragmented society into self-contained and mutually indifferent groups, such a fellow feeling did not develop among the Hindus. 'Caste has killed public spirit. Caste has destroyed the sense of public charity. Caste has made public opinion impossible. A Hindu's public is his caste. His responsibility is only to his caste'.[12] Indeed the very term 'Hindu society' was an oxymoron because there could be no 'society' in the absence of shared sympathies. 'In India people are treated with contempt, yet it does not sicken an Indian with disgust, rouse his sense of justice and fair play, and his humanity does not rise in protest at what is going on around him.'[13] Being entrenched within a way of thinking that reduced human beings to their membership of particular castes, caste Hindus could not see the untouchables as human beings like

---

[10] Ambedkar (1976: 3).

[11] Ambedkar (1976: 3). See also Kshirsagar (1991: 61). For Ambedkar, an 'active' conscience drives a man to 'undertake a crusade to eradicate the wrong' and 'fires him with a righteous indignation' (Ambedkar 1945: 197).

[12] Ambedkar (1945: 197).

[13] Ambedkar (1945: 197).

them, let alone as fellow members of a shared community. Not surprisingly, they rarely took interest in, let alone campaigned against their degrading and inhuman status.

Ambedkar's analysis of how untouchability had been enforced so long shaped his views on how it could be ended. For him, its eradication did not just mean ending a social practice; it involved nothing less than a social revolution, a radical restructuring of the very foundations of the Hindu society. It involved 'relentless struggle', an uncompromising, determined, and organized movement by the Dalits with a view to acquire political power, 'the key to all social progress', and using the institutions of the State to create an egalitarian and casteless society. As Ambedkar said in a Dalit meeting,

> You should realise what our objective is. It is not fighting for a few jobs here and there or for a few concessions. It is the highest cause that we have cherished in our heart, that is to see that we are recognised as the governing community.[14]

The Dalits could not mount such a struggle unless they broke the hold of the dominant ideology and realized that their lowly status was not their destiny or a result of their karma but the product of an externally imposed unjust and exploitative system. As Ambedkar observed on several occasions, slaves must be convinced 'that they need not be slaves',[15] that their slavery can be ended, and that it is within their power to do so, as the first necessary step towards their emancipation. It was equally important that the untouchables should develop a sense of self-respect, which alone can generate a 'divine discontent' with their current condition and a 'burning desire' to change it.[16] 'Self-respect is the most vital

---

[14] Das (2011, Volume 1: 34–5). A patriot is one who cares for his countrymen, whose 'humanity rises in protest against injustice', who is outraged by the harm done to them, and cannot bear to see them 'treated as being less than man'. See also Moon (1979–96, Volume 3: 44, 97), where Ambedkar says that fellow feeling is 'a sentiment which leads an individual to identify with the good of others', a 'disposition ... to treat man as the object of reverence and love'.

[15] Keer (1990: 71). As he once said, 'Tell the slave he is a slave and he will revolt' (Keer 1990).

[16] Keer (1990: 67, 124, 143, 581).

factor in life. Without this man is a mere cipher.'[17] The untouchables must realize that they were fighting not so much to 'improve' their material condition as to regain their 'honour' and 'dignity' and reclaim the 'title deeds' of their humanity.[18]

For Ambedkar, one's sense of dignity depends on others' recognition of it and their corresponding behaviour. People may assert their dignity but that has no value if it receives no response or affirmation from others. Their recognition is withheld because it is in their interest to see some as inferior, as legitimate subjects of domination. The latter need to mount a collective and determined struggle which both affirms their sense of dignity and is a means to secure its recognition. It would develop their sense of agency and power, build up their strength and self-confidence, demonstrate to their opponent that one will not be taken for granted or dismissed as inconsequential, and demand and secure his respect and recognition. Every gain in the struggle would reinforce one's self-respect and generate the energy to continue it.

It was important to Ambedkar that the Dalits should also take a critical look at themselves and ensure that they were worthy of respect in their own and others' eyes. Over the centuries, they had developed 'evil habits and bad ways of living', ugly customs, passivity, a sense of helplessness, the tendency to pursue their narrow self-interest, hierarchical gradation among themselves, low ambition, and so on.[19] As a result they were unable to not only unite for a common cause but also respect themselves and command the respect of others. They had developed deep and subtle forms of self-contempt, and half-believed that they were worthy of nothing better. While fighting against the wider society and as a necessary

---

[17] Keer (1990: 127).

[18] As Ambedkar said on 1 September 1951 while laying the foundation stone of Milind Mahavidyalaya at Aurangabad:

> The problem of raising the lower order in India ... is to remove from them that inferiority complex which has stunted their growth and made them slaves to others, to create in them the consciousness of the significance of their lives for themselves and for the country, of which they have been cruelly robbed by the existing social order. Nothing can achieve this purpose except the spread of the higher education. (Keer 1990: 551)

[19] Ambedkar, 'Who Were the Shudras', cited in Keer (1990: 143).

precondition of it, they needed to fight against themselves and acquire the intellectual and moral qualities of free men.

Ambedkar thought that while concentrating on their own liberation, the Dalits should also aim higher. Like Marx, by whom he was deeply influenced, he thought that being the most oppressed group, they constituted a negative class, a concentrated expression of the evil of the prevailing system, and should become the vanguard of all the oppressed groups in Hindu society.[20] They should form alliances with them and set up a political party committed to the cause of social and political revolution. This is what his Independent Labour Party and, later, the Republican Party of India were in their own different ways meant to do. Once the oppressed groups were united, the State was theirs to take. As he put it in one of his optimistic moods:

> [T]he scheduled castes and the backward classes form majority of the population of the country. There is no reason why they should not rule the country. All that is necessary is to organise for the purpose of capturing political power which is your own.[21]

Ambedkar argued that the Dalits could not change the Hindu social order without getting the caste Hindus to change their beliefs and practices. Like all privileged groups, caste Hindus would not do so unless they felt convinced that the Dalits were deeply serious and would not rest until the prevailing social order was radically restructured. For Ambedkar, a 'sense of crisis' brought about changes in days which the slow reformist pressure could not achieve in decades. The 'great defect of the policy of least resistance and silent infiltration of rational ideas', on which in his view Gandhi and the liberals relied, 'lies in this that they do not produce a sense of crisis'.[22] The Dalits were to create a sense of crisis by concentrating on strategically significant issues, mounting carefully planned struggles throughout the country, and refusing to be satisfied with concessions and compromises. While violence was to

---

[20] 'It is to the lower classes that we must look for the motive power of progress' (Rodrigues 2002: 82). This was so because they challenged the established social order, sought equality, and possessed the solidarity and the organizational strength required for political struggle (Rodrigues 2002: 82).

[21] Rodriges (2002: 82).

[22] Ambedkar (2014: 136).

be scrupulously avoided, some might regrettably occur. Ambedkar thought that such a determined challenge to Hindu society was bound to trigger intense introspection in it and throw up a movement for change. That should in turn pave the way for a democratic polity in which all citizens including the Dalits would enjoy equal civil and political rights.

Although universal franchise was the sine qua non for the liberation of the untouchables, it was not enough. As a minority, they were powerless before the Hindu majority, which could use the 'weapon' of democracy to continue to oppress them. In a mature democracy, the danger of this happening was mitigated by two factors. First, the majority was 'political', made up of shifting alliances and interest groups, and hence contingent and fluid. Second, it had at least some fellow feeling for the minorities and could be depended upon to pay some regard to their interests. These conditions did not apply in India, where the majority was 'communal', and hence permanent and entrenched, and did not have a fellow-feeling for the minorities. It was a 'vested corporate interest group', a 'closed governing class', before which the minorities including the untouchables were totally helpless. Ambedkar wondered how to deal with such a situation.

He conceded that the principle of majority rule lay at the heart of democracy and should be respected by anyone who valued the latter. He thought that the best way to guard against majority domination was to devise an institutional mechanism under which the majority could not rule on its own and needed to share power with the minorities, that is, to make it what Ambedkar called a 'relative majority'. He relied on two devices, the policy of reservation and weighted representation in the legislature, both already in force in some form in colonial India.

The policy of reservation involved several things, one of which involved giving the untouchables a proportionate number of constitutionally guaranteed seats in the legislature and a measure of political power. Similar reservations in the administrative structure gave them some control over the formulation and implementation of government policy.[23] Finally, reservations in educational

---

[23] Ambedkar wanted a 'proper admixture of different communities' in civil service. This might have lead to a 'small degree of inefficiency' but would correct caste biases of officers and inspire public confidence in the

institutions, especially their higher echelons, ensured that they were able to acquire the qualifications necessary to rise to the highest positions in all areas of life.

Since the danger of minorities being systematically outvoted by the majority still remained, Ambedkar proposed weighted representation. The majority was to be given fewer seats than its number warranted, and the minorities were to receive more seats than their proportion in the population. Ambedkar proposed that the Hindus who constituted 55 per cent of the population should have 40 per cent of the seats in Central Assembly. By contrast Muslims, who were just over 28 per cent of the population, were to be allocated 32 per cent of the seats; the SCs, just over 14 per cent of the population, were to be allocated 20 per cent of the seats; and so on. Under this scheme, the majority community still remained a majority in the legislature, but it was no longer an 'absolute' majority, able to get its way without the help of the minorities. The executive, too, was to be so constituted that it did not draw all its members from the majority and feel accountable only to that group. As to why the majority would accept such a reduced political representation and power, Ambedkar argued that it would otherwise face minority resistance and civil unrest. Although weighted representation did not violate the democratic principle of 'one person, one vote', it violated the equally, perhaps even more, important principle of what Ambedkar called 'one vote, one value'.[24] While conceding the point, he argued that weighted representation checked the abuse of majority power, gave the minorities an effective share in the

---

system. He agreed that the 'best' candidate should be selected for a job but insisted that one important feature of the 'best' candidate was impartiality and freedom from caste and class based antipathies and prejudices. Even the 'best' man shares the moral feelings of his class 'and may turn out to be the worst from the point of view of the servile classes'. Intellectual merit or professional qualification was necessary but not sufficient, and the definition of 'merit' or 'best' candidate should take full account of the required moral dimension. 'Mere efficiency', 'naked efficiency and nothing but efficiency' cannot be the only consideration (Moon 1979–96, Volume 9: 476–7).

[24] Ambedkar ([1947] 2017: 47). The Lucknow Pact of 1916 endorsed weighted or disproportionate representation of provincial minorities in the assemblies constituted after the 1919 reforms in Bombay; 20 per cent of Muslims had 33 per cent of assembly seats.

government of the country, safeguarded their interests and rights, and, in these and other ways, respected the fundamental principles and served the basic objectives of democracy.

For Ambedkar, this was not, however, the end of the matter. While weighted representation protected and empowered the Dalits, it did not ensure that their representatives would promote their interests. Since they depended on the majority community to get elected, they would court its goodwill and compromise the interests of their constituents. The only way to guard against this was to free them from the electoral pressure of the majority. Ambedkar thought that a separate electorate for the untouchables, to which he was once opposed, was the best way to do so, and made it one of the major planks of his political strategy. Such a provision already existed in relation to Muslims and others, and he could not see why it should not be extended to the untouchables as well.

Ambedkar insisted on a separate electorate for the untouchables at the Second Round Table Conference and secured the Communal Award of 1931. Under the Award, the SCs were to choose their own representatives as well as to have a vote in the general constituency, thus having two votes. Gandhi took the strongest objection to a separate electorate, some of his reasons being the same as those Ambedkar himself had given a year earlier when he too was opposed to it. In Gandhi's view, it was demanded by a very small minority and lacked general support among the Dalits. It assumed that caste Hindus could not be trusted to represent the interests of the untouchables, and insulted the efforts of many who were actively fighting for them. The separate electorate polarized the two communities, sharpened their differences, and hindered the development of common interests and mutual trust. It also did little to improve the condition of the untouchables, the main reason for its demand. Once they became a separate electoral unit, caste Hindus would have no incentive or reason to end the practice of untouchability and would continue to discriminate against and even ostracize them as before. Indeed they could be more brutal, especially in the exercise of their very considerable economic power, now that the restraining influence of even the minimum sense of community was replaced by resentment and hostility.

Gandhi argued that the advocates of the separate electorate were wrong to look at the issue only from the standpoint of the untouchables. Untouchability gravely damaged the caste Hindus as well both psychologically and morally. They needed to be liberated from it just as much as the untouchables, giving both a shared moral interest in ending it. Rather than break away from the Hindu society, the untouchables should work with caste Hindus and mount a common struggle against a system that diminished the humanity of both. Gandhi also had strong political reasons for rejecting the separate electorate. He thought it would encourage the untouchables to define themselves as non-Hindu or even anti-Hindu. This would make them an easy target for conversion with predictable social tensions and political consequences. It would also fuel their hostility to the Hindus and lead to alliances with other minorities that could systematically outvote the Hindus and pose a threat to their interests.

For these and related reasons, Gandhi thought he had no choice but to pit all his might against the Communal Award by embarking on an indefinite fast, something he could have avoided by showing a better understanding of and winning over Ambedkar at the Second Round Table Conference. Ambedkar condemned the fast in the strongest terms, fought hard, and secured a compromise. The separate electorate for the untouchables was rejected but the number of their representatives was considerably increased and they were to be elected in two stages. In the primary election, four untouchable candidates were to be elected by the untouchables themselves. Based on a joint electorate, whoever among them secured a majority in the general election was the winner. Although Ambedkar accepted the compromise, he continued to feel unhappy about it. It prevented an independent political movement among the untouchables based on a strong collective identity, left the election of their representatives in the hands of the Hindu majority, and denied them the benefit of a second vote. To counter this, he demanded that the winning candidate must secure at least a certain percentage of untouchable votes in the general election, but found no support in the Congress Party.

Ambedkar refused to give up and made his last attempt to secure such a provision by getting Sardar Nagappa to introduce a Bill in the Constituent Assembly. Since the term 'separate electorate' aroused deep fears, Nagappa said that his Bill involved a 'qualified joint electorate'. Voters were to be issued two ballot papers, a white one for the general and a coloured one for the SC voter. Candidates securing the minimum of 35 per cent of the SC votes were 'qualified' for election. Their general votes were then counted, and one who got the majority was declared elected. Nagappa's Bill met strong opposition and was dropped to Ambedkar's great disappointment. As he watched post-Independence India, he became bitterly disillusioned with the 'careerism' and 'hunger for power' of the SC representatives and their neglect of their communities.[25] It seems that he was no longer sure that a separate electorate would remedy the situation.[26] He could think of no other alternative than to urge the SC to choose their representatives with great care, to keep a keen eye on them, and to ensure by means of organized pressure that they did not betray their communities.

Conversion

As we saw earlier, Ambedkar took the view that untouchability was bound up with the caste system, that the latter was integral to the Hindu society, and that the untouchables would always remain such within the Hindu social framework. However, he did not entirely give up on the Hindu society, and hoped to transform it from within. He knew it had thrown up reformist movements in the past, and Gandhi's vigorous campaign against untouchability 1932 onwards gave him some hope. He supported temple-entry satyagrahas, joined the popular Ganapati festivities in Bombay (now Mumbai), arranged inter-caste dinners and meetings, and so

[25] In 1956, Ambedkar complained to his secretary Nanak Chand Rattu that 'the educated few have proved to be a worthless lot, with no sympathies for their downtrodden brethren'. They were busy 'fighting among themselves for leadership and power' (see Rattu 1997: 93). Ambedkar was acutely aware of the ways in which an individual's place in the social system shaped the structure of his thought and imposed what he called 'internal' limitation. As he once put it, 'People sometimes ask the idle question why the Pope does not introduce this or that reform. The true answer is that the revolutionist is not the kind of man who becomes a Pope, and that the man who becomes a Pope has no wish to be a revolutionist' (Rodrigues 2002: 145).

[26] The Working Committee of his Scheduled Caste Federation (SCF) resolved on 27 August 1955 that reservations for SCs in the central and state legislatures should be abolished. In his *Thoughts on Linguistic States* ([1955] 1977), written four months later, Ambedkar advanced a similar view and favoured plural member constituencies over separate electorates.

on. Increasingly, he came to feel that all this was leading nowhere. Gandhi's Harijan Sevak Sangh, which replaced the more radical Anti-untouchability League, neither involved the untouchables in their own emancipation nor confronted caste prejudices. However, the mere existence of Harijan Sevak Sangh alarmed orthodox Hindus, who intensified their resistance, spread malicious stories about Gandhi's private life, and even threatened his life. Ambedkar concluded that the Hindu society was beyond hope and that the untouchables would never achieve social equality with caste Hindus. As he remarked with considerable bitterness and exaggeration, 'There can be a better or a worse Hindu. But a good Hindu there cannot be.'[27]

Around 1935 onwards, Ambedkar began to lose interest in temple-entry satyagrahas and fostering better inter-caste relations, and talked instead of converting to another religion. He put the point well in a speech in April 1942: 'I thought for long that we could rid the Hindu society of its evils and get the Depressed classes incorporated into it on terms of equality.... With that objective in mind we burned the Manu Smriti and performed mass thread ceremonies. Experience has taught me better ... we no longer want to be part of the Hindu society.'[28] Pride and self-respect too played a part as he felt that a religion that had for centuries treated his people so abominably did not deserve their allegiance. Although born a Hindu, he said he did not want to die as one.

For Ambedkar, it was not enough to reject Hinduism; conversion to another was crucial for two important reasons. First, since Hinduism was not defined by a set of core beliefs whose rejection amounted to an exit from it but was rather acquired by birth, one could cease to be a Hindu only by explicitly embracing another religion. Second, religion for him was not so much a matter of personal belief as of social belonging and collective solidarity. To profess a religion was to belong to a particular community, to enjoy a sense of fellow feeling with its members, and to derive strength from their support. Conversion meant acquiring not just a new set of beliefs but a new community, a new source of solidarity. For Ambedkar, unless the untouchables aligned themselves with and derived collective strength from an established

[27] Moon (1979–96, Volume 1: Appendix II).
[28] Kunte (1982: 250).

religion, they risked perpetuating their current social isolation and powerlessness.

Ambedkar asked which religion the untouchables and even perhaps other backward castes should convert to. He ruled out Christianity and Islam, the preference for many of them in the past, on several grounds. Since they had gone for mass conversions, they needed to accommodate the caste consciousness of their new converts and remained deeply infected by it. Although their caste system was 'fundamentally different' from its Hindu counterpart and did not involve religious sanction, excommunication, pollution, and inequality of status, it too was hierarchical and discouraged easy social contact. Ambedkar also thought that Christianity and Islam tended to 'denationalize' converts. Religions in India had a strong cultural, historical, and political content, and signified distinct nationalities. Since Ambedkar saw Islam and Christianity as 'foreign' religions, he thought that to convert to them was to step out of not only the Hindu society but also the Indian nation, something the untouchables did not and should not wish to do.

Ambedkar's choice of religion was limited to Sikhism and Buddhism. He was sympathetic to the former in his early years, but felt that it too was tainted by the caste system, though not to the same extent as Christianity and Islam, and carried a good deal of Hindu philosophical and cultural baggage. He preferred Buddhism, a 'truly egalitarian' religion that had emerged in direct opposition to Hinduism without losing its Indian roots. It placed morality at its centre instead of God, concentrated on social ethics rather than divine worship and the other-worldly destiny of the human soul, involved no theological beliefs, and was not so much a religion as *dhamma* (ethics). Since Ambedkar took the view that the untouchables were originally Buddhists and had been made to suffer because of that, conversion to Buddhism also had the advantage of returning to their roots and settling historical scores with Brahmanic Hinduism. He converted to it himself and encouraged thousands of his followers to do the same in Nagpur on 14 October 1956, nearly twenty years after he had first raised the subject. He called the conversion 'rebirth'—an 'end' to one form of life or mode of existence and the 'beginning' of another. It is arguable whether the Buddha himself would have been sympathetic to mass conversions, especially on the advice of a leader and at public meetings.

Vision of India

Ambedkar's vision of Independent India was articulated in terms of the three interrelated ideas of liberty, equality, and fraternity, familiar since the French Revolution but which he attributed to the Buddha. In a broadcast in 1954, thinking of the Buddha, he said, 'positively my social philosophy may be said to the enshrined in three words, Liberty, Equality and Fraternity. Let no one, however say that I have borrowed my philosophy from the French Revolution. I have not. My philosophy has roots in religion.'[29] Liberty stood for self-determination and the ability to lead a life of one's choice. It required a constitutionally guaranteed body of legal, political, and other rights, and depended on a well-structured State. Equality meant 'one man, one value'. It involved not only political equality or equality of rights and political power, but also social and economic equality. Social equality referred to equality of status and respect based on acknowledgement of the equal dignity and shared humanity of all human beings, and involved absence of all forms of discrimination, hierarchy, and exclusion in formal and informal relations. Economic equality meant equality of life chances and a broad equality of economic power. It required that no individual or group should be at mercy of or exercise disproportionate power over others. Ambedkar called this 'socialism' or 'State socialism' and distinguished it from the welfare State, which provided a safety net to the poor but took little interest in the inequality of economic power and wealth.

The programme of the Independent Labour Party on which he fought the elections of 1937 included a planned economy, nationalization of key industries including land and insurance, extensive State-supported industrialization, agricultural cooperatives, land mortgage banks, guaranteed workers' rights, land settlement and public works to relieve unemployment, and free and compulsory primary education. Ambedkar wanted socialism to be enshrined in the Constitution so as to place it 'beyond the reach of a Parliamentary majority to suspend, amend or abrogate it'.[30] He later changed his mind on both. He diluted the socialist programme when he set up the Republican Party of India, and decided against giving socialism a constitutional status in order to respect

---

[29] Keer (1990: 459).
[30] Ambedkar ([1947] 2017: 46).

genuine differences of views on the subject and to allow the electorate to make its own choice.

For Ambedkar, fraternity meant fellow feeling, a sense of concern for and an active interest in the well-being of the members of one's society. It presupposed, but went beyond, equality and involved a sense of common belonging. People could be equal yet avoid living together, inter-dining, inter-marriage, and other forms of social intercourse. For him, mere citizenship—a relationship based on common political allegiance—was not enough. It needed to be embedded in and complemented by 'kinship', fraternity, mutual concern, shared nationhood, or what John Stuart Mill called a 'sentiment of nationality'. A sense of common belonging referred to 'a longing not to belong to any other group' but this one, a 'corporate sentiment of oneness'.[31] Unlike nationalism, which reified the nation and was aggressive and collectivist, the sentiment of nationality or nationhood meant no more than feeling at home with and caring for the well-being of people inhabiting a common territorial unit. It fostered social cohesion, mutual trust, a willingness to make sacrifices for others, and above all a 'public conscience'.

Fraternity underpinned liberty and equality and realized them in areas lying beyond the reach of the law for Ambedkar. Take something as basic as the rule of law, which is at the heart of liberty and equality. It implies that all are equally subject to the law, that none are above the law, and that it is enforced in a non-discriminatory manner. In the absence of fraternity, a law might satisfy these formal requirements, but be so designed as to serve the interests of a particular group or oppress a minority. Even if it was just in its content, the judges and the police might subvert it in practice. Judges necessarily enjoyed some degree of discretion in all legal systems, and had to decide who to accept as witnesses, how much credence to give to their testimonies, what counted as evidence, how to weigh it up, and so on. They might use their discretion to the detriment of those with whom they shared no fellow feeling or against whom they harboured prejudices. Similarly, if the police despised certain groups, they might distort evidence, ignore their complaints, record things that were never said, and harass them in ways too subtle to prove in a court of law. Furthermore, several areas of human life lay beyond the reach of

---

[31] Moon (2002, Volume 8: 143).

the law. If a fellow passenger vacates her seat or mumbles abuses when a member of the despised group sits next to her, or when a man refuses to rent his property to a member of the minority community, the law offers the victim little to no protection. As Ambedkar put it:

> It is striking that the worst injustice and persecution can be perpetrated within the limits of the law and in the name of the law, and a Hindu may well say that he will not employ an untouchable, that he will not sell him anything, that he will evict him from his land, that he will not allow him to take his cattle across his land, without offending the law in the slightest degree because the law is limited to the state, and in civil society oppression reigns rampant.[32]

For Ambedkar, then, liberty, equality, and fraternity were inseparable. Without equality, liberty was precarious and at the mercy of the dominant group and without liberty, equality led to uniformity and killed individuality, initiative, and creativity. Without fraternity or identification with other members of one's society, equality and liberty would be subverted in subtle ways and remain 'no deeper than coats of paints'.[33] Conversely, fraternity was impossible in the absence of liberty and equality that removed artificial barriers between individuals and groups, facilitated easy interactions between them, and fostered a common sense of belonging.

It is hardly surprising that the Preamble to the Constitution of India, which bears Ambedkar's unmistakable fingerprints, enjoins the State not only to secure justice, liberty, and equality to its citizens but also to 'promote among them all fraternity'. He was convinced that unless Indians rose above castes and creeds and discarded the deeply ingrained ideas of inequality and hierarchy, they could never become a 'united people'. He was also convinced that what mattered most to the people, especially the oppressed minorities, was that the government should be 'for' them, and it was to be 'of' or 'by' them largely because that was the best way to make it work 'for' them. Democratic procedures and institutions did matter, but so too did the objectives pursued and the ultimate outcome.

Ambedkar argued that this was not going to be easy because of a deep tension at the very heart of the Indian polity. Its Constitution

---

[32] Moon (1979–96, Volume 5: 270–1).
[33] Moon (1979–96, Volume 13: 1217).

committed it to the great ideals of liberty, equality, and fraternity, but these were largely absent in its daily life. As a result, the State and society pulled in opposite directions. Ambedkar put the point well in his important speech in the Constituent Assembly on 25 November 1949:

> On 26th January, which is our Republic Day, the country is going to enter a life of contradictions. In politics, we will have equality but in social and economic life we will have inequality.
>
> In politics, we will be recognising the principle of 'one man one vote' and 'one vote one value'. In our social and economic life, we shall by reason of our social and economic structure continue to deny the principle of 'one man—one value'. How long shall we continue to live this life of contradiction? How long shall we continue to deny equality in our social and economic life? If we continue to deny it for long, we will do so only by putting our political democracy in peril. We must remove this contradiction at the earliest possible moment, or else those who suffer from inequality will blow up the structure of political democracy which this Assembly has so laboriously built up.[34]

For Ambedkar, the contradiction could only be resolved by the State dominating and systematically shaping society in the desired direction. Since the objectives of the State were alien to the conservative Indian society, the State must be led by a determined elite. If the State became a hostage to society, as was the case for centuries in premodern India, or was led by men and women with no commitment to these objectives as in colonial India, Ambedkar saw no hope for the country.

Critical Appreciation

Ambedkar's thought was born in the crucible of personal experience and shows remarkable originality and insight. He was primarily concerned with the analysis of the causes, modes of legitimation, mechanisms of oppression, and ways of eradicating the practice of untouchability. He rightly located untouchability within the larger discussion of inequality, and examined the latter without losing sight of the specific form it had taken in the Hindu society. His

---

[34] Moon (1979–96, Volume 13: 1216).

analysis of the graded nature of Hindu inequality is profound, and explains why it was largely taken for granted for centuries and made organized opposition difficult. He skilfully traced its cultural, economic, and political roots and showed how they reinforced each other. Ambedkar was right to argue that the rigid compartmentalization of society brought about by the caste system and the resulting ethos of mutual indifference militated against any kind of fellow feeling and common life. This partly explains why, in the vast Brahmanic literature on the subject, there was very little criticism of the caste system. The critique was first mounted by the Buddhists. Even they were not as radical as they could have been, and their ideas were marginalized once the Brahmanic orthodoxy regained its domination.

So far as the eradication of untouchability was concerned, Ambedkar rightly stressed that the untouchables were not and should not see themselves as its passive victims waiting for others to liberate them. His great contribution lay in forging among them a sense of collective identity. He traced their origins and history, highlighted the specificity of their experiences, offered them a vision of their radical social mission, reminded them of their earlier acts of resistance, and located their current struggle within an inspiring tradition. He mounted a powerful critique of the Dharmashastras and gave the Dalits badly needed critical tools to attack the dominant religious ideology. In these and other ways, he sharpened and raised their self-consciousness and helped them become a self-determining collective subject. This extraordinary achievement has largely been responsible for a strong sense of Dalit identity reflected in the most welcome emergence of Dalit politics, a distinct body of Dalit literature, and a distinct Dalit perspective on Indian history.

Unlike many radicals, Ambedkar refused to romanticize the Dalits or nurture their sense of victimhood and self-pity, and urged them to put their own house in order. They needed to change their ways of thought and life and equip themselves intellectually and morally for their emancipatory struggle. He stressed that their struggle had to be conducted at several levels, including the ideological, social, political and economic, and that it was closely bound up with those of other backward castes and classes. He strove all his life to bring them together within a single political party committed to a radical economic programme.

Approaching democracy, equality, nationhood, State, and so on from his unique perspective, Ambedkar was able to highlight and offer new insights into their neglected dimensions. More than any other Indian leader, he stressed the vital importance of social equality and showed that in its absence, political equality remained ineffective. As he argued, social inequality humiliates and degrades its victims, undermines their pride and self-respect, and even breeds self-contempt. It also profoundly distorts their formal and informal relations with other groups and makes their lives a veritable nightmare. While political and economic equality can facilitate social equality, they cannot by themselves create and sustain it. This was why Ambedkar was highly critical of liberals and Marxists who respectively put their faith in political and economic equality, took a reductionist view of social equality, and failed to appreciate its specificity and complexity.

The idea of fraternity is neglected in much of the modern especially liberal political theory, and Ambedkar was right to stress its importance. A victim of inequality and social rejection himself, he appreciated the role of fellow feeling in shaping our ideas of justice, influencing the content and enforcement of law, and inspiring the struggle against injustices. Although one can be moved by an abstract commitment to the ideals of equality and justice, one's pursuit of them is energetic and tenacious when one is able to see the victims in their concreteness, identify with them, feel their pain and sorrow, share common emotional bonds with them, and is thus driven by what Ambedkar called fellow feeling or fraternity. He was right to stress the importance of moral emotions and a shared collective identity, and reject a narrowly rationalist view of human conduct.

Ambedkar's analysis of nationhood, with which he associated the idea of fraternity, is equally rich and suggestive.[35] A nation for him was not an abstraction, a transcendental entity hovering over

---

[35] As mentioned in Pal (2017: 193):

Without social union political unity is difficult to be achieved. If achieved, it would be as precarious as a summer sapling ... With mere political unity India may be a state. But to be a state is not to be a nation, and a state, which is not a nation, has only small prospects of survival in the struggle for existence.

Ambedkar thought that a multi-ethnic or 'composite' State needed to develop a strong sense of social unity to counter ethnic nationalism.

and dominating its members, but a community of men and women bound together by the ties of mutual concern and commitment. To serve the nation was nothing more and nothing less than to promote their well-being. This is why he felt that India's independence struggle could not be conducted in isolation from the internal struggle against its own oppressive social order. As he observed on many occasions, a nation is not a primordial entity but a political project, not given by nature but a collective creation of the moral imagination of its members, and has claims on them only to the extent that it includes them fully in its self-understanding. Like Tagore and Gandhi, his view of nationhood had a humanist orientation and was remarkably free from the collectivism, narrowness, and aggressiveness that are generally associated with it.

While much in Ambedkar's social and political thought is valuable and needs to be built upon, it has its limitations. I shall briefly highlight four of these. First, Ambedkar relied too heavily on intricate institutional mechanisms and devices to promote the interests of the untouchables, and did not fully appreciate the importance of changing the moral culture of the wider society and Gandhi's role in it. To be sure, he did say that the 'Hindu mentality' needed to change, and that their 'outlook, traditions ... and social philosophy'[36] had to be transformed, but these were passing remarks and he did not explore how this was to be done and what it entailed. Not all his institutional mechanisms would make much difference to the plight of the Dalits if the Hindu majority remained implacably hostile to them. It might refuse to establish them in the first instance and suppress the likely resistance, or accept and subvert them in all too familiar ways. Even the separate electorate on which he pinned all his hopes would not have been of much help. There was no reason to believe that the untouchables would necessarily elect radical leaders and that, even if they did, the Hindu majority could not outvote, buy off, or co-opt them. A profound cultural change was needed among the caste Hindus, and that could be best brought about by their leadership.

Gandhi saw this and insisted that the Hindus must put their house in order. Untouchability was a Hindu practice, and it was their duty to 'repent', 'do penance', express regrets, and fight it. This might involve suffering and bloodshed, but it 'should be theirs'

---

[36] Kunte (1982: 250).

not the untouchables'. The practice went against not only the great moral values of human dignity and equality but also many of their own great ideals, and they owed it to 'Hinduism and themselves' to mobilize its reformist resources. The fight against untouchability was a struggle for the very soul of their religion. It was moral and spiritual not just political in its nature, and required the involvement of every one of them.

Gandhi led the campaign with great zeal and deployed a wide variety of strategies. When a textual exegesis did not help in his debates with the orthodox, he appealed to the 'spirit' of Hindu religion, and when that failed to work, to universal morality and conscience. He also appealed to Hindu pride, guilt, shame, self-interest, and the good name of their religion, and generated enormous moral and political energy in support of his reformist cause. He set a personal example by adopting an untouchable girl, cleaning latrines, living and sharing meals with the untouchables, attending marriages only when one of the parties belonged to them—all in themselves trivial but symbolically significant and subversive of deeply ingrained taboos. Although his endorsement of some version of the caste system until the last few years of his life, his concern not to alienate the conservatives and weaken the unity of the independence struggle, and his tendency to view the untouchables as a 'poem of pity' and failure to involve them in their struggle meant that his campaign was not as radical as it should have been, it nevertheless had a transformative effect on the Hindu society. Inspired by him, thousands of Hindus, mainly middle class, carried his campaign to the remotest parts of the country, threw up reformist movements, and weakened the foundations of the practice of untouchability. It is, of course, more than likely that he would not have given the subject high priority without Ambedkar's pressure. But equally the latter would have been marginalized like other such leaders and movements in the past without the profound cultural change brought about by Gandhi. The two played complementary roles, one concentrating on caste Hindus and the other on the untouchables, one exerting moral and social and the other political pressure on the Hindu orthodoxy.

Second, Ambedkar homogenized both Dalits and caste Hindus, and ignored their internal differences and common concerns. He was convinced that the Dalits had common interests and a common enemy, and that they should all unite behind the banner of 'one party, one leader, one programme'. He saw himself as their only true spokesman, and his programme as the master key to their liberation. Although he was one of their best spokesmen and shoulders above their other leaders, he was not the only one and his views were not shared by all. The Dalits in different parts of India had different histories, different patterns of interaction with caste Hindus, and, beyond a certain point, faced different problems. Their leaders disagreed about the causes and the best ways of eradicating untouchability, including such questions as the separate electorate, the policy of reservation, socialism, the role of the State, and the nature of the Hindu society. Ambedkar tended to challenge their representative credentials and sometimes dismissed them as Congress stooges or victims of false consciousness. Apart from being unfair, such an approach tended to discourage a vigorous and healthy debate among the untouchables, and suppress genuine differences of views.

Ambedkar showed the same homogenizing tendency in his discussion of caste Hindus. Almost all his proposals, such as the separate electorate and weighted representation, were based on the assumption that caste Hindus were almost all hostile to the untouchables, that they formed a solid faction, and that no justice could be expected from them. This is why he dismissed Nehru, the communists, and others as unreliable friends, dubbed them and almost all upper caste Hindus as 'Brahmins', and once even said that no Hindu judge could be trusted to do justice to the untouchables, a widely resented remark for which he later apologized. Ambedkar's view did great injustice to large groups of Hindus. While some Hindus approved of untouchability, others did not. Among the latter, some were for the caste system, some against it, yet others opposed its current form but not the allegedly egalitarian classical *varna*s (castes). Furthermore, caste Hindus belonged to different castes, and had their own conflicts of interests and disputes about their relative hierarchical status. The same minutely graded inequality that hindered lower-caste unity also prevented that of the upper castes. Caste Hindus were neither a homogenous and cohesive group nor an implacable enemy of the untouchables. This is not to say that Ambedkar was wrong to attack high-caste domination, but rather that he was wrong to take a quasi-Manichean view of Hindu society and make it the sole basis of his emancipatory strategy.

Third, Ambedkar's thought had a strong statist and elitist bias. Like many modernists he drew too neat a contrast between State and society, seeing the former as a rational progressive agency and the latter as reactionary and blighted, and relied on the coercive power of the State to transform society. He preferred a centralized State, a unitary form of government, and opposed devolution of power to the villages that he dismissed as a 'sink of localism' and a 'den of narrow mindedness'.[37] The State for him could only play a radical reformist role if it was led by a Westernized elite free from the limitations of the vast majority of their fellow citizens and acting in an authoritarian manner. True to the logic of this view, Ambedkar once suggested that the caste system and untouchability could be eradicated summarily if only India could throw up its equivalent of Mustapha Kamal Pasha or even Mussolini! He even wanted the State to regulate and rationalize the Hindu religion, lay down its central principles, proscribe some of its beliefs, and monitor the training and conduct of its priesthood. He did not ask what competence the State had in religious matters, how this kind of theological engineering was possible in a liberal democratic society, or whether it should be done in relation to other religious communities as well. Ambedkar was right to stress the State's emancipatory role but wrong to not see that force alone could not secure or sustain large-scale changes. Furthermore, to turn to the Westernized social and political elite as the sole agent of social transformation was not only to condemn the vast majority of Indians to the status of passive objects but also to alienate them from the State and weaken its legitimacy in their eyes.[38]

Fourth, although Ambedkar was right to emphasize the importance of fraternity or collective fellow feeling, he gave very little thought to how to develop and nurture it. Castes obviously stood in the way, but their abolition did not guarantee it. Equal citizenship facilitated it but it too was not enough. Ambedkar was silent on what else needed to be done to build common bonds of sympathy and mutual concern among citizens. What is worse, some of his own proposals seemed to militate against it. He relied on, among other

[37] Moon (1979–96, Volume 13: 62).

[38] In spite of his strong commitment to the socialist economy, Ambedkar placed great emphasis on individual liberties and rights and called Article 32, which protected them, 'the soul of the Constitution' (Pal 2017: 593).

things, the separate electorate to safeguard Dalit interests, but that could ghettoize them and hinder their normal interactions with the majority without which no common belonging is possible. One might argue that the separate electorate builds up their strength and confidence, empowers them, commands majority respect, and facilitates their integration. However, its dynamics can also work in the opposite direction, as it did in the case of Muslims in colonial India. It might heighten the sense of separateness, intensify the caste-based identity, and give the Dalit leadership a vested interest in perpetuating it. Even the conversion to Buddhism can have a similar effect. While giving the Dalits a strong sense of collective pride and identity, it can also distance them from the Hindu society and hinder common belonging. This is not at all to argue against conversion, but rather to suggest that separation, whether political, social, or religious on which Ambedkar so heavily relied, sits uneasily with the goal of fraternity.

★ ★ ★

I have so far highlighted Ambedkar's important insights and limitations. He was a product of his age and made assumptions typical of it. Like any great thinker he needs to be periodically reinterpreted and revised in the light of the changing circumstances. Some of his limitations are adventitious and can be easily overcome. Others such as his statism and quasi-Manichean view of Hindu society are integral to his thought, and require rethinking the fundamentals of his basic approach.

References

Ambedkar, B.R. 1917. 'Castes in India'. *Indian Antiquary* XLI (May).
———. 1945. *What Congress and Gandhi Have Done to the Untouchables*. Bombay: Thacker and Co.
———. 1946. *Who Were the Shudras? How They Came to Be the Fourth Varna in the Indo-Aryan Society*. Bombay: Thacker and Co.
———. 1948. *The Untouchables: Who Were They and Why They Became Untouchables*. Delhi: Amrit Book Company.
———. 1976. *Conditions Precedent for the Successful Working of Democracy*. Nagpur: Y.M. Panchbhai.
———. [1955] 1977. *Thoughts on Linguistic States*. Jalandhar: Bheem Patrika.

———. 1979–96. 'Annihilation of Caste'. In *Dr. Babasaheb Ambedkar: Writings and Speeches*, Volume 1, edited by Vasant Moon, pp. 23–96. Bombay: Dept. of Education, Government of Maharashtra.

———. 2014. *Dr. Babasaheb Ambedkar: Writings and Speeches*, Volume 9, edited by Vasant Moon. Bombay: Dept. of Education, Government of Maharashtra.

———. [1947] 2017. *States and Minorities: What Are Their Rights and How to Secure Them in the Constitution of Free India*. Delhi: Kalpaz Publications.

Das, Bhagwan. 2011. *Thus Spoke Ambedkar: A Stake in the Nation*, Volume 1. New Delhi: Navayana Publisher.

Keer, Dhananjay. 1990. *Dr Ambedkar: Life and Mission*. Bombay: Popular Prakashan.

Kshirsagar, R.K. 1991. *Political Thought of Dr Babasaheb Ambedkar*. New Delhi: Intellectual Publishing House.

Kunte, B.G. (comp.). 1982. *Source Material on Dr. Babasaheb Ambedkar and the Movement of Untouchables*, Volume 1. Bombay: Education Department, Government of Maharashtra.

Moon, Vasant (ed.). 1979–96. *Dr. Babasaheb Ambedkar: Writings and Speeches*. 10 Volumes. Bombay: Dept. of Education, Government of Maharastra.

——— (ed.). 2002. *Dr. Babasaheb Ambedkar: Writings and Speeches*, Volume 8. Mumbai: Education Department.

Pal, Samaraditya. 2017. *Indian Constitution, Origins and Evolution: Constituent Assembly Debates*, Volume 7. Nagpur: Lexis Nexis.

Rattu, N.C. 1997. *Last Few Years of Dr Ambedkar*. New Delhi: Amrit Publishing House.

Rodrigues, Valerian (ed.). 2002. *The Essential Writings of Ambedkar*. New Delhi: Oxford University Press.

2

B.R. Ambedkar and Antonio Gramsci

Justice for the Excluded, Education for Democracy*

COSIMO ZENE

> Educate yourselves because we'll need all your intelligence. Rouse yourselves because we need all your enthusiasm. Organise yourselves because we need all your strength.
>
> *Antonio Gramsci*[1]

> Educate, Organise, Agitate!
>
> It might be asked why the principle of equal justice has failed to have its effect. The answer to this is simple. To enunciate the principle of justice is one thing. To make it effective is another thing...
>
> *Bhimrao Ramji Ambedkar*[2]

Ambedkar and Gramsci were both born in 1891, but this is not the most relevant feature that unites them. They both lived in a

---

* An earlier version of this chapter appeared as 'Justice for the Excluded and Education for Democracy in B.R. Ambedkar and A. Gramsci' in *Rethinking Marxism* 30 (4): 494–524 in 2018; © Taylor & Francis. Used with permission from the author. Quoted material from Paik (2014) has been reproduced with permission from Routledge.

[1] Gramsci (1992: 71).
[2] Ambedkar (1989: 71).

period of great change and upheaval, culminating in two World Wars and both participated intensively to respond to the challenges their respective countries were facing. And yet, their involvement in high-level politics did not prevent them from engaging with the status of those who were placed 'on the margins of history' and 'out of the temple', deprived of any agency to live a decent, human life. Both of them understood that democracy, in order to be true, cannot generate inevitable casualties. True democracy cannot afford to allow the exclusion of groups and entire communities from participating in the democratic process.

Both leaders concur that education is indispensable for Dalits and subalterns so as to achieve self-awareness and consciousness of their active role in society. These leaders' own individual experiences of education as a tool to achieve political mastery and effectiveness can be very revealing. Gramsci, although a very successful student, had to struggle to make progress and, given his political and journalist interests[3] as well as lack of means, never managed to finish his degree at the University of Turin, Italy. This did not prevent him, however, from learning, cultivating his mind, and probing 'intellectuals' while also instructing them. When reading Gramsci's jail sentence, the fascist prosecutor said, 'We must prevent this brain from thinking for 20 years.'[4] If anything, life in prison motivated Gramsci to think even more intensively, not solely about himself but also about others, and especially those robbed of their freedom. Similarly, the prison of untouchability did not prevented Ambedkar from thinking. He was more fortunate than Gramsci, completing his education with high achievements in world-renowned universities. Yet he never conceived his education as a personal gain and property but as a gift to be shared with others, especially those less privileged. In this sense, he provides us with a clear example of the Gramscian 'integral historian' and 'democratic intellectual'.

For both leaders, education came top of the agenda and, far from representing a mere acquisition of erudition, it must become an engine that transforms reality and a wisdom which inspires further praxis. Education in itself is a dead end, if it does not make

---

[3] As Carlucci (2017: 36) notes: 'The student of linguistics consecrated himself entirely to political activity.'

[4] Gramsci (1971: lxxxix). Gramsci (1971) will be referred hereafter as SPN.

the 'principle of justice' effective for all, in the plural. Ambedkar and Gramsci as 'collective thinkers' knew that the achievement of real 'social justice' would come to fruition only when Dalits and subalterns were able to engender their own intellectuals, their very 'collective thinkers'. At a time when the whole educational system seems to be moving globally towards the marketization of knowledge, the danger that the 'weaker sections' will be once again robbed of their ability, opportunity and right to think, runs high. Statistics tell us that 130 million girls worldwide are not in education. I wonder—and Ambedkar would too—how many Dalit girls contribute to the soaring of that staggering data. And yet, some Dalit women who have taken to writing their life-experience (*testimonios*[5]) help us to reflect on the significance of untouchability as a social and a political reality. They have even provoked further reflection among Indian feminist intellectuals.[6] As part of our education policies, are we ready to listen to their voices and willing to learn from them?

The proposed 'rapprochement' (not a 'comparison') between Ambedkar and Gramsci is not invoked here so as to validate the praxis of one vis-à-vis the other, but to celebrate their mutual accomplishments and, possibly, to find inspiration in their deep ethical commitment towards those who have been excluded from social justice and community life, and prevented from being active members of the history and life of one's country.

To dispel all doubts regarding the aforementioned, it will suffice to quote Article 46 of the Indian Constitution, since this bears the mark of Ambedkar's signature throughout:

> The State shall promote with special care the educational and economic interests of the weaker section of the people, and in particular, of the Scheduled Castes and the Scheduled Tribes, and shall protect them from social injustice and all forms of exploitation.

Not only is Ambedkar here urging the State to care for the education of the 'weaker sections', but he is also educating the State to be truthful to democracy and social justice and reminding us that it is not enough to 'enunciate the principle of

---

[5] See Nayar (2012).
[6] See Arya and Singh Rathore (2020).

justice', but commitment to praxis is needed so as 'to make it effective'.[7]

In a previous work, I have attempted to bring together the political philosophies of Gramsci and Ambedkar,[8] mostly in connection with their mutual interest in the status of subalterns and Dalits, in the specific cases of Italy and India, but applicable also to a wider scenario, as both of them envisaged. In this first effort in 2010, I invited a group of Gramscian and Ambedkarite scholars to reflect upon some aspects of the two leaders' political philosophies revolving around the emergence of subaltern/Dalit subjectivity and historical agency, the function of intellectuals and the interpretation of 'common sense', the experience of subalternity and consciousness in Dalit literature, and the role of religion in subaltern and Dalit lives. Following this, more recently, I reflected on the relevance of an innovative, transforming, and immanent 'spirituality' of subalterns and Dalits, which provides support for their struggle to return from 'the margins of history' to the centre of human life and politics, thus reaffirming the dignity of their full-humanity.[9] Gramsci's notion of the 'creative spirit of the people' (*spirito popolare creativo*) and Ambedkar's search for an alternative and transformative Buddhism bear witness to the continuity of a journey very much still in progress. In order to make this immanent spirituality operative for individuals and entire groups of subalterns and Dalits, education is a must.

Gramsci: The Power of Education, the Struggle for Hegemonies, and Educating to Democracy

Gramsci's writings on schooling and education, which underscore his political pedagogy, are disseminated within his journalistic, pre-prison works, as well as his *Letter from Prison* and *Prison Notebooks*. Particularly in the latter work, Gramsci provides his most incisive and mature thoughts on this argument, which must at any rate be considered not as an isolated treatise but as part of the totality of his political vision and action—in one word, as an

---

[7] Ambedkar (1927).
[8] See Zene (2013).
[9] Zene (2016).

integral part of his philosophy of praxis, as the following oft-quoted paragraph from *Notebook 10* makes clear:

> The educational relationship should not be restricted to the field of strictly 'scholastic' relationships.... This form of relationship exists throughout society as a whole and for every individual relative to other individuals. It exists between the intellectual and non-intellectual sections of the population, between the rulers and the ruled, élites and their followers, leaders and led [*dirigenti e diretti*] and the vanguard and the body of the army. Every relationship of 'hegemony' is necessarily an educational relationship and occurs not only within a nation, between the various forces of which the nation is composed, but in the international and world-wide field, between complexes of national and continental civilization. (Q10 §44, 1331; SPN: 350)[10]

Although this paragraph must be read diachronically in conjunction with other writings of Gramsci, it contains in a nutshell the essence of his demanding pedagogy: The ubiquity of hegemony in all spheres, from the classroom to international relations, demands ideally the presence of an 'educational relationship' when the State is set to become an integral democracy. Since history is always in the making and given that 'everyone can be a philosopher/intellectual', everyone can also (learn to) be a 'leader', even (or especially) the subalterns, given that everyone has the right to exercise 'the fundamental power to think' (Q12 §2).

In a recent short but dense article, aptly entitled 'Hegemony and Pedagogy' [*Egemonia e pedagogia*], Baldacci retraces the strong link between the two concepts to a felicitous period of around fifty years ago, when the pedagogical interest in Gramsci's work gained prominence.[11] In the 1967 'Convegno di Studi Gramsciani di Cagliari', two sessions discussed the topic of education, schooling,

---

[10] References to Gramsci's *Prison Notebooks* will follow the internationally established standard of notebook number (Q), number of note (§), and page number, according to the Italian critical edition (see Gramsci 1975). The English translation of this edition, currently including Gramsci's first eight notebooks in three volumes, is still a work in progress (see Gramsci 1992, 1996, 2007). A partial English translation is also available (see SPN).

[11] See Baldacci (2016).

and culture in Gramsci.[12] In the same year as the Cagliari Convegno, the anthology *La formazione dell'uomo*[13]—a detailed compilation of Gramsci's writings on schooling and educational issues—was also published. In this essay, Baldacci retraces the initial relevance of the concept of hegemony in Gramscian thought to soon after 1956, when Togliatti—leader of the Italian Communist Party (PCI [Partito Comunista Italiano])—proposed a 'Leninist Gramsci' while affirming that in Gramsci there was no 'substantial difference' between hegemony and dictatorship. However, the socialist historian Tamburrano insisted that there was in fact a substantial difference, 'since Gramsci puts the accent on the need to obtain the consensus of the masses, which means a democratic conquest of power and an equally democratic preservation of it'.[14] According to Baldacci, at that point, there seemed to be two different interpretations of the concept of hegemony in Gramsci: (*i*) a (Marxist) continuity with the concept borrowed from Lenin (Togliatti and Luciano Gruppi); and (*ii*) a more liberal-socialist position (Bobbio and Tamburrano), which underlines 'the novelty of Gramscian thought and its distance form Leninist orthodoxy'.[15]

This rich background provided the favourable conditions for Giovanni Urbani, the editor of the anthology *La formazione dell'uomo*, to bring hegemony and pedagogy together in his extensive introduction, clarifying that 'it would not be possible to understand Gramsci's special interest shown towards pedagogical problems ... nor the solution he puts forward concerning the "schooling question", if both instances are not reconnected with the political problem'.[16] Hence, Urbani, while interpreting Gramsci's pedagogy through the leitmotif of hegemony, analyses the 'dynamic of the process according to which the subaltern class acquires leadership', clarifying that 'this is perhaps the "core" of Gramscian politics'.[17] According to him, while a younger Gramsci

---

[12] Rossi (1969–70).
[13] Urbani (1967).
[14] Tamburrano ([1959] 1976), quoted in Baldacci (2016: 143).
[15] Baldacci (2016: 144).
[16] Urbani (1967: 14), quoted in Baldacci (2016: 143). The 'schooling question' refers here to the reform of the educational system—known as *Riforma Gentile*—devised and implemented in 1923 by the minister of education of the fascist government, philosopher Giovanni Gentile.
[17] Baldacci (2016: 144).

was concerned with 'spontaneity' and the initiative from below, in his later years he unifies this with the demands coming from leadership: 'The concept of hegemony is therefore born as a solution to the relationship between direction and spontaneity, between leaders and led, between initiative from above and the one from below.'[18] In this context, Gramsci sees also the power of the State (the dominant classes) as both an exercise and a combination of domination (including coercion) and consent. When subaltern groups are ready to challenge the dominant hegemony, the 'class struggle' becomes a 'struggle of hegemonies', in which individual and social development concur to the transformation of history and achievement of autonomy, thanks to a newly acquired critical consciousness by the subalterns.

Baldacci maintains that Urbani, privileging a 'wider concept of hegemony', highlights its pedagogical profile, thus revealing the propensity of the led as 'growth towards autonomy' and a progressive overcoming of the division between leaders and led, according to the normative historical and political principle as 'an ideal of human formation according to which all men ... must become leaders'.[19] This happens, according to Urbani, with the formation of a new State, following a new 'human ideal' in which the former 'anonymous conformism' becomes a new and 'superior social conformism'.

At the basis of Urbani's interpretation of Gramsci's thought lies the solution to the problem of democracy, in the relationship between spontaneity and direction, between leaders and led: 'On an individual (molecular) level, the hegemonic relationship always presents itself as an educational rapport, since through this the leader aims to modify the conscience of the led "arousing their initiative and active participation".'[20] Commenting on Gramsci's note (Q10 §44), Baldacci said, 'Urbani seems to suggest [perhaps over-interpreting Gramsci] that the pedagogical relationship must be assumed to be the model for any relationship of hegemony, and that therefore this is truly such only if it takes on an educational profile, thus promoting a growth of the subject being led.'[21] In other

---

[18] Baldacci (2016: 144).
[19] Urbani (1967: 59), quoted in Baldacci (2016: 147).
[20] Baldacci (2016: 148–9).
[21] Baldacci (2016: 149).

words, according to Urbani, Gramsci 'conceives the educational relationship ... in the strict sense as a particular and specific form of the general hegemonic relationship'.[22]

Baldacci also discusses Angelo Broccoli's work *Antonio Gramsci e l'educazione come egemonia* (1972), in which the author wishes to provide 'a dynamic interpretation of the concept of hegemony' by suggesting a relevant passage of the *Notebooks* (Q11 §12)[23] to be read in conjunction with Q10 §44, and concludes: 'The emergency of hegemony cannot fail to take into account changes in the masses, which must modify the concrete way in which it [hegemony] is set.'[24] Baldacci sees in this a development in the masses of a process of critical self-consciousness, with which the masses overcome 'folklore', moving towards 'a rational vision of reality', thus overcoming the dichotomy between leadership and spontaneity, while 'reaching ever more advanced forms of critical and conscious participation and active consent by the masses'.[25] This 'authentically' dialectic form of hegemony—more Gramscian than Lenin's—must inform also the pedagogic relationship, given that 'for Gramsci the pedagogic relationship is an active and reciprocal relationship'.[26] According to Baldacci, by underlining the active, dynamic and reciprocal character of the pedagogic relationship, Broccoli seems to postulate that the central note in Q10 §44—'Every relationship of "hegemony" is necessarily an educational relationship'—can also be reversed to 'Every educational relationship is necessarily a relationship of hegemony'.

---

[22] Urbani (1967: 69), quoted in Baldacci (2016: 149).

[23] As per Q11 §12, 1386:

The development process is dependent on a dialectic between the intellectuals and the masses; the stratum of intellectuals develops both quantitatively and qualitatively, but every jolt towards a new 'breadth' and complexity of the stratum of intellectuals is linked to a similar movement made by the mass of the simple, which rises to higher levels of culture and simultaneously enlarges its circle of influence towards the stratum of specialized intellectuals, producing outstanding individuals and groups of greater or less importance.

[24] Broccoli (1972: 140), quoted in Baldacci (2016: 151).

[25] Baldacci (2016: 151).

[26] Broccoli (1972: 155).

In his critique of the two authors, Baldacci suggests that one of the limits of Urbani and Broccoli is their use of the first thematic edition of Gramsci's *Prison Notebooks* rather than the critical edition of 1975, which thus prevents them from applying a diachronic reading to Gramsci's thought. Furthermore, Urbani seems to support an idealized understanding of the pedagogic relationship, and, as a consequence, seems to 'transpose onto hegemony this emancipative virtue, thus naturally becoming a device for the development of self-consciousness and autonomy'.[27] Gramsci, Baldacci maintains, seems to conceive the pedagogic–hegemonic relationship in a more problematic fashion. In fact, a pedagogic rapport could also trigger subordination, rather than promote emancipation: 'Therefore, a given pedagogical relationship can in fact become a factor of subjection and maintenance in a state of minority, rather than a factor of emancipation',[28] thus becoming a '(tendentious) renunciation to educate the people' (Q11 § 1).

Broccoli, referring to the note Q11 §12, highlights the dynamic aspect of hegemony, thus indicating how the dialectic relationship between intellectuals and masses provides a parallel and interdependent growth in both groups. However, according to Baldacci, it is not hegemony per se that delivers this dynamism; this could be possible only through the intervention of the 'philosophy of praxis', according to a passage closer to the one quoted by Broccoli, which states: 'The philosophy of praxis does not tend to keep the "simple" in their primitive philosophy of common sense, but instead [wishes] to lead them to a higher conception of life' (Q11 §12, 1384).

We could say, at least provisionally, that hegemony is a double-edged sword in the hands of intellectuals (and the masses alike): it can be used to preserve the status quo of subalterns, to crystallize their condition through both coercion and consent or it can be applied to promote their emancipation, depending on the final goal to be achieved. In Gramsci's case, as Baldacci makes clear, it is the steady commitment to the philosophy of praxis that 'sets in motion this evolutionary dynamism, because this philosophy is intrinsically connected to a project of emancipation of subaltern social groups, and is aimed at overcoming the division between

---

[27] Baldacci (2016: 155).
[28] Baldacci (2016: 156).

leaders and subalterns'.[29] The very 'pedagogical ideal' that Gramsci proposed for his own time, at a particular historic juncture in Europe—a 'moral and intellectual reformation'—was meant to involve both intellectuals and subalterns. This could simply mean that 'in Gramsci there is a correspondence between authentic pedagogical relationship and pedagogical relationship conceived according to the philosophy of praxis'.[30]

Baldacci dedicates his latest book (*Oltre la subalternità. Praxis e educazione in Gramsci*[31]) to discuss his thesis—the democratic emancipation of subalterns through the pedagogy of the philosophy of praxis—in detail, bringing together in a true Gramscian fashion philosophy, history, politics, and pedagogy. *Oltre la subalternità* (*Beyond Subalternity*) points towards formative process and pedagogy as democratic educational practices in which subjects are invited to overcome subalternity, thus becoming citizens, as Gramsci had hoped, who are able 'to think, to study, to direct, or to control those who direct' given that 'every "citizen" can become a "ruler"' (Q12 §2, 1547), even the 'subaltern-citizen'. From this perspective, we might wish to expand a narrow definition of 'subalternity', or even to 'refiguring the subaltern', as suggested by Peter Thomas, so as to reconsider its 'potential to cast light both on the contradictory development of political modernity and on contemporary political processes'.[32] Proposing a return to Gramsci's texts, Thomas concludes that:

> [A] study of Gramsci's integral development of this notion [subalternity] reveals a much richer field of reflection on the contradictions and forms of political modernity than became apparent during the first season of engagement with his texts. Subalternity for Gramsci is an experience of marginality, in terms of the subalterns' relations to the centers of political power, but it is not a marginal experience, in terms of the political relations and forms to which the majority of the inhabitants of modern political communities are subjected, in the West and North just as much as the East and South.[33]

---

[29] Baldacci (2016: 157).
[30] Baldacci (2016: 157).
[31] Baldacci (2017b).
[32] Thomas (2018: 3).
[33] Thomas (2018: 14).

If, following Gramsci, '"The end" of subalternity is conceived not in terms of an exit from this condition, but as the internal transformation of the hegemonic relations that structure it',[34] then Baldacci's conclusion that 'only education can allow one to go beyond subalternity' indicates the way to put in motion this 'internal transformation'.

It is not the purpose of this chapter to give a complete overview of scholarly works dedicated to Gramsci's pedagogic–educational thought, especially, in our case, in the Anglophone world. I would like, nonetheless, to bring to the attention of the reader two edited volumes which somehow have marked the pace of scholarly commitment to the debate. In their introduction to the first book, *Gramsci and Education*, Borg, Buttigieg, and Mayo, in addition to reiterating the relevance of the concept of hegemony as central to Gramsci's discussion of education, insist on the need to adopt a 'holist approach', being mindful 'to incorporate different aspects of Gramsci's large *oeuvre* and to deal with a broad range of areas'.[35] This is widely reflected in the compendium of essays written by a group of international scholars, many of whom had already 'contributed to the growing international literature on Gramsci's work' and thus reaffirming that 'Gramsci remains a key point of reference in the literature of education, especially literature that deals with radical and transformative approaches to education'.[36] Among the innovations brought about by this collection, when compared to the Italian debate, are the areas dealing with popular and workers/adult education (referring to Gramsci's experience with the factory councils in Turin, starting in June 1919, and the 'Prison School' on the island of Ustica),[37] with radical adult education, with multiculturalism, and with the cultural production of dominant and subaltern groups. In relation to the present chapter,

---

[34] Thomas (2018: 14).

[35] Borg, Buttigieg, and Mayo (2002: 19).

[36] Borg, Buttigieg, and Mayo (2002: 19).

[37] From 7 December 1926 to 20 January 1927, Gramsci spent forty-four days on the island of Ustica, off the northern coast of Sicily, in political confinement. Here, with Amedeo Bordiga, he organized 'prison school' for the inmates (*Scuola dei confinati*). Bordiga was in charge of the sciences while Gramsci took care of history and literature. The story is recounted in the recent documentary film *Gramsci44* (2016).

the essay by Joseph Buttigieg is particularly relevant.[38] Here, the author not only reconnects the main topic of education with the essential themes of democracy and the role of intellectuals, but he does so by addressing the specific problematic at that point in time of how traditional American intellectuals lamented the loss of litterae humaniores and promoted conservative forms of schooling, even at the cost of making a partial and selective use of Gramsci, so as to defend their position. Unfortunately, Buttigieg's conclusion ('According to Gramsci's criteria, we are still a long way from an educational system worthy of a true democracy'[39]) not only reflects the situation at present in USA, but its neoliberal underpinning has been exported elsewhere.

The second, more recent, book which addresses our topic is *Antonio Gramsci: A Pedagogy to Change the World* (2017), edited by Nicola Pizzolato and John D. Holst. In their comprehensive introduction, the editors offer a thorough review of the literature to date but also interweave Gramsci's biography and activity as journalist and later party leader with his educational views and pedagogical-political interests. A great merit of this introduction is to provide a broad summary of the Italian debate on the subject, which is also carried out by some of the articles in the volume, and to put this in dialogue with the English-speaking reflection on Gramsci's pedagogy. By following a narrative of historical progression—from the 'early years' in Sardinia to the political commitment as journalist at the *Ordine nuovo* in Turin, during the beginnings of the Communist Party, and to the prison years and his reflections in the *Notebooks*—Pizzolato and Holst show a steady growth towards a 'mature Gramsci' whose legacy is still informing contemporary developments in the fields of critical pedagogy and radical adult education, which is mainly happening outside of Italy. Yet, it was Gramsci's 'Italian experience', mediated by constant and progressive conceptualizations, which provided the backdrop for his 'philosophy of praxis' in dialectical tension with the 'constellation of concepts'[40] that supported this philosophy. While practical applications of Gramsci's thought to specific historical and geographically diverse situations might favour one

---

[38] Buttigieg (2002).
[39] Buttigieg (2002: 132).
[40] Thomas (2009: 134).

or a variety of concepts so as to highlight a meaningful learning and teaching experience, one must take into account the totality of Gramsci's thought[41] in order not to betray the motivations which inspired the 'hermeneutical circle' of praxis supported by philosophy, which in turn is tested by further praxis and shared reflections of the 'integral historian' and the 'collective thinker' (Q11 §12). No better example to illustrate these concepts than the article by André Tosel in this collection on the 'formation of a collective will and of individual personality', or the displacement from the individual to the social, which 'is conceptualised through a twofold theoretical and political objective: to think and to operate at the same time for the construction of a collective will of the subaltern masses to become hegemonic as well as for the construction of a human personality that attunes the mass with the individual'.[42] As we shall see, Dalit women are faced with the same problematic challenge, while being supported by Ambedkar's idea concerning the coincidence of the individual working for the group and equally developing a personal character.[43]

Learning from History: Education to Democracy through 'Third Eye' (*Trutya Ratna*) and 'Self-Respect' (*Svaabhimaan*), 'Self-Reliance' (*Svaavalamban*), 'Daring/Courage' (*Dhaadas*)[44]

While the literature discussing educational and pedagogical policies in Ambedkar seems in general to be rather fragmented,[45] there are some recent publications that, while addressing the specific issue

---

[41] See the subheading 'Reading Gramsci Holistically' in Mayo (2017: 36–8).

[42] Tosel (2017: 173).

[43] Only lack of space prevents us from discussing here the relevant essay by Pietro Maltese (2017) that also appears in the edited collection by Pizzolato and Holst (2017).

[44] This terminology, coming from vernacular Marathi, has been brought to light by Shailaja Paik (2007, 2014) so as to underscore—as we shall see—conceptual frames used by Dalit themselves, thus revealing a remarkable level of self-consciousness and self-determination.

[45] For a general discussion on Ambedkar's vision on Dalit education see Chalam (2008), Mahapatra (2004), and Shukla (1998). For the wider context

of Dalit women's education, are able to provide a deeper analysis of Ambedkar's thought on the subject. Padma Velaskar, building on her previous work on Dalit women's education,[46] provides an informative summary of Ambedkar's thought while defining him as 'one of the finest examples of an organic intellectual leader that India has seen'[47] as a stimulus for the education and social liberation of Dalit women. Velaskar laments that while Ambedkar and his philosophy have attracted 'great scholarly attention', still 'few studies have delved into his thoughts on education ... A more comprehensive and complex reading of the corpus of Ambedkar's educational work is eminently warranted' given that 'education was of central significance to his revolutionary project'.[48] Rightly, Velaskar reminds us that the 'Emancipatory Educational Project' of Ambedkar 'is not a simple borrowing of Western ideas as is sometimes assumed' but part of 'a unique synthesis of the reconstruction of liberalism, socialism and Buddhism as the new moral basis of social living'.[49] In a sense the historical reality lived by Dalits prompted Ambedkar to find a local response to the solution of local problems such as the persistence of the caste system and untouchability, as supported by Hindu ideology. In other words, 'Ambedkar was clear that a system that bred division and hierarchy, caste was unworthy of a place in a democratic order.'[50] Although 'concerned by issues of class exploitation and poverty', and being 'not unsympathetic to Marxism' while recognizing 'capitalism as an enemy of the dalits', Ambedkar 'saw caste as the fundamental and autonomous building block of the Indian social structure that was not reducible to class'.[51] It was perhaps the religious sanctioning of caste that made him turn to another religion (Buddhism) as part of an overall solution: 'The need for an anchoring in religion was acutely felt by Ambedkar, not only for providing solace and spiritual regeneration for a religiously abused people but also for

---

of education, see also Bhattacharya and Chinna Rao (2017), Jondhale and Beltz (2004), Rodrigues (2002), and Thorat and Kumar (2008).

[46] Velaskar (1998, 2005, 2006).
[47] Velaskar (2012: 246).
[48] Velaskar (2012: 248).
[49] Velaskar (2012: 249).
[50] Velaskar (2012).
[51] Velaskar (2012: 250).

providing a stronger ethical and moral basis for "reconstructing the world"'.[52] This choice, no doubt, would appear controversial from a Gramscian perspective, but it became almost indispensable for Ambedkar in order to overcome 'the perilous contradiction that existed in society between political equality and social [and religious] inequality',[53] if Independent India were to establish a real political democracy. The root of Ambedkar's educational thought is a 'recasting educational aims for establishing social democracy'.[54] Velaskar provides also a pertinent summary of Ambedkar's vision for the empowerment of Dalit women through education which precedes a section on Dalit women's active participation, emerging as political activists and leaders during the 1930s and 1940s, thus giving an indispensable contribution to the future of education for Dalits and subalterns.

In a recent book, *Dalit Women's Education in Modern India* (2014), Shailaja Paik not only provides an excellent historical investigation on the topic under examination, but she does so highlighting the most crucial issues encountered by Dalit women in their educational experience in modern India and into the present. In fact, by concentrating on Dalit women, Paik manages to show us the positive but often also contradictory effects of education regarding this particular group being subjected to 'double discrimination': a discrimination fostered by caste and gender inequality and by the presence of a 'double patriarchy', internal and external to the Dalit community.[55]

Moreover, Paik is, to my knowledge, the first scholar who openly refers to Gramsci's ideas on education to support Ambedkar's views. At various points in her book, Gramsci is invoked to highlight crucial issues. For instance: 'Like Gramsci, Ambedkar asserted that the first stage in raising subaltern consciousness was schooling for all classes (Gramsci 1971, 30–31).'[56] This is in stark contrast with Gandhi who 'pathologised Shudra education while Ambedkar supported it. Gandhi argued that injunction against Shudras studying Shastras or

---

[52] Velaskar (2012: 250). See also Fiske and Emmrich (2004) and Jondhale and Beltz (2004).

[53] Velaskar (2012: 251).

[54] Velaskar (2012: 251).

[55] This is indeed similar to what, elsewhere, I have labelled as the 'double burden of untouchability' for Dalit women.

[56] Paik (2014: 86).

Vedas were justified' simply because 'a Shudra would completely misread the Shastras'.[57] 'Yet, in order to even misread the Shastras, we have to allow not only Shudras but also Dalits to access and read them. For them the right to reading *at all* came before the question of misreading any text.'[58] This is indeed a major issue which, for Dalits, might go hand in hand with the question of the 'temple entry': The effort by the Brahmins to keep Dalits separate from the divine and the sacred scriptures, on account of their 'impurity' and deficient humanity, serves also as a symbolic and ritual validation for the 'exclusion of Dalits from knowledge', resulting in punishment for 'their attempts to seek any sort of education'.[59]

While discussing the transnational connection of Phule's and Ambedkar's ideas on subaltern education, Gramsci is mentioned again, together with the other influential contemporary educationist, John Dewey, and latter ones, such as Fanon, Freire, and Foucault. Importantly, 'all of these theorists were concerned about the double colonisation (internal and external) of the subordinated and struggled to look upon education as a tool of emancipation',[60] thus questioning educational structures contemporary to them. In particular, Paik refers to Phule's concept of *Trutya Ratna* (third eye, or, literally, 'third jewel'), derived from Phule's homonymous play, as an apt metaphor for critical thinking or critical consciousness, and part of 'his agenda of building a critical consciousness among those excluded from education for centuries'.[61] Ambedkar was certainly inspired by this concept and by Phule's decision to implement such ideas by opening the first school for Dalits in 1848 and for women in 1852.

Regarding independent and critical thinking, the other major inspiration for Ambedkar was, as we shall see, his teacher at Columbia, John Dewey. Rightly, Paik points out that Ambedkar 'had no such connection with his contemporary Gramsci, nor had [he] read any of his work'.[62] Nonetheless, 'Gramsci greatly emphasised supporting and encouraging free, creative thinking among

---

[57] Paik (2014: 86).
[58] Paik (2014: 86).
[59] Paik (2014: 86).
[60] Paik (2014: 75–6).
[61] Paik (2014: 76).
[62] Paik (2014: 76).

all citizens as "vital to future society and government" (Gramsci 1971, 31–33)'.[63] Moreover,

> [l]ike Phule and Ambedkar, Gramsci advocated that pupils should criticise the curricula and the disciplinary structure of the old system and thus participate actively (Gramsci 1971, 37, 42). All of them understood the difficulties of the task, the 'extra effort' to be made in order to inculcate self-discipline and self-control. According to them this was significant in allowing the subaltern to compete successfully with more privileged classmates. Gramsci also went on to analyse how education frequently endorses structures of power, stating that the 'new type of school is advocated as democratic, while in fact it is destined not merely to perpetuate social differences but to *crystallise* them' (Gramsci 1971, 40, emphasis added).[64]

Paik, elaborating Gramsci's pivotal concept of 'praxis', underlines the Gramscian 'practical exploration of what would constitute a more egalitarian and liberating system of schooling'.[65] In fact, 'Both Gramsci and Ambedkar clearly recognised that schooling constituted only one form of social activity within a broader network of experience, history and collective struggle (Gramsci 1971: 29).'[66] One major question bringing together Phule, Ambedkar, and Gramsci is their common interests on the 'interlinkage between political hegemony and pedagogic practices'.[67] For Ambedkar the ability of Dalits to gain political power (*sattaa*) rests on their skilfulness to occupy 'effective positions in the government' (*maaranyachya jaagaa*), as a result and fulfilment of successful education.[68]

> Unlike Tilak and Gandhi, they [Phule and Ambedkar] concurred with Gramsci that 'education was a prerequisite for everybody in society, a right for all its members (Gramsci 1971: 41–43)', especially for women and low castes. Both Ambedkar and Gramsci also underlined the importance of 'common schools' for all classes in order to undercut rank and hierarchy.[69]

---

[63] Paik (2014: 76).
[64] Paik (2014: 76).
[65] Paik (2014: 77).
[66] Paik (2014: 76).
[67] Paik (2014: 77).
[68] See *Janata*, 15 December 1945, quoted in Paik (2014: 77).
[69] Paik (2014: 77).

With a strong commitment to political democracy, education for both Ambedkar and Gramsci was also geared towards this aim, being facilitated by democratic teachers. While Paik underlines that 'Almost half a century before Foucault's theoretical insights, Ambedkar and Gramsci (Gramsci 1971: 37, 41–43) underscored that some "special training" and "discipline" were necessary for the disadvantaged',[70] she rightly insists on how Ambedkar 'encouraged efforts to develop a more democratic and empowering approach that looked to teachers as leaders in transforming educational practice'.[71] Invoking Gramsci's insights once again, she points out that '[t]eachers were indeed "cultural workers" and "transformative intellectuals" who supported the oppressed and remained committed to advancing progressive projects through the educative process'.[72]

There is no doubt that Paik's work has brought to the surface a variety of relevant issues, concerning Dalits in general and Dalit women's education in particular—issues that previously were either ignored or remained hidden under more compelling disciplinary concerns of historians, anthropologists, and scholars of cultural, gender, and Dalit studies. For instance, the re-reading of Phule's and Ambedkar's activity and works in their respective milieu and their relevance for Dalit women offers a new glimmer of light through which the experience and activity of these women can become meaningful and present novel interpretations. In the same way as Ambedkar learned from Phule and improved the latter's commitment for the uplifting of women and untouchables, Dalit women have been able to carry on Ambedkar's insights, thus becoming agents and subjects of their own and their communities' progress. Being doubly discriminated against—on grounds of caste and gender—Dalit women would represent, in Gramscian terms, one of the lowest levels of subalternity. Conversely, they seem to

---

[70] Paik (2014: 94).

[71] Paik (2014: 96). 'Teachers were in fact *saarathi* [guides and leaders] who were to mould individuals and societies' (Ambedkar [1927], quoted in Paik [2014: 96]).

[72] Paik (2014: 96). Paik mentions here that Gramsci 'refers to teachers as "cultural workers" actively involved in a cultural struggle of the oppressed', and inspiring some contemporary authors (Apple 1988; Giroux 1988, 2002) to consider the teacher as 'transformative intellectual' (Paik 2014: 104n28).

manifest, according to Paik, a high degree of self-awareness in the process of overcoming subalternity.[73]

There are a variety of novel findings in Paik's work which would need to be discussed in depth, and I will try to return to these in the final part of this chapter. For the time being, it suffices to say that Paik does more than merely using Gramsci to validate Ambedkar's educational thought. By adopting, albeit unintentionally, a Gramscian methodology in her historical-ethnographic research, she is also endorsing Gramsci's insights useful to analyse a given reality altogether different from the Italian scene for which they were mainly originally intended. The special *Notebook 25*, titled *On the Margins of History. The History of Subaltern Social Groups*, at §2, provides an indispensable methodological direction, as Gramsci writes: 'Every trace of independent initiative on the part of subaltern groups should ... be of incalculable value for the integral historian. Consequently, this kind of history can only be dealt with monographically, and each monograph requires an immense quantity of material which is often hard to collect.' (Q25 §2, 2284).

In fact, when collecting these 'traces' of the dispersed, multi-sighted histories, Paik and Gramsci seem to coincide on one very relevant conclusion: For Gramsci, the subalterns 'have no history: [that is to say] there are no traces of their history in the historical documents of the past' (Q14 §39). Equally, Paik is able to confirm that 'studying Dalit history also means using materials that may not exist in official archives: historians have to make extensive use of "unofficial" or even "unarchived" or "trivial" sources as well as oral history and thus engage with hitherto-unfamiliar spaces of knowledge production.'[74] Again, she needs 'to underscore that there is sparse or diffused evidence on the biographical background of these women because the presence and voices of women are often marginalised or silenced in the historical record'.[75] Additionally,

---

[73] However, Paik also recognizes that '[t]he shame of being a Dalit and a woman is thus implanted in the classroom—and a consciousness is forged. A girl, as she becomes a woman, may use this consciousness to fight back, as some have done, or she may—as most do—keep her head down and get on with her life' (Paik 2014: 341).

[74] Paik (2014: 333).

[75] Paik (2016b: 16).

she points out that, 'Unlike middle-class, upper-caste women, Dalit women moreover never figured as subjects or agents in the historical accounts of anticolonial nationalist struggle or women's reforms.'[76]

This problematic background, however, does not prevent Paik from finding those 'traces of independent initiative' that allow her to reconstruct an improbable history of Dalit women's education. The benefits of education, however, are not achieved without great hardship: 'It was a rarity indeed to come across a Dalit woman who enjoyed her school experience',[77] although, as Paik's study has shown, 'Dalit women were challenged by multiple forms of power which repressed them and at the same time produced numerous possibilities for political transformation'.[78] One can see at play here these 'multiple forms of power' controlling Dalits, men and women alike, not only in the educational arena but in other spheres of life. This is, in Gramscian terms, the 'struggle of hegemonies', operating between Dalits and others but also within the Dalit community itself, which for Paik is highlighted through the 'Paradox of Education': 'It is clear that for many Dalits, the liberation which education promised to achieve has been only partial.'[79] Moreover, 'While education allowed Dalit women to form united communities to achieve rights and power, it also reproduced differentiations and inequalities, sometimes even at a cost of Dalit identity, something neither Phule nor Ambedkar could have anticipated or desired.'[80] If some women decided to help their immediate community first, 'rather than the Dalits or oppressed in general', it was likewise the case that 'some women also turned whatever little education they had back into the larger oppressed community of women irrespective of caste',[81] thus bringing them closer to the Gramscian ideal of 'democratic intellectuals' and 'collective thinkers'.

Whatever the results of the educational effort set in motion by Phule, continued by Ambedkar, and carried out by Dalit women

---

[76] Paik (2016b: 16).
[77] Paik (2014: 330).
[78] Paik (2014: 331).
[79] Paik (2014: 341).
[80] Paik (2014: 341).
[81] Paik (2014: 340–1).

may be—while taking into account the shortcomings, contradictions and paradoxes—I substantially agree with Anupama Rao's comment that 'Dalit women's education was forged in the context of viewing education as the right to think'.[82] Rao adds here a pertinent note: 'The political philosopher Jacques Rancière (2012) reminds us that the right to think also involves the right to think otherwise as he engages with what might be termed an intellectual history of subaltern thought.'[83] The recognized ability to think and the right to think also set in motion for both Ambedkar and Gramsci the ability and the right to participate in the democratic process, which is largely a recognition of the right to self-rule, which in Paik's narrative involves also and starts with 'self-respect' (*svaabhimaan*) and 'self-reliance' (*svaavalamban*), and also 'daring' and 'courage' (*dhaadas*), so as to achieve 'improvement' (*sudhaaranaa*) for oneself and the community. Paik summarizes this in a remarkable way: 'To Ambedkar the self and community were compatible ... We can ill afford to forget Ambedkar's earlier advice and strategies to work simultaneously on the emancipation of the self and the community, in order to constitute Dalit power and a political "Dalit community" in early twentieth-century western India, however fuzzy and fragile it may be.'[84] This is markedly close to the Gramscian idea and principle of the 'democratic intellectual' and the 'integral historian' who, by necessity, becomes also a 'collective thinker': 'For a mass of people to be led to think coherently and in the same coherent fashion about the real present world, is a "philosophical" event far more important and "original" than the discovery by some philosophical "genius" of a truth which remains the property of small groups of intellectuals' (Q11 §12, 1378).

I would like to bring to an end this part of the chapter by quoting an extended and intensive passage from Paik's PhD thesis—rather than its published and perhaps more polished version—that conveys with immediacy her commitment as 'integral historian' and

---

[82] Rao (2016).

[83] Rao (2016). A parallel reflection on this score is offered by Gopal Guru (2002) who, commenting on the academic hierarchies present within social sciences in India which divides a few privileged theorists from a vast mass of empiricists ('theoretical brahmins and empirical shudras'), maintains that 'Dalits need theory as social necessity' as much as they need it for 'inner necessity', while appealing also to Gramsci to make his point.

[84] Paik (2014: 341).

her activity as a 'collective thinker' among Dalit women, but no doubt within the spirit of Ambedkar's legacy:

> It has been a challenging task to intricately weave through the life stories of our 'unheard,' 'unsung,' 'forgotten' Dalit women through my own subjectivation. Such a study requires not only a reflection on certain fundamental issues of Dalit self and society, but also a careful handling of their 'diverse' thoughts and experiences, including those localized and scattered. I have had some very intriguing and engaging experiences while conducting ethnographic interviews with 'my' Dalit women which the elite scientist is unable to share. I have been able to enter their 'sequestered spaces,' restricted to elite scholars and successfully unpack their experiences, making them reflect on their past history. I have seen and known some of my informants since my childhood. Most of the time my informants used the collectives 'aaplyat' (in our community), 'aapan' (we), 'aaplasamaj' (our community); thus talking to me as a Dalit woman. Being a Dalit woman certainly helped me easily intrude into their private lives and engage with them fully. My fieldwork has been my life itself, the experiences of growing up as a Dalit in Pune. It has required me to seriously take into account the question of experience; wherein the deconstruction and reconstruction of history can take place, in order to develop critical knowledge and a critique of knowledge itself.[85]

Dewey, Ambedkar, and Gramsci: An Improbable Dialectical Triangle?

According to several scholars,[86] there is little doubt that John Dewey had an enormous impact on Ambedkar, in addition to Ambedkar himself acknowledging, both directly and indirectly, Dewey's influence on his activity not only as an educationist and political leader, but also as compiler of the Indian Constitution. The connection between Dewey and Gramsci is certainly more tenuous, although a number of authors have discussed possible commonalities and divergences.[87] Whilst the Dewey–Gramsci

---

[85] Paik (2007): 34.

[86] See Queen (2004, 2015), Mukherjee (2009), Maitra (2012), and Stroud (2016, 2017).

[87] See West (1988), Semeraro (2008), Liguori (2015), Baldacci (2014), Hogan (2015), Holma and Kontinen (2015), and Hinchliffe (2016).

connection is itself interesting, for the purpose of our discussion I am obviously more interested in establishing the Ambedkar–Gramsci link, for which Dewey could provide a possible bridge. It might be the case, in fact, that while there is a very strong intellectual and theoretical affinity between Dewey and Ambedkar, at the level of praxis and experience, Gramsci and Ambedkar seem to share a good number of similarities: both of them were living through difficult political situations in their respective countries (fascism and prison for Gramsci; colonialism, early period of independence, and untouchability for Ambedkar); both were committed to providing guidance and leadership to those excluded from political participation and emancipation; both believed in the possibility of these groups achieving full social and political recognition; both fought tenaciously, with the means provided by the State, to improve the circumstances of 'weak democracies', so as to accomplish a sound, real, 'organic' democracy; and for both of them, education played a crucial and indispensable role in order to attain tangible results. We must also recognize that their lives were mostly paved with struggle and suffering, and often loneliness, rather than easy success, but we equally appreciate that their legacy is still a source of hope for many.

In a recent and original essay, 'What Did Bhimrao Ambedkar Learn from John Dewey's *Democracy and Education?*,' Stroud sets out to reply to a question that proves very relevant to our reflection, both because the terms in question (if not Dewey's book itself)—democracy and education—were occupying the minds of three committed intellectuals in three different continents, and because of similarities and differences in their theoretical and practical conclusions.[88] In addition to highlighting Dewey's strong influence on Ambedkar as leader and reformer, Stroud is eager to prove that Ambedkar acquired in the process a new dimension becoming 'the Indian pragmatist'.[89] Christopher Queen had already retraced 'Dewey's presence in the texts and theories of Ambedkar, especially

---

[88] Moreover, rather than confining their thoughts to the archives of history, we might want to find inspiration for the solution to problems which still affect our contemporary situation, given the little progress made in affirming democracy and education—also taken in conjunction—as cornerstones of our common living.

[89] Stroud (2017: 84).

in relation to how Ambedkar reconstructs Buddhism in accord with a Deweyan sense of education and pedagogy',[90] and how 'his later retellings of Buddhist doctrines are shown to extend Deweyan themes concerning pedagogy, reconstruction and democratic community-building'.[91] Following a method complementary to Queen's, Stroud retrieved Ambedkar's personal copy of *Democracy and Education*—which Ambedkar had acquired in London in 1917 and which was stored at Siddhartha College in Mumbai[92]—and established Ambedkar's serious engagement with this book, more than any other book, since he marked and annotated the text in grey, blue, and red pencil. In order to 'track what themes or ideas appear to have captivated Ambedkar', Stroud arranged his discussion into three emergent themes: 'the idea of education as serving the needs of society as a purposive means of transmission, the relation of past to present in the idea of reconstruction and the interrelation of communities and individual dispositions'.[93] Regarding 'Education as Transmission', Stroud remarks the relevance given by Ambedkar to certain passages on 'experience' and the idea that 'experience goes beyond the biological into the realm of the cultural',[94] commenting on the 'thousands of years of Hindu tradition' Ambedkar had 'to resist and reform to remove present stigma and social injustice'.[95] This is not very dissimilar from Gramscian 'common sense' or a 'traditional popular conception of the world', which mostly tends to preserve the status quo, especially for Dalits or those living in cultures of subordination. Often

> [T]he subordinated come to see the hierarchies of the world they inhabit as inevitable and inescapable, the will of God or the law of nature. They may not like their subordination, but they cannot see how things could possibly be other than as they are. Any

---

[90] Queen (2015), quoted in Stroud (2017: 82).

[91] Stroud (2017: 80).

[92] The Siddhartha College contains Ambedkar's personal books 'on Indian culture and philosophy, communism, religion, and philosophy ... as well as books by J.S. Mill, Jeremy Bentham, and Vladimir Lenin' (Stroud 2017: 81).

[93] Stroud (2017: 84).

[94] Stroud (2017: 85).

[95] Stroud (2017: 85).

revolutionary transformation both brings about and depends on the transformation of the existing culture of subordination.[96]

For this very reason, Ambedkar underlines in red Dewey's sentence: 'Society exists through a process of transmission quite as much as biological life' since this process 'makes possible through transmission of ideas and practices the constant renewing of the social fabric'.[97] Transmission and communication was the style used by Ambedkar to address thousands of mostly illiterate untouchables, often addressing them in Marathi. Ambedkar used Dewey's ideas in a very pragmatic way, finding inspiration in them when addressing the needs of untouchables, given that '[t]hey wanted a message that moved them to emancipation … What they wanted was a path to freedom and respect, and Ambedkar gives them this in the form of religious conversion.'[98] This choice has been very controversial, especially for a 'secular' leader like Ambedkar who believed in the human values of the Enlightenment. However, we should not underestimate that communicating his message through the idiom of 'religion' was one way to alter the transmission of Hinduism and to disrupt the perpetuity of the caste system and untouchability. In this case, indeed 'communication was educative' because 'in a deep sense, Ambedkar can be seen as *living* Dewey's philosophy more often than merely *talking* about it in the Indian context'.[99] Ambedkar acknowledged Dewey's distinction

---

[96] Crehan (2011: 245). I certainly agree with Hinchliffe (2016) that '[f]or Gramsci, an educative order simply fails if it merely consolidates common sense. Pedagogies that fail to move learners on from common sense, no matter how benign and comfortable, also fail to recognise that "all men are philosophers".'

[97] Dewey ([1916] 1985: 6), quoted in Stroud (2017: 85).

[98] Stroud (2017: 86).

[99] Stroud (2017: 86). From a Gramscian perspective, as Crehan maintains, we could add that

> [T]here is no simple recipe, however, for cultural transformation; it is a complex historical process in which there needs to be an active dialogue between intellectuals and nonintellectuals. Those who live the harsh realities of subordination, however capable they may be of everyday resistance, cannot, in Gramsci's view, themselves come up with the coherent, effective counter-narratives necessary if the existing hegemony is to be overcome'. (Crehan 2011: 245)

between formal and informal education. However, 'whereas Dewey was so often interested in reforming formal schooling for better transmission and revision of society, Ambedkar was often focused on experimental means of forming and reforming society outside of the classroom',[100] a choice to which Gramsci would have certainly subscribed. Both Gramsci and Ambedkar were very aware of the powerful influence of 'the social settings created by religion'.[101] However, while Gramsci's aim was to replace religion altogether with a 'higher ideology' (philosophy of praxis), Ambedkar reverted to activism, starting in the 1920s and early 1930s, 'recrafting social environments through caste integration of temples ["temple entry protest"[102]] and water source usage, as well as inter-caste dining' so as 'to interfere with the transmission of certain pernicious aspects of Indian culture'.[103] This, for Ambedkar, was closely connected to the concept of democracy and of belonging to one 'Hindu community'. To this end, Ambedkar established traditional places for education, such as providing libraries and lecture halls, but also creating social and educational institutions and hostels, all of which were meant 'to interrupt old harmful ways of living and to transmit in their place reconstructed or improved manners of living in community with others'.[104] Dewey's ideas of transmission and reconstruction were essential to Ambedkar not only 'to purifying these traditions', but most of all 'to alter the harmful transmission of culture and religion'.[105]

In 1936, a reform group of upper-caste Hindus invited Ambedkar to talk about caste reform at the Jat-Pat-Todak Mandal in Lahore. But the 'Indian pragmatist' Ambedkar had no intention of providing some 'cosmetic adjustments' to the caste system. His message would have been very clear: 'individuals must renounce the holy

---

For this very reason, Gramsci insists on the importance for subaltern groups to create and promote their own intellectuals.

[100] Stroud (2017: 87).
[101] Stroud (2017: 87).
[102] On 2 March 1930, Ambedkar led a satyagraha 'temple entry protest' at Nashik in order to allow Dalits to enter the Kalaram Temple. As Ambedkar later explained, it was not a matter of 'entering the temple' but to have the right to do so.
[103] Stroud (2017: 87).
[104] Stroud (2017: 90).
[105] Stroud (2017: 90).

texts of Hinduism (and effectively Hinduism itself) to purge society of the scourge of the caste system'.[106] The Lahore conference was cancelled and the speech never delivered.[107] Towards the end of his speech, he quoted from Dewey's *Democracy and Education*: 'Every society gets encumbered with what is trivial, with dead wood from the past, and with what is positively perverse....'[108] Roughly at the same time (1932), Gramsci was writing in his prison cell about past philosophy, including its 'errors', in these terms:[109]

> It is this history [of philosophy] which shows how thought has been elaborated over the centuries and what collective effort has gone into the creation of our present method of thought which has subsumed and absorbed all this past history, including its follies and mistakes [*i suoi errori e i suoi delirii*]. Nor should these mistakes themselves be neglected, for, although made in the past and since corrected, one cannot be sure that they will not be reproduced in the present and once again require correcting. (Q11 §12, 1379–80; SPN: 327)

Although looking at history from a more secular perspective, Gramsci knew how much religious ideology also contributed to support the 'follies and mistakes' of the past philosophy that in Europe supported the 'slave trade' and internal and external colonialisms. In other words, 'our present method of thought' cannot do without critical awareness, so as to provide a response to the reproduction of past errors into the present, both for Gramsci and Ambedkar. For this reason, Dewey's emphasis on formal schooling is supplemented by Ambedkar 'through other means such as mass organising, social centers, and political speeches ... for the needs of India'.[110] (Moreover, 'Ambedkar's notion of reconstruction is oriented towards effectiveness, and not simply a parochial maintenance of the traditional value of certain ways of doing things'.[111]

---

[106] Stroud (2017: 91).

[107] 'This speech was published and sold in print versions, including Gandhi's negative response and Ambedkar's rebuttal in later editions' (Stroud 2017: 102n51). The speech text can be found in Ambedkar (1979), under the title 'Annihilation of Caste'.

[108] Dewey ([1916] 1985: 24), quoted in Stroud (2017: 91).

[109] See Francioni and Frosini (2009: 3–6).

[110] Stroud (2017: 91–2).

[111] Stroud (2017: 92).

Ambedkar's deep commitment to interpreting *Democracy and Education* prompted him to do so by engaging imaginatively with the present, critically addressing the traditions, laws and, customs based on Hindu holy scriptures, which endorsed the caste system, including untouchability. Ambedkar was really enthused by Dewey's 'democratic ideal', which highly contrasted with his daily experience as an untouchable living in a non-egalitarian and non-democratic milieu. For this reason, he was determined to uphold the ideal of his former teacher and mentor of 'democracy as a way of life', but in a pragmatically real way: '[A]s a way of interacting with others that allow each a role in the group's activities and that does not oppress or crush any individual'.[112] While Dewey gives great relevance to formal education so as to create a democratic community, 'Ambedkar postulates religious renunciation and conversion as a means to eradicate the mental disposition that perpetuates caste oppression.'[113] As he clarifies in 'Annihilation of Caste': 'Caste is a notion, it is a state of mind. The destruction of Caste does not therefore mean the destruction of a physical barrier. It means a *notional* change.'[114] We could almost hypothesize that Ambedkar here is trying, in a very utopian way, to democratize 'religion' and to educate not solely his fellow untouchables but caste Hindus as well, given that he had been invited by upper-caste Hindus to deliver a speech that later became 'Annihilation of Caste'. In Gramscian terms, this is clearly a 'struggle of hegemonies', even though here we find ourselves in an environment different from the 'scientifically inflected pragmatism of Dewey's work',[115] and equally distant from Gramsci's Marxian philosophy of praxis. However, 'it should be clear that Ambedkar's use of Dewey is not mechanical or unoriginal, and it should grant him entry into the pantheon of those we consider to be pragmatists',[116] or even 'as perhaps the most significant pragmatist in India'.[117]

To my knowledge, the first author who brings together Dewey and Gramsci is Cornel West, when critiquing Roberto Uber's 'Emancipatory Experimentalism', which he characterized as

---

[112] Stroud (2017: 96).
[113] Stroud (2017: 97).
[114] Ambedkar (1979: 68).
[115] Stroud (2017: 98).
[116] Stroud (2017).
[117] Stroud (2017: 99).

third-wave Left romanticism.[118] What is missing in Uber's plan, according to West, is the contribution of 'the two great figures of the third-wave of Left romanticism', John Dewey and Antonio Gramsci, since they 'partly set the agenda for any acceptable and viable third-wave ... in our time'.[119] There is not, however, a direct comparison between Dewey and Gramsci, since West's interest, on this occasion, was to provide a corrective to Uber's theories. The only moment when differences between the two were discussed— in an effort not to dismiss both Gramsci and Dewey—is when West comments that 'Gramsci tenaciously holds on to Marxist theory even in those areas where it is most problematic, such as politics and culture' while Dewey 'simply limits [Marxist theory] explanatory scope, circumscribes his area of application, and rejects its imperial monistic and dogmatic versions'.[120] Guido Liguori, in a chapter following an introduction on Marxism and Pragmatism (and the reception of the latter in Italy), and a brief discussion of American Pragmatism in the *Prison Notebooks*, considers the closeness between Gramsci and Dewey—notwithstanding obvious differences—deriving from their common Hegelian background but most of all by Gramsci's polemic with Bertrand Russell's 'objectivism' and the latter's attack on Dewey.[121] All in all, although 'Gramsci's evaluation of pragmatism was not a positive one ... it was not entirely negative.' Liguori continues: 'After all, themes like "secular morality", "popular philosophy" and philosophy-as-politics, which Gramsci aptly attributed to pragmatism, were not in reality so distant from some of the fundamental points elaborated by Gramsci in the Notebooks'.[122] After emphasizing Cornel West's remarks regarding 'Dewey's lack of knowledge of Marx' while he remained 'an extreme critic of Marxism', Liguori sums up West's pragmatism and the latter's choice to proclaim himself a neo-Gramscian: 'Unlike *monocausal* Marxism ... [Gramsci] helps him to read the specific conflicts of the society in which he lives, in the first place the racial struggle.'[123] According to Liguori, while West 'uses Gramsci to provide a corrective to post-structuralism' or

---

[118] West (1988).
[119] West (1988).
[120] West (1988: 13).
[121] Liguori (2015).
[122] Liguori (2015: 195).
[123] Liguori (2015: 199).

the 'cognitive nihilism' of Foucault and Derrida, he also *'translates the categories and the sense of the Notebooks'* studies into American', the reality of the modern-day USA, although 'something is always lost in translation'.[124]

It is surprising, from our point of view, that while valuing Gramsci's contribution to the 'race question', the West does not seem disturbed by Dewey's lack of concern with the problem of racism in USA. Implicitly, this appears to be the main criticism levelled by Semeraro against Dewey's concept of democracy, derived from a pragmatic philosophy of science and flowing into the holism of the great society, when compared to Gramsci's idea of democracy resulting from his philosophy of praxis: 'When Gramsci speaks of democracy, he does not do it in a neutral and generic way, but he places himself from the point of view of the subalterns, he takes into consideration the concrete reality of those who are deprived of it.'[125]

We will return to further discuss the question of race while we consider other scholars more inclined to stress similarities between Dewey and Gramsci. For instance, writing on what brings Gramsci and Dewey together from a pedagogical perspective, Baldacci underlines, in addition to a strong component in favour of democracy, their methodological stance around an 'educational principle' for the school in its totality.[126] Moreover, this 'educational principle' must not be applied in an abstract way, but in a historicized fashion, given that education responds to the 'social context'—that is, 'industrialism' for Dewey and 'Americanism' for Gramsci[127]—thus addressing the novelty of the situation that necessitates the adoption of a 'new human type'.[128] Equally, Holma and Kontinen find in Dewey's idea of the 'method of democracy' complemented with critical perspectives inspired by Gramsci, a response to the impasse caused by frustrated political engagement as experienced by citizens.[129] In sum, they wish 'to contribute in establishing a

---

[124] Liguori (2015: 201).
[125] Semeraro (2008: 13–28).
[126] Baldacci (2014).
[127] See Manacorda (1970).
[128] Baldacci (2017a) develops even further Dewey's pedagogical insights in a chapter, as part of the edited volume *John Dewey e la pedagogia democratica del '900*.
[129] Holma and Kontinen (2015).

framework for understanding the role of adult education in the process of ensuring a functional democratic society'.[130]

Hogan offers a very balanced, articulate, and convincing discussion on a 'dialogue between Gramsci's thought and John Dewey', with their common ground in the Left Hegelian traditions, and despite all their differences, highlighting 'the strong family resemblance between their positions' as being 'rooted in their conception of social creative intelligence advanced by critical self-consciousness'.[131] What mostly emerges in Hogan's script is the determination of both Gramsci and Dewey—as a strong conviction and almost a faith, despite all shortcomings—to provide viable, concrete, historical ways of making democracy effective in their respective environments. If, for Dewey, 'the cure for the ills of democracy is more democracy',[132] Gramsci contributes to a solution through the unity between theory and practice, philosophy and politics, and both agree that collective thinking and action is the 'democratic' cure for these ills. Our troubled and fragile democracies are still affected today by the influences of the final example provided by Hogan, which concerned both Dewey and Gramsci: the shortcoming of *Homo economicus* and the failure of neoclassical economics when this introduced methodological individualism and the proximity of value-free inquiry as in natural sciences.

As Eddie Glaude comments, 'No one really questions John Dewey's commitment to democracy', although he continues: 'But Dewey was never truly attentive in his philosophical work to the problem of racism in America; in none of his major books on democracy did he grapple with the challenge that race presents to his ideas.'[133] Sam Stack, who initially seems more lenient towards Dewey's position regarding racism,[134] notwithstanding the latter's involvement in the 'Odell Waller case', maintains that 'Dewey neglected the true significance of color in his analysis of

[130] Holma and Kontinen (2015: 24).
[131] Hogan (2015: 108–9).
[132] Hogan (2015: 112).
[133] Glaude (2008: 17–18).
[134] Stack (2009). 'By the onset of World War II, Dewey seemed on the verge of a better understanding of American racism ... He challenged the belief that racism could be grounded in nature and used the experience of women's suffrage to prove his point, that women were not by nature inferior to men' (Stack 2009: 25).

the problem'.[135] Quoting William Paringer, Stack says that 'Dewey was not radical enough in his approach to racism, sexism, poverty, and inequity', while Charlene Siegfried 'believes Dewey failed to grasp the power behind the oppression of racism and that Dewey took too much from a neo-Marxist analysis, taking an economic inequality approach to the problem of racism'.[136] In one line, for Stack, 'Dewey and other liberals of the era failed to see how deeply racism was embedded in every aspect of Jim Crow society and, it was education, often informal and non-formal, that embedded these cultural mores in southern society that reinforced tradition, living patterns, relationships, and community.'[137] Nevertheless, Stack is also adamant that '[a]lthough Dewey never fully grasped the deep seated sociocultural prejudice of the Jim Crow south, and did not push his own vision of pragmatic inquiry far enough, his philosophy of pragmatism lays down a framework for continuing to reflect, question, imagine, and inquire into the causes and manifestations of racism'.[138] It might then be the case, that Ambedkar in fact saw the validity of Dewey's pragmatism to address racism, sexism, and inequality in India. Moreover, while Ambedkar found inspiration in Dewey's *Education and Democracy* as a platform to address the 'Dalit question', he pushed its pragmatism to achieve new frontiers through a creative combination of theory and praxis. If we take, for instance, Dewey's relevant book *Experience and Education* ([1938] 1997) and apply it to the Indian environment, it seems clear to me that Ambedkar's direct experience of untouchability, going well beyond formal education and the classroom, bears a decisive relevance when setting an educational plan of action for the Dalit community: Ambedkar was never ready to accept a partial, individual solution to 'racism' by agreeing to be recognized as an 'honorary touchable' by the ruling class. His experience of untouchability was so deeply-felt ('enliving'[139]) that even his becoming an 'ontic touchable' would not have 'cleansed' him from his 'ontological untouchability'. Hence, his radical position and the strong political determination and commitment to pursue

---

[135] Stack (2009: 25).
[136] Paringer (1983) and Siegfried (1998), quoted in Stack (2009: 28).
[137] Stack (2009: 29).
[138] Stack (2009: 30).
[139] See Hohr (2013).

the 'annihilation of caste'. In this sense, Ambedkar offers an illuminating example of a Gramscian 'democratic intellectual' and 'collective thinker' who is able to inspire masses and Dalits to struggle for political recognition and the attainment of freedom.[140] Although Ambedkar never commented directly on racism in USA and on Dewey's shortcoming in addressing this, he did make a direct comparison between Gandhi's idea of Swaraj (independence/self-rule) and President Lincoln's attitude toward the 'Negroes question'.[141] The Gandhi–Ambedkar protracted dispute over these issues offers a case study at the highest political and State level, while illustrating also the relentlessness of Ambedkar's commitment.[142]

(Re-)Educating Gandhi and Dewey, among Others

In his *Indian Political Theory* (2017), Aakash Singh Rathore warns us about the unduly prolonged presence in India—in the name of 'comparative political theory'—of theories that are totally foreign to India's everyday people. In view of this, he suggests redirecting our attention regarding Indian political theory towards the lived experience of Indian political life, thus proposing a 'return to

---

[140] In Chapter 5 of *Experience and Education* ('The Nature of Freedom'), Dewey asserts that the freedom of intelligence—the act of freely thinking, observing and judging—is the only freedom of enduring importance. He discusses this within the schooling system and the relationship between student and teacher. Once again, Ambedkar would have taken the discussion beyond formal education so as to include all spheres of Dalits' life where freedom and the ability/right to think were not solely at risk but often negated.

[141] According to Ambedkar (2009: 4409), quoted in Singh Rathore (2017: 204n9).

> Mr. Gandhi wants Swaraj as did President Lincoln want Union. But he does not want Swaraj at the cost of disrupting the structure of Hinduism ... as President Lincoln did not want to free the slaves if it was not necessary to do so for the sake of the Union ... Mr. Gandhi's attitude is, let Swaraj perish if the cost of it is the political freedom of the Untouchables'.

[142] It would be pertinent to discuss at this point also Gramsci's writing on the question of race in USA, but I prefer to refer here to the excellent article on this topic by R.A. Judy (2020).

tradition', but with a caveat and a principle which would guide this return: 'The principle that any modification to be made must benefit the least advantaged and that those changes that do benefit the least advantaged are legitimate.'[143] The 'return' would justify Singh Rathore's plan to examine 'the inadequacy of transatlantic political theory', exemplified by Habermas's post-secular turn, Žižek's critique of 'human rights', global justice and international relations (Sen and Rawls, including the 'global justice industry'), and transatlantic theories of intervention (Marxism, post-structuralism, postcolonialism). This process makes it possible to lay the ground for the 'preconditions of *svaraj*', as 'the activity of being oneself' through a 'look within' and an 'excavation downwards'. While a 'thick svaraj' insists on the 'nature and purity' of Indian tradition, a 'thin svaraj' points towards hybridity and pluralism. Singh Rathore considers Gandhi and Ambedkar as the most prominent representatives of these two positions. Would it be possible to reconcile their divergent views on Swaraj (and those of their present-day followers), given the well-known antagonism between the two? Having examined Thomas Pantham's, Ramachandra Guha's, and Partha Chatterjee's attempts to resolve the tension between Gandhi and Ambedkar, Singh Rathore concludes that he is 'quite sceptical about the validity of such attempts of reconciliation'.[144] Even Gandhi's and Ambedkar's mutual aim in wanting to abolish untouchability does not go far enough to match Ambedkar's determination to annihilate caste altogether.

Singh Rathore provides a wealth of evidence to prove the 'irreconcilable differences' between Gandhi and Ambedkar, despite the fact that Gandhi 'moved closer to Ambedkar in the last years of his life',[145] or so it seemed. But while Gandhi was against the 'sin' and the 'curse' of untouchability, no real action followed to address this. For instance, the Bardoli Programme (1922–3), designed for the benefit of untouchables, including their education, resulted in total failure. The satyagrahas organized by Ambedkar and untouchables at Mahad and Nasik (1927 and 1930, respectively), to affirm the untouchables' right to use public water tanks and temple-entry, respectively, were opposed by Gandhi and the Congress, thus failing

---

[143] Singh Rathore (2017: 2).
[144] Singh Rathore (2017: 170).
[145] Singh Rathore (2017: 186).

to achieve any result. A major failure was perhaps that the demands made by Ambedkar at the Round Table Conference (1930–3) to allow 'adequate representation' for Dalits and a 'separate electorate for a period of ten years' were forfeited when Ambedkar agreed to sign the 'Poona Pact' so as to break Gandhi's fast unto death. In this case, Gandhi's non-violent satyagraha against the British became an act of violence against the Dalits, while Ambedkar acted in a true non-violent manner towards Gandhi. Singh Rathore welcomes, nonetheless, the rapprochement between Gandhi and Ambedkar as a 'strategic collaboration,' but suggests remaining 'attuned to the fundamental, irresolvable differences between them', while bringing them 'into a *constellation*' (a term borrowed from Hent de Vries, Adorno, and Benjamin), implying 'something *less* than identification, less than reconciliation, but still overcoming the chasm of separation'.[146] This 'dialogue within difference' was the result of the irresolvable paradox of the double-bind that entrapped Ambedkar and the Dalits as 'Slaves of slaves', as even Gandhi had recognized. Ambedkar had no doubts, as he made clear in the opening address at the Round Table Conference in London (1930), that 'nobody can remove our grievances as well as we can, and we cannot remove them unless we get political power in our own hands'.[147] Roughly at the same time (1934), in a fascist prison cell, Gramsci was writing: 'Subordinate groups always endure the initiative of the dominant groups, even when they rebel and arise: only a "permanent" victory breaks, and not immediately, their subordination' (Q25 §2, 2283); a few lines into his discussion, he adds: 'Subaltern classes are not, by definition, unified and cannot coalesce until they are able to become "State"' (Q25 §4, 2286). Both leaders were fully aware of the dynamics behind subalternity, since both had researched into its causes within the history of their respective countries. That is why, in that same opening address, Ambedkar could confirm: 'It is only in a Swaraj constitution that we stand any chance of getting the political power into our own hands, without which we cannot bring salvation to our people.'[148]

[146] Singh Rathore (2017: 188).
[147] Ambedkar (1982: 503–6), quoted in Singh Rathore (2017: 195).
[148] Ambedkar (1982: 503–6), quoted in Singh Rathore (2017: 195–6).

These very concepts have been translated by Singh Rathore into 'Dalit svaraj', which, in his theory, becomes also 'the precondition of Indian political theory', since 'svaraj without Dalit svaraj is tantamount to liberty without equality'.[149] So as to clarify 'Dalit svaraj', Singh Rathore appeals to Ambedkar's idea of Swaraj—'a Government of the people by the people and for the people'—which is well beyond the promise of accepting social ameliorations for Dalits, since 'not bread but honour, is what they want'.[150] British rule had not changed the situation of Dalits, and only 'Dalit svaraj, or free, equal, and agent-centred participation in the political sovereignty of a free sovereign nation works Ambedkar and the Dalits out of the double-bind that they had found themselves ensnared in for so long.'[151] As we know, Ambedkar never managed to win a separate electorate for the Dalits and he opposed a 'Hindu svaraj' for the rest of his life, until, a few months before his death, he opted for conversion, because 'just as Swaraj is necessary for India, so is also change of religion necessary for untouchables. The underlying motive in both the movements is the desire for freedom'.[152]

I do agree with Singh Rathore that India must find its own way for a sound and effective 'political theory' rather than relying on political theories, comparative or otherwise, coming from 'the West'. I would, however, tend to take a more radical approach to the problem and apply some caveats when discussing 'Eurocentrism'. Presumably, political theories are based and rest on a supporting philosophy, as much as educational philosophies are grounded on a given philosophy or 'school of thought'. The problem we have been facing for some centuries now is that Western or Anglo-European philosophy has been portraying itself as a 'universal philosophy'—the only 'philosophy', in fact[153]—rather than the historical or localized philosophy of the West, or Europe.[154] There

---

[149] Singh Rathore (2017: 192).
[150] Ambedkar, quoted in Singh Rathore (2017: 192).
[151] Singh Rathore (2017: 202).
[152] Ambedkar, quoted in Singh Rathore (2017: 203).
[153] See Zene (2015).
[154] For instance, this is the case for the philosophy underpinning the 'Universal Declaration of Human Rights', in which the 'universality' is provided almost exclusively by Anglo-European philosophy.

is no doubt that the philosophy that motivated the expansion of European empires, with the acquisition of political, economic, and military power imposed itself as the highest—if not the sole—'way of thinking', thus imposing also a 'colonization of minds' or an intellectual subordination. My contention is that although we can safely affirm that 'the history of European philosophy has been a history of "egology"',[155] there have been moments of sanity and self-reflexivity within this philosophy, despite its 'follies and mistakes' (Q11 §12), and that some philosophers have resisted the temptation to impose on to others the all-powerful, domineering western 'logos'. Otherwise, it would make little sense to bring Ambedkar and Gramsci together, given the transatlantic origin of the latter. On the other hand, we must also recognize that colonialism, subalternity, sexism, and racism happened in Europe prior to being exported elsewhere. There is, however, a tentative way to 'provincialize Europe': by acknowledging and accepting that its philosophy is not universal but regional and historically bound. In this way, we can welcome Singh Rathore's suggestion to 'open a window of opportunity for new or hitherto ignored conceptions to be brought into play', thus provoking 'the thought, or at least the possibility, that some aspects of "Eastern" thought may hold resources towards a more sustainable future'.[156] (I would venture to call this exchange an inter-philosophical critical dialogue taking place within the field/environment of world philosophies and thus recognizing the presence of multiple ontologies and epistemologies, rather than one single philosophical tradition dictating the pace of reasoning to the whole world.) This is not very dissimilar to the closeness Singh Rathore finds between the concepts of *pratyahara* and decoloniality,[157] as a central component of contemporary Latin American philosophy, and in particular the difference between postcolonial theory and decoloniality, is 'that very inward turn of decoloniality, a turn toward indigeneity and alternative epistemologies, and a disavowal of futile attempts to elbow in to transatlantic institutional and academic discourses'.[158] Indeed, as Singh Rathore suggests, '[a] thin svarajist Indian political

---

[155] Levinas (1979).
[156] Singh Rathore (2017: 208).
[157] See Walter Mignolo (2008), Miguel Quijano (2007), and others.
[158] Singh Rathore (2017: 214n4).

theory will find deep resonance with the fruit of decolonialist work, despite being grounded half a world away',[159] given that it is not distance that can prevent the transformation of the at-times equivocal Heideggerian *Mit-sein* (co-being) into a fruitful *Mit-denken* (thinking-with), promoted by the encounter of different epistemologies and world philosophies. As the Argentinian-Mexican philosopher Enrique Dussel suggests, there is 'the need to undertake and deepen permanent South–South dialogue, in order to define the agenda of the most urgent philosophical problems in Africa, Asia, Latin America, eastern Europe, etc., and discuss them together philosophically'.[160]

Our reflection in this chapter has been inspired by two pioneering intellectuals and leaders, Ambedkar and Gramsci, who, in their own ways, anticipated Dussel's line of reasoning in their educational philosophies as well. Ambedkar, in dialogue with Dewey's work on education, adapted the findings to the Indian milieu—also in line with Phule's tradition—so as to provide a platform for Dalits' political activity and direct involvement in Independent India. Despite many setbacks and being ignored by Indian academia in the social sciences and humanities,[161] he still motivates Dalits to carry on their quest for a real Dalit Swaraj as well as independent thinking. Gramsci would have certainly supported the idea of Dalit Swaraj as a democratic educational practice conducive to overcoming subalternity by becoming subaltern-citizens who are able 'to think, to study, to direct, or to control those who direct' given that 'every "citizen" can become a "ruler"' (Q12 §2, 1547). Moreover, Gramsci and Ambedkar alike struggled to become 'collective thinkers' for the subalterns, for those excluded from 'thinking'—not an easy task. The clear position and strong conviction of the two leaders rest on their ethical standing reflected in Gramsci's calling for 'intellectual and moral reform' and Ambedkar's prompting for a 'social and moral consciousness of society'—both very much in line with the principle announced by

[159] Singh Rathore (2017: 214n4).

[160] Dussel (2009: 511). For a reflection on Ambedkar's contribution to cosmopolitan insights and his thought 'on promoting democratic unity across linguistically and culturally diverse political units, as well as on pursuing domestic rights protections through suprastate institutions', see Cabrera (2017).

[161] Singh Rathore (2017: 186–7).

Singh Rathore at the outset of his reflection: '[T]he principle that any modification to be made must benefit the least advantaged and that those changes that do benefit the least advantaged are legitimate'.[162] Similarly, Dussel reminds us that '[a]n essential element of such a critical stance is for philosophers to assume the responsibility for addressing the ethical and political problems associated with the poverty, domination, and exclusion of large sectors of the population, especially in the global South (in Africa, Asia or Latin America)'.[163]

Concluding her review of Paik's book, Anupama Rao comments that 'the publication of Paik's book coincides with a rise of Dalit activism. Many recall the suicide of the doctoral student Rohith Vemula in Hyderabad after a lifelong experience with caste discrimination and social exclusion.'[164] Shailaja Paik wrote an online comment on Vemula's 'story of triumphs and tribulations' titled 'Education and Exclusion of Dalits: A History of Hurt and Humiliation'.[165] She quotes from the letter Rohith wrote before killing himself: '[M]an [Dalit] is never treated as a mind, but only a thing ... to a vote. To a number. To a thing. As a glorious thing made up of star dust. In every field, in studies, in streets, in politics, and in dying and living.' He thus mentions how the ruling classes objectify and 'thingify' Dalits by reducing them to mere 'items'. Paik continues her reflection with some piercing questions, which remain open also for us to ponder, since the 'task of education' for Dalits and other subalterns is still a daily struggle: 'In his life and death, Rohith Vemula forces us to raise some difficult and important questions: what does education mean to Dalits? What are the costs they have to pay, in order to seek higher education? Why do Dalits feel being reduced to mere "things"? What effect does such a thingification and itemisation have on Dalits?'[166] No doubt these are the very questions Ambedkar would have addressed to intellectuals, party leaders, politicians, and Dalits themselves, not solely 'to enunciate the principle of justice', but in his endeavours 'to make it effective.'[167]

[162] Singh Rathore (2017: 2).
[163] Dussel (2009: 514).
[164] Rao (2016).
[165] Paik (2016a).
[166] Paik (2016a).
[167] Ambedkar (1989: 104).

References

Ambedkar, B.R. 1927. 'Nayaya Tari Dya' ['At Least Give Justice']. *Bahishkrut Bharat*, 3 June.

———. 1979. 'Annihilation of Caste'. In *Dr. Babasaheb Ambedkar, Writings and Speeches*, Volume 1. Mumbai: Education Department, Government of Maharashtra.

———. 1982. *Dr. Babasaheb Ambedkar, Writings and Speeches*, Volume 2. Mumbai: Education Department, Government of Maharashtra.

———. 1989. *Dr. Babasaheb Ambedkar, Writings and Speeches*, Volume 5. Mumbai: Education Department, Government of Maharashtra.

———. 2009. *Selected Works of Dr B.R. Ambedkar*. Available at https://drambedkarbooks.files.wordpress.com/2009/03/selected-work-of-dr-b-r-ambedkar.pdf; last accessed 30 May 2020.

Apple, M.W. 1988. *Teachers and Texts*. New York: Routledge.

Arya, S. and A. Singh Rathore. 2020. *Dalit Feminist Theory: A Reader*. London and New York: Routledge.

Baldacci, M. 2014. *Per un'idea di scuola. Istruzione, lavoro e democrazia*. Milano: Franco Angeli.

———. 2016. 'Egemonia e pedagogia. Una critica delle interpretazioni di Gramci'. *Materialismo Storico* 1 (1–2): 142–60.

———. 2017a. 'Democrazia ed educazione: una prospettiva per i nostri tempi'. In *John Dewey e la pedagogia democratica del '900*, edited by M. Fiorucci and G. Lopez, pp. 21–38. Roma: TrePress.

———. 2017b. *Oltre la subalternità. Praxis e educazione in Gramsci*. Roma: Carocci editore.

Bhattacharya, S. and Y. Chinna Rao (eds). 2017. *The Past of the Outcaste. Readings in Dalit History*. Hyderabad: Orient Blackswan.

Borg, C., J. Buttigieg, and P. Mayo (eds). 2002. *Gramsci and Education*. Lanham, MD: Rowan & Littlefield Publishers.

Broccoli, A. 1972. *Antonio Gramsci e l'educazione come egemonia*. Firenze: La Nuova Italia.

Buttigieg, J. 2002. 'Education, the Role of Intellectuals, and Democracy: A Gramscian Reflection'. In *Gramsci and Education*, edited by C. Borg, J. Buttigieg, and P. Mayo, pp. 121–32. Lanham, MD: Rowan & Littlefield Publishers.

Cabrera, L. 2017. '"Gandhiji, I Have No Homeland": Cosmopolitan Insights from BR Ambedkar, India's Anti-caste Campaigner and Constitutional Architect'. *Political Studies* 65 (3): 576–93.

Carlucci, A. 2017. 'Egemonia e linguistica nella ricerca internazionale'. *Filosofia Italiana* (2): 31–45.

Chalam, K.S. 2008. *Modernization and Dalit Education: Ambedkar's Vision*. Jaipur: Rawat Publications.

Crehan, K. 2011. 'Gramsci's Concept of Common Sense: A Useful Concept for Anthropologists?'. *Journal of Modern Italian Studies* 16 (2): 273–87.
Dewey, J. [1916] 1985. *Democracy and Education, The Middle Works*. Volume 9: 1916 of *Collected Works of John Dewey*, edited by Jo Ann Boydston. Illinois: Southern Illinois University Press.
———. [1938] 1997. *Experience and Education*. New York: Macmillan.
Dussel, E. 2009. 'A New Age in the History of Philosophy: The World Dialogue between Philosophical Traditions'. *Philosophy & Social Criticism* 35 (5): 499–516.
Fiske A. and C. Emmrich. 2004. 'The Use of Buddhist Scriptures in B.R. Ambekar's *The Buddha and His Dhamma*'. In *Reconstructing the World: B.R. Ambedkar and Buddhism in India*, edited by S. Jondhale and J. Beltz, pp. 97–119. New Delhi: Oxford University Press.
Francioni, G. and F. Frosini. 2009. 'Quaderno 11. Nota introduttiva'. In *Antonio Gramsci—I Quaderni del Carcere, Edizione anastatica dei manoscritti*, a cura di Gianni Francioni, Volume 15, pp. 1–22. Rome: Biblioteca Treccani—L'Unione Sarda.
Giroux, H. 1988. *Teachers as Intellectuals: Toward a Critical Pedagogy of Learning*. Gramby, MA: Bergin and Garvey.
———. 2002. 'Rethinking Cultural Politics and Radical Pedagogy in the Work of Antonio Gramsci'. In *Gramsci and Education*, edited by C. Borg, J. Buttigieg, and P. Mayo, pp. 41–65. Lanham, MD: Rowan and Littlefield.
Glaude, E.S. 2008. *In a Shade of Blue: Pragmatism and the Politics of Black America*. Chicago: University of Chicago Press.
Gramsci, A. 1971. *Selections from the Prison Notebooks* (SPN), edited and translated by Q. Hoare and G. Nowell-Smith. London: Lawrence and Wishart.
———. 1975. *Quaderni del carcere*, edited by V. Gerratana. Torino: Einaudi.
———. 1992. *Prison Notebooks*, Volume 1, edited and translated by J.A. Buttigieg. New York: Colombia University Press.
———. 1996. *Prison Notebooks*, Volume 2, edited and translated by J.A. Buttigieg. New York: Colombia University Press.
———. 2007. *Prison Notebooks*, Volume 3, edited and translated by J.A. Buttigieg. New York: Colombia University Press.
Guru, G. 2002. 'How Egalitarian Are the Social Sciences in India'. *Economic and Political Weekly*, 14 December, 5003–9.
Hinchliffe, G. 2016. 'John Dewey and Antonio Gramsci: Thinkers for Our Times'. In *Dewey's 'Democracy and Education' 100 Years On*. Paper presented at the Dewey Conference in Cambridge, UK, 28 September–1 October 2016. Available at https://ueaeprints.uea.ac.uk/64160; last accessed 30 May 2020.

Hogan, B. 2015. 'Pragmatic Hegemony: Questions and Convergence'. *The Journal of Speculative Philosophy* 29 (1): 107–17.

Hohr, H. 2013. 'The Concept of Experience by John Dewey Revisited: Conceiving, Feeling and "Enliving"'. *Studies in Philosophy and Education* 32 (1): 25–38.

Holma, K. and T. Kontinen. 2015. 'The Rocky Road of Growth into Contemporary Citizenship: Dewey, Gramsci, and the Method of Democracy'. *Studier i Pædagogisk Filosofi Årgang* 4 (2): 24–37. Available at www.ojs.statsbiblioteket.dk/index.php/spf; last accessed 30 June 2020.

Jondhale, S. and J. Beltz (eds). 2004. *Reconstructing the World: B.R. Ambedkar and Buddhism in India*. New Delhi: Oxford University Press.

Judy, R.A. 2020. 'Gramsci on *la questione dei negri*: Gli Intellettuali and the Poesis of Americanization'. In *Gramsci in the World*, edited by F. Jameson and R. Dainotto, pp. 165–78. Durham: Duke University Press.

Levinas, E. 1979. *Totality and Infinity: An Essay on Exteriority*. The Hague: M. Nijhoff.

Liguori, G. 2015. 'Dewey, Gramsci and Cornel West'. In *Gramsci's Pathways*, edited by G. Ligouri, translated by David Broder, pp. 192–201. Leiden: Brill.

Mahapatra, B.C. 2004. *Dalits in Third Millennium*. New Delhi: Sarup & Sons.

Maitra, K. 2012. 'Ambedkar and the Constitution of India: A Deweyan Experiment'. *Contemporary Pragmatism* 9 (2): 301–20.

Maltese, P. 2017. 'A Pedagogy of the Subalterns: Gramsci and the Groups "On the Margins of History"'. In *Antonio Gramsci: A Pedagogy to Change the World*, edited by N. Pizzolato and J.D. Holst, pp. 185–97. Geneva: Springer International Publishing Switzerland.

Manacorda, M.A. 1970. *Il principio educativo in Gramsci. Americanismo e conformismo*. Roma: Armando.

Mayo, P. 2017. 'Gramsci, Hegemony and Educational Politics'. In *Antonio Gramsci: A Pedagogy to Change the World*, edited by N. Pizzolato and J.D. Holst, pp. 35–47. Geneva: Springer International Publishing Switzerland.

Mignolo, W. 2008. 'La option de-colonial: Desprendimiento y apertura. Un manifesto y un caso'. *Tabula Rasa* 8: 243–81.

Mukherjee, A.P. 2009. 'B.R. Ambedkar, John Dewey, and the Meaning of Democracy'. *New Literary History* 40 (2): 345–70.

Nayar, P.K. 2012. 'The Poetics of Postcolonial Atrocity: Dalit Life Writing, Testimonio, and Human Rights'. *Ariel: A Review of International English Literature* 42 (3–4): 237–64.

Paik, S. 2007. 'Daughters of a Lesser God. Dalit Women's Education in Postcolonial Pune'. PhD Thesis, Department of History, University of Warwick, UK. Available at http://wrap.warwick.ac.uk/1157/1/WRAP_THESIS_Paik_2007.pdf; last accessed 3 January 2020.

———. 2014. *Dalit Women's Education in Modern India. Double Discrimination*. London and New York: Routledge.

———. 2016a. 'Education and Exclusion of Dalits: A History of Hurt and Humiliation'. *The Wire*, 14 May. Available at https://thewire.in/education/education-and-exclusion-of-dalits-a-history-of-hurt-and-humiliation; last accessed 30 May 2020.

———. 2016b. 'Forging a New Dalit Womanhood in Colonial Western India: Discourse on Modernity, Rights, Education, and Emancipation'. *Journal of Women's History* 28 (4): 14–40.

Paringer, W.A. 1983. *John Dewey and the Paradox of Liberal Reform*. Albany, New York: State University of New York Press.

Pizzolato, N. and J.D. Holst (eds). 2017. *Antonio Gramsci: A Pedagogy to Change the World*. Geneva: Springer International Publishing Switzerland.

Queen, C.S. 2004. 'Ambedkar's Dhamma: Source and Method in the Construction of Engaged Buddhism'. In *Reconstructing the World: B.R. Ambedkar and Buddhism in India*, edited by S. Jondhale and J. Beltz, pp. 132–50. New Delhi: Oxford University Press.

———. 2015. 'A Pedagogy of the Dhamma: B.R. Ambedkar and John Dewey on Education'. *International Journal of Buddhist Thought and Culture* 24 (1): 7–21.

Quijano, M. 2007. 'Coloniality and Modernity/Rationality'. *Cultural Studies* 21 (2, 3): 168–78.

Rancière, J. 2012. *Proletarian Nights: The Worker's Dream in Nineteenth-Century France*, translated by John Drury. London: Verso.

Rao, A. 2016. 'Review of Paik, Shailaja, *Dalit Women's Education in Modern India. Double Discrimination*'. H-Net, November. Available at https://networks.h-net.org/node/22055/reviews/151266/rao-paik-dalit-womens-education-modern-india-double-discrimination; last accessed 30 June 2020.

Rodrigues, V. (ed.). 2002. *The Essential Writings of B.R. Ambedkar*. New Delhi: Oxford University Press.

Rossi, P. (ed.). 1969–70. *Gramsci e la cultura contemporanea: Atti del Convegno di studi gramsciani di Cagliari, 1967*. 2 Vols. Rome: Editori Riuniti.

Semeraro, G. 2008. 'Il pragmatismo di J. Dewey e la filosofia della praxis di A. Gramsci'. In *Ripensare Gramsci: tra idealismo, pragmatismo e filosofia della prassi*, edited by I. Di Vora and U. Margiotta, pp. 13–28. Lecce: Pensa Multimedia.

Shukla, J.J. 1998. *B.R. Ambedkar, Gandhi & Tagore. A Comparative Study on Education*. Ahmedabad: Karnavati Publication.
Siegfried, C. 1998. 'John Dewey's Pragmatist Feminism'. In *Reading John Dewey*, edited by Larry Hickman, pp. 187–216. Bloomington: Indiana University Press.
Singh Rathore, A. 2017. *Indian Political Theory: Laying the Groundwork for Svaraj*. London and New York: Routledge.
Stack, S.F. Jr. 2009. 'John Dewey and the Question of Race: The Fight for Odell Waller'. *Education and Culture* 25 (1): 17–35
Stroud, S.R. 2016. 'Pragmatism and the Pursuit of Social Justice in India: Bhimrao Ambedkar and the Rhetoric of Religious Reorientation'. *Rhetoric Society Quarterly* 46 (1): 5–27.
———. 2017. 'What Did Bhimrao Ambedkar Learn from John Dewey's Democracy and Education?'. *The Pluralist* 12 (2): 78–103.
Tamburrano, G. [1959] 1976. 'Fasi di sviluppo del pensiero politico di Gramsci'. In *La città futura*, edited by A. Caracciolo and G. Scalia, pp. 45–67. Milano: Feltrinelli.
Thomas, P.D. 2009. *The Gramscian Moment. Philosophy, Hegemony and Marxism*. Leiden: Brill.
———. 2018. 'Refiguring the Subaltern'. *Political Theory* 46 (6): 816–84.
Thorat, S. and N. Kumar. 2008. *B.R. Ambedkar. Perspectives on Social Exclusion and Inclusive Policies*. New Delhi: Oxford University Press.
Tosel, A. 2017. 'Hegemony as Pedagogy: The Formation of a Collective Will and of Individual Personality According to Gramsci'. In *Antonio Gramsci: A Pedagogy to Change the World*, edited by N. Pizzolato and J.D. Holst, pp. 173–84. Geneva: Springer International Publishing Switzerland.
Urbani, Giovanni. 1967. 'Introduzione: Egemonia e pedagogia nel pensiero di Antonio Gramsci'. In *La formazione dell'uomo Scritti di pedagogia*, edited by G. Urbani. Roma: Editori Riuniti.
Velaskar, P. 1998. 'Ideology, Education and the Political Struggle for Liberation: Change and Challenge among the Dalits of Maharashtra'. In *Education, Development and Underdevelopment*, edited by S. Shukla and R. Kaul, pp. 210–40. New Delhi: Sage.
———. 2005. 'Education, Caste, Gender: Dalit Girls' Access to Schooling in Maharashtra'. *Journal of Educational Planning and Administration* 19 (4): 459–82.
———. 2006. *Inequality, Opportunity, Emancipation: The Education of Dalit Men and Women in India*. New Delhi: Institute of Human Development.
———. 2012. 'Education for Liberation: Ambedkar's Thought and Dalit Women's Perspectives'. *Contemporary Education Dialogue* 9 (2): 245–71.

West, C. 1988. 'Between Dewey and Gramsci: Unger's Emancipatory Experimentalism'. *Northwestern University Law Review* 81 (4): 941–52.

Zene, C. ed. 2013. *The Political Philosophies of Antonio Gramsci and B.R. Ambedkar. Itineraries of Dalits and Subalterns.* London; New York: Routledge.

———. 2015. 'World Philosophies in Dialogue: A Shared Wisdom?'. *Confluence: Online Journal of World Philosophies* 1 (2): 11–32.

———. 2016. 'Inner Life, Politics, and the Secular: Is There a "Spirituality" of Subalterns and Dalits? Notes on Gramsci and Ambedkar'. *Rethinking Marxism* 28 (3–4): 540–62.

3

Ambedkar and Democracy
Critical Reflections

ANAND TELTUMBDE

> A democracy which enslaves the working class ... is no democracy but a mockery of democracy.
>
> B.R. Ambedkar[1]

It may be ironical to recall Ambedkar's conception of democracy at a time when we are condemned to experience its total antithesis in the country that claims to be running on the Constitution architected by him. Before going into the details how the extant constitutional democracy came to be constituted in the name of Ambedkar, it may be worth explicating this irony first with reference to the very commonplace definition of democracy given by Abraham Lincoln, as a form of government that is *of the people, by the people, and for the people*. Democracy, by this definition places people at the centre; its raison d'être therefore becomes empowering people. Democracy must be receptive to the people's views and respectful to their dissent. Does Indian democracy, flaunted as the largest democracy in the world by its rulers, qualify this familiar definition of democracy? In theory, the existence of the Constitution that professes itself in the name of the people as

---

[1] Ambedkar (2014: 217).

the 'sovereign, socialist, secular, democratic republic'; the existence of operative structure of legislative institutions comprising Parliament, assemblies, and local bodies; regularly held elections to elect peoples' representatives; and the professional bureaucracy and judicial pyramid comprising lower courts to the Supreme Court may not leave much scope for dispute. But beyond this façade, if one takes cognizance of the real content of this structure as it operates, one would not find *demos* anywhere except during the ritual of elections. Right from the beginning, the manner in which this structure itself is designed enables the entrenched classes and castes to rule the country, monopolizing the mandate of people. Over the years, it has become a plutocracy and criminocracy, the rule of money bags and criminals!

Philosophic Distillate

With regard to the relation between Ambedkar and democracy, it may be said that his entire philosophy can be distilled into a single word, *democracy*. At various times, Ambedkar explicated his conception of democracy, every time with wider meaning than before, transcending all its familiar contours given in the books. His democracy was closely related to his ideal of a 'good society', based on 'liberty, equality, and fraternity'. These three words comprised his fond phrase, which, as he claimed, itself had an entirely different meaning than it received from its progenitor, the French Revolution. In a speech on All-India Radio on 3 October 1954, he declared:

> Positively, my social philosophy may be said to be enshrined in three words: Liberty, Equality and Fraternity. Let no one, however, say that I have borrowed my philosophy from the French Revolution. I have not. My philosophy has roots in religion and not in political science. I have derived them from the teachings of my Master, the Buddha. In his philosophy, liberty and equality had a place.... He gave the highest place to fraternity as the only real safeguard against the denial of liberty or equality or fraternity which was another name for brotherhood or humanity, which was again another name for religion.[2]

---

[2] Ambedkar, quoted in Kadam (1997: 26).

His conception of liberty was 'not merely the negative conception as absence of restraint' or 'confined to the mere recognition of the right of the people to vote', it was very positive. It involved the idea of government by the people.[3] Likewise, his conception of equality meant 'abolition of privileges of every kind in law, in the civil service, in the Army, in taxation, in trade and in industry: in fact the abolition of all processes which lead to inequality'.[4] He defined fraternity as 'an all-pervading sense of human brotherhood, unifying all classes and all nations, with "peace on earth and goodwill towards man" as its motto'.[5]

Democracy, as he saw it, was both the end and the means of this ideal. It was the end because he ultimately considered democracy as coterminous with the realization of liberty, equality, and fraternity. Democracy was also the means through which this *ideal* was to be attained. Lofty conception indeed but smacking of a chicken and egg problematic to translate it in to practice!

Beyond Government

Ambedkar's notion of 'democratic government' conformed to the previously cited dictum of Abraham Lincoln. For major part of it, he saw such a government coming in the form of parliamentary democracy. But he was acutely aware of its limitation. It may sound strange that he defended parliamentary democracy in the Constituent Assembly, but had opined, not many years before, that parliamentary democracy was not the government by the people.[6]

> Parliamentary Democracy is a form of Government which the function of the people has come to be to vote for their masters and leave them to rule. Such a scheme of Government, in the opinion of Labour, is a travesty of Government by the people. Labour wants Government which is Government by the people in name as well as in fact. Secondly, liberty as conceived by Labour includes the right to equal opportunity and the duty of the State to provide

[3] Ambedkar (1991a: 37).
[4] Ambedkar (1991a: 37).
[5] Ambedkar (1991a: 37).
[6] Ambedkar (1991a).

the fullest facilities for growth to every individual according to his needs.[7]

But 'democracy' as such meant much more to him than a democratic government. 'A democratic form of Government presupposes a democratic form of society. The formal framework of democracy is of no value and would indeed be a misfit if there was no social democracy. The politicals never realized that democracy was not a form of Government: it was essentially a form of society.'[8] It was a way of life. He would say, borrowing the words of his favourite professor, John Dewey: 'Democracy is not merely a form of government. It is primarily a mode of associated living, of conjoint communicated experience.'[9] It is essentially an attitude of respect and reverence towards fellow men.[10] This expression reflected his aspiration to see a casteless society in India. It tends to value fraternity over the other two tenets in his value triad. While liberty as a value would not be objected to by anyone, there could be doubts about equality. Some would think that men are differentially endowed and hence equality is an artificial value. Ambedkar conceded that men were 'undoubtedly unequal' but he raised a pertinent question whether they should therefore be treated unequal. He sees that if they were treated unequally, those who were privileged with better endowment, personal as well as social, would keep winning but that would not mean the victory of the best. It means society will increasingly be saddled with suboptimal choices and in course, will plummet to its dysfunctional low. This was, therefore, why he argued in favour of giving incentives to those who were unprivileged or underprivileged—so that they come on par with others.[11] It is a powerful pragmatist argument for equality but is still rooted in paradigm of competition and lacks in moral basis as contained in Marxian dictum of 'species being'. Humans are equal not from some instrumental logic but by virtue of being humans, by the measure of their self-worth. He problematized equality, particularly economic equality, again

---

[7] Ambedkar (1991a: 37).
[8] Ambedkar (1979c: 222).
[9] Dewey (2001: 91).
[10] Ambedkar (1979a: 57).
[11] Ambedkar (1979a: 58).

from a pragmatist viewpoint: while it was desirable, it might take a long time because socialist revolution that would ensure this equality would not happen as the proletariat was not ready for such a revolution:

> Believing as I do in a socialist ideal, inevitably I believe in perfect equality in the treatment of various classes and groups. I think that Socialism offers the only true remedy for this as well as other problems.... Now it is obvious that the economic reform contemplated by the Socialists cannot come about unless there is a revolution resulting in the seizure of power. That seizure of power must be by a proletariat. The first question I ask is: Will the proletariat of India combine to bring about this revolution? What will move men to such an action?[12]

This argument stretches to a fault the Marxist dictum, 'It is not the consciousness of men that determines their existence, but their social existence that determines their consciousness,[13] and the claim that political revolutions have always been preceded by social and religious revolutions.[14] He envisaged such a revolution so as to establish fraternity among people even before equality materialized. This formulation may beg for an answer to the question: What is the motive force to bring about such social and religious revolutions? History does not reflect a compartmental view of social life to discern such order of priority; at best, it depicts a dialect build up through which material and non-material aspects of life spiral up.

Social Transformation

Another crucial feature of Ambedkar's conception of democracy is that it is geared towards social transformation and human progress. He defined democracy as '[a] form and a method of Government whereby revolutionary changes in the social life are brought about without bloodshed. That is the real test. It is perhaps the severest test. But when you are judging the quality of the material you must

---

[12] Ambedkar (1979a: 46).
[13] Marx (1977).
[14] Ambedkar (1979a: 43).

put it to the severest test.'[15] It was obviously a response to a communist challenge that promised such a change through revolution, which appeared to be necessarily associated with violence. He convinced himself that his democracy could achieve the same results: it is clear through his reference to economic democracy as the necessary prerequisite to political democracy. Socialism was just another name for economic democracy. In a speech he delivered in 1943 at the All India Trade Union Workers' Study Camp held in Delhi, he conveyed his observation as to why parliamentary democracy collapsed in many European countries:

> There is a great need of someone with sufficient courage to tell Indians: Beware of Parliamentary Democracy, it is not the best product, as it appeared to be.... The idea became sanctified and was upheld in the name of liberty. Parliamentary Democracy took no notice of economic inequalities and did not care to examine the result of freedom of contract on the parties to the contract, should they happen to be unequal. It did not mind if the freedom of contract gave the strong the opportunity to defraud the weak. The result is that Parliamentary Democracy in standing out as protagonist of Liberty has continuously added to the economic wrongs of the poor, the downtrodden and the dis-inherited class. The second wrong ideology which has vitiated Parliamentary Democracy is the failure to realize that political democracy cannot succeed where there is no social and economic democracy. Some may question this proposition. To those who are disposed to question it, I will ask a counter question. Why Parliamentary Democracy collapsed so easily in Italy, Germany and Russia? Why did it not collapse so easily in England and the U.S.A.? To my mind there is only one answer—namely, there was a greater degree of economic and social democracy in the latter countries than it existed in the former. Social and economic democracy are the tissues and the fiber of a Political Democracy. The tougher the tissue and the fiber, the greater the strength of the body. Democracy is another name for equality. Parliamentary Democracy developed a passion for liberty. It never made even a nodding acquaintance with (10/108) equality. It failed to realise the significance of equality, and did not even endeavour to strike a balance between Liberty and Equality, with the result that liberty swallowed equality and has left a progeny of inequities.[16]

---

[15] Ambedkar (1994: vii).
[16] Ambedkar (1991c: 107, 108).

The importance of this longish citation couched with pragmatist logic should not be seen in its assessment of historical facts but in its inference how this contrivance of 'political' democracy actually works to perpetuate social and economic inequalities. We may empirically see its proof in the cases of England and USA, marked by Ambedkar as relatively better parliamentary democracies.

Roots in Rationality

Dr Ambedkar's passion for democracy was also rooted in his commitment to rationality and scientific outlook. Democracy may be seen as premised on them. The sound conduct of democracy depends on dialogue and deliberation, which in turn depend on some shared common sense—logical norms that could only be provided by rationality. There cannot be any meaningful discussion if people are free-wheeling and behave irrationally. History reveals this in various ways. It is commonly held that the scientific outlook is inherently anti-authoritarian; in the normal course of scientific progress, nothing gets accepted simply in the name of authority unless there is a coherent analysis and a cogent proof. Irrationality could lead to authoritarian structures as they existed in the ancient world. In my view, theocracy and the caste system were the natural products of irrationality and absence of a scientific ethos.

For instance, in the West, the birth of experimental science coincided with the rise of democratic accountability in politics. Even today, where democracy is strong, there science also enjoys a respected place.[17] Arguably, with the strengthening of democratic values, we also renew the preconditions for scientific discovery and technological innovation.

Ambedkar may have imbibed these values from his professor, John Dewey. Dewey's experimentalist model views democracy as an institution for pooling widely distributed information about problems and policies of public interest by engaging the participation of epistemically diverse knowers. Democratic norms of free discourse, dissent, feedback, and accountability function to ensure collective, experiment-based learning from the diverse experiences of different knowers. If democracy is to succeed, it needs two things

---

[17] Jonathan (2017).

that veer in different directions. On the one hand, every individual needs to have a certain degree of self-reliance and self-confidence, a certain willingness to back his own judgement and to set forth his own point of view, to defend it, to organize the propaganda if necessary, and so on; all the ordinary business of democratic politics implies confidence in his/her judgement. On the other, an individual must be willing to submit to the authority of the majority. One or the other of these two things is bound to fail. This can only be achieved by cultivating rationality and scientific attitude through proper education.

Ambedkar also reflects the influence of Dewey's pragmatism, which provides flexibility without sacrificing a scientific and rational attitude. Charles Sanders Peirce, credited as the originator of pragmatism, originally conceived it as a philosophy of science with enquiry at its centre. To Peirce, the scientific method unlocks or at least leverages the power of individualism as people work together to address problems.[18] Dewey preferred to characterize his philosophy as experimentalism or instrumentalism that sought both creation of generalized knowledge and testing in actual context.[19] For pragmatists, science is distinguished from all other methods of enquiry by its cooperative or public character.[20] It also guards off the risk of individual rationality distorting the truth. A classic Buddhist parable of the three blind men confronting the 'problem' of describing an elephant (in the Udana Sutta) illustrates the need for a community of enquiry. Each one characterized the elephant from his own limited perspective: the tail as a rope, the ear as a fan, and the leg as a trunk. The moral of this story is that we are all trapped inside our limited selves and cannot know the truth. If, however, the three blind men were members of a community or enquiry, they would behave differently. They would talk to each other, compare perspectives, argue, and test hypotheses as they touched, smelled, and listened to the elephant (gathered facts). Under these circumstances, it is possible to imagine that the blind men will eventually overcome the limited perspective and come to a truer sense of elephant. Ideally, members of the community or enquiry recognize the value of uncertainty. Democracy thus filters

---

[18] Shields (2003: 512).
[19] Vo and Kelemen (2014: 246).
[20] Bucheler (1955: x); Vo and Kelemen (2014: 246).

out dogma, prejudices, constricted perspectives, and all kind of irrationality from the management processes of society.

The discussions and debates are the life source of democracy, and they are premised on a platform of shared common sense, logic, and critical enquiry. Scientific outlook and rational thinking are the biggest defence against propaganda and manipulation, the common tools of subjugation. The anti-democratic trend since 2014 under the Bharatiya Janata Party (BJP) rule in India can be easily correlated to the growth of irrationality. Scientific outlook and rational thinking grants equality to all beings which is the prerequisite for the feeling of fraternity. Dr Ambedkar's attraction to Buddhism was basically because of its rational and scientific temper. Many centuries before Descartes, the Buddha urged his followers to use their reason and not to believe anything without proof. The Kalama Sutta insists on a proper assessment of evidence, rather than a reliance on faith, hearsay, or speculation:

> Yes, Kalamas, it is proper that you have doubt, that you have perplexity, for a doubt has arisen in a matter which is doubtful. Now, look you Kalamas, do not be led by reports, or tradition, or hearsay. Be not led by the authority of religious texts, not by mere logic or inference, nor by considering appearances, nor by the delight in speculative opinions, nor by seeming possibilities, nor by the idea: 'this is our teacher'. But, O Kalamas, when you know for yourselves that certain things are unwholesome (akusala), and wrong, and bad, then give them up ... And when you know for yourselves that certain things are wholesome (kusala) and good, then accept them and follow them.[21]

The Buddha consistently reflected such scientific methodology in his exhortations to his disciples. It does not mean that Buddhism, which was a religionized form of the Buddha's teachings, is entirely rational and non-dogmatic. Even Ambedkar had to acknowledge this fact and write his own interpretation of Buddhism in *The Buddha and His Dhamma* (1957). Dr Ambedkar's devotion to the Buddha's teachings reflects his own commitment to critical enquiry and independence of mind, which did not accept the text as sacrosanct. Although not a Marxist, Ambedkar reflects Marx's motto, *De omnibus dubitandum*: doubt everything. When he

---

[21] Verhoeven (2001: 77–97).

declared that he would make entire India Buddhist, it was not as much in terms of religious conversion but in terms of making it enlightened, adopting rationality and scientific temper, and developing critical faculties. It is reflected in naming his last weekly newspaper as *Prabuddh Bharat* or Enlightened India, after *Janata* and *Bahishkrut Bharat*. It was not only an equalitarian, free, and fraternal India that he sought to achieve, but also an enlightened one, an India of rationality and science.

Ambedkar believed that the scientific temper and rationality also required a glue of social ethics and viewed religion to provide the same. While the former recognizes the importance of 'social' in reaching the truth as in the fable of the three blind men, Ambedkar thought that this *social* needs an ethical code to sustain itself. Following the path of social morality results perforce in the temper if not the practice of the democratic spirit, for it implies that diversified human experience and resultant sympathy which are the foundation and guarantee of democracy. The identification with the common lot which is the essential idea of democracy becomes the source and expression of social ethics.

The Buddha, following this methodology, evolved a code of social ethics which Ambedkar considered an essential ingredient of democracy. Without social ethics, democracy is reduced to a political contest between individuals, as it has been all over the world and particularly in India. Democracy then becomes just the façade identified with periodical elections but without any content. The elections, particularly the first-past-the-post type elections that India adopted, tend to valorize voters' collectivities, which are mostly conceived in terms of primordial identities like castes and communities and, as such, automatically privilege the majority (natural or constructed) community at the cost of minorities. They demand huge investments which invariably come from big capitalists who recover it through policy favours for five years, leaving huge personal pay-offs to politicians. This investment and payback cycle is pushed upwards spirally over the years to make Indian democracy a pure plutocracy, where the entire lower strata of people are effectively excluded. Ambedkar perhaps had an inkling of this power dynamic of the entrenched classes and hence envisaged the need for social ethics which would restrain them from misusing 'democracy' as a ladder to attain their selfish ends.

Ethical Foundation

The model of democracy based on the ethical code that Dr Ambedkar found was in the Buddhist sangha. Ambedkar's projection of the Buddhist sangha as an ethics-based model superior to that of Marx's communist model may be easily faulted simply for its lack of scalability. However, his insistence that society needs ethical glue to sustain itself is incontrovertible. Whence this glue is to be secured, how it is produced there, and what is its shelf-life are the relevant questions, however, in this regard. Religions in general and Buddhism in particular dwelt upon developing this ethical code to sustain human society, but their reference frame has been the societies of their time. Whether the 'human' constituent of this frame remained unchanged since then, through the momentous changes that occurred around Ambedkar so as to work as its premise, is also questionable.

However, one may concede that as a model, the form of governance of the Buddhist sangha was conducive to maintaining plurality of discourse, though in a bounded sense, as it adhered to a single ideology open only to variant interpretations. It was certainly more akin to the Socratic method of dialogue than the prevalent prescriptive doctrinaire approach of the Brahmanism. The underlying logic and rationale of governance was that it was a form of 'deliberative democracy' which was participatory and permitted accommodating differences of opinion and even dissent without imposing majoritarian decision-making principles. Irreconcilable dissent as that which occurred at meetings of the several councils of the monastic fraternity (for example, at the Third Council during the reign of Asoka) led to an amicable agreement to differ and the formation of different sects. The ideals of democracy manifest in Buddhist social and political philosophy were seen as the best principles of governance to the extent that they generated 'principles of statecraft [denoting] a democratic welfare state',[22] mainly embodied in terms of a specific understanding of kingship. Contrary to the prevailing idea of a divinely ordained monarch, the idea of a king as a chosen leader, it was argued, has arisen historically as a social contract. In many respects, Buddhist ideals of Statecraft-embodying principles and practices such as the rule of law, deliberative democracy,

---

[22] Jayatilleke (1967: 81).

procedures of governance, and the social policies of the Asokan welfare State bear a striking similarity to the Enlightenment values in Europe.[23]

Ambedkar's conception of democracy embeds human dignity, which depicts belief in the inherent value of human life. Democracy constantly raises the value and function of each member of the community, however humble he/she may be. The principle of one vote, one value is not just in the political context but reflects the ethical value that must pervade the society. It is not to concede the man's right to be respected, but because we are convinced that the social order is not possible without his special contribution. It is a belief that man's moral idealism is the constructive force of progress, as it has always been; this is because every human being is a creative agent and a possible generator of fine enthusiasm.

Justice, Social and Economical

According to Ambedkar, political democracy rests on four premises: (*i*) the individual is an end in himself; (*ii*) the individual has certain inalienable rights which must be guaranteed to him by the Constitution; (*iii*) the individual shall not be required to relinquish any of his constitutional rights as a price of any privilege; and (*iv*) the State shall not delegate power to private persons to govern others.[24] Ambedkar's vision of democracy encompassed political, social and economic democracy. As he saw it, political democracy alone could not be expected to go very far if glaring economic and social inequalities remained.

This has been his insightful contribution to the concept of democracy, which transcended the boundaries of liberalism. He wanted the future Constitution to hard code the economic structure of the country. He observed that

> [O]ld time Constitutional Lawyers believed that the scope and function of Constitutional Law was to prescribe the shape and form of the political structure of society. They never realized that it was equally essential to prescribe the shape and form of the economic structure of society, if Democracy is to live up to its principle of one

---

[23] Jayasuriya (2008: 41–74).
[24] Ambedkar (1979b: 409).

man, one value. Time has come to take a bold step and define both the economic structure as well as the political structure of society by the Law of the Constitution. All countries like India which are late-comers in the field of Constitution making should not copy the faults of other countries. They should profit by the experience of their predecessors.[25]

As for social democracy, he problematized the caste system and wanted its annihilation. The caste system basically violated the soul of Democracy, which according to him is 'the doctrine of one man, one value'.[26] Democracy desired population without any permanent fissures. He wrote, 'History shows that democracy cannot work in a State where the population is not homogeneous.'[27] He also problematized the religious division among people, which created a problem of communal majority and minority. He wanted due safeguards to minorities in the democratic set up. He said,

> The British System of Government imposes no obligation upon the Majority Party to include in its cabinet the representatives of Minority Party. If applied to India the consequence will be obvious. It would make the majority community a governing class and the minority community a subject race. It would mean that a communal majority will be free to run the administration according to its own ideas of what is good for the minorities. Such a state of affairs could not be called democracy. It will have to be called imperialism.[28]

Towards bringing about economic democracy, Ambedkar prepared a memorandum as the draft for the future Constitution of India on behalf of the Scheduled Caste Federation (SCF), which was later published as 'States and Minorities' (1979b). It proposed the framework of State socialism to be incorporated into the Constitution. His State socialism included salient provisions like nationalization of land with compensation to the landlords in terms of debentures, parcelling out of this land to village cooperatives on lease with the State undertaking supply of finance, and other inputs, along with

[25] Ambedkar (1979b: 412).
[26] Ambedkar (1979b: 412).
[27] Ambedkar (1979d: 103).
[28] Ambedkar (1979b: 413).

basic and key industries to be owned and operated by the State and insurance to be nationalized and made compulsory to all people. He argued that the State should have control on the economic sphere because if in the name of liberty, which meant liberty from the control of the State, it would be 'another name for the dictatorship of the private employer'.[29]

He then himself pondered over the issue of bringing about such a structural change and State exercising effective control in preserving it, which appeared feasible only under dictatorship. This dictatorship, however, would contradict individual liberties. He found the way out in terms of hard-coding such a structure into the Constitution, which would not be alterable by any future majority. He wrote:

> The way out seems to be to retain Parliamentary Democracy and to prescribe State Socialism by the Law of the Constitution so that it will be beyond the reach of a Parliamentary majority to suspend, amend or abrogate it. It is only by this that one can achieve the triple object, namely, to establish socialism, retain Parliamentary Democracy and avoid Dictatorship.[30]

By 1948, he had reconciled with parliamentary democracy that he was critical of for having sacrificed equality for liberty. Instituting equality through constitutional law was his way to overcome the deficiency of parliamentary democracy. There are numerous problems with this proposition, but the foremost question in this regard is how the ruling classes would agree to write their own death warrant in the Constitution. If it had been so easy, there would not have been any necessity for revolutions. Elsewhere, he himself acknowledges the truth that the 'vested interests have never been known to have willingly divested themselves unless there was sufficient force to compel them'.[31] Interestingly enough, he realized the impossibility of it when heavens showered all opportunities on him beyond his own imagination.

The first opportunity came almost immediately in the Constituent Assembly. He voiced this idea of State socialism when he was called upon to speak on the Objective Resolution proposed

---

[29] Ambedkar (1979b: 410).
[30] Ambedkar (1979b: 412).
[31] Ambedkar (1991b: 197).

by Jawaharlal Nehru on 13 December 1946. Ambedkar had managed to get himself elected to the Constituent Assembly with the help of Jogendranath Mandal from Jessore–Khulna constituency in East Bengal. On 17 December he spoke on Nehru's Resolution alluding to his plan of 'economic democracy':

> I do not understand how it could be possible for any future Government which believes in doing justice socially, economically and politically, unless its economy is a socialistic economy. Therefore, personally, although I have no objection to the enunciation of these propositions, the Resolution is, to my mind, somewhat disappointing.[32]

But surprisingly, he hastened to add the next sentence, 'I am however prepared to leave this subject where it is with the observations I have made.'[33] Of course, he continued his speech which was hugely applauded by the Constituent Assembly. But it also marked some kind of patch up between him and the Congress. The very invitation to Ambedkar to speak on the Objective Resolution surprised many, including himself.[34] Later developments confirmed this patch up. When Ambedkar's membership was invalidated by Mountbatten's 3 June plan for the partition of India, which located Ambedkar's then-constituency in Pakistan, the Congress had got him elected from Bombay (now Mumbai) before the next session of the Constituent Assembly convened. The Congress, which was hell bent to ensure that Ambedkar did not enter the Constituent Assembly, had deferred its plan to get Mavlankar inducted into the Constituent Assembly by making Barrister Jayakar resign, and got Ambedkar elected instead. There is no clear evidence to explain this significant volte face on the part of the Congress. However, anyone having a strategic hang of the political situation back then could make out that only Gandhi could have such a strategic masterstroke. Ambedkar was not only elected to the Constituent Assembly but also inducted into the first all-party cabinet headed by Nehru and subsequently made the chairman of the most important committee of the Constituent Assembly, the Drafting Committee.

[32] Ambedkar (1994: 9).
[33] Ambedkar (1994).
[34] Ambedkar (1994: 7).

Constitution sans 'Ambedkar'

It is important to understand why the Constitution, which is supposed to be architected by Ambedkar, does not have any of his most radical ideas. He could never even voice his idea of hard coding a socialistic structure in the Constitution in the Constituent Assembly and rather had to be satisfied with some passing references to it relegated to Part IV ('Directive Principles of State Policy') of the Constitution, which would remain as mere moral precepts to be wilfully ignored by the ruling classes. Ironically, when someone proposed it, he had to oppose it. In 1946, K.T. Shah had proposed an amendment seeking to declare India as a 'Secular, Federal, Socialist'[35] nation, it was he who forcefully opposed it.[36] Ambedkar argued that the amendment was 'purely superfluous' and 'unnecessary', as 'socialist principles are already embodied in our Constitution' through Fundamental Rights and the Directive Principles of State Policy.[37] Referring to the Directive Principles, he told Shah, 'If these directive principles to which I have drawn attention are not socialistic in their direction and in their content, I fail to understand what more socialism can be.'[38] Shah's amendment failed to pass. The Directive Principles merely express the desire that the policies of the State should strive to do social and economic justice but cannot be said to constitute socialist structure as claimed by Ambedkar.

Ambedkar had criticized parliamentary democracy in 1943 for the neglect of economic inequalities as observed before. However, in the Constituent Assembly, he pleaded for it as more appropriate for the country and for running the administration efficiently and effectively. Ironically, both Gandhi and Ambedkar cohered in upholding the idea of parliamentary democracy, the former seeing its roots in the age-old system of the village panchayats and the latter seeing its origins in the Buddhist sanghas. These elements in our heritage, said Ambedkar, made it possible and easy for India to adopt the parliamentary system of democracy. Besides, as he told the Constituent Assembly, the Drafting Committee chose this system because they preferred more responsibility to stability which could

---

[35] See https://www.constitutionofindia.net/blogs/assembly_member_of_the_week___k__t__shah; last accessed 4 April 2020.
[36] Ambedkar (1994b: 326).
[37] Ambedkar (1994b).
[38] Ambedkar (1994b: 327).

slip into authoritarian exercise of power. Ambedkar observed while introducing the Draft Constitution in the Constituent Assembly on 4 November 1948, 'The Draft Constitution in recommending the parliamentary system of executive has preferred more responsibility to more stability.'[39]

Contradictions or inconsistencies were not uncommon with Ambedkar, who dismissed them invoking Emerson's dictum that consistency was a virtue of an ass.[40] His pragmatism, which relied on choosing the best course of action in an unfolding situation intrinsically did not care for the choices in the past just for the sake of consistency. It rather characterized evolution of Ambedkar along many dimensions. However, these apparent contradictions during the Constitution-making process perhaps alluded to his compulsions to pilot the discussions of the Constituent Assembly along the charted course which was definitely laid down by Nehru and Patel, who presided over most subcommittees of the Constituent Assembly. There is a reason to believe that he was happy with the outcome. In the euphoric shower of praise on the Constitution and on him as its chief architect, he had even exhorted his followers to shun the path of agitation and satyagraha and get resolution of their demands through constitutional means. However, it did not take long for him to get disillusioned with it. On 2 September 1953, during a debate on the power of governor in the Rajya Sabha, he responded to the charge that he was the architect of the Constitution by saying, 'My answer is I was a hack. What I was asked to do, I did much against my will.... Sir, my friends tell me that I have made the Constitution. But I am quite prepared to say that I shall be the first person to burn it out. I do not want it. It does not suit anybody.' When a member reminded him that he defended it, he snapped back to the dismay of the house, 'We lawyers defend many things.'[41]

Despite the disownment of the Constitution, the Ambedkarite Dalits swear by the Constitution and uphold it just because they believe that it was written by Ambedkar. This is the precise outcome of the Gandhian strategy. The Constitution, which would essentially adopt colonial framework of governance (adopting almost three-fourths of the India Act 1935, complete colonial

[39] Ambedkar (1994b: 52).
[40] Ambedkar (1979e: 139).
[41] Ambedkar (2003: 388–9).

institutional structure of governance, the Indian Penal Code [IPC], and so on) to push the policies of the government to serve the interests of the incipient bourgeoisie, would have to be fortified with emotional attachment of the lower strata, its victims. Ambedkar, who had emerged as the icon of the majority of the Dalits and had all the potential to be the icon of the entire lower strata, could be such an emotional anchor. It has worked perfectly. The Dalits, first, do not wish to know Ambedkar's aforementioned remarks disowning the Constitution and, if at all known, would take shelter in his following explanation.

Two years later, on 19 March 1955 in the Lok Sabha, Anup Singh, a Rajya Sabha member from Punjab, asked him, 'Last time when you spoke, you said that you would burn the Constitution.' Ambedkar shot back:

> Do you want a reply to that? I would give it to you right here. My friend says that the last time when I spoke, I said that I wanted to burn the Constitution. Well, in a hurry I did not explain the reason. ... The reason is this: We built a temple for god to come in and reside, but before the god could be installed, if the devil had taken possession of it, what else could we do except destroy the temple? We did not intend that it should be occupied by the Asuras. We intended it to be occupied by the Devas. That's the reason why I said I would rather like to burn it.[42]

They would simply believe that the Constitution was good but the implementers have been vile. They would not even faintly doubt that if the rulers were all godly men, there might not be any need for the Constitution itself.

Conditions for Successful Democracy

Ambedkar had very explicitly stated the conditions which are very much necessary for the successful working of democracy. They can be stated in brief as follows:[43]

1. Equality: For the success of democracy the first and foremost necessary element is equality. He said, '[T]here must

---

[42] Ambedkar (1989: 860).
[43] Kshirsagar (1992: 56–61).

not be an oppressed and suppressed class. There must not be a class which has got all the privileges and a class which has got all the burdens to carry. Such a thing, such a division, such an organization of a society has within itself the germs of a bloody revolution, and perhaps it would be impossible for the democracy to cure them'.[44] According to him, 'where equality is denied everything else may be taken to be denied'.[45]

2. Two-party system: The second important condition for the successful working of democracy is the existence of strong opposition to the ruling majority.[46] 'Democracy means a veto of power. Democracy requires that not only that the Government should be subject to the veto, long term veto of five years, at the hands of the people, but there must be an immediate veto. For this, there must be an Opposition in the Parliament to challenge the Government.'[47]

3. Equality in law and administration: There must be not only equality before law, but also equality of treatment in administration. Ambedkar said:

> We must have a Government in which the men in power will give their undivided allegiance to the best interest of the country. We must have a Government in which men in power, knowing where obedience will end and resistance will begin, will not be afraid to amend the social and economic code of life which the dictates of justice and expediency so urgently call for.[48]

4. Constitutional morality: Ambedkar said that '[a] Constitution which contains legal provisions, is only skeleton. The flesh of the skeleton is to be found in what we call constitutional morality.'[49] According to him, the Constitution is important for the success of democracy, but more important was constitutional morality in polity and society.

---

[44] Ambedkar (2003: 475–6).
[45] Ambedkar (1987a: 66).
[46] Kshirsagar (1992: 57).
[47] Ambedkar (2003: 477).
[48] Das (1977: 22).
[49] Kshirsagar (1992: 59).

5. No tyranny of majority: Ambedkar said, 'The minority must always feel safe that although the majority is carrying on the Government, the minority is not being hurt.'[50] He insisted that

> [T]here is one other thing which is very necessary in the working of Democracy, and it is this that in the name of democracy there must be no tyranny of the majority over the minority. The minority must always feel safe that although the majority is carrying on the Government, the minority is not being hurt, or the minority is not being hit below the belt.[51]

6. Moral order: Ambedkar said, 'A politician dose not merely trade in politics, but he also represents a particular faith covering both the method as well as the metaphysics of politics.' He further said that '[p]olitics has become a kind of sewage system intolerably, unsavoury and insanitary. To become a politician is like going to work in drain.' According to him, politics is the key of all emancipation. Therefore, he asked depressed classes to capture political power for the realization of social democracy in its true spirit. He emphasized on moral order in politics just because he wanted democracy to be implemented in the true sense.
7. Public conscience: According to Ambedkar Public Conscience means, 'Conscience which becomes agitated at every wrong, no matter who is the sufferer; and it means that everybody whether he suffers that particular wrong or not is prepared to join him in order to get him relieved.' Ambedkar considered public conscience as an essential condition for the successful working of a democracy. It is the will of the people that makes a healthy democratic atmosphere.

Prophetic Warning

While opposing incorporation of the 'secular and socialist' character of the Constitution during its making, Ambedkar, in his last speech in the Constituent Assembly on 25 November 1949, issued three warnings towards maintenance of democracy 'not merely in form,

---

[50] Kshirsagar (1992: 60).
[51] Ambedkar (2003: 482).

but also in fact': the first was to 'hold fast to constitutional methods of achieving our social and economic objectives. It means we must abandon the bloody methods of revolution. It means that we must abandon the method of civil disobedience, non-cooperation and satyagraha'; the second was not 'to lay their liberties at the feet of even a great man, or to trust him with power which enable him to subvert their institutions ... in politics, Bhakti or hero-worship is a sure road to degradation and to eventual dictatorship;' and the third was 'not to be content with mere political democracy. We must make our political democracy a social democracy as well. Political democracy cannot last unless there lies at the base of it social democracy.'[52] Surprisingly, in this celebrated speech, the absence of economic democracy is conspicuous. However, he seems to include economic democracy in social democracy itself when he explained social democracy as 'a way of life which recognises liberty, equality and fraternity as the principles of life'.[53] He elaborated: 'These principles of liberty, equality and fraternity are not to be treated as separate items in a trinity. They form a union of trinity in the sense that to divorce one from the other is to defeat the very purpose of democracy.'[54] He prophetically warned:

> On the 26th of January 1950, we are going to enter into a life of contradictions. In politics we will have equality and in social and economic life we will have inequality. In politics we will be recognising the principle of one man one vote and one vote one value. In our social and economic life, we shall, by reason of our social and economic structure, continue to deny the principle of one man one value. How long shall we continue to live this life of contradictions? How long shall we continue to deny equality in our social and economic life? If we continue to deny it for long, we will do so only by putting our political democracy in peril. We must remove this contradiction at the earliest possible moment or else those who suffer from inequality will blow up the structure of political democracy which is Assembly has to laboriously built up.[55]

How could these contradictions be removed? Since he had forbidden extra-constitutional methods (including not only violence

---

[52] Ambedkar (2003: 1215, 1216).
[53] Ambedkar (2003: 1163).
[54] Ambedkar (2003: 1216).
[55] Ambedkar (2003: 1163).

but also 'satyagraha'), the answer presumably lay in laid-down democratic practice. However, Ambedkar himself warned that the whole process of democratic practice in an unequal society was vulnerable to being derailed by vested interests. It thus posed a chicken-and-egg problem: What came first, democracy or socialism? Initially, Ambedkar had rightly envisaged that socialism would come first and set the stage for political democracy. His hope, at that time, was that 'State socialism' would be enshrined in the Indian Constitution. Without constitutional protection for socialist principles, socialism in a democratic society was likely to be derailed by vested interests.

While socialism first may resolve this dilemma, the problem of achieving it craves an answer. Ambedkar's proposal for State socialism had little chance of being accepted by the Constituent Assembly, where privileged interests actually dominated. The Constituent Assembly comprised the members elected by the provincial assemblies which were themselves elected by limited franchise with just about 28 per cent population having voting rights. Of the total 389 members, 292 were representatives of the states, 93 represented the princely states, and 4 were from commissioner provinces. Of the 292 elected members, the Congress had 208 representatives, and the Muslim League 73. But as the Muslim League refused to participate, there was overwhelming domination of the Congress in the Constituent Assembly that prompted Granville Austin to comment, 'The Assembly was the Congress and the Congress was India.'[56] As such, there was no possibility of any such proposal denting the interests of the privileged classes being considered in the Constituent Assembly. However, it was not even given a chance. When a member of the Left wanted it, ironically Ambedkar himself opposed it in the name of democracy.[57]

The idea of Directive Principles of State Policy was taken from the Irish Constitution and the content from the Declaration of the Rights of Man proclaimed by Revolutionary France, the Declaration of Independence by the American Colonies, and the United Nations Universal Declaration of Human Rights. The Nehru Committee Report of 1928 and the Congress Resolutions

[56] Granville (1966: 9).
[57] Ambedkar (1994: 351).

of 1931, and later, in 1936, its commitment inter alia to socialism, inspired by the Constitution of the USSR, had also influenced the Directive Principles. Ambedkar had this to say about them:

> In my judgment, the directive principles have a great value; for they lay down that our ideal is economic democracy ... [Our] object in framing this Constitution is really twofold: (1) to lay down the form of political democracy, and (2) to lay down that our ideal is economic democracy and also to prescribe that every Government ... shall strive to bring about economic democracy.[58]

As it turned out, they remained good but empty words in the Constitution. Directive Principles were not taken seriously in Independent India. They were not enforceable in a court of law, and nor did electoral politics succeed in holding the State accountable to their realization, as Dr Ambedkar had envisaged.

Interrogating Democracy

The question that Ambedkar raised but avoided to answer in unequivocal terms, 'Is there democracy in India?', perhaps because of his role in the making of the Constitution, can be answered now by any common man in India.

As a matter of fact, Indian postcolonial State, having essentially adopted the colonial State structure, could not be expected to be a democracy. With the coexistence of a plethora of draconian laws in place that nullify fundamental rights and mark individuals targeted by the State as defenceless, the Indian State becomes antithetical to democracy. Its character rather has been more oppressive to people with addition of Brahmanic cunning to the colonial ethos. Castes and religion, the classical barriers to liberty, having been given a new lease of life in the Constitution, exist as a backdrop. Dalits, Adivasis, and Muslims continue to suffer multi-dimensional oppression. For instance, among undertrials in Indian prisons, the SCs, STs, and Muslims account for 55 per cent, a disproportionate number to their total population of 39 per cent.[59] Muslims are easily labelled as terrorists and

---

[58] Ambedkar (1994: 352).
[59] Tiwary (2016).

incarcerated for years in jails and even hanged with impunity. Adivasis, who are struggling to protect their habitat, become Maoists and could be exterminated by unleashing the State military might against them. Dalits who are the pervasively suffer caste atrocities are also being selectively targeted by the State as Maoists.[60] There is no liberty for workers to go on a strike to protest against their exploitation. The plight of the Maruti Suzuki workers in Manesar who dared to struggle for wage hike and abolition of contract labour is a case in point in recent years! Even those who organize themselves to raise voice against the suppression of peoples' democratic rights find themselves without liberties and are victimized with impunity. The cases of Binayak Sen and Saibaba, who stand convicted for life imprisonment, and recent ones against activists-intellectuals, all under fabricated charges, illustrate the fascist core of India's democracy.[61]

Decimating Dissent

The liberty in the country is symbolized by small spaces marked out in every state capital, like Azad Maidan in Mumbai. Even these areas are fenced off and surrounded by the armed posse of police, ready to pounce upon people under one or the other pretext of violation of some draconian law. The constitutional dictum that rights are not absolute is used by the State to the hilt in denying those very rights. Most rights can be easily ignored in the name of national security. Apart from the processual denial of liberty, there are a plethora of draconian laws, some of which are inherited from the colonial rule and many are added by the 'democratic republic' of India. The first such law that flowed from the colonial statutes is the Section 124 A of the IPC or the Sedition Act, which Gandhi termed as 'the prince among the political sections of the IPC designed to suppress the liberty of the citizen'.[62] On the one hand, Article 19A grants the freedom of speech and expression but on the other hand, Section 124A incriminates it. In 2014, Kashmiri students were charged for sedition when they allegedly cheered for

---

[60] Teltumbde (2018).
[61] FPJ Web Desk (2020); Mustafa (2020).
[62] See https://www.mkgandhi.org/voiceoftruth/greattrial.htm; last accessed 4 April 2020.

Pakistan during a cricket match. The arrest of the Jawaharlal Nehru University (JNU) students like Kanhaiya Kumar, Omar Khalid, and Anirban Bhattacharya, or Hardik Patel, of the Patel agitation fame in Gujarat, were charged for sedition along with hundreds of thousands in jails labelled as Maoists and terrorists. Another Act that has colonial connection is the Armed Forces Special Powers Act (AFSPA), which was promulgated on 15 August 1942 in the wake of emergency declared by the Viceroy Lord Linlithgow when the Indian National Army (INA) marched into India and the launch of the Quit India Movement by Gandhi. It conferred vaguely defined special powers to the armed forces to arrest and use force (even kill) civilians on mere suspicion. Modelled on these lines, four ordinances—the Bengal Disturbed Areas (Special Powers of Armed Forces [SPAF]) Ordinance, the Assam Disturbed Areas (SPAF) Ordinance, the East Bengal Disturbed Areas (SPAF) Ordinance, and the United Provinces Disturbed Areas (SPAF) Ordinance—were issued by the central government to deal with the internal security situation arising out of the partition of India. After Independence, the legal architecture for the paramilitary forces and the armed State police to combat insurgency in the region was created in the wake of the Naga National Council (NNC) movement to form a 'Free Sovereign Naga Nation' with Assam Maintenance of Public Order (Autonomous District) Act in the Naga Hills in 1953 and thereafter the Assam Disturbed Areas Act of 1955. It paved the way for AFPSAs in various regions like Assam, Manipur, Punjab, Chandigarh, and Jammu and Kashmir. It continues to deny democracy to all these regions.

Beyond these few Acts as colonial legacy, dozens of Acts in antidemocratic category were promulgated by the 'democratic republic' of India. One of the first such Acts was the Madras Suppression of Disturbances Act (1948) that authorized the use of military violence against the peasants in Telengana. The peasant struggle in Telengana which began in 1946 was against forced labour, illegal exactions, evictions by feudal landlords, and oppression by village Patels (officers), among other things. Later, it developed into an agrarian liberation struggle to get rid of feudal landlordism and the Nizam's dynastic rule in the state. The struggle continued even after the Nizam's rule ended with the entry of Indian troops in September 1948 and the merger of the Hyderabad State into the Indian Union. As many as 4,000 communists and peasant activists were killed and more than 10,000 communist and sympathizers were put behind the bars. A spate of Acts followed purely to suppress peoples' movements that broke out from the late 1960s. The Maintenance of Internal Security Act 1973 (MISA), the Terrorism and Disruptive Activities (Prevention) Act 1987 (TADA), the Prevention of Terrorist Act 2001 (POTA), National Security Act 1980 (NSA; amended 1984 and 1987), the Essential Services Maintenance Act 1981 (ESMA), and the Maharashtra Control of Organised Crime Act 1999 (MACOCA) are some of the draconian central as well as State Acts. There are multiple of them all over India to terrorize people into submission.

Wither Rule of Law

One of the tests of democracy is the rule of law. With such an arsenal at the disposal of the State the 'rule of law' is the inevitable casualty. The Constitution of India vide Article 14 asserts the principle of the rule of law to protect the citizen from the arbitrary power of the State. The Supreme Court, at various times, has reiterated the 'rule of law' to be the 'basic feature' of the Constitution, which cannot be destroyed even by an amendment of the Constitution under Article 368.[63] Equality before law means subjection of all classes to the ordinary law of the land administered by ordinary law court. In reality, is there the rule of law in India? The VIP/VVIP syndrome in the country, the menace of which might make the bygone feudal era of monarchies look better, may perhaps be enough to expose it. Then there are occurrences such as custodial torture, extrajudicial murders, and encounters, which is the order of the day in India that decries its rule of law.[64]

Procedurally, law excludes most people from its purview. First, it has a high socio-economic barrier that may not be crossed by potential victims, and second, its outcome would depend upon the moneybags backing it. The poor people who are mostly wronged scarcely get justice. At the very first encounter of people with the police, experience of lawlessness is the rule. The police responses are conditioned by the class, caste, and community of people.

---

[63] Baxi (1980: 81).
[64] Pillai (2019); Human Rights Watch (2016).

Kuldip Nayar, a noted journalist, had perceptively observed on this relationship between police and people, 'An ordinary person's introduction to a police station begins with the beating.'[65] It is notable that the Indian police have been called 'the largest gang of organized criminals' by none other than the head of the only Police Commission ever constituted after Independence. Even after a vicious police encounter, the justice delivery system is manoeuvrable with money. Even discounting corruption, the rich hire expensive lawyers to exploit law, whereas the poor cannot even afford to access the courts. The corruption further aggravates this intrinsic inequality before law. As per a report on *Corruption in Judiciary*, Volume 1, by the Centre for Media Studies in 2005, 33 per cent of the people had bribed judiciary to the extent of Rs 3,817 crore in just one year.[66] No wonder there is abysmally low conviction in cases of atrocity. In the cases of major crimes, it is negligible. Most infamous cases of atrocities, Kilvenmeni included, rather exposed the systemic bias in the justice delivery system, which leads to summary acquittals of the perpetrators. In Kilvenmeni, poor Dalits were punished for a murder of a landlord's henchman who was killed in the clash that took place that evening. All the landlords accused were acquitted, with the Madras High Court simply dismissing the charges against them saying that the 'respected' landlords, some of whom owned cars, could not have committed such a ghastly act of burning forty-four Dalit women and children.[67] The judicial injustice is repeated in case after case. In Bihar, there was a virtual caste war over two decades (1990s and 2000s) in which hundreds of Dalits were massacred by private armies of the upper-caste landlords. These cases have reached in appeal to Patna High court after decades but instead of regretting its own flaw, the Patna High Court has been acquitting all the murderers with a ditto judgements amounting to saying that it did not see enough evidence for their conviction. The Dalit rape victims met a similar judgment: In the Bhawari Devi rape case, the court observed that the high-caste people could not rape a low-caste woman. In cases under the Atrocity Act, the judicial

---

[65] See https://www.asianage.com/india/all-india/240818/kuldip-nayar-a-peoples-journalist-enters-eternal-sleep.html; last accessed 4 April 2020.
[66] Gadhia (2009: 35).
[67] Kandasamy (2015).

bias is revealed in the repeated observation that the crime is not committed because of the victim's caste. In ghastly cases like Khairlanji[68] and Jajjhar,[69] the judges did not see the murders were because of caste!

★ ★ ★

As seen previously, Ambedkar's conception of democracy, while termed as a liberal or bourgeois democracy, tends to transcend their familiar boundaries and aspires to get closer to any radical concept of democracy. Its apparent contradiction necessarily suffers from impracticability. Particularly, when he envisions democracy in terms of 'liberty, equality, and fraternity', representing political, economic, and social democracies, respectively, one wonders how they all, particularly economic and social democracies, are to be accomplished. His answer that economic democracy necessitated socialistic society, which could be created by hard-coding economic structure into the Constitution is historically as well as practically problematic. Even his model of State socialism providing for continuation of private enterprises and industry is too radical to be accomplished through constitutional law. It poses a problem of how the entrenched propertied and powerful people, who constitute majority in the Constituent Assembly would accept such a Constitution that takes away their power and property. It could only be possible when the people who did not possess any property win political power. As he acknowledges elsewhere, people would not easily part with their property just by asking for it, they will have to be forced to do so; the Constitution will have to be backed by such a force that compels them to accept the new order of equality. Likewise, social democracy necessitated annihilation of caste as minimal prerequisite. How would this be accomplished is not explicated.

The problem of social democracy is rather aggravated by consecrating caste and religion in the Constitution. But can we even think of social democracy in exclusion of other two? The answer will have to be in negative. The battles to bridge and eliminate social divisions like caste and communities have to contend with

[68] *The Hindu* (2010).
[69] Dalit History Month (2019).

the resistance of the entrenched powers that favour status quo. Mere feel of disturbance will actuate them to defeat such attempts, unless they are convinced that those attempts are in their long term interests. The social reforms that Ambedkar desired to precede the political reforms also may not be possible unless there are commensurate changes brought about in the economic relationships. For instance, in order to annihilate castes, the economic structure of the society that subsumes social relationships based upon castes will have to be suitably altered, which in turn would affect the political relationships. A brief history of Ambedkar's own struggle reveals it. The social struggles that he led initially to sensitize the Hindu society to realize the importance of reforms in their society did not work and rather made him to turn towards political prospects. His struggles on this terrain brought him certain success but proved inadequate to attain the goal of annihilation of castes. Eventually, he tried out the religious method, not merely in terms of reform but total change of religion but arguably, it also failed to make dent on the caste structure of the society. Whatever changes in it have crept in may rather be attributed to the changes that came in economic structure of the society, first when capitalism entered India under colonial cover, and later spread across rural area during the postcolonial decades. The only inference that could be drawn from this experience is that unless people wage simultaneous struggle for changing economic aspects of their lives, exclusive struggles for change in social and cultural terrain may never succeed.

Even the political democracy that Ambedkar thought is brought about by the Constitution suffers from infirmities on account of the electoral mechanism it adopted for operationalizing democracy. The first-past-the-post type of electoral system actually valorizes management strategies than peoples' will and as such negates the basic premise of representation. As we have been experiencing the aftermath of our democracy based on such a principle, 'political democracy' invariably accentuates and perpetuates the existing economic inequality and even jeopardizes social democracy. This has been seen happening in all constitutional democracies world over. Howsoever the game may be configured, it cannot eliminate influence of money and, as they say, he who pays the piper calls the tune: The rich people make the system subservient to their interests. The elections need communication to the masses through an organization (party), which in turn needs money to sustain it.

Those who supply this money would certainly expect the elected representatives to do their bidding. With such a propelling power of money, the entire State becomes subservient to the rich and turns oppressive to the poor. None other than the Indian democracy makes it clearer. The electoral dynamics imperatively resorts to manipulation of people along the familiar fault lines and induces animosities among them vitiating what little spirit of fraternity or community (as people prefer it to be substituted) might have prevailed.

Ambedkar's struggle for democratizing Indian society is a valuable text for us to read and reread. Past always showcases itself to the present to learn from, both from its successes as well as from failures, and never to emulate. Among the two, failures are more important than successes because they propel us to think through and alert us about possible follies. Success, on the other hand, could daze us into emulating it and push us to sure failure because the situational combination of the factors that produced success in the past would not be the same in the present. Ambedkar's vision of democracy may likewise serve as the beacon. India made significant progress but on dimension of democracy has regressed even faster. The onslaught of the right-wing Hindutva forces is out to decimate it in their zeal to transform this country into a Hindu Rashtra. But as the visionary Ambedkar warned, it would be a great calamity. We have to rise to thwart this imminent danger.

References

Ambedkar, B.R. 1979a. 'Annihilation of Caste'. In *Dr. Babasaheb Ambedkar: Writings and Speeches*, Volume 1, edited by Vasant Moon, pp. 23–96. Mumbai: Education Department, Govt. of Maharashtra.

———. 1979b. 'States and Minorities'. In *Dr. Babasaheb Ambedkar: Writings and Speeches*, Volume 1, edited by Vasant Moon, pp. 381–449. Mumbai: Education Department, Govt. of Maharashtra.

———. 1979c. 'Ranade, Gandhi and Jinnah'. In *Dr. Babasaheb Ambedkar: Writings and Speeches*, Volume 1, edited by Vasant Moon, pp. 205–40. Mumbai: Education Department, Govt. of Maharashtra.

———. 1979d. 'Maharashtra as a Linguistic Province'. In *Dr. Babasaheb Ambedkar: Writings and Speeches*, Volume 1, edited by Vasant Moon, pp. 99–128. Mumbai: Education Department, Govt. of Maharashtra.

———. 1979e. 'Thoughts on Linguistic States'. In *Babasaheb Ambedkar: Writings and Speeches*, Volume 1, edited by Vasant Moon, pp. 137–201. Mumbai: Govt. of Maharashtra.

———. 1987a. 'Philosophy of Hinduism'. In *Dr. Babasaheb Ambedkar: Writings and Speeches*, Volume 3, edited by Vasant Moon, pp. 3–92. Mumbai: Education Department, Govt. of Maharashtra.

———. 1989. *Dr Babasaheb Ambedkar: Writings and Speeches*, Volume 15, edited by Vasant Moon. Mumbai: Education Department, Govt. of Maharashtra.

———. 1991a. 'Why Indian Labour Is Determined to Win the War'. In *Dr. Babasaheb Ambedkar: Writings and Speeches*, Volume 10, edited by Vasant Moon, pp. 36–43. Mumbai: Education Department, Govt. of Maharashtra.

———. 1991b. 'What Gandhi and the Congress Have Done to the Untouchables'. In *Dr. Babasaheb Ambedkar: Writings and Speeches*, Volume 9, edited by Vasant Moon, pp. 1–387. Mumbai: Education Department, Govt. of Maharashtra.

———. 1991c. 'Labour and Parliamentary Democracy'. In *Dr. Babasaheb Ambedkar: Writings and Speeches*, Volume 10, edited by Vasant Moon, pp. 106–112. Mumbai: Education Department, Govt. of Maharashtra.

———. 1994a. 'B.R. Ambedkar's Address at Poona District Law Library on December 22, 1952'. In *Dr Babasaheb Ambedkar: Writings and Speeches*, Volume 13, edited by Vasant Moon, p. 287. Mumbai: Education Department, Govt. of Maharashtra.

———. 1994b. *Dr. Babasaheb Ambedkar: Writings and Speeches*, Volume 13, edited by Vasant Moon. Mumbai: Education Department, Govt. of Maharashtra.

———. 2003. *Dr. Babasaheb Ambedkar: Writings and Speeches*, Volume 13, Part 3, edited by Vasant Moon. Mumbai: Education Department, Govt. of Maharashtra.

———. 2014. 'On The Industrial Disputes Bill'. In *Dr. Babasaheb Ambedkar: Writings and Speeches*, Volume 2, edited by Hari Narke, pp. 201–33. Mumbai: Education Department, Govt. of Maharashtra.

Baxi, Upendra. 1980. *The Indian Supreme Court and Politics*. New Delhi: Eastern Book Co.

Bucheler, Justus. 1955. *Philosophical Writings of Peirce*. New York: Dover

Das, Bhagwan (ed.). 1977. *Thus Spoke Ambedkar*, Volume 1. Jalandhar: Bheem Patrika.

Dalit History Month. 2019. 'Dulina—The Long History of Lynching Dalits'. *Medium*. Available at https://medium.com/@dalithistorynow/dulina-the-legacy-of-a-long-history-of-lynching-dalits-7c3c51a2f180; last accessed 27 March 2020.

Dewey, John. 2001. *Democracy and Education*. Electronic Classics Series. Pennsylvania: The Pennsylvania State University.
FPJ Web Desk. 2020. 'Over 130 Intellectuals Write to President, CJI Asking for Release of Prof Saibaba, Varavara Rao'. *The Free Press Journal*. Available at https://www.freepressjournal.in/india/over-130-intellectuals-write-to-president-cji-asking-for-release-of-prof-saibaba-varavara-rao; last accessed 20 June 2020.
Gadhia, Harish R. 2009. *Judicial Accountability: Re-visioning the Role of Judiciary*. New Delhi: AIR, P-Journal.
Granville, Austin. 1966. *The Indian Constitution: Cornerstone of a Nation*. Oxford: Oxford University Press.
Hindu, The. 2010. 'Khairlanji Case: HC Commutes Death Sentence for Six'. Available at https://www.thehindu.com/news/national/Khairlanjicase-HC-commutes-death-sentence-for-six/article16196520.ece; last accessed 27 March 2020.
Human Rights Watch. 2016. *"Bound by Brotherhood": India's Failure to End Killings in Police Custody*. Available at https://www.hrw.org/sites/default/files/report_pdf/india1216_web_0.pdf; last accessed 25 March 2020.
Jayasuriya, L. 2008. 'Buddhism, Politics, and Statecraft'. *International Journal of Buddhist Thought & Culture* 11: 41–74.
Jayatilleke, K.N. 1967. 'The Contemporary Relevance of Buddhist Philosophy'. In *The Wheel*, p. 248. Kandy: Buddhist Publication Society.
Jonathan, S. 2017. 'The Common Origins of Science and Democracy'. *Brookings*. Available at https://www.brookings.edu/blog/techtank/2017/03/08/the-common-origins-of-science-and-democracy/; last accessed 23 March 2020.
Kadam, K.N. 1997. *The Meaning of the Ambedkarite Conversion to Buddhism and Other Essays*. Mumbai: Popular Prakashan.
Kandasamy, M. 2015. 'No One Killed the Dalits'. Seventh Anuradha Ghandy Memorial Lecture. Available at http://sanhati.com/wp-content/uploads/2015/11/lecture-with-footnotes.pdf; last accessed 27 March 2020.
Kshirsagar, Ramchandra Kamaji. 1992. *Political Thought of Dr. Babasaheb Ambedkar*. New Delhi: Intellectual Publishing House.
Marx, Karl. 1977. *A Contribution to the Critique of Political Economy*. Moscow: Progress Publishers. Available at https://www.marxists.org/archive/marx/works/1859/critique-pol-economy/; last accessed 7 April 2017.
Mustafa, F. 2020. 'Strange and Arbitrary Bail Orders: Are Indian Judges Going Too Far?'. *The Wire*. Available at https://thewire.in/law/judges-bail-orders; last accessed 20 March 2020.

Pillai, P. 2019. 'Extrajudicial killings: India's Long History of "Fake Encounters"'. *The Interpreter*. Available at https://www.lowyinstitute.org/the-interpreter/extrajudicial-killings-long-history-fake-encounters; last accessed 20 March 2020.

Shields, Patricia M. 2003. 'The Community of Inquiry: Classical Pragmatism and Public Administration'. *Administration & Society* 35 (5): 510–38.

Teltumbde, A. 'Labelling Dalits and Adivasis as Maoists Is an Old State Strategy for Crushing Dissent and Criticism'. *Scroll*. Available at https://scroll.in/article/881626/labelling-dalits-and-adivasis-as-maoists-is-an-old-state-strategy-for-crushing-dissent-and-criticism; last accessed 22 March 2020.

Tiwary, Diptiman. 2016. 'Over 55 per cent of Undertrials Muslim, Dalit or Tribal: NCRB'. *Indian Express*, 1 November.

Verhoeven, Martin J. 2001. 'Buddhism and Science: Probing the Boundaries of Faith and Reason'. *Religion East and West* (1, June): 77–97.

Vo, Linh-Chi and Mihaela Kelemen. 2014. 'John Dewey (1859–1952)'. In *The Oxford Handbook of Process Philosophy and Organization Studies*, edited by Jenny Helin, Tor Hernes, Daniel Hjorth, and Robin Holt, pp. 236–54. Oxford: Oxford University Press.

4

Repairing Complex Historical Injustice

NEERA CHANDHOKE

The twin concepts of historical injustice and social justice are inextricably associated with the name 'Dr Bhimrao Ambedkar', the role he played in shaping the freedom struggle, and his contributions to the conceptualization and making of the Indian Constitution. Dr Ambedkar's attacks on caste system compelled the nationalist movement to recognize that it was simply not enough to fight for the freedom of Indians from colonial rule. Indians had to be liberated from the shackles that bound them to an indefensible caste system.

Dr Ambedkar, in effect, gave a new twist to the concept of freedom. Freedom from colonialism had to be accompanied by freedom from social fetters that had truncated the ability of vulnerable sections of society to come into their own. Delivering his address at the opening plenary session of the First Round Table Conference on 20 November 1930 as the representative of the Depressed Classes, Dr Ambedkar expressed precisely this point of view.

> We know that political power is passing from the British into the hands of those who wield such tremendous economic, social and religious sway over our existence .... But we will consent to that on one condition and that is that the settlement of our problems is not left to time. I am afraid the Depressed Classes have waited too long for time to work its miracle. At every successive step taken by the British Government to widen the scope of representative government, the Depressed Classes have been systematically left out.

No thought has been given to their claim for political power ... we will not stand this any longer. The settlement of our problem must be a part of the general political settlement and must not be left over to the shifting sands of the sympathy and goodwill of the rulers of the future.

The message had important implications for the concept and the practices of justice. Substantive freedom for the Dalit community could only be achieved when the upper castes recognized their own complicity in the perpetuation of injustice on their own people. And substantive concepts of freedom, equality, rights, and fraternity could only be achieved when Indians realized that they must compensate for historical injustice through affirmative action policies.

The politics of substantive freedom acquired a sharp political edge because questions relating to how equal political status for all in an independent India could be achieved was catapulted to the forefront of the agenda. How would a democratic India go about acknowledging and remedying historical injustice? What were the roads society had to follow to deliver social justice for the most disadvantaged? These questions were tackled through the concept of social justice.

The first section of the chapter explores the concept of historical injustice and the second section that of social justice. The argument is that the concept of social justice is composed of at least three sets of rights, if not more. These are the rights to material goods that are essential to well-being, the right to voice or to participate in the multiple deliberations of society as an equal, and the right to respect. The concept of social justice is thus an umbrella concept. The problem is that social and political recognition and realization of all three sets of rights may not occur in tandem. A community may be granted the first and second rights, but not the third right. Denial of even one right compromises the principle of social justice. There is, in effect, more to the concept of social justice than we have assumed initially.

Complex Injustice in History

Skilled historians lay before us the intricate details of the past in all its richness and intricacies much as Titian's wonderful Renaissance painting 'Fall of Man' (1550) depicted the minutiae of the exile of Adam and Eve. Political theorists who choose to address present predicaments are generally concerned with *why* certain forms of injustice continue to be reproduced in the present.[1] History matters but, for the most part, contemporary political theory, despite the warnings of many scholars, does not try to reconstruct the languages and the practices of the past. Most approaches to historical understanding are presentist, perhaps even instrumental, that is, we read the past through the prism of contemporary understandings, categories, concepts, and concerns. Irrespective of the methodology we prefer to come to terms with the past, we must know where we have come from and how we arrived from there to here. Even as she warned against excessive preoccupation with the history of injustice, Iris Marion Young suggested that it is both a mad and dangerous wish to break with the past and make it irrelevant. If we do not face the facts of historical injustice, we may be 'haunted by victim's ghosts and destined to repeat the perpetrator's wrongs'.[2] For this reason, a brief foray into history can be justified.

It is universally accepted that the history of social orders is embedded in injustice done to groups for no reason other than birth into a community typed as the 'enemy', as 'inferior', or as the 'polluting'. In India, Bangladesh, Pakistan, Sri Lanka, and Nepal, a rigid, hierarchical, and exclusionary caste system has, for at least two centuries, subjected Dalits to three-fold injustice: extreme economic deprivation; institutionalized social discrimination; and lack of voice. The history of the sub-continent brought to the community little but torn feet and bleeding hands.

The precise nature of the caste system is a matter of considerable debate, whether the system is sanctioned by religious texts or is the outcome of a division of labour. What is clear is that untouchability developed alongside, with an entire group being exiled to a space outside the caste system. If there is one thing that is worse than birth *into* a system where caste governs access to opportunities and status, it is birth *outside* the system. Stigmatized as the outcasts and 'untouchables', Dalits were expected to perform menial

---

[1] I speak of political theorists who address contemporary political predicaments. Historians of ideas are of course interested in recapturing the sense of the past.
[2] Young (2012: 171–2).

tasks, prohibited from participating in collective life or occupying the same residential space, and condemned by rigid and inhuman codes of pollution and purity to live lives stripped bare of dignity and meaning.

Witness the paradox: Dalits performed tasks that were crucial to the reproduction of the Hindu community, from cleaning filth, to labouring on land, to leather working, but the community itself was sequestered socially and spatially. Historians have discovered that the caste system was fluid, and members of one caste could, in some circumstances, move to an upper caste. The one feature that prevented the Dalits from doing so was the line of pollution. Nowhere in the hierarchy of caste, suggests Jodhka, is the rigidity of the line as sharp. The line of pollution and impurity is absolute.[3]

Practices of discrimination were consolidated over time, even though protest stalked the practice of untouchability, much as Nemesis single-mindedly pursues hubris. In the sixth century, philosophers belonging to the Charvaka school of materialist philosophy and Buddhism attacked caste and untouchability among other precepts of Brahmanical Hinduism. From the sixth to the sixteenth century, the Bhakti movement of devotional mystics launched a powerful and concerted attack on caste-based discrimination. Till today, the poetry of the sixteenth-century weaver Kabir, who exposed the hollowness and the hypocrisy of organized religion and its gatekeeper's is remembered, recited, and sung. 'Pandit,' he addressed the Brahmin, 'look in your heart to know. Tell me how untouchability was born—Untouchability is what you made so.'[4]

Right up till the turn of the twentieth century, a number of social-reform groups, driven by the quest for a moral order and the belief that untouchability was a later appendage to Hinduism, tried to retrieve the essence of the religion. Others threw up their metaphorical hands in despair, broke away, and established new religions such as Sikhism, Jainism, and Buddhism. A 'divinely ordained' social hierarchy and practices of exclusion became the object of struggle, the target of social reform movements, and often the butt of ridicule.

[3] Jodhka (2012 71).
[4] Cited in Omvedt (2008: 99).

Contemporary understandings of untouchability as historical injustice were consolidated in the opening years of the twentieth century through political mobilization of the community and the initiation of several debates within the freedom struggle. In the early decades of the twentieth century, the political leader of the Dalits, Dr Ambedkar, interpreted untouchability as a violation of civil rights, and advocated constitutional and legal remedies. In a caste-bound society that had raised inequality and injustice to the status of a binding moral norm, and fine-tuned it as a moral virtue, the issue at stake was politically significant, equal status for all in an independent and democratic India.

The Present of Redistributive Justice

In few newly independent countries were equality and redistributive justice given such centrality in the political imaginary. Independent India adopted an ambitious programme of redistributive justice, which sought to turn existing inequities and hierarchies on their head. To accomplish this task, the project had to take cognizance of background inequalities, many of which were composed of little but layers of historical injustice.[5] It 'looked backwards' to identify historical injustices. It simultaneously 'looked forward' to estimate how accumulated disadvantages could be tackled through appropriate means, in this case redistributive justice.

Redistributive justice ensures the right of all citizens to privileges, opportunities, income, voice, and recognition. Most of the goods to which people have a right can be placed in the meta-category of redistribution of resources and wealth, voice, and recognition. Within the project of redistributive justice, affirmative action policies guaranteed the physical presence of Dalits in State-maintained educational institutions, public employment, and elected bodies. This was accomplished through reservations or quotas, fixed in proportion to the demographic strength of the community. The Constitution and laws criminalized the practice

---

[5] Not all background inequalities have their root in the past; many of them are specific to particular phases of capitalist accumulation, such as dispossession from mineral-rich land that is appropriated by capitalists.

of untouchability, and in the interests of affirmative action, exceptions were made to Article 14 of the fundamental rights chapter of the Constitution that guarantees the right to equality.

Undeniably, affirmative action policies that centre on the politics of presence and acknowledgement of harm done, as well as the dynamics of democracy and electoral calculations, have contributed to the repair of historical wrongs. The advantages of these policies are, however, unevenly spread out. The constituency of affirmative action has benefited, but in bits and pieces.

For instance, we see the making of an educated and professionally qualified Dalit middle class. Magazines run cover page stories on the rise of Dalit millionaires and the establishment of a Dalit Chamber of Commerce and Industry.[6] A Dalit movement has succeeded in prising open worlds that for long had been closed to the community. Activists have seized the right to voice through collective action, and now influence and even shape public debates. The last three-and-a-half decades have witnessed the Dalit movement and political parties moving to the centre-stage of Indian politics. The caste question has been foregrounded in public consciousness in and through a series of meaningful political interventions. Widely respected Dalit intellectuals and activists aggressively fight out the caste issue in political and intellectual circles[7] and bring offenders to heel. Prominent Indian writers in English invariably place a Dalit protagonist in mid-flow of the narrative pace Rohinton Mistry and Arundhati Roy.[8] In regional literature, upper-caste writers have, for some time now, poignantly narrated the sufferings of Dalits.[9]

Today, Dalits write their own histories and biographies. A vibrant literary movement denounces the ostracism of an entire community from mainstream society, and chronicles the nerve-wracking

---

[6] Khandekar (2013).

[7] Kancha Ilaiah (1996). This text is a sharp, emotional, and often bitter polemic against everything that symbolizes upper castes: from their Gods, to cuisine, to the position of women, to marriage rituals.

[8] The kind of visibility that has attached itself to contemporary Indian writing in English makes engagement with the caste question both perceptible as well as public.

[9] For example, see Premchand on Dukhi (Chattopadhyay 2017), Mulk Raj Anand ([1935] 2014) on Bakha, and Mahasweta Devi (2017) on Doulati.

experience of being treated as an 'outcaste'. Challenging prevailing literary conventions, rewriting the script of literary and poetic production, inserting the community into critical narratives of the Indian nation, and intent on representing their own community, writers have profoundly dented the way we think of others and of ourselves. This genre of literature has gained considerable acclaim, and English translations of Dalit literary works, for example Narendra Jadhav's *Untouchables* (2005), Omprakash Valmiki's *Jhoothan* (2003), and Baby Kamble's *The Prisons We Broke* (2009), have expanded the canon of postcolonial literature and aesthetics in Indian and Western universities. Above all, electoral politics, affirmative action, and the space afforded by civil society for mobilization have enabled a suppressed community to recover agency and speak back to codified power.

In many ways, caste-based practices have changed for the better at least in in urban India. Yet the practice of untouchability, often palpable, sometimes masked, persists in significant areas of social interaction. Studies have shown that the community continues to be underrepresented in industry, and Dalits confront formidable obstacles in the field of entrepreneurship.[10] In the geographical and political heart of the country (central India), in 'tribal India', members of the Adivasi community suffer from a triple disadvantage.[11] In some parts of the country, attempts by Dalits to assert their constitutional right to equality have fetched terrible backlashes and caste riots.

In short, the one vital good that redistributive justice tries to secure, recognition, continues to elude attempts at repair. Empirical work on the practice of untouchability bears this out. In 1969, the sociologist I.P. Desai, presenting the findings of his research project in rural Gujarat, told us that in public arenas governed by law, untouchability was least practiced. When it came to the private sphere of personal transactions, matters were different.[12] In 90 per cent of the villages he surveyed, Desai found that Dalits were not allowed to enter houses of caste Hindus, and were kept away from service providers such as barbers and shopkeepers. They were not allowed access to village wells and prevented from entering

---

[10] Iyer, Khanna, and Varshney (2013).
[11] Chandhoke (2015).
[12] Desai (1976).

temples. In the public sphere, Dalits had come into their own as citizens of Independent India. The private sphere, the domain where social transactions not only foster friendship, companionship, and intimacy but also govern life chances, Dalits are still discriminated against.

In 1999, Shankar Gaikwad, after interviewing 200 employed and college-going Dalits, reported that the attitude of caste Hindus had not changed.[13] Dalit students and colleagues were not invited into homes of caste Hindus and were barred from worlds of friendship and familiarity. In 2006, a research project conducted by scholars and social activists in 565 villages in 11 states of India revealed systematic evidence of untouchability and infliction of atrocities on the lower castes, despite a powerful Dalit movement, and in defiance of laws that render untouchability an offence.[14] Matters are not much better nine years on. On 12 May 2015, a Dalit bridegroom was forced to wear a helmet over his traditional bridal headgear, as he was pelted with stones by upper-caste Hindus because he had dared to mount a horse and lead his marriage procession; the determined bridegroom reached the venue of the wedding under police protection.[15]

The Disjunctions of Redistributive Justice

The disjunction between the right to basic goods and the right to recognition, despite the fact that Dalits have secured the right to voice, complicates the project of redistributive justice a great deal. The impact of the denial of recognition cannot be underestimated. For one, lack of recognition reinforces other injustices confronted by the community in everyday life from the politics of the workplace, to the politics of the neighbourhood. Two, denial of recognition disrupts social relationships based on the reciprocal obligation to see each other as equal and as worthy of dignity. Three, disrespect and humiliation demoralize and diminishe human beings and erode their confidence to participate in the multiple transactions of society with a degree of assurance. Honneth tells us that since the self-image of individuals is based upon experiences of recognition,

[13] Gaikwad (1999).
[14] Shah et al. (2006: 165–6).
[15] *The Hindu* (2015: 7).

disrespect carries its own form of injury. That is why individuals describe experiences of non-recognition as insult or humiliation. The consequences are serious, 'psychological death' of those whose bodily integrity has been violated, 'social death' for victims of slavery, and 'scars' for those whose cultures have been denigrated.[16]

Apart from the reproduction of harm caused by discrimination, the disjunction in the outcome of redistributive justice highlights the complex nature of historical injustice, the semi-autonomy one form of injustice acquires from other forms, and resistance to repair. Jeff Spinner-Halev, who has argued that 'enduring injustice' rooted in the past persists over time and over space as well, ruefully accepts that 'what makes an enduring injustice particularly perplexing is how difficult it is to repair'.[17]

We have to accept, equally ruefully, that the Indian experience bears out this conclusion. Despite struggles against rank discrimination in words, verse, and collective action since the sixth century, despite acceptance of historical wrong by the leaders of the freedom struggle, despite the mobilization of the Dalit community, and despite affirmative action, caste-based discrimination continues to relentlessly stalk the political biography of Independent India. Sixty-five years after the Constitution and a series of laws criminalized the practice of untouchability and prescribed affirmative action policies, matters remain grim. Till today, what caste we belong to continues to profile social relations, codify inequalities, and govern access to opportunities and privileges. 'Caste as a specter', writes the anthropologist Nicholas Dirks, 'continues to haunt the body politic of postcolonial India'.[18]

It is time to ask what we expect of redistributive justice. The agenda of 'redistributive justice as repair' is fairly clear. One, we accept that society has wreaked harm on a section of people for morally arbitrary reasons. The acknowledgement simply holds up a mirror to the ugliness that societies are capable of. Two, the text of history is read as a narrative of collective guilt and complicity on the one hand, and collective harm on the other. There are no individual exceptions to this story. Injustice is an integral part of the way society is reproduced over time, and those who benefit from

---

[16] Honneth (1995: 131).
[17] Spinner-Halev (2012: 56).
[18] Dirks (2001: 17).

history participate in this injustice. Three, if injustice continues to track the lives of members of the community, society is obliged to support policies intended to repair harm. In a democracy, this is the least we owe to fellow citizens who continue to labour under inherited injustice. Four, affirmative action, which is a group right not an individual one, does not only atone for past wrongs by providing preferential access to certain basic goods. The objectives of the project are much wider. The short-term objective of redistributive justice is to ensure that the triply disadvantaged secure access to goods through affirmative action and through the politics of presence. The long-term objective is to create a level playing field that enables people to participate in the multiple transactions of society as equals.

The generic goal of redistributive justice, in sum, is the realization of equality by taking note of, and by repairing background inequalities. Marc Galanter, author of an acclaimed work on 'compensatory discrimination' in India, argues that the objective of the Constitution was to establish a regime of formal equality and mitigate prevailing inequalities in wealth, education, and power. The government was forbidden to employ ascriptive categories of caste, race, and religion to realize this goal. 'This ban on "communal" measures was subject to a massive and singular exception: the state was employed to utilize these forbidden categories to remedy the accumulated disabilities suffered by those at the bottom of the caste hierarchy (the Scheduled Castes).'[19]

For the makers of the Constitution, the least that Indian society owed to people who had been unjustly wronged is to see that they are given what is due to them. If the norm of equality (in its fundamental avatar of one-person-one-vote) is pivotal to democracy, each person is owed equality of status. This is borne out by the concept of justice, according to which no one will receive more than his/her fair share of benefits and no one will be made to shoulder more than his/her fair share of burdens. That is, every person should be given his/her due: equality of status and equal rights to basic material needs, voice, and recognition.

It follows that the concept of equality, as a companion concept of justice, is not primarily about the right to X, Y, and Z, that is, the norm of equality cannot be reduced to redistributive justice.

---

[19] Galantar (2002: 306).

Whereas redistributive justice ensures that the burdens and the benefits of society are fairly distributed, its companion concept, equality, assures something more than the right to 'this' or the right to 'that'. It assures equality of status. Certainly the right to 'this' good or 'that' is an essential precondition of equality. However, equality is not fundamentally about the distribution of goods, but about the status people occupy relative to each other. A person may be skilled and competent, but if he/she is discriminated against on the basis of caste, religion, gender, or race, he/she is certainly not equal to his/her colleagues in the workplace. It seems to me that among the ideals of democratic life, priority should be given to equality of status because it is status that enables people to realize personhood and take part in social, political, economic, and cultural dealings with confidence that his/her voice counts and counts equally. It is counterproductive to reduce equality to redistributive justice.

Jonathan Wolff, intervening in the debate on what came to be known as 'luck egalitarianism', emphasizes precisely this point. He suggests that egalitarians should not only be motivated by a concern for fairness but also by the idea of respect. There is more to a society of equals, argues Wolff, 'than a just scheme of distribution of material goods. There may also be goods that depend on the attitude people have towards each other.'[20] In cases of conflict between these two values, respect should take priority over equality. Without going into the precise merits or demerits of Wolff's intervention, I think he has managed to pinpoint the insurmountable obstacles faced by the project of redistributive justice. Let us phrase the core issue as thus: Is there any relationship between redistribution of resources/wealth and recognition?

It is admittedly difficult to establish a relationship between the right to tangible things such as education, income, and representation, and the extension of respect to others or recognition. Presumably, however, the deeper logic that informs egalitarian philosophies and policies is targeted towards the inculcation of precisely these sentiments. For liberal theorists, the provision of basic needs is a necessary precondition for expanding the realm of choices and enabling agency. Marxists argue that redistribution of resources is an essential prerequisite for equality.

[20] Wolff (1998: 104).

This is the *maximal* take on redistribution. *Minimally*, if I do not have to beg for my daily food or clothing, if I am not dependent on the charity of others for the satisfaction of my daily wants, and if I can provide for my own social reproduction as well as that of my family, I acquire a sense of self-respect, which is arguably integral to recognition.

The link between redistribution and recognition has, however, proved rather tenuous in India, as well as elsewhere. Think of racism in USA despite affirmative action. This, perhaps, is not surprising, for not only is recognition an intangible concept inasmuch as it is shaped by human prejudice, attitude, and group identities, it is a matter that is not so easily commanded by politics. Politics can negotiate the distribution of resources. The matter requires vision, courage, and commitment, but as history has shown, it can be done. How does politics negotiate recognition? How does it lay down parameters of what human beings owe each other simply because each of us is human? For, too many troubling factors cast their dark shadow on this precise issue, factors that relate to the stereotyping of others as the polluting, the untouchable, the inferior, or indeed the 'enemy at the gates'. These stereotypes are not easily amenable to political negotiation or intervention. And for precisely this reason, recognition manages to dodge the project of redistributive justice, leaving the main value of equality unfulfilled.

Equality and Redistributive Justice

The task at hand is to whether it is possible to design a principle of redistributive justice that validates the precept of equality. Redistributive justice must not slide into the conviction that people should be given enough to eat and offered a subsistence wage, and that their status simply does not matter. In the section that follows, I offer six suggestions on how possibly this link might be forged.

1. Perhaps we can begin our task by taking a look at the vocabularies we employ to capture the intent of affirmative action. I am not for a moment suggesting that a shift in our conceptual languages, and, therefore, a change in our linguistic approach to redistributive justice, will solve all

dilemmas, but it might be a beginning. Even if the debate on the implications of the linguistic shift from the victim to the agent and the survivor is inconclusive, we can learn a great deal from the preoccupations of the feminist movement. Will casting victims as agents, asks Dunn, minimize the effects of the forces arrayed against them? 'Calling battered women "survivors", while granting them agency, may only shift responsibility and attention back to them as individuals and away from the social structures and forces that they must overcome.' But she continues, 'there is the possibility that the social construction of victims as survivors ... will ultimately result in what social movement activists and victim advocates in everyday life increasingly refer to as empowerment.'[21] The emphasis on the way we frame the issue might just transform the terms of engagement.

What are these terms of engagement? In popular perceptions, affirmative action policies are understood as compensation for past wrongs, hence the terminology of compensatory discrimination. The terminology is unfortunate. The very idea that 'we' who have benefited from history owe 'those' who have lost out raises a host of doubts about the project. The idea that 'we' owe something to 'them' divides society along the axis of 'we-ism' and 'they-ism'. These attitudes not only polarize society but also diminish the status of beneficiaries of affirmative action to either victims, a term that breeds nothing but condescension, or as recipients of unjustified rewards.

Since affirmative action has not folded up after ten years as hoped by the makers of the Constitution, younger generations have begun to ask the question, how long? Why should our generation be made responsible for the sins of our forebears? And why should someone whose family has benefited from these policies continue to enjoy advantages? Why, they ask, is intra-caste inequality not worthy of comment the way inter-caste inequality is? They are not completely wrong, not if we frame the issue in terms of formal equality or that each gets one. How we should go about framing the problem is dealt with in point three; here I just want to emphasize

[21] Dunn (2005: 21).

that affirmative action has to be conceived as part of a larger project—redistributive justice, at the heart of which lies the concept of equality. There is nothing quite as demeaning as the term 'compensation': it might belong to the school of legality not to that of ethics. People cannot be compensated for past wrongs; these wrongs will remain as blots on the face of history howsoever we may read it. All that we can do is to see that they get what is due to them as citizens in a democracy, the right to material goods, voice, and recognition. All that we can do is to ensure that structural injustice is destroyed through intentional political action.

And it is precisely this dimension of social change that is missing in notions of compensation. In a hard-hitting critique of the 'choice and circumstance school' or that of 'luck egalitarianism', Elisabeth Anderson suggest that 'recent egalitarian writing has come to be dominated by the view that the fundamental aim of equality is to compensate people for undeserved bad luck'.[22] But the proper aim of egalitarian justice, Anderson reminds us, is 'not to eliminate the impact of brute luck from human affairs but to end oppression'.[23] The proper aim of egalitarianism is to allow people to live in a democratic community instead of a hierarchical one. Similarly, the objective of redistributive justice that seeks to equalize unequal constituencies is not to pay off people for historical wrongs, but to ensure that they can participate in the various transactions of society as equals. Even as we understand the significance of history, we have to begin from the here and the now, from democratic contexts, from the promises of the Constitution, and from the vocabularies of social movements.

2. When we begin our reflections on what is to be done by recalling our political context, democracy, and perhaps a compelling case for redistributive justice, can be articulated as an integral part of the generic right to substantive equality, which of course is the linchpin of democracy. The notion of one-person-one-vote is not only an electoral ploy, it is shorthand for the status individuals secure for themselves

---

[22] Anderson (1999: 288).
[23] Anderson (1999: 288–9).

in highly unequal societies. Persons are equal because each human being has the capacity to make his/her own history in concert with other similarly endowed human beings. Of course, the histories that persons make will not be the histories they chose to make, but this is not the issue at hand. What is important is that each person possesses this ability. Two implications follow the presumption of equality. One, equality is a default principle. Two, background inequalities or accumulated historical injustices *have* to be tackled in order to realize equality. It is, accordingly, incumbent upon the State, as the codified power of society, to take on the responsibility of neutralizing background inequalities. It is only then that the precepts of equality and the mandates of redistributive justice can be realized.

3. Howsoever powerfully political theorists articulate the significance of equality and redistributive justice, howsoever elegantly they make their case, these norms can hardly be left to do their own work of garnering a degree of social and political acceptance and legitimacy. Political theory is important, constitutional and legislative provisions are important, Supreme Court judgments are important, but they are simply not enough. If the right to equality is violated, citizens should be exercised and agitated about this violation. For this to occur, for the society to feel deeply about the right on offer and even more deeply about violations of the right, the incorporation of a right into political thinking, into our values, and into vocabularies that are ritually employed in and through politics, requires a great deal of hard work. Redistributive justice and the companion concept of equality have to be underpinned by a political consensus on the significance of the norm.

The construction and the consolidation of this political consensus is, of course, a project that requires the harnessing of creative imaginations and courage on the one hand, and careful reasoning, persuasion, and dialogue on the other. The task also demands the investment of rather high degrees of energy and time. But this is essential because a political consensus on what constitutes or should constitute the basic rules of society is central to our collective lives. The political is not a given; it has to be constructed, as Marx had told us long ago, through determined and sustained political intervention.

This makes sense because reasoning, persuasion, and dialogue constitute far more effective ways of making equality a predominant value and redistributive justice as its companion concept politically acceptable than mere enactment of laws. Support for the project can only be fashioned through political mobilization in civil society. Lea Ypi's suggestion that 'once an attempt to develop a fundamentally appropriative normative interpretation of the function and purpose of political institutions has been made, avant-garde agents join the theorists' activist effort to render normative views politically effective and motivationally sustainable' is well taken.[24] Whether political theorists think that activists should join in at the phase of formulating principles or at the stage of implementing them is a significant debate, but this is not the issue I wish to take on at this moment.[25]

All I wish to suggest is that it is only a wide-ranging network of social movements that can remind people that denial of recognition is a problem of and for the society and not only for the class that is discriminated against. In pre-Independence India, such movements had been inaugurated and gained considerable steam. In post-Independence India, the onus of battling discrimination has fallen onto the shoulders of Dalits, and the rest of society wends its way through the world without regard for the infirmities it has subjected its own people to. Redistributive justice and the significance of equal status for people who have suffered historical injustice has to be legitimized by every generation for each generation simply because public memory is short. Of course we find a plurality of social movements, each of which struggles to realize equality for its constituency. The same value can be expressed in different terms and different ways. It is time

[24] Ypi (2012: 5).
[25] Rahul Rao, in his otherwise sympathetic review of Ypi's book, suggests that in her theory, the avant-garde seems less relevant to conceptualizing principles of egalitarian justice and more relevant to the construction of forms of political agency that could help give effect to those principles (Rao 2013: 105).

that these issues, these terminologies, and these struggles link with each other in overlapping networks that ensure a regime of equality and of redistributive justice. More significantly, the conceptualization of redistributive justice has to validate the precept of equality of status as the main objective of political theory and political struggles.
4. The link between equality and distributive justice can perchance be realized when we shift the terminology of affirmative action from compensation for past wrongs and conceive of human beings as bearers of rights, including the right to a fair share in the collective resources of society. If, in history, these resources have been disproportionately monopolized by upper-caste and upper-class groups, and if others have been historically subjected to triple injustice, disadvantaged persons have the right to demand that they be granted their rightful share by virtue of a right. A fair share in the resources of a society can be conceptualized as ownership of enough resources that allow human beings to have a reasonable chance of making their histories, irrespective of the kinds of histories they make. The objective of redistributive justice is to ensure that persons should participate in social, political, and cultural transactions as equals. This is the *first* stage of realizing equal status.
5. Once each citizen has secure rights to goods, the special circumstances of groups whose life chances have been impaired by complex forms of historical injustice have to be addressed. To embrace affirmative action, policies in the abstract or in isolation from a political consensus on equality provoke nothing but acrimony. Arguably, affirmative action policies in India have been embroiled in controversy, and the beneficiaries of these policies subjected to humiliation and disrespect, because policies have been instituted in a political space that is not informed by this consensus. Affirmative action should, perhaps, occupy the second stage in the project of redistributive justice.
6. If we bring about these two linguistic turns, dropping the vocabulary of victim and compensation, and adopt the concept that each human being is by right a co-sharer in the collective resources of society, we might accomplish a third linguistic turn. The historically disadvantaged stake a claim to goods, not as 'victims' but as bearers of rights that have

been unjustly denied to them, not as people whom fate has consigned to a lowly and inferior place in the caste and class hierarchy, but by virtue of their right to equal status.

The former compromises the tenets of egalitarianism because it reinforces patronizing and humiliating attitudes that reinforce denial of recognition. There is, arguably, a considerable difference between collectively participating in the reconstruction of a society that has been unequally and unfairly organized, and demanding compensation for victimhood. The first road to egalitarian democracy may reinforce equality of status and the second serve up sympathy, not solidarity.

In sum, affirmative action forms the central plan of redistributive justice. We recognize that some of our fellow citizens have been subjected to historical injustice; the recognition places an obligation on us to rectify a wrong. Recognition of an obligation is important but not enough. We have to work towards the creation of a political consensus in society that historical injustice violates the basic principle of constitutional equality. If historical injustice that results in background inequalities compels people to live lives that are below our considered convictions of what it means to be human, this should be seen as constituting a serious violation of basic entitlements.

One last word to end the argument: At some point we have to ask whether our task as egalitarians end with the proposition that people have the right to redistributive justice as a remedy for persistent historical wrongs. Should we disclaim any further responsibility for the historically disadvantaged after providing them with the minimum of material needs? Should all of us not be moving constantly towards a shared vision of egalitarian democracy where people can live fulfilling lives instead of remaining mired in notions of minimal reparation or remedies? Should we not strive to strengthen a political consensus on the desirability of foregrounding the value of equality, of essaying obligations to people whose rights have been seriously hampered and persuading other citizens to participate in debates on what constitutes a just society? It is only when we concentrate on the construction of a political consensus in society that the uncomfortable distinction between 'us' and 'them' that bedevils much of the case for redistributive justice can be dissolved.

It might be far better for our task, let me suggest, to situate and to ground the right to remedial justice in a political consensus that in an egalitarian democracy persons *have* to be treated in 'this' way not 'that'. This is the least we owe to people who have been historically disadvantaged.

★ ★ ★

Communities that have suffered from multiple historical injustices are not only likely to be economically deprived but also socially marginalized, made politically insignificant in terms of the politics of 'voice' as distinct from the 'vote', humiliated, dismissed, and subjected to intense disrespect in and through the practices of everyday life. Anyone who suffers from these multiple disadvantages will find it impossible to participate in social, economic, and cultural transactions as equals. Efforts have been made to repair historical injustice. But the ideology of discrimination continues to dominate Independent India despite a multitude of constitutional provisions, laws, affirmative action policies, and political mobilization.

Ideologies, or so it appears, are just not reducible to the domain of the economy. We cannot assume that redistribution of resources and wealth to benefit people who have been deprived in the past will lead to respect or recognition. The politics of voice can achieve a great deal in the public sphere, but if the ideology of discrimination continues to shape social relations in the private domain, much of the gains are lost. Studies tell us that whereas a Dalit may be able to access the worlds of education and employment through reservations, he/she may not be able to access the domain of private transactions, that is, friendships, associational life, dining with others, inter-marrying, or indeed membership of exclusive clubs. Does the world of the private matter? It matters for two reasons. One, it is essential that no one should be barred from worlds of friendship and intimacy that make for emotional support systems. Two, market exchanges do not always fall entirely in the public domain. Who our friends and acquaintances are, which school and universities we have attended, and which social network we are located in have a major effect on opportunities or lack of opportunities in the marketplace. Old school ties still count, even in worlds of democracy.

To put the issue starkly, if equality is compromised, the project of redistributive justice will bear inadequate results. One of the most essential goods human beings are entitled to, the right to recognition, has not been realized. For this right to be recognized, social movements that speak the language of equality for their own particular constituencies have to come together and support the idea of building a political consensus on what is due to all human beings, what should be done for them, and what should not be done to them.

A word on historical injustice: Undoubtedly, political theorists have to take history seriously. But the focus of concern is the here and now—the democratic context that shapes collective lives and aspirations. Comprehension of how deep the roots of injustice are is important. But it is also important not to get trapped too much in the past and in the politics of recrimination and resentment that divides society irremediably and prevents the consolidation of a consensus on the need to battle discrimination. As Iris Marion Young suggests, history matters, 'but not in order to reproach, punish, or demand compensating damages'.[26] After acknowledging the enormity of harm complex historical injustice heaped on the backs of groups, we have to move forwards to alter what appears to be unalterable, taking as our reference point the main precepts of democratic life.

Finally, Dr Ambedkar had insightfully remarked in 1946 that the problem of the Dalits is not social in nature; it is completely unlike the problem of dowry, widow remarriage, and age of consent. The problem is different from that of securing to the community liberty and equality of opportunity at the 'hands of a hostile majority which believes in the denial of liberty and equal opportunity to the minority and conspires to enforce its policy on the minority. Viewed in this way the problem of the Untouchables is fundamentally a political problem.'[27] The political problem has been negotiated by constitutional precepts and practices in different ways. Yet a major problem tracks affirmative action policies, the disjuncture between access to material redistribution, and the right to voice and the right to respect.

---

[26] Young (2012: 172).
[27] Ambedkar ([1946] 1991: 190).

References

Ambedkar, B.R. [1946] 1991. *What Congress and Gandhi Have Done to the Untouchables.* Bombay: Thacker.

Anand, Mulk Raj. [1935] 2014. *Untouchable.* New Delhi: Penguin Random House.

Anderson, Elizabeth S. 1999. 'What Is the Point of Equality?' *Ethics* 109 (2): 287–337.

Chandhoke, Neera. 2015. *Democracy and Revolutionary Politics.* London: Bloomsbury.

Chattopadhyay, Bhaskar. 2017. 'Sadgati: Based on Premchand's Story Satyajit Ray Took a Scathing Look at the Tragic Lives of Untouchables'. *Firstpost.* Available at https://www.firstpost.com/entertainment/sadgati-based-on-premchands-story-satyajit-ray-took-a-scathing-look-at-the-tragic-lives-of-untouchables-4115527.html#:~:text=While%20Premchand's%20story%20is%20a,Dukhi%20is%20alive%20%E2%80%94%20as%20if; last accessed 1 July 2020.

Desai, I.P. 1976. *Untouchability in Rural Gujarat.* Bombay: Popular Prakashan.

Devi, Mahashweta. 2017. 'Douloti the Bountiful'. In *Imaginary Maps,* translated by Gayatri Chakravarti Spivak, pp. 19–94. Kolkata: Theme.

Dirks, Nicholas. 2001. *Castes of Mind, Colonialism and the Making of Modern India.* Princeton: Princeton University Press.

Dunn, Jennifer L. 2005. '"Victims" and "Survivors": Emerging Vocabularies of Motive for "Battered Women Who Stay"'. *Sociological Inquiry* 75 (1): 1–30.

Gaikwad, Shankar L. 1999. *Protective Discrimination Policy and Social Change. An Analytical Study of State Action on Scheduled Castes in Aurangabad City.* Jaipur: Rawat.

Galantar, Marc. 2002. 'The Long Half-Life of Reservations'. In *India's Living Constitution: Ideas, Practices, Controversies,* edited by Zoya Hasan, E. Sridharan, and R. Sudarshan, pp. 306–18. London: Anthem.

Hindu, The. 2015. 'Dalit Groom Attacked for Riding a Horse'. 13 May, p. 7.

Honneth, Axel. 1995. *The Struggle for Recognition: The Moral Grammar of Social Conflicts,* translated by Joel Anderson. Cambridge: Polity.

Ilaiah, Kancha. 1996. *Why I Am Not a Hindu: A Sudra Critique of Hindutva Philosophy, Culture, and Political Economy.* Calcutta: Samya.

Iyer, Lakshmi, Tarun Khanna, and Ashutosh Varshney. 2013. 'Caste and Entrepreneurship in India'. *Economic and Political Weekly* XLVIII (3): 52–60.

Jodhka, Surinder S. 2012. *Caste.* Oxford India Short Introductions. New Delhi: Oxford University Press.

Khandekar, Milind. 2013. *Dalit Millionaires.* New Delhi: Penguin.

Omvedt, Gail 2008. *Seeking Begum Pura: The Social Vision of Anti-Caste Intellectuals*. Hyderabad: Navayana.

Rao, Rahul. 2013. 'Listening to the Avant-Garde'. *Ethics and Global Politics* 6 (2): 101–7.

Shah, Ghanshyam, Harsh Mander, Sukhdeo Thorat, Satish Deshpande, and Amita Baviskar. 2006. *Untouchability in Rural India*. New Delhi: Sage.

Spinner-Halev, Jeff. 2012. *Enduring Injustice*. Cambridge, UK: Cambridge University Press.

Wolff, Jonathan. 1998. 'Fairness, Respect, and the Egalitarian Ethos'. *Philosophy and Public Affairs* 22 (2): 97–122.

Young, Iris Marion. 2012. *Responsibility for Injustice*. Oxford: Oxford University Press.

Ypi, Lea. 2012. *Global Justice and Avant-Garde Political Agency*. Oxford: Oxford University Press.

5

Dr Ambedkar and the Trio of Principles

*Liberty, Equality, and Fraternity**

PRADEEP GOKHALE

A Methodological Issue

While studying Ambedkar's thought, we have to face two types of questions.

1. One question is that of giving an internally consistent and coherent picture of Ambedkar's thought. Ambedkar's intellectual career was multidimensional. He was an economist, a religious thinker, a lawyer, a constitutionalist, and a dynamic sociopolitical thinker. He was vibrantly and militantly responding to the complex and turbulent sociopolitical situation, often with equanimity. Therefore, his thought reveals apparent tensions and a multipolar effort to balance individual, group, and national interests, as well as interests of the humankind as a whole. In doing so, he was trying to maintain a balance among contradictory interests with a

---

* A slightly revised version of the chapter was published in 2016 in *Dialogue Quarterly, A Journal of Astha Bharati* 17 (3): 66–80. An earlier version of the chapter was presented in Acharya Nagarjuna University, Guntur on 8 October 2014.

focus on the interests of the downtrodden. We also find that his thought was firmly grounded in materialism but it was not anti-religious. In spite of accepting a materialist explanation of consciousness, he emphasized the importance of mind in bringing about social transformation. Hence, it is a challenging task to give a consistent and coherent picture of the diverse thought of Dr Ambedkar. One has to see whether and how 'the thought' of Dr Ambedkar can be reconstructed from his 'thoughts'. Giving a consistent and coherent picture of Ambedkar's thought is particularly important in the present context because one of the common threads running though his diverse thoughts has been the trio of liberty, equality, and fraternity. It is common to Ambedkar's sociopolitical, religious, and constitutional thought. But in giving a consistent and coherent picture there is a risk (which is explained later) and this poses the second challenge before an Ambedkar theorist.

2. Bringing out consistency in what is dynamic and even dialectical may amount to treating dynamic as static, what is changing as constant. While theorizing Ambedkar's thought, one has to keep track of its dynamism and dialectical development. I suggest that we can identify three major phases in Ambedkar's intellectual development. The first phase could be called the Hindu Reformist phase, which continued up to 13 October 1935, when in a conference at Yeola he declared that though he was born as Hindu, he would not die a Hindu. The second phase marks Ambedkar standing at the threshold of Hinduism with one foot outside Hinduism, but without a firm decision as to which religion is to be embraced. It can be called the phase of transition during which Ambedkar's inclination towards Buddhism steadily increased. This phase continues up to 1948[1] or 1950,[2] by which time he made up his mind about joining Buddhism. The last phase can be called the Buddhist phase,

---

[1] This was the year when he wrote an introduction to Laxmi Narsu's book, *The Essence of Buddhism*, where he declared that he was working on Buddhism independently.

[2] This was the year in which his article 'Buddha and the Future of His Religion' was published in *Mahabodhi Society Journal*, where he argued that Buddhism is the ideal religion.

though technically it consists of two sub-phases—would-be Buddhist and Buddhist. For the sake of brevity, we call the three phases the Reformist phase, the Threshold phase, and the Buddhist phase. Though Ambedkar's thought consistently revealed some core elements during these phases and sub-phases, it was also discontinuous in some important ways. The point is that Ambedkar's thought should be studied not as a crystallized or fossilized body of ideas but as a dynamic, flawed, and developing intellectual process. It is against this general background that I want to study Ambedkar's theorization of the trio of principles. What was Ambedkar's approach to the three principles? In this context, scholars often quote the statement in which he correlates his social philosophy and the three principles with Buddhism. He says,

> Positively my social philosophy may be said to be enshrined in three words—liberty, equality and fraternity. Let no one, however say that I have borrowed my philosophy from the French Revolution. I have not. My philosophy has roots in religion and not in political science. I have derived them from the teachings of my master, the Buddha.[3]

How we should interpret this statement is a crucial problem. Dr Ambedkar has referred to these principles at different stages of his life. I am suggesting that Ambedkar's aforementioned statement may not be taken as applicable to all the phases of the development of his thought. Ambedkar makes this statement in a talk which he gave in 1954 on All India Radio. At this stage, he had made up his mind that he was going to adopt Buddhism. Before that, in his article 'Buddha and the Future of His Religion', he refers to these principles, but there he regarded adherence to these principles as a criterion of ideal religion. He also claims that Buddhism fulfils this criterion. But he does not say that he has derived these principles from Buddhism.

Ambedkar's earliest reference to the three principles can be found in his masterpiece 'Annihilation of Caste', which he wrote in 1936.[4] In this speech, he refers to the three principles as foundations of an

---

[3] Ambedkar's address on All India Radio, 3 October 1954, quoted in Ambedkar (2003: 503).

[4] 'Annihilation of Caste' is originally an undelivered speech.

ideal society. But he does not refer to Buddhism in this context. However, he does refer to the French Revolution. While discussing equality as one of the principles of an ideal society, he admits that it had been the most contentious part of the slogan of the French Revolution.[5] Therefore, at this stage, he was treating these principles as occasioned by the French Revolution. Even at a later stage, when he wrote 'The Hindu Social Order: Its Essential Principles', originally an unpublished essay, he discusses the three principles in the context of the French Revolution.[6] Even here he does not refer to Buddhism as the source of these principles. Though the date of this work is not known to us, it is much later than 'Annihilation of Caste'. Hence, when Dr Ambedkar says that he has derived his social philosophy, which was enshrined in the three principles of liberty, equality, and fraternity, from the teachings of the Buddha, his statement is not to be taken literally; it should be interpreted in the context of the would-be Buddhist phase in which he was making this statement.

I want to suggest that though primarily Ambedkar accepted these sociopolitical principles from the context of the French Revolution, gradually he reinterpreted them as religious principles, and when he came to the conclusion that Buddhism is the ideal religion, he reappropriated them as principles rooted in the Buddha's message. I would say that in the post-1950 phase, he rediscovered these principles as those rooted in the Buddha's message. This once again underlines the need to understand Dr Ambedkar's thought, not as a static or constant viewpoint, but as a dynamic flow of thought. Hence, in the present context we need to do two things:

1. We need to see how Ambedkar's thinking about the three principles developed and matured over a period of time. Here, we will be dealing with Ambedkar's texts belonging to the Threshold phase.
2. Given that Ambedkar finally said that the principles are rooted in the Buddha's teachings, we need to see in what form they can really be found in the Buddha's teachings. Here, we will have to deal with the texts belonging to Ambedkar's Buddhist phase.

[5] Ambedkar (2011: 49).
[6] Ambedkar (1987, Volume 3: 95–115).

This chapter will be an attempt to accomplish the aforementioned tasks.

Development of Ambedkar's Thinking

The development of Ambedkar's analysis of the three principles can be sketched on the basis of his relevant writings. When he presented them first in 'Annihilation of Caste', he may not have been fully clear about all aspects of these principles. He was convinced that they were centrally important as the basic principles of an ideal society, an ideal democracy, and an ideal religion. But he was also facing some issues concerning them. In later formulations, he seems to have found an answer to some of the issues. So we can at least say that though his understanding of the principles did not undergo a radical change, it at least got matured and enriched in later formulations. Broadly speaking, Ambedkar addressed three theoretical issues concerning the three principles:

1. What is the exact nature of the three principles?
2. Are these principle justified? If they are, on what grounds?
    The question of the nature of the principles and the question of their justification are interrelated because a principle may be justified if its nature is understood is one way, but may not be justified as having some other nature.
3. The third issue pertains to the interrelation among the three principles. This issue is theoretical as well as practical. Theoretically, the question is whether the three principles are independent of each other or one of them is basic and others can be derived from it. Practically the question is whether these principles, when brought into practice, are necessarily in harmony with each other or in conflict. Which principle should have an upper hand in order to resolve the conflict is also an important practical issue.

All these are complex issues. The issues occur in Ambedkar's writings in various places and they were handled by him in various ways. His various formulations of the issues, at least prima facie, are not fully consistent. However, enquiring into these formulations, the consistency and inconsistency among them and their developmental order is important for having a realistic picture of Ambedkar's thought.

Though Ambedkar has referred to the three principles in numerous places, he has discussed them together in three works. It is important to consider the three discussions together because the three works have a common pattern.

1. 'Annihilation of Caste': In 'Annihilation of Caste', Ambedkar raises a question regarding the principles foundational to an ideal society and answers it in terms of the three principles. He argues how Hindu scriptures, such as the Manusmriti, violate all the three principles.
2. 'Philosophy of Hinduism': This book, originally an unpublished manuscript, is included in *Dr. Babasaheb Ambedkar: Writings and Speeches*, Volume 3 as Chapter I.[7] The aim of this work is to critically examine the philosophical position of Hinduism. The central argument of this book is as follows. Any religion can be critiqued in terms of two criteria: utility and justice. Which criterion is to be applied is determined by the question as to what is central to the religion—society or the individual. In ancient religions, society was at the centre. Hence, while critiquing such religions, utility would be the main criterion. In contrast, modern religions are individual centric. Hence, modern religions can be critiqued by using justice as the criterion. Against this background, Ambedkar critiques Hinduism first by applying justice as the criterion and then by applying the criterion of utility. Ambedkar shows that Hinduism does not measure up to either of the two criteria. This is because, according to him, Hinduism is neither individual centric nor society centric: It is class-centric. Here, by 'class', Ambedkar means 'caste'. The relevant question here is: What does Ambedkar mean by justice? In his works, he identified justice with three principles of liberty, equality, and fraternity. Like in 'Annihilation of Caste', Ambedkar explains in this book how the three principles are violated in Hinduism.
3. 'The Hindu Social Order—Its Unique Features': This essay is included in *Dr. Babasaheb Ambedkar: Writings and*

---

[7] Ambedkar (1987, Volume 3: 1–92).

Speeches, Volume 3 as Chapter II.[8] The central concern of this essay is whether Hindu social order can be called a free social order. Naturally, the question is: What are the essentials of a free social order? Here Ambedkar states two essentials: (*i*) an individual is an end in himself/herself and the development of the individual is the aim of society; (*ii*) the associated life of the members of a society should be based on liberty, equality, and fraternity. Having explained the essentials, Ambedkar examines Hinduism in their light and shows how these essentials are not found in Hinduism.

The feature shared by these three texts is that they are critical estimates of Hinduism. 'Annihilation of Caste' is the first of these texts. But the exact chronology of the later texts is not known. In the manuscript, since 'Philosophy of Hinduism' occurs before 'The Hindu Social Order' and have been published in that order, it is very likely that they were written in that order as well. If we read the three texts in this order, it appears clear that Ambedkar's thoughts on the three principles must have gradually developed through these three texts. So let us briefly see how the discussion of the three principles develops in the three texts.

1. Fraternity: In *Annihilation of Caste with a Reply to Mahatma Gandhi*, Ambedkar discusses fraternity first. He describes it as associated life, mobility, consciously communicated interests. He also describes it as an attitude of respect and reverence towards fellowmen.[9] In 'Philosophy of Hinduism', he identifies it with fellow feeling and also contrasts it with individualism. 'Individualism would produce anarchy. It is only fraternity which prevents it and helps to sustain the moral order among men.'[10] He also claims that fellow feeling is a natural sentiment.[11] In 'The Hindu Social Order', he brings out the religious element in fraternity.[12] Hence, we find a gradual development of the concept of fraternity from

[8] Ambedkar (1987, Volume 3: 95–115).
[9] Ambedkar (2011: 48).
[10] Ambedkar (1987, Volume 3: 44).
[11] Ambedkar (1987, Volume 3: 44).
[12] He explains fellow feeling in Christian religious terms in Ambedkar (1987: 97).

an emphasis on the social aspect to the moral aspect and then to the religious aspect.

2. Liberty: In *Annihilation of Caste with a Reply to Mahatma Gandhi*, Ambedkar introduces the concept of liberty as right to life and limb and also as the right to property and the right to choose one's profession.[13] In the later texts, he reflects on the concept by bringing out other aspects of it. In 'Philosophy of Hinduism', he discusses the conditions which make liberty possible. These conditions include social equality, economic security and knowledge.[14] In 'The Hindu Social Order', he classifies liberty into civil liberty and political liberty and elaborates on it. Civil liberty includes liberty of movement and liberty of speech. They imply freedom of action and freedom of opinion. Freedom of action, when fully realized, implies absence of exploitation, suppression, unemployment, and poverty. Political liberty consists in the right of the individual to share in the framing of laws and in the making and unmaking of governments.[15] Hence, we can say that the concept of liberty does not change substantially but only gets clarified and refined.

3. Equality: Ambedkar's discussion of equality is most complex and challenging. In *Annihilation of Caste with a Reply to Mahatma Gandhi*, Ambedkar admits the problematic character of the principle of equality and accepts equality not on factual grounds, but as a pragmatic necessity.[16] In later writings, we find that he was still struggling with the problematic character and trying to find a solution. In those writings, he was aware that we cannot talk of equality among human beings in the way we can talk about equality in physics or mathematics. But in 'Philosophy of Hinduism', he is more constructive and affirmative about the notion. He defines equality among human beings as their common

---

[13] Ambedkar (2011: 48).

[14] Ambedkar (1987, Volume 3: 38–9).

[15] Ambedkar (1987, Volume 3: 98–9).

[16] Ambedkar (2011: 49–50). His conclusion there is: 'The doctrine of equality is glaringly fallacious, but taking all in all it is the only way a statesman can proceed in politics, which is a severely practical affair and which demands a severely practical test.'

essence which entitles them to the same fundamental rights and equal liberty.[17] In 'The Hindu Social Order', he accepts Professor Beard's view[18] that the fundamental common characteristic among human beings is moral equality which has to be accepted against the inequalities in terms of physical strength, talents, industry and wealth. It is due to this moral equality that no one has a right to oppress others, however superior he may be in terms of physical strength, talents, industry, or wealth.[19] I suggest that this moral equality can be understood as equality of human beings qua human beings or equality of moral status or moral worth of human beings, which is rather abstract in nature. Hence, we can say that Ambedkar's approach to equality, which was initially negative and pragmatic, becomes constructive, moral, and abstract in the later period. He must have thought that it is only in this way that equality can be justified.

The Question of Justification of the Three Principles

As already noted, in 'Annihilation of Caste', Ambedkar expresses doubt about acceptability of equality as a principle. The question was, if equality is contrary to facts, how can it be a value? Ambedkar's answer in 'Annihilation of Caste' seems to be that sometimes a value can be accepted if it is beneficial to humanity, even if it is not supported by facts. In later writings, as we saw, he gives a more sophisticated justification by distinguishing what he calls moral equality from other kinds of equality such as physical, intellectual, and economic equality. It seems that at this stage, he equates moral equality with the essence of a human being. With regard to the justification of the other two principles, Ambedkar does not seem to have any serious problem. In *Annihilation of Caste with a Reply to Mahatma Gandhi*, he asserts that there need not be any question about their acceptability.[20] He raises the

---

[17] Ambedkar (1987, Volume 3: 25).
[18] See Beard ([1942] 2019).
[19] Ambedkar (1987, Volume 3: 96–7).
[20] 'What objection can there be to fraternity? I cannot imagine any.'; 'Any objection to Liberty? Few object to liberty in the sense of a right to free movement, in the sense of a right to life and limb…' (Ambedkar 2011: 48).

question of the essential character of these principles in 'The Hindu Social Order'. Here, his justification of the principles is moral and religious in nature. He does not just talk about each principle separately but all the principles together and claims that they follow from a more fundamental tenet, namely, that of the individual as an end in himself. He describes this tenet as the sacredness of human personality and in this way suggests a kind of religious justification of these principles.[21]

Here, the notion of religious justification needs clarification. Ambedkar's notion of religion in its ideal form does not imply a belief in transcendent metaphysical entities such as God, soul, or other worlds. Even his notion of the sacred does not imply them. Similarly, in the Buddhist phase, the distinction Ambedkar makes between religion and *dhamma* is meant to draw a line of demarcation between the popular concept of religion and Ambedkar's understanding of the ideal religion. At this stage, Ambedkar defines dhamma as morality which is universal and sacred. Dhamma as morality was sacred not because it implied God, an immortal soul, or any such transcendent element, but because it was inviolable and universal. Further, when Ambedkar says that the three principles can be derived from the sacredness of the human personality, his use of the term 'sacred' connotes nothing beyond the universal human essence. As a modernist thinker, Ambedkar believed in such an essence and tried to derive the three principles from it. For Ambedkar, religion in this sense was a secular or this-worldly force, leading to the progress and well-being of humankind. To him, religion in its ideal form was a progressive social force.

Interrelation among the Three Principles

We find that in his later writings Ambedkar was also concerned with the question of interrelation among the three principles. He approaches the issue in diverse ways and it is difficult to decide as to what was his exact answer. Sometimes he regards one of the principles as fundamental and derives other principles from it. Sometimes he asserts interconnectedness or interdependence instead of any kind of reductionism. In 'Philosophy of Hinduism',

---

[21] Ambedkar (1987, Volume 3: 99).

he asserts that fraternity and liberty are derivative notions; the basic and fundamental notions are equality and respect for human personality. Then he goes one step ahead and says that equality is the original notion and respect for human personality is a reflection of it. In 'The Hindu Social Order', while discussing the principles of a free social order, Ambedkar does not stop at the trio but acknowledges another principle, namely that the individual is an end in himself. We have seen that he explains the principle as sacredness of human personality and regards this principle as basic to the trio of principles.[22] We find that, in his later thought, Ambedkar attaches special importance to the principle of human being as an end in himself. For example, it is the first pillar of political democracy which he states in the memorandum submitted to the Constituent Assembly.[23] This makes the picture more complicated. I think the complexity can be reduced if we consider this principle and the principle of fraternity in their interrelation. Fraternity implies treating human beings as objects of reverence and love, paying regard to others, seeking the good of others and so on. Similarly, treating human beings as ends in themselves implies sacredness of human personality. Both these attitudes—of treating human beings as ends in themselves and of treating them as objects of veneration, respect, and love—are at par, as they attach intrinsic value to human beings. In this way, the question of interrelationship of principles can be brought back within the jurisdiction of the three principles. Now we can say that within the framework of the three principles, Ambedkar presents three different approaches.

1. We have seen that in 'Philosophy of Hinduism' he regards equality as basic.
2. In 'The Hindu Social Order', he regards 'the individual as an end in himself' as the basic principle, which means in a sense that fraternity is the basic principle. Another important text in this context is Riddle No. 22 in Ambedkar's work 'Riddles in Hinduism'. Here, Ambedkar regards fraternity as the basic principle which sustains equality and liberty. He says:

[22] Ambedkar (1987, Volume 3).
[23] Joshi (2008: 169).

> Without fraternity, liberty would destroy equality and equality would destroy liberty. If in Democracy liberty does not destroy equality and equality does not destroy liberty, it is because at the basis of both there is fraternity. Fraternity is therefore the root of Democracy.[24]

This raises a problem. Is equality basic or is fraternity basic? I think that the apparent paradox can be resolved by regarding both equality and fraternity as basic but in two different ways. I think equality is basic from a logical point of view. For example, fraternity as a principle logically presupposes equality because fellow feeling consists in regarding the other as equal to oneself. Liberty in itself, if it is a self-regarding principle, will come in conflict with equality, but it will be a harmonious principle if it is understood as equal liberty to all. In this sense, equality is logically at the basis of the other two principles. But at practical and psychological levels, fraternity is basic. According to Ambedkar, equality and liberty can be sustained if they are practiced through fellow feeling.

3. This brings us to the third approach which is more comprehensive. According to this approach, when Ambedkar says that equality is basic or when he says that fraternity is basic, it is not reductionism, nor is there any paradox. Ambedkar was trying to articulate the complex relation of interaction and interdependence between the three principles. Ambedkar expresses this complex relation in his concluding speech given in the Constituent Assembly in 1949. He says:

> These principles are not to be treated as separate items in trinity. They form a union of trinity in the sense that to divorce one from a union of trinity in the sense that to divorce one from the other is to defeat the very purpose of democracy. Without equality, liberty would produce the supremacy of the few over the many. Equality without liberty would kill individual initiative. Without fraternity, liberty and equality could not become a natural course of things.[25]

As a general comment on the development of Ambedkar's analysis of the trio of principles, I will say this: Ambedkar's theorization

---

[24] Ambedkar (1987, Volume 4: 283).
[25] Joshi (2008: 168).

on the trio of principles was initially focused on a critique of the unjust social order legitimized by Hindu religion. He used the trio as a three-fold measuring rod for this critical estimate. But as an independent social thinker, he was also concerned with the question of the exact nature of the three principles, their justifiability, and their interrelation. The guiding framework in which he theorized the three principles was that of social democracy. Social democracy was a continuing theme in Ambedkar's thought. In his formulation, social democracy has two correlates. One correlate is political democracy. According to Ambedkar, political democracy is not sufficient; it should be transformed into social democracy, or rather political democracy cannot last unless it is based on social democracy.[26] The other correlate of social democracy is religion. In Riddle No. 22 of his work 'Riddles in Hinduism', Ambedkar discusses the three principles, underscores fraternity as the sustainer of the other two principles, and locates the roots of fraternity in religion.[27] In this way, religion becomes the basis of social democracy. This, I think is a culmination of Ambedkar thought. It is at this stage that Ambedkar said in 1954 on All India Radio that his philosophy had roots in religion and not in political science. At this stage, Ambedkar was convinced that the Buddha's dhamma is the ideal religion. Therefore, I would like to say that at this stage Ambedkar relocates the three principles as those rooted in Buddhism. So let us consider in brief how the three principles can be found in Buddhism according to Ambedkar.

The Trio of Principles as Found in Buddhism

Here we have to note one point at the very outset. We have seen that Ambedkar tries to show systematically and elaborately how all the three principles are violated in Hinduism. However, we do not find Ambedkar making such a systematic endeavour to show how all the three principles are rooted in Buddhism. We find him making a general claim to that effect, but not arguing it out. Among the three principles, we find him making an explicit case

[26] Joshi (2008).
[27] 'That question is—wherein lie the roots of fraternity without which Democracy is not possible? Beyond dispute, it has its origin in Religion.' (Ambedkar 1987, Volume 4: 284).

for equality as advocated by the Buddha. But about the two other principles, Ambedkar is more suggestive and cryptic rather than explicit and elaborate. Hence, it is necessary to carry forward and complete Ambedkar's task of demonstrating how the three principles can be found in Buddhism. For doing this, we have to depend mainly on the texts he has presented in his last phase which I have called the Buddhist phase. The main text of this period is *The Buddha and His Dhamma*, but we can also refer to two other texts which Ambedkar cites/invokes in the 'unpublished preface' of this text.[28] They are (*i*) 'Buddha and Karl Marx', and (*ii*) 'Revolution and Counter-Revolution in Ancient India'. Both are available in an incomplete form. I will also add another text to this list, namely, 'Riddles in Hinduism'.[29]

In *The Buddha and His Dhamma*, Ambedkar gives a new perspective to understand Buddhism. After narrating the traditional approaches to Buddhism, Ambedkar asks new questions about Buddhism in the light of which a social perspective on Buddhism can be developed. He asks: Did the Buddha teach liberty? Did the Buddha teach equality? Did the Buddha teach fraternity?[30] Obviously, Ambedkar's answers to all these questions were in the affirmative, though he did not explicitly say so.

Equality

Out of the three principles, Ambedkar explains how the Buddha teaches equality explicitly and elaborately. Book III, Part V, Section IV of the text is devoted to the discussion of equality in the Buddha's teaching.

The Buddha, as interpreted by Ambedkar, also advocates gender equality. According to Ambedkar, the Buddha offered to Ananda the following clarification of his position on Mahaprajapati's conversion: 'Ananda! Do not misunderstand me. I hold that women are

---

[28] Initially, the preface was not published along with *The Buddha and His Dhamma*. It was discovered later on. It has been included in Rathore and Verma (2011).

[29] This is my conjecture based on the reference Ambedkar makes in this book (Ambedkar 1987, Volume 4: 214n1) to a work published in 1947 (Radha Kumud Mookerjee, *Ancient Indian Education*, Macmillan and Company, London).

[30] Ambedkar (1974: 159).

as much capable as men in the matter of reaching Nibbana ... I am not an upholder of the doctrine of sex inequality.'

Fraternity

Ambedkar does not talk explicitly about fraternity as discussed in Buddhism. But in another work, namely 'Riddles in Hinduism' (Riddle No. 22) Ambedkar explicitly identifies fraternity with the Buddhist principle called *maitri*. I quote:

> [W]hat sustains equality and liberty is fellow feeling what the French Revolutionists called fraternity. The word fraternity is not an adequate expression. The proper term is what the Buddha called Maitree.[31]

This gives us a key to understand how Ambedkar was locating fraternity in Buddhism.

Liberty

Like fraternity, Ambedkar also does not discuss liberty explicitly in Buddhism. Here we have to notice one problem about liberty as a principle of social life. The concept of liberty can be understood in terms of freedom of speech, freedom to choose one's profession, and so on, even if we avoid the language of rights. So the question of liberty can be reframed in terms of freedom. Now we can ask the question whether the Buddha supported freedom of thinking, freedom of speech, freedom to choose one's profession, freedom to acquire property, and so on. In *The Buddha and His Dhamma*, Ambedkar tries to show that the Buddha did support freedom of various kinds. The universal and sacred morality and the way of moral disciplining which he propagated were consistent with freedom of thought and action; they were not based on scriptural authority or divine commandment. It was based on free and rational thinking. Hence, in the Buddha's thought, human freedom and morality went together.

In his interpretation of Buddhism, Ambedkar highlighted freedom of thought. He depicted the Buddha as anti-authoritarian. He insists that the Buddha claimed no place for himself in his own dhamma.[32]

---

[31] Ambedkar (1987, Volume 4: 283).
[32] Ambedkar (1974: III.I.1).

Again, there is no explicit discussion of freedom of speech or freedom of action in *The Buddha and His Dhamma*, but the way Ambedkar depicts the personality and life of the Buddha shows how Bodhisattva Gotama emphasized these democratic forms of freedom. When there was a conflict between the Shakyas and the Koliyas over the distribution of the water of the river Rohini and there was pressure on Bodhisattva Gotama to participate in the ensuing war, the Bodhisattva opposed this pressure by exercising the freedom of speech and action. Even after attaining enlightenment, the Buddha did not thrust his views on others by working miracles or claiming a supernatural authority, but by entering into dialogue and discussion and by encouraging discussion.

Again with reference to the right to choose one's profession, there is no explicit statement to that effect in *The Buddha and His Dhamma*, but the principle of right livelihood (*samyak-ajiva*) implies that one may choose one's profession by applying moral criteria. This can be contrasted with the Brahmanical approach to the choice of profession which imposed caste criteria, gave more freedom to higher castes, and no freedom to the lowest caste and in this way imposed an immoral and unjust hierarchy.

Last in the list would be the right to property. Ambedkar has a complex approach (which could be called an ambivalent approach as well) to this and it is also reflected in his writings on Buddhism. As an advocate of liberty, he advocates the right to property but due to the influence of Marxism, he has also before him the ideal of abolition of private property. And he sees both these approaches reflected in Buddhism. In his interpretation of Buddhism, Ambedkar emphasizes that the Buddha did not glorify poverty.[33] This was indirectly the Buddha's acknowledgement of the right to property. On the other hand, the Buddha exhibited an ideal form of social life through the establishment of the sangha in which the members possess the bare minimum private belongings. Ambedkar assimilated this ideal with the Marxist ideal of abolishing private property. Ambedkar was clearly aware of this duality of approaches in Buddhism[34] and he seemed to appreciate both. In fact, this was

---

[33] 'The Buddha has not said, "Blessed are they who are poor"' (Ambedkar 1974: III.III.4.4).

[34] 'A Bhikkhu cannot have private property, a layman can have' (Ambedkar 1974: V.IV.3.46).

the question of a possible tension among the two principles and of cutting a balance between them. Ambedkar seems to have believed that the balance between liberty and equality can be reached through fraternity which was another name of the Buddhist principle of maitri.

I will conclude simply by saying that the Buddhist phase of Dr Ambedkar's thought is marked by the inclusion of the trio of principles namely liberty, equality, and fraternity in dhamma, which is elevated to saddhamma. In this way, the three principles get re-rooted in an ideal religion. Here it should be noted that though Ambedkar distinguishes between dhamma and religion, it only means that dhamma is not religion in the narrow sense of the term. But Ambedkar also defines dhamma as universal and sacred morality, which amounts to saying that dhamma is religion in its wider and nobler sense.

References

Ambedkar, B.R. 1974. *The Buddha and His Dhamma*, Second Edition. Bombay: Siddharth Publication.

———. 1987. *Dr. Babasaheb Ambedkar: Writings and Speeches*, edited by Vasant Moon. Mumbai: Education Department, Government of Maharashtra.

———. 2003. *Dr. Babasaheb Ambedkar: Writings and Speeches*, Volume 17, Part 3, edited by Vasant Moon. Mumbai: Education Department, Government of Maharashtra.

———. 2011. *Annihilation of Caste with a Reply to Mahatma Gandhi*. Mumbai: Dr Bhalchandra.

Beard, Charles. [1942] 2019. 'Freedom in Political Thought'. In *Freedom: Its Meaning*, edited by Ruth Nanda Anshen. Routledge.

Joshi, B.R. 2008. 'The Philosophy of Dr. B.R. Ambedkar as Reflected in the Indian Constitution'. In *The Philosophy of Dr. B.R. Ambedkar*, edited by Pradeep Gokhale, pp. 155–80. Pune: Sugava Prakashan.

Rathore, Akash Singh and Ajay Verma (eds). 2011. *B.R. Ambedkar: The Buddha and His Dhamma*, Critical Edition. New Delhi: Oxford University Press.

6

Discrimination, Colonial Injustice, and the Good Society[*]

VIDHU VERMA

The last decade has seen a great interest in some issues on a scale ranging from the local to the global. A widespread conviction of the centrality of humans' embeddedness within the social and political world has led to writings that accept the ethical obligations it imposes on all of us. However, to what extent are these actions importantly driven by normative assumptions shared with others remains unclear. What is clear, however, is that these obligations cannot be fulfilled through technological change or be translated into intergenerational moral norms by a vocabulary of rights, needs, and duties. The distinction is often complicated and no one was more aware of the dilemmas than B.R. Ambedkar, the Dalit movement's most significant political thinker and the chief architect of the Indian Constitution. For long his work was rarely incorporated within the multiple genealogies and mappings of Indian political thinkers. The reason was that the actual situation of the Dalit lifeworld regarding its institutional locations, disciplinary logic, and discursive procedures was not theorized even though Ambedkar's journey from a Mahar community to the London

---

[*] Arguments presented in this chapter are from a project on Indian political theory titled 'A Theory of Social Action: Exploring the Political in Gandhi, Ambedkar and Tagore'. Many thanks to Aakash Singh Rathore for encouraging me to complete the chapter for this volume.

School of Economics and the Constituent Assembly was well documented.[1] Ambedkar's philosophical and polemical attacks on the Indian National Congress (INC) were universally derided while his adversaries were admired. In recent years, however, some studies outlining the entanglement of nationalist thought with colonialism have led to a reassessment of the very ideas which Ambedkar presented while reconsideration of the nature of oriental studies has initiated a re-evaluation of his problematic legacy.[2] Renewed interest in Ambedkar's work has coincided with a questioning of the colonial discourse in which the dichotomy of the stagnant East and the dynamic West has remained a structuring principle of domination.[3] It coincides with the examination of the ideological hold of Eurocentrism in which there is a failure to engage with the political concerns of thinkers and activists within the colonial context.[4]

This revival has mainly been carried out in the register of contemporary political philosophy with its divisions between liberal and communitarian visions of a moral subject. This chapter argues that such approaches tend to bypass the questions of how a practitioner of moral individualism should be so solicitous of the welfare of the State, and so ready to part with religion to reinvent it in another. Recent work draws upon Ambedkar's interest in classical literature to invent a new philosophical framework.[5] Many writings argue that Ambedkar's politics was conditioned by the anger he experienced in the course of his schooling and life in the village which was dominated by Brahmin orthodoxy.[6] It brought with him unique cognitive resources that exploded the traditional categories for understanding politics, laws and, morality.[7] Some studies reflect on the organization, networks, and institutions that he developed. His influence on many scholars can be seen in all the disciplines of social sciences, in a massive Buddhist conversion, and in the content, purpose, and aesthetics that underlie Dalit literary expressions.[8]

[1] Ahir (1990); Keer (1995).
[2] Fitzgerald (1996).
[3] Bilimoria and Irvive (2009).
[4] Jefferess (2008).
[5] Vajpeyi (2012).
[6] Kumar (2014).
[7] Rao (2009).
[8] Zelliot (1996).

However, Ambedkar's importance goes well beyond the question of his influence. The significance of life, dignity, and self-respect created a set of new concepts in the political vocabulary of Indians, but not before Ambedkar questioned the assumption that existing concepts were not only exemplary but also, in complex ways, representative of more general values connected to or even forming a group identity. More than this, his acute liberal sensibilities, coupled with an abiding admiration for English and American intellectuals and ruthless puncturing of the nationalist pretensions to universality, challenged colonial discourse as a closed system of knowledge. He disagreed with the nationalist opinion that social divisions and caste identities would disappear after consolidating India's nationhood. Along with this stance, Ambedkar opposed the colonial policy of divide and rule that saw India as made of many distinct interests which could not be united in a nation. By analysing the historical problem of Dalit subjectivity in the context of dominant political traditions and transformations, Ambedkar demolished existing categories and concepts that led him to a critique of colonial injustice and the nationalist discourse while offering philosophical perspectives on the self.

Nevertheless, the relationship between the social and political remains puzzling insofar as his theory of action identifies both the mechanisms by which moral norms can be developed in society and the content of those norms; this would appear to leave no doubt about the widely divergent life choices people make through 'conversion' to Buddhism. It is important to note that even if agents were unanimous in their moral norms to which they subscribed, the motives of the conversion are more significant than the practical result of these actions.[9] Once individual members relate to one another with a new set of norms, political subjects newly acquire a moral obligation to adhere to the decisions they have made. Thus, contemporary agents are not responsible for the wrongdoing of past agents but they are responsible for reproducing caste injustices that mediate their identities, agency, social positions, and outcomes of interaction. How does Ambedkar's idea of agency which is constituted by choosing actions in accordance with principles of practical reason (liberalism and later Buddhism) get linked to his account of social justice that draws on experience of discrimination? How

[9] Ambedkar (1936).

does a free agent account for the personal conflict between his motivations and its demand for truthfulness and on the other the propensity to obey existing social and political rules?

With these questions in the background, I will try to give an understanding of Ambedkar, the discursive and cognitive framework in which his work unfolded, and the historical significance of his overall intellectual trajectory. Unlike many political leaders who shared the view of caste harmony and saw differences as primarily the result of demographic and political dynamics of different groups (Gandhi, for example), Ambedkar saw these groups as marginalized within Hindu society. Now, although Ambedkar's work offers invaluable insights into problems of representation of groups under colonial domination, his framework suggests the unfolding effects of Dalit subjectivity as a vehicle for political claims-making and collective identification in the democratic set up of a postcolonial State.

In the first section, I analyse the process through which some of these claims become legitimated as a category of political contestation in the eyes of other powerful political actors in the national movement. I argue how some of the complex issues of 'discrimination' expanded the very concept of social justice in terms of admitting groups as appropriate subjects of justice and their placement in a diverse society. In focusing on social justice, this section attempts to reconsider a historical relationship, in which difference in access to positions of authority due to caste and class is associated through dependency and antagonism, and in which Dalit critiques on aspects of nationalism may also be, in some important senses, its affirmation. Ambedkar speaks to the intricacies of Hindu society and the meanings of equality and freedom through the experiences of the 'depressed classes' and their relations to each other. As individuals and groups are mobilized through the nationalist discourse, how do subaltern communities become disenfranchised from the promises of equality espoused within liberal forms of governmentality? Once civil rights are systematically accepted in the Constitution, how might the legacies of historical injustice give meaning, urgency, and spaces for resistance?

The second section explores his critique of caste within the paradigm of modernity based on the three principles of liberty, equality, and fraternity as well as on his adherence to the principle of historical injustice. I endorse the claim that in most of the speeches and writings, Ambedkar often debated the social preceding over political issues in colonial modernity. This chapter refers to his insurgent and heterogeneous responses that may help us in renegotiating the way social is related to the political in newer ways. He makes politics coextensive with concerns in the social, cultural, and economic life that open these domains to public scrutiny, which is not the same as conflating the political and social or separating them.

In the last section, I examine some challenges to Ambedkar's theory of social justice. The first is about the burdens of being an ethical agent and the transition to another possible self. The second is the place of utopian ideals that can no longer claim transhistorical validity but show a vision to inspire many.[10] How might an account of what is good for humans shape just social and political arrangements in the future? Can Ambedkar be seen to develop accounts of the human good along perfectionist lines?[11] What kind of perfectionism is held to be true and what views of political morality are anchored in this perfectionism? What are the empirical conditions for setting of such perfectionism that shapes the political? The third challenge is about the role of violence in Ambedkar's understanding of colonial injustice. In our reading, Ambedkar's concept of social justice carries an unwavering commitment to difference within marginalized groups, yet it equally rejects radical cultural essentialisms that refuse to engage in ideals of exchange across a plurality of subject positions. My contention is that these political commitments and his orientation for a critical perspective call for alternative ontologies. Not only is it misleading to attribute to Ambedkar a theory of perfectionism but it conflicts with his use of terms in the discussion over the idea of the good society. This theory not only makes claims about the root of marginality and discrimination but affirms Dalit subjectivity as a political process. Entirely, we must hold it neither as a useful dream or an ideal nor as an attempt to flee the demands of the present life, but as a fundamental way of life holding in poetic tension both civic life and life of the self.

[10] Omvedt (2016).

[11] In this chapter, I use the term 'perfectionism' to refer generally to accounts of the human good that relate perfectionist goods to the development of human nature.

Favouring an 'exceptionalist' reading of Ambedkar, I argue that the popularity of the nationalist leaders and thinkers has tended to overshadow the pertinent work of Ambedkar. What the chapter suggests is that we understand the political lexicon differentiating the texts 'Annihilation of Caste' from 'The Buddha and His Dhamma' as an audacious effort by Ambedkar to fashion the definitive theory of Dalit struggle in India. His original reading of nationalism heralded the Dalit's exceptional status as the only group capable of addressing the social question in a postcolonial liberal polity.

Caste Discrimination and the Informal Local Configurations of Power

One of the most critical ways of carving group identities during the national movement was to embrace violent and insurrectionary resistance. Another was to assert an indigenous autonomy through tradition, religion, and moral values in the face of colonial modernity. Orientalists inspired many upper castes who brought their knowledge of ancient texts into the reform movements, propelled by the desire to acquire qualifications for various jobs under the colonial government.[12] Liberal reformers and militant leaders criticized the colonial regime, but equally, they legitimized ideologies of Hindu supremacy.[13] The hegemony of the colonial powers affected the nationalist intellectuals who appropriated the methodological assumptions of Europeans. They claimed the historical legitimacy of their nation through their derivation from ancient religious and cultural groups. Thus, the scholarship of this time provided the basis upon which leaders and activists created a utopian image of the ancient Aryan civilization governed by the true religion.[14]

Dalit leaders who neither supported the imperial State nor the weak bourgeoisie were concerned with composing a voice of protest against privileged Brahmins who had monopolized the dominant

---

[12] Mani and Frankenberg (1985).

[13] B.G. Tilak argued that Asiatic Aryans had maintained their original civilization. Later, M.S. Golwalkar sought to uphold this idea by maintaining that Aryans were native to India.

[14] Figueira (2002). For instance, an Aryan–Semite dichotomy is evident in some of the writings of Justice Ranade (1842–1901).

trends of intellectual tradition in India. Against this background, Ambedkar's hostility towards the Indo-European paradigm and the danger of its assimilation by nationalists is quite understandable. In fact, Ambedkar's counter-history that reveals the annexation and usurpation hidden in Hindu myths sets out to subvert the authority of Brahmin nationalists; he was incensed by the failure of political organizations led by upper castes to address issues of social change. Dalits could translate the meaning of anti-colonial struggles in a way that nationalists failed to do. So Ambedkar would argue that people in colonies can attain Swaraj successfully, but they must set themselves against the dominating upper castes and still manage to live in the same democratic polity.

The most explicit goal for Ambedkar was to apply historical lessons as crucial to the development of Dalit politics. By analysing the historical problem of Dalit subjectivity in the context of dominant political traditions and transformations, he emerged as a critic of the intellectual practices of the past. In his political commitment to redemptive political theory—for it is the latter that led him to privilege the forms of polemical and rhetorical address and to fall back upon the politics of minoritarianism—he contests the hegemonic ideologies of national belonging.

One of the distinct ways to articulate Ambedkar's contribution to social justice is to contrast it with the political and ethical theories that flank it. In the early part of the twentieth century, a significant number of leaders emerged that defended an egalitarian tradition of political thought but with a different political context. During this period, the 'idioms, and irascible idiosyncrasies, of communitarian identities and national ideologies were sought to be given a semblance of coherence and structure'.[15] A wholesale construction of Hinduism had taken place as part of the nationalist discourse, and new organizations of the left intelligentsia had emerged. The left viewed caste issues as subordinate to class exploitation, so it was left to Dalit leaders to project a minimum acceptable programme for the rights of lower castes. They argued that the notion of class failed to explain the dominating role of the intellectual or middle-class elite. The risk for Ambedkar was that a Brahmanical elite's lifeworld may implode into a tight defence of its corporate caste interests.

[15] Bose and Jalal (1999: 107–8).

Zelliot argues that one of the important critiques of Brahmanical hegemony based on radical egalitarianism is found in the ideologues of Dalit Bahujan thought.[16] Unlike the Bhakti saints that attempted to purify Hinduism, they endeavoured to create an independent Dalit perspective of Indian society which demonstrated that Hindu society was based on social discrimination. Unlike the Bhakti tradition that paid heed to personal salvation, and the social reformers who saw personal responsibility in the revolt against archaic customs, the Dalit Bahujan thinkers felt the need to interpret the intellectual and moral basis for liberation from caste system. In short, the challenge was of restoring dignity, recognition, and cultural continuity to the Dalits, but also for discovering themselves in a postcolonial context.[17]

The Dalit Bahujan tradition challenged the conception of citizenship as populations of the lower castes became more politicized. The political awakening of lower-caste groups under colonial rule took shape through expansion of public spaces and selective access to education, employment, and public places. The case for liberal equality was reinforced as questions were raised about 'priestly privilege and the ideas, norms and practices which had been instituted to consecrate these privileges as given and indestructible'.[18] The ideology of political nationalism gave rise to mass movements that articulated the need for an equitable distribution of power. For many scholars, the struggle of social egalitarianism was out of step with the juridical–administrative structure of bourgeois democracy or of liberal modernity that upholds a notion of right-holding individuals. Partha Chatterjee writes of this articulation as a desire 'in an admittedly abstract and undifferentiated sense, a desire for democratization, where rights and the application of justice are open to a broader basis of consultation, disputation and resolution, but this democratization falls short of bourgeois democracy'.[19] The external critique of caste drawn from the liberal ideology of Europe suggests that a legal framework of bourgeois freedom and equality provides an alternative and, in principle, a more democratic basis

---

[16] Zelliot (1996: 43).
[17] Verma (2010).
[18] Geetha and Rajadurai (1998: 430).
[19] Chatterjee (1995: 197).

for this unification.[20] However, Anupama Rao argues that political equality requires 'acts of commensuration'.[21] If commensuration presupposes the 'logic of equivalence', then minority as a category indicates a qualitative difference, what we might call a subject's singularity, which cannot be fully commensurable within political space. When particularities outside the liberal-political commensuration become sites around which demands for dignity and respect occur, they pose a problem for the abstract citizenship formulated in the Indian Constitution.

Despite the significance of the battles fought during colonial times by the 'depressed classes' to gain entry into educational institutions, much against the resistance of dominant high castes, these were erroneously seen as demands for a better just order based on liberal equality of opportunity. The economic changes during the British rule opened up only marginal avenues for vertical social mobility among the lower classes. However, it was the nationalist reading of 'equality' that was seen to threaten formal privileges and claim redress of disadvantages; this reading ignored hereditary occupations that had been the hallmark of the caste system in which depressed classes were born to serve higher castes.

In this attempt to test the practicability of the European Enlightenment paradigm, Ambedkar acknowledged that 'equality may be a fiction', but one must accept it as a 'governing principle'.[22] He broadly proposed a legal and social conception of equality, which entailed the elimination of arbitrary advantages in any social and economic system, irrespective of whether the inequality results from natural differences, social endowments (family, parental care, education), or individual effort. What he also found desirable was the idea of equality of opportunity for all human beings in the social and political sphere in as much as it involved 'liberty to choose one's profession'.[23] Applauding these conceptions, he was aware that if the core of justice is a rejection of principles whose attempted universal adoption would injure at least some people, then one needs to add another claim: He declared that democracy was not 'merely a form of government'. It was, according to him,

[20] Chatterjee (1995: 197).
[21] Rao (2009).
[22] Ambedkar ([1936] 1989b: 58).
[23] Ambedkar ([1936] 1989b: 57).

'primarily a mode of associated living, of conjoint communicated experience. It was essentially an attitude of respect and reverence towards fellowmen'.[24]

In 'Annihilation of Caste', Ambedkar offers a genealogy of Dalit cultural life to overturn the nationalist narrative of 'formal equality' and a united front with a consensus to compel the disadvantaged social groups to reconsider their discourse. As I have argued elsewhere, Ambedkar's work reveals a profound conceptualized scope as he critiques the classical political texts to account for Dalit subjectivity within colonialism. In 'The Path to Salvation', he argues that Hinduism is unacceptable as it does not recognize the importance of an individual. He laments the way the Hindu religion keeps people in 'perpetual slavery' and ignores their material needs: 'A religion which opens the path of acquiring property for some and compels others to depend on these few even for the daily necessities of life, is not a religion, but an utter selfishness'.[25]

The Limits of Colonial Modernity

Although Ambedkar is well known for his attack on the caste system and its practices of untouchability, the philosophical justifications for some of these struggles are deeply contested. Assumptions that his emphasis on the social domain missing in the nationalist discourse was misleading or disempowering continue to be debated.[26] In many works, there has been a realization that the split between the social and political has led to epistemic inconsistencies over time that is historically difficult to transcend. Scholars argue that the identification of political power with social issues has exhibited a tendency that leads to political absolutism.[27] In contrast to this identification, constitutionalism checks such tendencies towards tyranny and absolutism if it ignores the social questions; the Constitution is able to secure the domain of public freedom, which was the only appropriate domain of power. On this view, a diverse society represented a divisive

[24] Ambedkar ([1936] 1989b: 57).
[25] Ambedkar (1936).
[26] Kapila (2014); Mehta (2010).
[27] Mehta (2010).

domain, a 'resistance to the political vision' of a unified nation and interests of the country.[28]

A puzzle lies in the way Ambedkar's early writings show little anxiety about the colonial State but much concern about the pragmatics of effective governance and representation. So, while Ambedkar opposed British colonialism and its economic exploitation of India, he did not join the INC. Ambedkar held the view 'that as no country was good enough to rule over another, no caste or class was good enough to rule over another'.[29]

This section explores the way Dalit leaders like Ambedkar neither fully accepted nor rejected the rationale of colonial rulers, but instead appropriated their claims in a novel approach to surpass the strictures of bourgeois modernity. This conceptualization proposes a deep ambivalence to the views and values of dominant groups and to that of the State. Given his subaltern position, the progressive analytical stance that Ambedkar develops helps him to transcend this position of subalternity by working through hegemonic claims. So, while Ambedkar repeatedly pointed out the deleterious cultural effects of Hinduism, he deployed his brand of critical, dissolvent rationality to show the origins of caste prejudices and to combat the cultural forces which waged war against conscience, faith, and morality. In this manner, Ambedkar offers significant assistance by the following three set of arguments through which he manages to fill in some major theoretical gaps.

The first argument is against colonial injustice, which Ambedkar raises through his attack on untouchability in 1927 in a presidential speech. He told his audience that the aim was not only to gain access to water, a natural resource, but also to break down the social inequalities perpetuated by the caste system.[30] He argues for the need to move away from individual to collective action, as mobilization among excluded groups is embedded in a system of domination. The multiple reverberations of injustice in this speech continue to resonate in the moving ceremonies and celebrations to mark that day a century later. For Ambedkar, the colonial power matrix was an organizing principle involving exploitation and domination exercised in multiple dimensions of social life over

---

[28] Mehta (2010).
[29] Mani (2015: 353–4).
[30] Ambedkar (2013).

political organizations and structures of knowledge. He situated colonial capitalist exploitation and domination alongside misrecognition as foundational sources of colonial injustice. Ambedkar was, for instance, unambiguous with respect to locating the cause of discrimination of the depressed classes in the caste structure and their marginalization by the colonial State. The challenge was that any problems that ensue, although socially constituted, could take on a life of their own and thus needed to be dealt with independently and in accordance with their specific logic. So, putting efforts into removing obstacles to participatory parity may not do anything to overcome unfreedoms related to misrecognition. Having said that, Ambedkar was of the view that restricting access to resources was not separate from discrimination, which means that empirical and analytical attention must be paid to local agricultural practices and regional imaginaries on water, as well as that urban spaces must adapt to changed circumstances to keep its commons and habitat from the scourge of untouchability.

The second argument in recognizing the right to repair for past historical injustices faced by the untouchables is that the very narrative of nationalist discourse on freedom and rights is at stake. Instead of understanding the colonial world in terms of the permanent opposition of settler and native—an opposition structured to help the former—Ambedkar draws attention to practices of representation that reproduce a logic of subordination that endures long after colonies gain independence. Rendering of a principle of equality only to the political sphere was a limited project as were the attempts to seek redress and compensation through the legal system. He fortified arguments for a rights-based system as an alternative to the failure of the current colonial rule to give a just response to the injustice perpetrated by Hindu society. In this way, the limitations of the law of the colonizer and the colonizer's inability to meet the demands for justice from the colonized could not be addressed within the solutions posed by nationalist leaders. The challenge to colonial injustices could not be addressed credibly without recalling the devastating effects of caste discrimination arising from centuries-long enslavement and domination. The nationalist leadership needed to show significant willingness to condemn caste discrimination perpetrated in many parts of India. Therefore, Ambedkar was opposed to the thesis that political reform was to have precedence over social change because being colonized, the subordinate groups were not only dehumanized by the violence of colonial discourse but also by the tyranny of society, which had made them lose their ability to interpret or describe their own image and philosophy.

While the idea of equality of opportunity that removed barriers based on direct and indirect discrimination was empowering for most groups, the Ambedkarite discourse attacked inequalities that arose from oppressive social and religious structures. Ambedkar realized that the creation of the modern public sphere by the colonial rule did promise the language of rights, hitherto unknown in Indian society, but he uncovers the basis of the nationalist critique of colonial rule; mainstream nationalists justified the fight against colonial rule on the grounds of inferior treatment and desire for self-governance whilst they continued to deny the same for the depressed classes. Rather than focusing on liberal democracy's ambition to forge a consensus, Ambedkar's aspiration was for the 'politicization of social justice' so that limitation of hegemonic theories of justice can be brought into view.

Both the terms of the debate and the intellectual genesis of the concept of social justice were contested in the early INC deliberations, where the emphasis was more on individual rights against arbitrary rule, respect for cultural diversity, and the collective freedom to participate in making of a new nation. The ideological stance of liberalism was submerged by historical events (Partition) and by the triumphalist ideas of nationalism. The idea of the nation-state was predicated on internal homogeneity even though this call for national identity was seen as tied to an ethnocentric denigration of minority groups. Despite this, the victory of democratic constitutionalism was made possible because it was designed not only to establish political structures and declare fundamental rights and freedoms but also to bring about changes in the social domain. Preferential discrimination for the benefit of the SCs, STs, and OBCs was meant to address some of these changes. The terms used for discussing the social policy of reservations for depressed classes covered the idea of compensation for indemnity for loss or damage done to certain Dalit groups in the past; the dominant concern was whether differences among groups should be taken into account to ensure substantive equality within a similar historical context.

The final argument is based on the premise that philosophy has a role in illuminating ways to understand our status as citizens and ends of our political institutions. Ambedkar claims that democracy and constitutionalism are coequal, rendering the 'terms' of political association—not merely the 'norms' delineated within— subject to democratic legitimation. This claim of Ambedkar's political philosophy breaks away from the confusing assessments that see him as placing importance on the social over the political. This transition constituted a significant shift in the 'caste question': In liberal terms, from veiled exclusion to assimilation, it represented a much more decisive break with the past for the Dalit communities. The argument for specific reservation policies under the British then presents a profound challenge as to how we have long thought of caste in political life. While Ambedkar saw caste-based movements as having no place in the future of democracy in India, the politics of claim-making has become a popular idiom for thinking about a more radical form of plural belonging in the Indian polity.

In 1936, seeing himself at that time as one to whom the slogan 'liberty, equality, and fraternity' appealed, Ambedkar wrote in 'Annihilation of Caste' about a community pierced with caste distinctions. The Jat-Pat-Todak Mandal, a social reformist organization based in Lahore, had found some of the views on social justice in this text unacceptable and did not allow him to deliver the presidential speech at their annual conference. This text attacked fixed accretive positions and religious practices and was about whether individuals or groups would be recipients of similar rights. Ambedkar draws attention to the devaluation of work that reinforces the secondary/subordinate status of specific social groups in Indian society. By describing the sheer degradation and subhuman, demeaning nature of the work, he critiques the hierarchical division of labour in which some jobs and offices carry more weight than others.

At first glance, this emphasis on moral commitments is misleading, of which I will say more in the last section. Let me clarify. Ambedkar's major premise is that there is a link between the absence of modern political beliefs and the ideals erected by Hinduism through the caste order. His critique of Brahmin domination and the colonial rule is driven not by identity concerns solely, but also by a clear sense of intellectual and moral integrity. He gave new impetus to the uncovering of self-deception in political life. For this, he turns to colonial domination which tends to oversimplify and disrupt the cultural life of a conquered people. From the moment the Dalit intellectual can produce work to be read exclusively by the oppressor, will he/she progressively take on the habit of addressing his/her people?

Notwithstanding the scepticism towards any religion's claim to absolute truth, many Dalit leaders in the past, like Jotirao Phule, spoke of a vision of truth (*satyashodh*) with a belief in the universal rights bestowed upon humankind. For Ambedkar, the objective was not to identify any unitary God-given truth but rather to begin a practice of self-transformation. His interest in the connections between consciousness and social order was by extension in the process whereby critical thought emerges. In 'Annihilation of Caste', as a part of the debate with Gandhi, Ambedkar writes that 'as a Mahatma he may be trying to spiritualise Politics. Whether he has succeeded in it or not, politics have certainly commercialised him. A politician must know that society cannot bear the whole truth and that he must not speak the whole truth; if he is speaking the whole truth it is bad for his politics.'[31] Ambedkar attacks him further on his position on caste system when he gives the reason 'why the Mahatma is always supporting Caste and Varna is because he is afraid that if he opposed them he will lose his place in politics'.[32] Thus, Ambedkar argues that by not attacking the foundations of caste, Gandhi is desisting from his truth-claim for the steadfastness to truth that he deploys against colonial rulers but is unwilling to use against Hindu caste supporters.

In the same text, Ambedkar stresses how the morality of Hinduism has cultivated the herd instinct of obedience and made the need for an entire command way of life. Hinduism builds these virtues on the need to obey giving it a transhistorical form that even those who command in life feel that they must be executors of a higher social and divine order. However, when this table of virtues is translated into democratic terms, then these virtues come into conflict with that required for creating active citizens.

---

[31] Ambedkar ([1936] 1989b: 93).
[32] Ambedkar ([1936] 1989b: 93).

Political Ontology and the Good Society

The preceding reading of Ambedkar will produce a new set of problems, not the least of which is how to square it against the thinker's own tendency to invoke 'conversion' in such a way that it does, in fact, appear as a real potential and not only about motivations of the agents. Political ontology does not hold up another world as an ideal to which the present one should be made to conform, but it demands the abolition of a 'religion of rules' that are not forced upon us but also create a normative demand on us as persons. It is associated with adjudicating the categories to which appeal might be made for analysing identities, individuals, social collectivities, regimes, or some combinations of these. Ontological choices affect our political theories substantively as they inquire into the continuity and diversity of personhood across societies, including how their inner processes are reshaped.

The first challenge is that the account that I defend in this chapter does not seek to appeal to the interests of actual ethical agents who, one might imagine, are concerned with advancing a unique set of human aims. While Ambedkar eschewed any attempt to ground Buddhist ethics in an external foundation, he continued to maintain that these claims can be validated in a just order. He propounds the doctrine that a comprehensive account of human good should inform a theory of justice. It would direct society to arrange institutions and to define the duties and obligations of individuals to maximize their contribution.

The second challenge following from the aforementioned one is to Ambedkar's theory of good that seems to be grounded in perfectionism. Let us recall that a perfectionist doctrine of human good holds that what is good for its own sake for a person is fixed independently of attitudes and opinions towards it and what constitutes an ideal way to live. Ambedkar's statements adumbrate a conception of moral personhood that embodies some ethical presuppositions. His theory includes views about what dispositions and attributes define human perfection. Resources should be distributed so that development of a thick theory of good can be encouraged in this direction. But in considering how political institutions will fare in the light of normative commitments, Ambedkar's theory does little work in advancing a shift of cognitive consciousness that permanently alters our way of being in the world to ensure individual, community, and societal properties do not remain the same as before. How might an account of what is objectively good for humans reasonably shape our views of future social and political arrangements is unclear?

The third challenge is about his view that Hindu religion is disruptive, humiliating, and often violent to members of lower castes. To what extent can they rid themselves of that violence? If force could facilitate colonizing expansion, frequently with violent consequences for the colonized, then it is impossible to eliminate such violence. The caste system involved physical and psychological violence against the lower castes because the fourfold nature of Hindu society assigned appropriate life duties to each person that had to be followed and obeyed. To what extent can the moral construction of caste be challenged by egalitarian ethics to counter forces of casteism today? At the heart of these challenges is the concern that if Ambedkar acknowledges the violence and force of British colonial rule, then he must view that the past acted as a foundation of this act in the colonies; on the other hand, he must appeal to the highest utopian ideals of the civilizational heritage in order to image a vibrant democratic polity in India which grounds itself in the acceptance of cultural inheritances that include religions.

These challenges are not quite as devastating as they might first appear, for in certain crucial respects, they reveal a misinterpretation of the nature of disputes we raised earlier in this chapter. But they prove quite useful in helping us establish what is at stake in debates about the relative significance of ideational and material or structural and agential factors. To begin with, in political analysis, the question raised by Ambedkar is whether social groups exhibit organic qualities and if such entities are appropriate subjects of political investigation. Ambedkar's arguments on tradition and religion, the denial of personhood to a human being because his actions are not following caste hierarchies, is worth noting. It means that, for many centuries, the high-caste members had greater status in society and viewed themselves as living by higher moral standards expected from them as members of a caste group. Ambedkar juxtaposes the 'untouchable group' and Brahmin groups in these writings to analyse the colonial situation.

He presents the 'depressed classes', who are confronted with an existential dilemma in a world divided into two: the social and historical exclusion from history, community, and citizenship; and the condition of living in two cultural realms. Now the psychological effects of this duality on these groups are devastating. Thus, to remind them of this construct, he continually urges them to take off the cloak of Hindu religion to be accepted as human. The mask of Hindu religion denies them their existence and reality. It would take generations to recover from the distortions of spirit and transform their physical and mental injuries into a struggle for humanity.

The next step is to turn to Ambedkar account of those who are placed and fixed in the caste system where the weightiness of 'imitation in the spread of these customs among the non-Brahmin castes, as means or as ideals', has been prevalent.[33] Instead of force or coercion, he brings up the virtue of 'self-duplication' that gives rise to entrenched ethical, religious, and social codes of castes. Experientially aware of the reality of socially constructed subjectivities, Ambedkar uses his schemata to explain the creation, maintenance, and eventual 'rigidification' of castes: 'caste in the singular number is an unreality. Castes exist only in the plural number. There is no such thing as a caste: There are always castes.'[34] According to him, 'while making themselves into a caste, the Brahmins, by virtue of this, created non-Brahmin caste' so that 'while closing themselves in they closed others out'.[35] Later, he argues that castes are enclosed units and the logic of this 'obdurate circumstance is merciless',[36] and it is in obedience to its force that some unfortunate groups find themselves enclosed because others in enclosing themselves have shut them out, with the result that new groups, by a mechanical law, are constantly being converted into castes to a bewildering multiplicity. This does not imply that politics is about rediscovery or a reaffirmation of original identity or lost purity. Here, he is emphasizing the unsettling effects as the 'mimetic' attitude is always partial even though it obstructs the path of resistance to injustice.

What emerges is a definite understanding of freedom as non-domination in social relations between human beings in a casteless

[33] Ambedkar ([1916] 1989a: 20).
[34] Ambedkar ([1916] 1989a: 20).
[35] Ambedkar ([1916] 1989a: 20).
[36] Ambedkar ([1916] 1989a: 21).

society. Ambedkar's case was that due to 'untouchability', two different views were concealed that had damaging implications for the political: one was that social relations with which the colonized were placed due to the caste system were immersed in a symbolic process that took the form of insults and humiliations; and second, in place of a recognition, there is the attribution of a meaning with which the depressed classes are placed and fixed.

In the text on salvation, Ambedkar quotes from the response by the Buddha to Ananda: 'Ananda, I have preached the Dhamma with an open heart, without concealing anything ... I tell to the Bhikkhu Sangha. So Ananda, be self-illuminating like the lamp. Don't be dependent for light, like the Earth ... But a light unto thyself. Believe in Self....' So Ambedkar concludes, 'be your own guide. Take refuge in reason. Do not listen to the advice of others. Do not succumb to others. Be truthful. Take refuge in truth. Never surrender to anybody.'[37]

While much has been made of the difference between political and social, his interpretation of Buddhism enquired into the normative claims of a caste-ridden society and the normative stance of its members.[38] During this period, Ambedkar expanded on an ethical and philosophical outlook drawn from various religious texts that could address the needs of the 'depressed classes' in India.[39] An example of what was alternative about the modernity to which he aspired was that he was not averse to including a religious element in his framing of modernity and its impact on the individual to exercise reason. Eventually, he creatively engaged with Buddhist doctrines to propose the idea of *dhamma* (justice). Ambedkar thus adds to the revisions of the history of Dalit emancipation offered by earlier thinkers like Phule, Pandita Ramabai, and Periyar; his profound depiction of the philosophical foundations of Buddhism; its rise and fall; and the ironies and contradictions of its history. Ambedkar reconstructs his critique of Gandhi and liberal politics in 'The Buddha and His Dhamma' with the call for humanity to

[37] Ambedkar (1936).
[38] Verma (2010).
[39] I use the term 'depressed classes' in this chapter as Ambedkar refers to them in his early writings. Race, conquest, and occupation seem to be the main factors in the early stages of development, followed by religion and philosophy that turned the divisions into the elaborate caste system into a rigid one.

adopt fraternity and transcend backward-looking resentment.[40] He recommends the existential stance of radical freedom and self-invention as one of *sadhamma* (true teaching). A radical leap out of this debased structure into a future where everyone recaptures the self will create the ideal conditions of existence for a more human world based on *maitri* (unconditional friendship/social fellowship).[41]

Hence, Ambedkar's theory does not suffer from an indeterminacy about the ontology to guide the agents to live their lives in ways they have good reason to value. He clearly does not regard ethical agents to be utility 'maximizers' or altruistic communitarians. Of course, it remains highly controversial as in 'Philosophy of Hinduism', he deals with ethics, values, principles, and rules intended to guide social and moral behaviour. We grapple to question our notions of a previous self with which we relate later selves and the way we relate ourselves to others. But the dangers of this are many, as a feeling of shame or despair might be needed to reach the good self we want.[42]

Returning to the challenge of perfectionism, in my reading, I am inspired by the work of R.W. Emerson who wrote an essay posing the problem of ideals. He argued that if we are helpless in the face of forces that constitute our destiny, 'we can recover power and freedom only by adopting another conception of the real'.[43] While Ambedkar carries an unwavering commitment to utopian ideals these can no longer claim universal, transhistorical validity, as in the tradition of the European Enlightenment. In later writings on Buddhism, Ambedkar draws attention to perfectionism as a dimension of the good life that involves a concern with soul transformation that places weight on the possibility of transforming oneself and one's society. Considering that expressing one's convictions is

---

[40] Ambedkar (1992).
[41] See satyagraha led by Ambedkar on 20 March 1927 in Mahad.
[42] See reasons why principle of perfection would be rejected and dismissed by Rawls (1973: 325–32). He argues that perfectionist achievements can be compared but they should not be tools of social justice. The reason is that 'criteria of excellence' are imprecise as political principles and their application to public questions is bound to be 'idiosyncratic' (Rawls 1973: 330). For a critique and defence of moral perfectionism, see Cavell (1990).
[43] Emerson (1984: 260).

itself an ethical demand, it is at this point that Ambedkar's approach is to proceed on a quest not with given principles but with the idea that one ought to look for one's own path that we are unceasingly trying to reach a better self. Gail Omvedt has rightly pointed out that such utopias 'are projected visions, sometimes imagined in the past, sometimes located in a different world, sometimes inscribed in the future possibility. However, they all claim to some kind of reality, the reality of being possible, and in so doing provide the motivation for efforts at social transformation'.[44]

Similarly, he engages with the limitations of democracy from within the constituent assembly. He addresses the aim of teaching the future citizens how to respond to the failure of genuine democracies to live up to their ideals. He suggests that accepting the contradiction in political and social life is not enough to contain the sense of compromise that results from the failure of societies to live up to their ideals. However inadequate an ethic specific to politics may be when it comes to curbing injustices, the articulation of this ethic is valuable. The cultivation of a new mode of being as tied to pursuit of objective goods gets very close to perfectionism. But we cannot compel another to develop their capacities for self-realization. We can only hope that the cultivation of these capacities might provide a robust way to close a violent chapter in caste-divided societies. This trend to undertheorize the perfectionist strain is a way to come to terms with evolving newer principles of rectifying injustice.

In the final step of meeting the challenge of perfectionism, we could turn to his early writings where Ambedkar raised questions about attributes of associations in a good society. For him, the problem is about 'how numerous and varied are the interests which are consciously shared by the groups'.[45] Related to this is the free interplay with other forms of associations as well as the social significance of group life. He argues that the strength of a society depends 'upon the presence of points of contact, possibilities of interaction between different groups which exist in it'.[46] Ambedkar finds missing 'organic filaments' or the threads which reunite disintegrating elements—the idea of which was borrowed from Carlyle—among the Hindus since 'religion compels the Hindus to treat isolation

---

[44] Omvedt (2016: 15).
[45] Ambedkar ([1936] 1989b: 64).
[46] Ambedkar ([1936] 1989b: 65).

and segregation of castes as a virtue'.[47] He also rejects views of a good society that has 'proven its fitness to survive'.[48] There is 'a gulf between merely living and living worthily' and, hence, he advances the need to change the social order for the future.[49] But he always insisted that to overcome caste, destruction of physical barriers were not enough. Trapped in various versions of representational paradigms, human beings are perfectly equipped to come out of it if they recognize that caste 'is a notion, it is a state of mind'.[50]

To that extent, then, Hinduism is incomplete as it is not derived from people's reflections on this complex world and their experiences in it. Side by side, the depressed classes do not nurture their reflections on living a harmonious and cooperative life as it is a society-oriented morality that arises from the existential conditions in which people conduct their lives. Ambedkar makes a lot of the equivocal status of the use of two terms—liberty and equality—in an ideal society for what is supposed to be a single referent here, arguing that there should be fraternity or 'varied and free points of contact with other modes of association', in other words, there should be 'social endosmosis'.[51] This represents for Ambedkar 'an attitude of respect and reverence towards fellowmen' denied when 'men are forced to accept from other the purposes which control their conduct'.[52] While he follows John Dewey in rejecting the 'dead wood from the past',[53] his whole schema is for a new doctrinal basis to religion, a basis that will be in consonance with liberty, equality, and fraternity. This means a conversion, or as he puts it, 'a new life' in defining the period in which the life of the human life takes on an unprecedented political significance.[54] The concept of fraternity features prominently in Ambedkar's social and moral thought and practice. It is among the human values that constitute the basic criteria that motivate but also justify human action in relations between members of the human species. But more than that, his statements imply that there are certain fundamental norms and

---

[47] Ambedkar ([1936] 1989b: 65).
[48] Ambedkar ([1936] 1989b: 65).
[49] Ambedkar ([1936] 1989b: 66).
[50] Ambedkar ([1936] 1989b: 68).
[51] Ambedkar ([1936] 1989b: 57).
[52] Ambedkar ([1936] 1989b: 57)
[53] Ambedkar ([1936] 1989b: 79)
[54] Ambedkar ([1936] 1989b: 78).

ideas to which a person ought to submit and that there are moral virtues that an individual can display in his conduct.

This means that human beings must be concerned with thinking about their political situation working on the premise that the blindness before the ontological question has real consequences for politics. It means that our political concepts have inherited a deep and problematic blind spot, since they come out from the very tradition of caste and class inequalities that we should all work to undermine. Hence, Ambedkar's claim is that, politically, Hindus have inherited a basic flaw following from the sanctity of the *shastras* (sacred books) on which their conduct is founded: 'Not to question the authority of the shastras, to permit the people to believe in their sanctity and their sanctions and to blame them and to criticise them for their acts as being irrational and inhuman is a incongruous way of carrying on social reform.'[55] This means that the political ontology for annihilating caste, coming as it does from the very tradition that sanctions such authority, is difficult to undermine. To act against fundamental religious notions is the paradox he finds at the heart of social reform. The natural life of individuals is excluded as something extraneous to the sacredness of the social order, yet constitutive of that divine order whose commands cannot be disobeyed.

Summarizing the aforementioned arguments, it would be a mistake to identify perfectionism directly with the claim that specific activities are good in themselves. As Ambedkar understands it, perfectionism is not so much a particular conception of the moral life but is a dimension that places weight on the possibility of transforming oneself and one's society. A moral person is oriented towards his or next unattainable self so one must have social liberty as opposed to slavery to make him or her fearless and restore his self respect. Above all, he acknowledges the role of the ongoing deliberation on justice in a democratic society because of the role that perfectionism plays in this conversation.

Lastly, the problem of violence that generates the third challenge is relevant to address as its engagement provides a serious contention to many of the presuppositions underlying conventional Western liberal political theory. The brief analysis presented here is designed to pick out only the salient elements of his argument to assess its role in a theory of social justice. He refers to the visible

[55] Ambedkar ([1936] 1989b: 68).

and mundane forms of violence meted out to the Dalits, in which exclusion, degradation, and humiliation are written into the very structure of their caste location. Gandhi's interpretation of the full requirements of Swaraj are in connection to the law of non-violence. Later, it becomes the basis for his constructive programme for social change. Ambedkar establishes a comparison between two modes of anti-colonial theory and practice, violence and non-violence, as competing 'ethics of resistance' that have become dominant in postcolonial studies.[56] In 'The Buddha and His Dhamma', Ambedkar points out that the Buddha did not make ahimsa a matter of rule but a matter of principle. Recalling the Buddha's reply to the senapati, the commander-in-chief of Vaisali, on practicing ahisma, he explains that this is a very important distinction as a 'principle leaves you freedom to act. A rule does not. Rule either breaks you or you break the rule'.[57] Gandhi's ideas on non-violence were derived from Jainism and not from the Buddha as, for the former, ahimsa is a concept and conduct where the principle becomes the rule. Since Ambedkar addresses the broader question of structural violence in Hinduism and under colonial domination, he finds that Gandhi's ideas on Swaraj fail to question the everyday violence faced by Dalits; no matter what interests Swaraj is to protect, it will be unable to give the guarantees necessary to make sure its proper recognition among Dalits. There is no cogent reasoning capable of justifying rules to protect upper caste interests.

Instead of violence, Ambedkar's focus naturally shifted to the electoral system and to the political institutions seen as sites for the norm and culture that framed Dalits as unable to rule. Although there is nothing to support the assumption that non-domination was the only goal with which he was concerned, the moral and political framework he adopted for reshaping institutions required promoting non-domination in social relations through representation in institutions. The difference between the numerical and substantive representations of lower castes was illustrated in Ambedkar's belief that representatives would be able to make use of their positions as elected candidates of their disadvantaged communities.

★ ★ ★

[56] Gandhi (2014: 19).
[57] Ambedkar (1992: 347).

The primary objective of this chapter was to trace the trajectory of Ambedkar's ideas of social justice as they moved from the margins of Indian society to get incorporated in a nationalist discourse. The decentring of Western classical liberalism resulted from a fundamental questioning of the vision of a just social and political order for all human beings. Towards this aim, I focused on selected themes in discourses on social vs. political reform, political ontology, and historical injustice; saw where they were located; and assessed the weakness and strength of their arguments. Social justice is rooted in the enlightenment that privileged a critical reflection on society and its traditions, but due to India's colonial context, it brought to the fore arguments that were specific in scope. As should have become clear from some of my arguments, justice is not only a matter of restitution, reparation, official apologies, and other forms of righting the wrongs of past colonialism, even though efforts of this kind are essential dimensions of all projects that work towards a more equitable present and future. Along with this, the pursuit of justice has to develop and, if possible, enact an interventionist critique of present dynamics and structures of neo-colonial injustice as well. Ambedkar's analysis of the Dalit movement documents the traumatizing effects of caste hierarchies and colonial injustices. The need for recognition implied a perspective constructed both in opposition to and independently from the Brahmanical social order, a parallel perspective in which Dalits could judge themselves and others through their own set of norms.

This chapter represents my attempt to awaken a different understanding of Ambedkar's political and intellectual legacy that has been conventional. This understanding of Ambedkar's political philosophy breaks with the confusing assessments that see him as placing great importance on the social over the political. While I endorse the claim that in most of Ambedkar's speeches and writings, the central theme is social reformism and that he often debated the precedence of the social over political issues, this chapter referred to his insurgent and heterogeneous response that may help in renegotiating the crisis of Indian political theory. By analysing the strategies of Ambedkar's reading practices as well as those of several key contemporaries, I demonstrate how negotiating in the culture of colonial rule was a political act itself.

Today, in India, the reality is that we have thousands of cases of caste violence and atrocities and the generation of statistics about them suggests the story of failure of our understanding of social justice as it is associated with emphasis on political and educational access, equity and economic life chances or the idea of *guna* (merit). Further, in the common focus on reservations in public offices, social justice discourse may hinder people from identifying and honouring other cultural ways of being. I submit that invoking Ambedkar without the critical discourse on social justice, that is, without giving careful attention to its assumptions and metaphors, runs the risk of reinforcing the very assumptions of individualism, competition, and consumerism that underlie and help to reproduce the current unjust divide.

References

Ahir, D.C. 1990. *The Legacy of Dr Ambedkar*. New Delhi: B.R. Publishing.

Ambedkar, B.R. 1936. 'What Path to Salvation?', Speech presented at Bombay Presidency Mahar Conference, 31 May. Translated by Vasant W. Moon. Available at http://www.columbia.edu/itc/mealac/pritchett/00ambedkar/txt_ambedkar_salvation.html; last accessed 22 August 2017.

———. [1916] 1989a. 'Castes in India. Their Mechanism, Genesis and Development'. In *Dr Babasaheb Ambedkar: Writings and Speeches*, Volume 1, edited by Vasanr Moon, pp. 3–22. Mumbai: Education Department, Government of Maharashtra.

———. [1936] 1989b. 'Annihilation of Caste. With a Reply to Mahatma Gandhi'. In *Dr Babasaheb Ambedkar: Writings and Speeches*, Volume 1, edited by Vasant Moon, pp. 23–96. Mumbai: Education Department, Government of Maharashtra.

———. 1992. 'The Buddha and His Dhamma'. In *Dr Babasaheb Ambedkar: Writings and Speeches*, Volume 2, edited by Vasant Moon. Mumbai: Education Department, Government of Maharashtra.

———. 2013. 'Mahad Satyagraha Not for Water but to Establish Human Rights'. In *Dr Babasaheb Ambedkar: Writings and Speeches*, Volume 17, edited by Vasant Moon, pp. 3–50. Mumbai: Education Department, Government of Maharashtra.

Bilimoria, Purushottama and Andrew B. Irvive (eds). 2009. *Postcolonial Philosophy of Religion*. New York: Springer.

Bose, Sugata and Ayesha Jalal. 1999. *Modern South Asia: History, Culture, Political Economy*. New York: Routledge.

Cavell, 1990. *Conditions Handsome and Unhandsome: The Constitution of Emersonian Perfectionism*. Chicago: Chicago University Press.

Chatterjee, Partha. 1995. *The Nation and Its Fragments: Colonial and Postcolonial Histories*. New Delhi: Oxford University Press.

Emerson, R.W. 1984. 'Power'. In *Essays & Lectures*, edited by J. Porte, pp. 969–86. Cambridge, NY: Press Syndicate of the University of Cambridge.

Figueira, Dorothy M. 2002. *Aryans, Jews, Brahmins: Theorising Authority through Myths of Identity*. New York: State University.

Fitzgerald, Timothy. 1996. 'From Structure to Substance: Ambedkar, Dumont and Orientalism, Contributions'. *Indian Sociology* 30 (2): 273–88.

Gandhi, Leela. 2014. *The Common Cause: Postcolonial Ethics and the Practice of Democracy 1900–1955*. Chicago: University of Chicago Press.

Geetha, V. and S.V. Rajadurai. 1998. *Towards a Non-Brahmin Millennium*. Calcutta: Samya.

Jefferess, David. 2008. *Postcolonial Resistance: Culture, Liberation and Transformation*. Toronto: University of Toronto Press.

Kapila, Shruti. 2014. 'Global Intellectual History and the Indian Political'. In *Rethinking Modern European Intellectual History*, edited by Darrin M. McMahon and Samuel Moyn, pp. 253–74. New York: Oxford University Press.

Keer, Dhananjay. 1995. *Ambedkar: Life and Mission*. Mumbai: Popular Prakashan.

Kumar, Krishna. 2014. *Politics of Education in Colonial India*. Delhi and UK: Routledge.

Mani, Braj Ranjan. 2005. *Debrahmanising History: Dominance and Resistance in Indian Society*. New Delhi: Manohar Publishers.

Mani, Lata and Ruth Frankenberg. 1985. 'The Challenge of Orientalism'. *Economy and Society* 14 (2): 174–92.

Mehta, Uday. 2010. 'The Social Question and the Absolutism of Politics'. *Seminar* 615, 15 November. Available at https://www.india-seminar.com/2010/615/615_uday_s_mehta.htm; last accessed 17 March 2020.

Omvedt, Gail. 2016. *Seeking Begumpura: The Social Vision of Anti-caste Intellectuals*. New Delhi: Navayana.

Rao, Anupama. 2009. *The Caste Question: Dalits and the Politics of Modern India*. New Delhi: Orient Blackswan.

Rawls, John. 1973. *A Theory of Justice*. Oxford: Oxford University Press.

Vajpeyi, Ananya. 2012. *Righteous Republic: The Political Foundations of Modern India*. Harvard: Harvard University Press.

Verma, Vidhu. 2010. 'Reinterpreting Buddhism: Ambedkar on the Politics of Social Action'. *Economic and Political Weekly* XLV (49): 56–65.

Zelliot, Eleanor. 1996. *From Untouchable to Dalit: Essays on the Ambedkar Movement*. New Delhi: Manohar.

7

Communication, Justice, and Reconstruction

*Ambedkar as an Indian Pragmatist**

SCOTT STROUD

By the 1950s, Bhimrao Ambedkar had experienced all the ranges of life's vicissitudes. He had felt the exclusion and pain of being an 'untouchable' in the Hindu caste system. He had seen electoral successes and setbacks as a representative of his people, now labelled as Dalits. He had come close to the sources of power, being the architect of Independent India's Constitution and an advisor, albeit an eventually estranged one, to Prime Minister Nehru. Few formally celebrated his legislative accomplishments in India, but the story was different elsewhere. In June 1952, Ambedkar was recognized by his alma mater, Columbia University in New York, with an honorary degree in recognition of his role in framing the Indian Constitution. New York was worlds away from his normal haunts in Bombay (now Mumbai) or New Delhi, but Ambedkar surely recognized its charms and vivacity; he studied there from 1913 to 1916 under some of the best professors USA had to offer. But on his visit in June 1952, there was one person whose absence he felt deeply:

---

* A shorter version of this chapter is available as Stroud, Scott R. 2017. 'The Like-Mindedness of Dewey and Ambedkar'. *Forward Press*. Available at https://www.forwardpress.in/2017/05/john-dewey-pragmatism-communication-and-bhimrao-ambedkar/; last accessed 21 March 2020. Published with permission from Forward Press.

John Dewey, the American pragmatist philosopher and former teacher from his days at Columbia University. As fate would have it, Dewey died after a short illness on 2 June 1952, as Ambedkar was on his way to New York. Writing to his wife, Savita, he lamented that 'there are many old friends who have gathered around me and [are] helping me in all sorts of ways. I was looking forward to meet[ing] Prof. Dewey. But he died on the 2nd when our plane was in Rome.' Ambedkar had many teachers in New York, but none compared to Dewey, as his next words to Savita reveal: 'I am so sorry. I owe all my intellectual life to him. He was a wonderful man.'[1] At this stage in his accomplished life, Ambedkar rarely showed absolute humility or inaccuracy, at least not in his private letters. We must take his words seriously and explore Ambedkar's debt to Dewey.

Other scholars have noticed this debt, but more must be said about its specifics. In the 1930s, Ambedkar would write that '[t]he best friends I have had in my life were some of my classmates at Columbia and my great professors, John Dewey, James Shotwell, Edwin Seligman and James Harvey Robinson.'[2] Eleanor Zelliot concludes her study of Ambedkar's education with the judgement that 'John Dewey seems to have had the greatest influence on Ambedkar.'[3] Dewey clearly influenced Ambedkar, but how? If we look at the relationship between these two original thinkers, we will see that Ambedkar is best understood as a *pragmatist* following in the line of John Dewey's philosophy, but with emphases and creative additions that could only come from his status as an untouchable (now Dalit) located in the Indian context. Ambedkar's urges to be an activist and an advocate also bring a communicative flavour to his form of pragmatism, something that is not emphasized in just this fashion in the thought of John Dewey. Ambedkar's pragmatism is a novel philosophical orientation that encourages vigorous engagement with others through certain types of communication.

John Dewey and American Pragmatism at Columbia University

Who was John Dewey? This may be a useful question to ask now, given the proliferation of philosophers and philosophies in the

---

[1] Rattu (1997: 35).
[2] *Columbia Alumni News* (1930: 12).
[3] Zelliot (2013: 69).

stories we tell about humankind's intellectual explorations, but in the 1910s, this query would be asking for the obvious. Dewey was a giant in philosophical circles. Having honed his philosophical positions at the University of Michigan, explored education by running the 'Laboratory School' at the University of Chicago, Dewey was hired by Columbia University with a halo of philosophical fame surrounding him. Like his fellow pragmatists William James (1842–1910) and Charles S. Peirce (1839–1914), John Dewey (1859–1952) emphasized community and experience in his philosophical writings. Rebelling against age-old European tendencies to fixate on the permanent, the changeless, and the certain, Dewey's philosophy emphasized the changing and uncertain nature of the world. He stressed the transactional character of our activities, including that of 'knowing', by frequently employing the notion of 'experience'. Experience was an interaction between an organism and its environment, and not simply a series of images inside an agent's head, as an idealist would put it. Humans, being living organisms, share much in common with the rest of the natural world: we are animated by purposes and desires and impulses, and these translate into paths of activities that make use of some aspect of our environment. These are called 'habits' by pragmatists. Habits are not merely physical, as there can be habits of how we talk to others or how we solve problems that perplex us. They are not negative traits, since habits serve as means to get to the ends we want. Life, for Dewey, was best seen as a quest to intelligently shape our habits such that we attain the individual and group goals that we see as worthy of our pursuit. Philosophy on such a scheme does not capture or recite timeless truths about the ever-changing world; instead, it serves as one tool among many to get what we want out of an uncertain environment.

Dewey lived a very long life, so this brief account of his philosophy is necessarily a simplification, but it captures its general orientation and is also an apt description of what Dewey was thinking when young Ambedkar first stumbled into his classes at Columbia University. Even though Ambedkar started his education at Columbia University in 1913, I have found no evidence that he was exposed to Dewey until 1914. Using a course list from Ambedkar's transcripts in connection with the original Columbia University bulletins, I have determined that Dewey's first lecture that Ambedkar attended was in the fall of 1914 titled 'Philosophy 231: Psychological Ethics and Moral and Political Philosophy'.

This was part of a year-long sequence of two courses, Philosophy 231 and 232, but the second course is not listed on the copies of Ambedkar's transcripts that we possess. Ambedkar is noted as taking two other courses in 1915–16 that we can verify as Dewey's courses: Philosophy 131 and 132, 'Moral and Political Philosophy'.[4] I have found the student lecture notes for the Philosophy 131 and 132 courses in which Ambedkar is listed as a substitute note taker for three days.[5] It was in the spring of 1916 that Ambedkar heard— perhaps for the first time—the motto of the French Revolution from Dewey: 'the *moral standard*, aim, as a *common good* ... the notion consequently of the *control of the individual in the name of the common good*. Liberty, equality, fraternity, and the name fraternity means common good.'[6] Ambedkar clearly absorbed these lectures; as K.N. Kadam tells us, 'Dr. Ambedkar took down every word uttered by his great teacher [Dewey] in the course of his lectures; and it seems that Ambedkar used to tell his friends that, if unfortunately Dewey died of a sudden, "I could reproduce every lecture verbatim."'[7] It is not surprising then that we are able to document their influence or even presence in vital later works or activities undertaken by Ambedkar.

These three central values that he most likely initially heard in Dewey's classroom would assume a grand prominence later in Ambedkar's life, explicitly orienting and guiding his quest for social justice. They would even find their way into the preface to

---

[4] For the courses that Ambedkar enrolled in while at Columbia, see Frances W. Pritchett, 'Courses Taken at Columbia'. Available at http://www.columbia.edu/itc/mealac/pritchett/00ambedkar/timeline/graphics/courses.html; last accessed 21 March 2020. I have gathered the course instructors from materials contained in *Columbia University Bulletin of Information: Division of Philosophy, Psychology, and Anthropology Announcement, 1914–1915*; *Columbia University Bulletin of Information: Division of Philosophy, Psychology, and Anthropology Announcement, 1915–1916*.

[5] For more details on these notes and the courses involved, see Stroud (2017b: 204–43).

[6] The original typed notes from Homer H. Dubs can be found at the Center for Dewey Studies at Southern Illinois University, Carbondale, USA. The original handwritten notes taken by Robert Lee Hale are located in the Butler Library Rare Book and Manuscript Collection at Columbia University, New York, USA.

[7] Kadam (1997: 1).

the Indian Constitution, a document orchestrated by Ambedkar in the 1940s. Pragmatists such as Dewey were not concerned with just one of these values, such as the individual notion of liberty or freedom of action. Such freedom must also be pursued along with the idea of creating certain sorts of community. Thus, the values of equality and the creation of feelings of fraternity are also important. As Ambedkar listened to this American philosopher expound on the motto from Europe, he was surely mentally connecting it to his past and future battles for social justice in the Indian context. Can one achieve equal rights for Dalits without sacrificing fraternity? This would be one of the most prominent balancing points in Ambedkar's later struggles against communism, a philosophical orientation that he believed could achieve equality (at least in terms of material wealth) only at the cost of fraternity. One cannot achieve one goal while destroying the hope of achieving the other goals, the pragmatist line of thought goes. Ambedkar, thereby, always sought to achieve freedom and equality for Dalits while preserving the conditions for fraternity. I submit that he gained this foundation from such sources as Dewey's lectures, even though Ambedkar would change and alter this way of thinking to fit the Indian context. Ambedkar was an original thinker, but his creativity extracted and appropriated vital values from American pragmatism.

Ambedkar, Dewey, and Everyday Democracy

Another way in which Ambedkar was influenced by Dewey's form of pragmatism was through his books. Ambedkar was a voracious reader, consuming knowledge from a huge range of areas in the form of books. One of his letters on the way to London later in his life complains of being unable to get into his trunk full of books, thereby forcing him to 'enjoy' the voyage without reading. What is left of Ambedkar's personal library is now largely preserved at Siddharth College in Mumbai, an institution his People's Educational Society founded in 1946. Other books can be found at the Symbiosis Institute in Pune and at Milind College in Aurangabad, another institution started by Ambedkar. In browsing all of these caches of books, I have come to the conclusion that no modern author is more represented or engaged with than John Dewey. In three separate visits to Siddharth College in Mumbai, I discovered the following books written by Dewey: *Ethics* (1908, two copies), *The Influence of Darwin on Philosophy* (1910), *German Philosophy and Politics* (1915), *Democracy and Education* (1916, 1925), *Experience and Nature* (1929), *The Quest for Certainty* (1930), *Freedom and Culture* (1939), *Education Today* (1940), and *Problems of Men* (1946). Books about Dewey and his pragmatism are also included in this collection: Sidney Hook's *John Dewey: Philosopher of Science and Freedom* (1950), Jerome Nathanson's *John Dewey: The Reconstruction of the Democratic Life* (1951), Paul Arthur Schilp's *The Philosophy of John Dewey* (1951), and A.H. Johnson's *The Wit and Wisdom of John Dewey* (1949). In another collection of Ambedkar's books preserved at the Symbiosis Institute in Pune, I identified other pragmatist works: Dewey's *Essays in Experimental Logic* (1953) and Joseph Ratner's edited collection of selections from Dewey's work, *Intelligence in the Modern World: John Dewey's Philosophy* (1939). At Milind College in Aurangabad, I discovered among the thousands of preserved books formerly owned by Ambedkar an unannotated 1948 edition of Dewey's *Human Nature and Conduct*.

Of all of these books, two of the most extensively annotated and underlined are works by Dewey. Inside the cover of the copy of *Democracy and Education* (1916) held at Siddharth College, Ambedkar notes that he acquired it in January 1917, while he was in London.[8] This book is an important work, as it is extensively annotated and underlined by Ambedkar in all the styles of his markings that survive. It was also worth engaging in, as it successfully crystalizes much of Dewey's thought in one treatise. Christopher Queen notes the importance of such annotated books: 'Ambedkar's habit of marking and annotating the texts he wished to consider most deeply offers us a rare opportunity to witness his way of entering into dialogue with the great thinkers of the past', including his teacher Dewey.[9] We can therefore infer from Ambedkar's markings in *Democracy and Education* what may have struck him as important; this importance is further confirmed when we are able to see echoes of these passages in Ambedkar's own speeches and activities after returning from his education abroad.

---

[8] For more on Ambedkar's engagement with this book, see Stroud (2017d: 78–103).

[9] Queen (2015: 12).

What did he learn from *Democracy and Education*? Ambedkar surely noticed its magisterial scope, as it synthesizes much of Dewey's thinking on moral philosophy, science, history, and career training to the general category of education. Education, according to Dewey's revision of his concept, is implicated in how societies transmit and preserve themselves. New members of a society are created in and through their experience in schools. Dewey argues in this work that only environments can educate individuals, but that agents can take a role in purposively shaping environments—such as that of the classroom—to make them more effective in creating the sorts of habits that we need in a democracy. Thus, education relates to democracy insofar as democracy denotes a *habit* of interacting with others and in solving problems in concert with one's peers. Democracy was a habit or a way of life and it was, for Dewey, an intensely personal affair that conditioned and created publics.

This notion of democracy as a way of life among others resonated with Ambedkar. The caste system violated such a communal situation and orientation by separating and ranking individuals based upon their birth castes. This ideal of democratic habits leading to democratic communities sank into his mindset such that he began to make these arguments naturally. For instance, in his 1919 testimony to the Southborough Committee on the issue of extending the franchise to Indians, Ambedkar utters a criticism of the caste system as destroying democratic like-mindedness:

> Men live in a community by virtue of the things they have in common. What they must have in common in order to form a community are aims, beliefs, aspirations, knowledge, a common understanding; or to use the language of the Sociologists, they must be like-minded. But how do they come to have these things in common or how do they become like-minded? Certainly, not by sharing with another, as one would do in the case of a piece of cake. To cultivate an attitude similar to others or to be like-minded with others is to be in communication with them or to participate in their activity. Persons do not become like-minded by merely living in physical proximity, any more than they cease to be like-minded by being distant from each other.[10]

These are largely Dewey's words from *Democracy and Education*, adapted to fit an instance of religious discrimination

---

[10] Ambedkar (2014: 248–9). For the passage of Dewey's that he is drawing up, see Dewey (1985: 7).

through the mechanism of caste. Dewey's conception of democracy clearly affected Ambedkar when he was asked to explain the evils of the caste system to a committee charged with extending the mechanisms of democracy to the various publics in India.

This Deweyan text also introduced Ambedkar to a unique notion of the endpoint of reconstruction. If reconstructive efforts do not abandon the past wholesale, they also do not transmit it completely, a question arises: Where do our ideals come from that animate and guide our efforts at improvement? This was an essential question for Ambedkar, as he was fighting against thousands of years of Hindu tradition. As I will discuss shortly, part of his strategy was to utilize a version of Buddhism to instantiate a critique of Brahmanical authority and praxis. Buddhism was valued by Ambedkar because of its curious status: it was both in and outside of the current Indian environment. It was a native religion of India, but in many ways, it had left the Indian lifeworld centuries ago. If one looks into the heavily annotated copy of *Democracy and Education* that Ambedkar possessed, we can see the impetus for this move. Ambedkar marks in his characteristic blue pencil the following passage on moral ideals in *Democracy and Education*:

> We cannot set up, out of our heads, something we regard as an ideal society. We must base our conception upon societies which actually exist, in order to have any assurance that our ideal is a practicable one. But, as we have just seen, the ideal cannot simply repeat the traits which are actually found. The problem is to extract the desirable traits of forms of community life which actually exist, and employ them to criticize undesirable features and suggest improvement.[11]

Reconstructive efforts must not look for ideals that transcend one's context on this pragmatist account. What Ambedkar sensed in Dewey was that one must extract or construct an ideal from the experienced good, all the while recognizing that one's experience was not going to be perfect or complete as is. Buddhism's connection to the South Asian subcontinent rendered it alive in people's memory, and thus a living option for reconstructing an ideal of how to behave and treat other denizens of one's community. Even in the years before Buddhism supplied his vocabulary of choice, the quest for respect and equal rights for his fellow untouchables in the

[11] Dewey (1985: 88–9).

1920s and 1930s was surely animated by his judgements of what respect upper castes gave themselves, as well as his experience of the relative equality in the western world that he experience in his education abroad.

Dewey's *Democracy and Education* also supplied a form for this communal idea. Looking at his annotations, one sees that Ambedkar highlighted Dewey's 'democratic ideal' in blue pencil. This serves as one of Dewey's fullest discussions of what the best community will be like:

> The two elements in our criterion both point to democracy. The first signifies not only more numerous and more varied points of shared common interest, but greater reliance upon the recognition of mutual interests as a factor in social control. The second means not only freer interaction between social groups (once isolated so far as intention could keep up a separation) but change in social habit—its continuous readjustment through meeting the new situations produced by varied intercourse. And these two traits are precisely what characterize the democratically constituted society.[12]

Dewey is pointing out that communities are at their democratic best when they have a free flow of communication and interaction among their parts. Ambedkar surely saw that the caste system destroyed such interaction, a point that he asserts in his text, 'Annihilation of Caste' (1936). But one also sees that the root of this ideal and free interaction is not merely political structures, but it is one of individual *habit* or *disposition*. This also is a prominent point in Ambedkar's epochal 'Annihilation of Caste', where he imports Deweyan political philosophy *and* psychology to make the point bluntly—instead of changing political structures or social settings, one must change the habits of high and low caste individuals. As Ambedkar puts it, 'Caste is a notion, it is a state of mind. The destruction of Caste does not therefore mean the destruction of a physical barrier. It means a *notional* change.'[13] This surely extends the Deweyan idea that democracy will relate to our habits of interaction, including those habits that cause us to see others as not worthy of interaction at all.

A related commitment of Dewey's philosophy of democracy was that democracy did not begin and end at the voting booth. It

[12] Dewey (1985: 92).
[13] Ambedkar (1989: 68).

was more than this as a habit of interaction that we could have or fail to possess. Indeed, Ambedkar saw this from his reading of *Democracy and Education*, noting in his own hand a vital line in his copy of this book: 'A democracy is more than a form of government; it is primarily a mode of associated living, of conjoint communicated experience.'[14] Caste destroys this habit that could create the shared interests and cooperation denoted by like-mindedness, and in the Indian context, Ambedkar saw that this schism between groups was furthered by a certain manner of use of religion. Thus, in his controversial undelivered speech from 1936, 'Annihilation of Caste', he shows the enduring importance of this democratic ideal as a way of life by echoing this very line from his teacher's great book. Ambedkar spoke Dewey's words, but in a different context— that of the battle against caste-based injustice. He did note his debt to Dewey in that speech, however, in one specific passage. This passage is also notable because it introduces the concept of 'reconstruction' as a method of social change:

> Prof. John Dewey, who was my teacher and to whom I owe so much, has said: 'Every society gets encumbered with what is trivial, with dead wood from the past, and with what is positively perverse .... As a society becomes more enlightened, it realizes that it is responsible *not* to conserve and transmit, the whole of its existing achievements, but only such as make for a better future society.[15]

The ellipses are Ambedkar's own, and they excise a phrase dealing with education in Dewey's original passage in *Democracy and Education*. Ambedkar's 1936 use of this passage cuts out mention of 'the school' with his use of ellipses. Dewey's original line read: 'The school has the duty of omitting such things from the environment which it supplies, and thereby doing what it can to counteract their influence in the ordinary social environment. By selecting the best for its exclusive use, it strives to reinforce the power of this best.'[16] Whereas Dewey emphasized the school as a means of reconstruction, Ambedkar reconstructed the range of means involved in pragmatic reconstructive efforts to be more general. One also sees Ambedkar's omission of Dewey's line directly after what he quotes

---

[14] Dewey (1985: 93).
[15] Ambedkar (1989: 57).
[16] Dewey (1985: 24).

in his 'Annihilation of Caste': 'The school is its chief agency for the accomplishment of this end.'[17] This selective quoting of Dewey's *Democracy and Education* shows that Ambedkar was enamoured with Dewey's reconstructive pragmatism, but also that he wanted to extend it and change it into a vehicle of reform that would be up to the challenges of the Indian context. Ambedkar clearly valued education, establishing many colleges and hostels for the support of Dalit students. But his emphasis was broader than just education, as the cause of caste oppression necessitated more than merely the education of Dalit youth. What remains common to Dewey and Ambedkar, however, is the pragmatist urge to not throw out everything from one's past tradition; one must save what is useful, fix what is damaged, and abandon that which is harmful. In other words, one does not *revolt* against the past in the present, one *reconstructs* the past for the needs of the present. This is why Ambedkar planned on asking his high-caste audience of reformers in this 1936 speech to abandon pernicious *shastra*s or sacred texts in an attempt to change the religiously infused mental habits that result in caste separation. Without such reconstruction, the hopes for instilling habits that create likeminded community members are minimal. This emphasis on reconstruction of the past as a way to a democratic future is clearly a Deweyan trace in the social outlook of Ambedkar.

This reconstructive method also explains why Ambedkar took so many passages from Dewey's *Democracy and Education* and, to a lesser extent, *Ethics* and *Experience and Nature*, and utilized them in his 'Annihilation of Caste' without attribution. This phenomenon of 'echoing' as I call it has been noticed by Arun Mukherjee, who explores the appropriation of Dewey's text by Ambedkar. Mukherjee notes that

> Ambedkar's writings mark his affiliation with Dewey through extensive quotations from Dewey's work. So deeply embedded is Dewey's thought in Ambedkar's consciousness that quite often his words flow through Ambedkar's discourse without quotation marks. Ambedkar not only borrowed concepts and ideas from Dewey, his methodological approach and ways of argumentation also show Dewey's influence.[18]

---

[17] Dewey (1985: 24).
[18] Mukherjee (2009: 347–8). Also see Stroud (2016: 5–27).

I want to argue here that this method is not a mere dependence on Dewey's arguments or texts, but instead represents an instantiation of the method of *reconstruction*, this time pursued through rhetorical or persuasion-focused means. One sees this method at work in 'Annihilation of Caste', for instance when Ambedkar attacks caste ideology:

> The Hindus often complain of the isolation and exclusiveness of a gang or a clique and blame them for anti-social spirit. But they conveniently forget that this anti-social spirit is the worst feature of their own Caste System ... An anti-social spirit is found wherever one group has 'interests of its own' which shut it out from full interaction with other groups, so that its prevailing purpose is protection of what it has got. This anti-social spirit, this spirit of protecting its own interests is as much a marked feature of the different castes in their isolation from one another as it is of nations in their isolation.[19]

This is often taken as merely Ambedkar's point, but the facts of the case are much richer than that. These are largely the words of Dewey's *Democracy and Education*, albeit shaped and adapted to fit the target of caste in Indian communities. One can see Ambedkar's adherence to the pragmatist method of reconstruction in light of present demands when one looks at the original passage that he pulls from in Dewey's work. Italicizing the phrases used in Ambedkar's speech, one can see the extent of Ambedkar's appropriative activity:

> *The isolation and exclusiveness of a gang or clique* brings its *antisocial spirit* into relief. But this same *spirit is found wherever one group has interests 'of its own' which shut it out from full interaction with other groups, so that its prevailing purpose is the protection of what it has got*, instead of reorganization and progress through wider relationships. It *marks nations in their isolation* from one another; families which seclude their domestic concerns as if they had no connection with a larger life; schools when separated from the interest of home and community; the divisions of rich and poor; learned and unlearned.[20]

The argument of 'Annihilation of Caste' is clearly drawn from Dewey's text, but it is altered to fit the specifics of caste oppression

[19] Ambedkar (1989: 51).
[20] Dewey (1985: 91).

in India. This is Ambedkar's version of reconstructive pragmatism in action—it aims to not only reconstruct the present communal situation into one of a more fulfilling democratic nature, but it reconstructs texts such as Dewey's *Democracy and Education* in order to serve as rhetorical or communicative means to achieve such ends. What Ambedkar gets from Dewey's *Democracy and Education* is therefore twofold: a reading of democracy as a habit-based endpoint of interacting agents, as well as a method of dealing with problems *and* textual interpretation. The pragmatist challenge for Ambedkar becomes finding—or creating—the right tools to meliorate one's present situations of injustice.

Towards a 'Religion of Principle'

Religion is not only a cause of social injustice for Ambedkar. It also assumes an increasing prominence as a means for the alleviation of social injustice. Later in his life, he talks more about Buddhism and how it can function as an egalitarian religion that guarantees equality, liberty, and fraternity among all members of society. It does this through doctrinal commitments, such as to the fundamental equality of all humans, but it receives a boost in these endeavours through a methodological tool that Ambedkar took from Dewey. Another pragmatist book that Ambedkar heavily annotated was *Ethics*, a book authored by John Dewey and James H. Tufts. The edition of the book that Ambedkar possessed was the 1908 one. The origins of this book in his collection are mysterious, but there is evidence that it was gifted to Ambedkar at an unknown time by the activist, K.A. Keluskar.[21] However he came into possession of it, this 1908 book is important because it shows Dewey's commitment to an individual transition from customary morality to reflective or reason-based morality. Moral progress happens, on this account, when individuals break free from custom and past ways of doing things and start to evaluate the comparative usefulness and worth of doing things in those ways. One may return to one's customary habits of thought and action, but only after reflectively analysing them. This surely grounds Ambedkar's critique in 'Annihilation of Caste', since his goal in that planned address was to

---

[21] For my speculations on the dating of this gift from Keluskar, see Stroud (2017a).

get orthodox Hindus to think about the roots of oppression within their customs and traditional texts. Ambedkar highlights the following passage that lists the three stages of cultivation of moral judgment: '1. Conduct arising from instincts and fundamental needs ... 2. Conduct regulated by *standards of society* ... 3. Conduct regulated by a standard which is both social and rational, which is examined and criticized.'[22] Communal contexts are important, but Dewey and Tufts are arguing for a vital role of the *individual* in the improvement of moral experience. Why? It is this individual who is the bearer of the habits that Dewey is so concerned with, and it is this individual that has painful or fulfilling experiences in a social and natural environment. Thus, Ambedkar continues this tradition of pragmatist ethics when he implores his upper caste audiences in the 1930s to increase their reflection on the standards of conduct that the Hindu tradition has forced on them from the past. He saw that reflective morality is a vital skill or habit to learn, encourage, and instantiate through one's reconstructive endeavours.

Later in his life, however, Ambedkar reaches back to Dewey's 1908 *Ethics* for another vital concept—the distinction between principles and rules in moral activity. Ambedkar extends this conceptual tool to fit his notion of religion and religious change. In his 'Annihilation of Caste' speech, Ambedkar challenges his upper caste audience (had they heard the speech) by stating, 'I do not know whether you draw a distinction between principles and rules. But I do.'[23] When Ambedkar continues, we see the exact, but unattributed, wording of Dewey and Tufts's explanation of rules and principles from their 1908 *Ethics*:

> Not only I make a distinction but I say that this distinction is real and important. Rules are practical; they are habitual ways of doing things according to prescription. But principles are intellectual; they are useful methods of judging things. Rules seek to tell an agent just what course of action to pursue. Principles do not prescribe a specific course of action.[24]

Ambedkar, like Dewey, asserts that rules are mechanical' and 'like cooking recipes'. Caste rules and regulations derived from

---

[22] Dewey and Tufts ([1908] 1985: 42).
[23] Ambedkar (1989: 75).
[24] Ambedkar (1989: 75). For more on this technique of 'echoing' in Ambedkar, see Stroud (2016).

the Manusmriti represent just this type of decree: 'Now the Hindu Religion, as contained in the *Vedas* and the *Smritis*, is nothing but a mass of sacrificial, social, political and sanitary rules and regulations, all mixed up. What is called Religion by the Hindus is nothing but a multitude of commands and prohibitions.'[25] This represents a 'religion of rules' for Ambedkar, and such a creed is not to be desired because it harms one's experience: '[T]he first evil of such a code of ordinances ... is that it tends to deprive moral life of freedom and spontaneity and to reduce it (for the conscientious at any rate) to a more or less anxious and servile conformity to externally imposed rules.'[26] Instead of a religion of rules, Ambedkar advises a religion of principles: 'Religion, in the sense of spiritual principles, [is] truly universal, applicable to all races, to all countries, to all times.'[27] Reconstructing the exact wording from Dewey's section of *Ethics*, Ambedkar claims that 'a principle, such as that of justice, supplies a main head by reference to which he is to consider the bearings of his desires and purposes, it guides him in his thinking by suggesting to him the important consideration which he should bear in mind'.[28] Ambedkar is merging the moral framework of Dewey's 1908 *Ethics* with his context of caste oppression. In doing so, Ambedkar combines the concerns of morality and the habits of reflective thinking into the concept of principle: principles are vital as they serve as *shared* methods for a range of *individuals* to habitually but thoughtfully engage a society which has inherited a problematic way of structuring its interactions. If reflective morality is central to the democratic idea as Ambedkar wants to instantiate it, principles become an important tool for realizing this state of affairs. Religion merely becomes the vehicle or bearer of such conceptual devices.

In his magisterial exposition of his chosen religion of principle, 'The Buddha and His Dhamma' (1957), Ambedkar tackles the challenging topic of ahimsa or non-violence using Dewey's distinction between principles and rules in his *Ethics*. In his posthumous work on the Buddha's doctrines, Ambedkar questions 'whether His Ahimsa was absolute in its obligation or only relative. Was it

[25] Ambedkar (1989: 75).
[26] Ambedkar (1989: 75–6).
[27] Ambedkar (1989: 75).
[28] Ambedkar (1989: 75).

only a principle? Or was it a rule?'[29] What Ambedkar is appealing to is a passage—underlined by Ambedkar in his personal copy of *Ethics*—authored by Dewey and Tufts: '*Rules are practical; they are habitual ways of doing things. But principles are intellectual; they are useful methods of judging things.*'[30] Rules are straightforward, but what they gain in explicitness they lose in flexibility and range of application. A rule may state 'do not kill', but one wonders what that means in situations of less-than-lethal harm. Rules simply tell one to do or not do some specific action. On the other hand, principles serve as methods to judge actions, situations, and events. These are more useful as they cover a variety of situations. Both the Buddha's and Dewey's view of experience entailed its ever-changing nature, a fact which rendered much of present and future life uncertain. Principles become our best intellectual tool to coalescing what we've learned from our past experiences and marshalling those resources for future success in unpredicted situations. Principles are more pragmatic and reflective than merely following the customary lines of acting and judging. As Ambedkar highlights in his copy of *Ethics*, reflective morality 'involves [the] power to see *why* certain habits are to be followed, what *makes* a thing good or bad. *Conscience* is thus substituted for *custom; principles* take the place of external *rules.*'[31]

Ambedkar appropriates this distinction in reconstructing the concept of ahimsa, indicating that it should be seen in the Buddha's hands as a principle, not as a rule. According to Ambedkar, the Buddha's teaching is to '"Love all so that you may not wish to kill any." This is a positive way of stating the principle of Ahimsa ... The doctrine of Ahimsa does not say "Kill not. It says love all."'[32] Love is a much more malleable and adaptive term, especially when compared to a mere prohibition on killing. On could refrain from killing another, yet still not instantiate a true Deweyan community of shared interests with that other person. This is the way that Dewey's thought gets adapted by Ambedkar into his view of Buddhism. The Buddha was proffering love, Ambedkar maintains, and this principle should be useful in a range of situations. A mere

---

[29] Ambedkar (1992: 345).
[30] Dewey and Tufts ([1908] 1985: 301).
[31] Dewey and Tufts ([1908] 1985: 167).
[32] Dewey and Tufts ([1908] 1985: 346).

rule to not harm would not enable the rich and deep sense of community that Ambedkar sought among all the publics in India.

One of the most important situations, of course, comes in the case of solving disagreements in situations of community. Ambedkar's reconstruction of Buddhism speaks to this challenge. At one point in 'The Buddha and His Dhamma', Ambedkar explains all the aspects to right speech in a way that is animated by the principle of loving others:

> one should speak only that which is true; that one should not speak what is false; that one should not speak evil of others; that one should refrain from slander; that one should not use angry and abusive language towards any fellow man; that one should speak kindly and courteously to all that one should not indulge in pointless, foolish talk, but let his speech be sensible and to the purpose.[33]

Located behind this is the idea that we should constantly be seeking ways to still our self-focused anger and to instead love others, even our enemies or those who disagree vehemently with us. This is non-violence, but a reconstructed form of it that de-emphasizes harm. Instead of killing, it centres on the maintenance and creation of *fraternity* among community members, now and in the future. Ambedkar's vision takes the Deweyan ideas of democracy, reconstruction, and reflective method and merges them with the distinctively Indian tradition of Buddhism. What emerges is a reconstructed sense of Buddhism that can serve a vehicle to empower Dalits and as a doctrine that hopefully creates more common ground among communal members. Ambedkar, like Dewey, did not want to solve a specific problem and create future ones by destroying needed relationships within one's community.[34]

---

[33] Ambedkar (1992: 121).

[34] There is a mystery here as to how much Ambedkar's vision of Buddhism changed in the 1950s until his death. Some portions of 'The Buddha and His Dhamma'—such as the section on ahimsa—are not present in an early draft he circulated for comments in 1951 (then titled 'The Buddha and His Gospel'). I argue elsewhere that some of these changes can be attributed to his later exposure to Dewey's 1939 essay, 'Creative Democracy—The Task Before Us', but it is clear that the larger question of the influence of Dewey's pragmatism in general is there from 1920 onwards. For more on the 1950s, see Stroud (2018: 61–80).

Instead, Ambedkar combines these lines of Deweyan thought and sees the Buddhist religious orientation as a way to communicatively solve one's problems now while maintaining needed relationships for future success. This was a point he noted even during the height of his political activity. When he addressed the student parliament of his newly formed Siddharth College on 25 September 1947, he pushed the attentive student leaders to respect their opponents:

> [A tyrant] need not pay any attention to eloquence because his will is law. But in a parliament where laws are made, no doubt by the wishes of the people, the man who succeeds in winning our opposition is the man who possess the art to persuade his opponent. You cannot win over a majority in this House by giving a black eye to your opponent.... You will have to carry a proposition only by the art of speaking, by persuading [your] opponent, by winning him over his side by argument, either gentle or strong, but always logically and instructively.[35]

Communication and advocacy can be vigorous, but it must not destroy the hope of creating common ground with one's opponents. Ambedkar's own heated rhetoric did not always live up to this charge, but one can see the Deweyan ideal that he shaped in the Indian context. If democracy is a matter of habits of interaction that preserve and promote community, and matters of community involve some amount of shared interest and like-mindedness, then one cannot totally disrespect or write-off one's opponents in their pushes for social justice. Justice is more than a matter of *equality* or *liberty*, it depends upon and requires *fraternity* among community members. Thus, communication becomes vitally important in Ambedkar's scheme of Buddhism because it is a means of social change that is susceptible to guidance by Buddhist views of loving one's interlocutors and opponents.

Much has been written on Ambedkar's innovative programme of social reform, and much more is left to write.[36] What the present work points to, however, is a new way of giving meaning to what Ambedkar was pursuing and why he did things in those ways.

---

[35] Ambedkar (2003: 378).

[36] See Queen (2004), Fiske and Emmrich (2004), Keer (1990), Jaffrelot (2005).

The point that I have tried to make is that we are best served to also consider Ambedkar's efforts in light of his continuous dialogue with pragmatism.[37] Thus, I argue that Ambedkar is best considered as the most prominent *Indian pragmatist* that one could identify, given the manner and extent to which Dewey's thought, method, and even words animated his writings and speeches. As I have shown, there is reason to believe that Ambedkar admired and internalized Dewey's ideas of deep democracy, reconstruction, and reflective morality and wove these into the tapestry of reform that his life represented. He was a pragmatist, albeit one with a distinctively Indian concern with the problems and boons of religions in a pluralistic community. He was no mere repetition or acolyte of Dewey's. His emphasis on religion and pursuit of social justice, merged with the unique mixing of orientations and beliefs resident in India, makes his version of pragmatism unique and valuable. Much more can be said about the relationship between Ambedkar the caste reformer and the American pragmatist Dewey, but it is now clear that Dewey's influence can be charted in specific and traceable ways in Ambedkar's writings, speeches, and activities. Like Dewey, Ambedkar was firmly committed to achieving equality, liberty, *and* fraternity; unlike Dewey, he had the traditional materials and imaginative resources to see Buddhism as the religious means that could be reconstructed and used for these meliorative ends. It is in acknowledging this debt and foundation that we can start to appreciate what Ambedkar does with American pragmatism when he adapts it to the Indian context.

References

Ambedkar, Bhimrao R. 1989. 'Annihilation of Caste'. In *Dr Babasaheb Ambedkar: Writings and Speeches*, Volume 1, pp. 23–96. Bombay: Government of Maharashtra.

———. 1992. 'The Buddha and His Dhamma'. In *Dr Babasaheb Ambedkar: Writings and Speeches*, Volume 11. Bombay: Government of Maharashtra.

---

[37] For some other explorations of this aspect to Ambedkar's development, see Stroud (2017b, 2017c), Mukherjee (2009), Maitra (2012), and Nussbaum (2016).

———. 2003. 'The Minority Must Always be Won Over. It Must Never be Dictated To'. In *Dr Babasaheb Ambedkar: Writings and Speeches*, Volume 17, Part 3, pp. 374–83. Bombay: Government of Maharashtra.

———. 2014. 'Evidence before the Southborough Committee'. *Dr Babasaheb Ambedkar: Writings and Speeches*, Volume 1, pp. 243–79. Mumbai: Government of Maharashtra.

Columbia Alumni News. 1930. '"Untouchables" Represented By Ambedkar, '15AM, '28PhD', 19 December.

Columbia University Bulletin of Information: Division of Philosophy, Psychology, and Anthropology Announcement, 1914–1915. New York: Columbia University, 30 May 1914.

Columbia University Bulletin of Information: Division of Philosophy, Psychology, and Anthropology Announcement, 1915–1916. New York: Columbia University, 27 February 1915.

Dewey, John. 1985. 'Democracy and Education'. In *The Middle Works of John Dewey*, Volume 9, edited by Jo Ann Boydston. Carbondale: Southern Illinois University Press.

Dewey, John and James H. Tufts. [1908] 1985. *Ethics*. In *The Middle Works of John Dewey*, Volume 5, edited by Jo Ann Boydston. Carbondale: Southern Illinois University Press.

Fiske, Adele and Christoph Emmrich. 2004. 'The Use of Buddhist Scriptures in B.R. Ambedkar's *The Buddha and His Dhamma*'. In *Reconstructing the World: B.R. Ambedkar and Buddhism in India*, edited by Surendra Jondhale and Johannes Beltz, pp. 97–119. New Delhi: Oxford University Press.

Jaffrelot, Christophe. 2005. *Dr. Ambedkar and Untouchability: Fighting the Indian Caste System*. New York: Columbia University Press.

Kadam, K.N. 1997. *The Meaning of the Ambedkarite Conversion to Buddhism and Other Essays*. New Delhi: Popular Prakashan.

Keer, Dhananjay. 1990. *Dr. Ambedkar: Life and Mission*. Bombay: Popular Prakashan.

Maitra, Keya. 2012. 'Ambedkar and the Constitution of India: A Deweyan Experiment'. *Contemporary Pragmatism* 9 (2): 301–20.

Mukherjee, Arun P. 2009. 'B.R. Ambedkar, John Dewey, and the Meaning of Democracy'. *New Literary History* 40 (2): 347–8.

Nussbaum, Martha C. 2016. 'Ambedkar's Constitution: Promoting Inclusion, Opposing Majority Tyranny'. In *Assessing Constitutional Performance*, edited by Tom Ginsburg and Aziz Huq, pp. 295–336. Cambridge: Cambridge University Press.

Queen, Christopher S. 2004. 'Ambedkar's Dhamma: Source and Method in the Construction of Engaged Buddhism'. In *Reconstructing the World: B.R. Ambedkar and Buddhism in India*, edited by Surendra Jondhale and Johannes Beltz, pp. 132–50. New Delhi: Oxford University Press.

———. 2015. 'A Pedagogy of the Dhamma: B.R. Ambedkar and John Dewey on Education'. *International Journal of Buddhist Thought and Culture* 24 (1): 7–21.

Rattu, Nanak Chand. 1977. *Last Few Years of Dr. Ambedkar*. New Delhi: Amrit Publishing House.

Stroud, Scott R. 2016. 'Pragmatism and the Pursuit of Social Justice in India: Bhimrao Ambedkar and the Rhetoric of Religious Reorientation'. *Rhetoric Society Quarterly* 46 (1): 5–27.

———. 2017a. 'The Influence of John Dewey and James Tufts' *Ethics* on Ambedkar's Quest for Social Justice'. In *Relevance of Dr. Ambedkar: Today and Tomorrow*, edited by Pradeep Aglave, pp. 32–54. Nagpur: Nagpur University Press.

———. 2017b. 'Pragmatism, Persuasion, and Force in Bhimrao Ambedkar's Reconstruction of Buddhism'. *Journal of Religion* 97 (2): 204–43.

———. 2017c. 'The Rhetoric of Conversion as Emancipatory Strategy in India: Bhimrao Ambedkar, Pragmatism, and the Turn to Buddhism'. *Rhetorica: A Journal of the History of Rhetoric* 35 (3): 314–45.

———. 2017d. 'What Did Bhimrao Ambedkar Learn from John Dewey's *Democracy and Education*?' *The Pluralist* 12 (2): 78–103.

———. 2018. 'Creative Democracy, Communication, and the Uncharted Sources of Bhimrao Ambedkar's Deweyan Pragmatism'. *Education & Culture: The Journal of the John Dewey Society* 34 (1): 61–80.

Zelliot, Eleanor. 2013. *Ambedkar's World*. New Delhi: Navayana.

8

Of Castes and Crowds
B.R. Ambedkar's Anti-colonial Endosmosis

J. DANIEL ELAM

> In other words, there must be social endosmosis. This is fraternity, which is only another name for democracy. Democracy is not merely a form of government. It is primarily a mode of associated living, of conjoint communicated experience. It is essentially an attitude of respect.
>
> B.R. Ambedkar[1]

> Now, between this succession without externality and this externality without succession, a kind of exchange takes place, very similar to what physicists call the phenomenon of endosmosis.
>
> Henri Bergson[2]

In receipt of a scholarship offered to him by the Maharaja of Baroda, a 22-year-old Bhimrao Ramji Ambedkar arrived at Columbia University in 1913. Under the guidance of John Dewey, James Shotwell, Edwin Seligman, and James Harvey Robinson, Ambedkar finished his MA in 1915 and his PhD in sociology in 1927 (he studied in London between the two degrees).

At that time, Ambedkar's arrival in Morningside Heights in 1913 went mostly unnoticed, in stark contrast to the concurrent celebration of the 1913–14 university visiting professor, Henri

---

[1] Ambedkar, cited in Rodrigues (2002: 276). See Dewey (1997: 97–8, 101–2).
[2] Bergson (2014: 63).

Bergson. The philosopher was greeted in New York by Columbia University's head librarian, who presented him with a bibliography of scholarship produced by American academics: 'A contribution to the bibliography of Henri Bergson', listing 496 entries. His lectures at Columbia were so popular that, James Shotwell writes, 'the largest hall in the university was crowded to overflowing' and 'a whole philosophical literature appeared'.[3]

Bergson's popularity in USA was due largely to William James's insistent championing of the young philosopher (especially in his lectures at Harvard, published in 1910, as *Pluralistic Universe*). In 1910, *Time and Free Will* was published in English twenty-one years after its publication in France (*Essai sur les données immédiates de la conscience*). English translations of his other books followed quickly: *Creative Evolution* and *Matter and Memory* were published in English in 1911. Philosophers at Harvard and Columbia were eager to welcome Bergson to New York.

This chapter imagines the likely encounter between the yet unknown Dalit thinker and the world-feted French philosopher, though by way of a much more circuitous path. Instead, it imagines this encounter as a conjuncture of philosophical, sociological, and political thought available in the 1910s, and articulated through a variety of interlocutors at the beginning of the twentieth century.

Ambedkar would return to India and lead one of the most significant civil rights movements in Independent India. Much less appreciated about Ambedkar is his role as a scholar of sociology at the moment of its institutional emergence, and, consequently, attention to Ambedkar as a scholar and reader. In this chapter, I analyse the conjuncture of social scientific/philosophic thought that reading Ambedkar reveals in retrospect—what I will call the vital pragmatism of John Dewey, Henri Bergson, and William James— with special focus on the term 'endosmosis'. Taken together, and under the particular strength of Ambedkar's analysis, this triptych forms the basis of a doubly anti-authoritarian politics: anti-colonial on the one hand, and anti-caste on the other. I hope to offer an Ambedkarite vision of Dalit aesthetic critique, indebted to the conjoined practices of sociology and extra-liberal egalitarian politics, available in the mid-1930s.

'Endosmosis' helps us isolate an intellectual conjuncture of early sociology, when the nascent field still grasped for metaphors from

---

[3] Shotwell (1964: 230).

other sciences, especially the natural sciences. Liberal thinkers like Herbert Spencer and metaphysical philosophers like Henri Bergson wrote in such a way that, to borrow a phrase from William James, 'made biology and psychology continuous'.[4] Because the precise unit of the human and human subjectivities had yet to fully be settled—and also because it was unclear whether human 'society' was indeed a separate entity from nature (despite Rousseau's claims)—it seems especially appropriate that early sociology and psychology relied on metaphors borrowed from the natural sciences. In biology, endosmosis is 'the process by which diffusion among substances occurs by a "push" from the outside of a membrane to the inside of the membrane.'[5] I will discuss the ways endosmosis settled in the social sciences and metaphysics at the beginning of the twentieth century. I argue that if we understand endosmosis as a matter of *contagion* and *interpenetration* rather than merely as 'social mixing', we recover a considerably more radical strain of political thought made possible by Ambedkar's Dalit critique.

Scholarship has tended to focus on Ambedkar's work in drafting the Indian Constitution, due in no small part because it reflects a singularly modern vision for Indian society and politics.[6] As the principal architect for a post-Independence Indian State, 'Ambedkar was an unalloyed modernist,' notes Partha Chatterjee.[7] Recently, a growing number of scholars have focused on Ambedkar's conversion to Buddhism as a symbolically important moment in Ambedkar's utopian vision for equality both in and beyond the restrictions of the Indian (and increasingly Hindu) State.[8] Ambedkar's role as a scholar of sociology is not very well appreciated, especially considering the moment of institutional emergence of this discipline, thereby minimizing Ambedkar's identities as a scholar and reader. As Christophe Jaffrelot has argued, Ambedkar's 'contribution to Indian sociology was overlooked for many years.... The founding fathers of Indian anthropology ... and most of their heirs, have ignored Ambedkar, even though he anticipated many of their arguments.'[9] Even while taking up this claim, scholars have failed

[4] James (1977).
[5] Howe (1987: 29–45).
[6] See Jaffrelot (2005); Rao (2009).
[7] Chatterjee (2004: 9).
[8] See Kadam (1997); Skaria (2015); Viswanathan (1990).
[9] Jaffrelot (2005: 31).

to pay attention to the historical specificity of 'sociology', which has had a circuitous career in the twentieth century. Attention to this overshadowed Ambedkar reveals a different formation of an anti-authoritarian sensibility that goes far beyond the alleged liberalism of his activism.

Sociology Hesitant

Ambedkar was a sociologist when sociology was, to quote his colleague and contemporary (and also underappreciated sociologist) W.E.B. DuBois, 'hesitant'.[10] Crudely put, sociology had yet to fully develop its own social scientific protocols necessary for disciplinary autonomy, and therefore revelled in a moment of philosophical social science which has since been sadly lost (or, more optimistically, shifted to more historically sensitive forms of cultural studies). A heady blend of empiricism, psychology, anthropology, vitalism, political theory, pragmatism, and metaphysics was the foundation to this *fin de siècle* sociology.[11] When DuBois and Ambedkar were sociologists, sociology was still pliable enough—'hesitant' enough—to be useful for a radical politics of anti-racism, anti-colonialism, and anti-casteism. For example, during Ambedkar's time at Columbia University, leftist scholars debated the political use of rendering parallel the functions of 'caste' in India and 'race' in USA: 'color-caste', thusly named, is still considered one of the foundational moments in Afro-Asian solidarity which emerged more fully in the wake of Cold War decolonization and the Bandung Conference in 1955.[12]

Of course, the social sciences were not always politicized in liberatory ways. The study of caste in India was often produced

---

[10] DuBois (2000: 37–44).

[11] See Anderson and Valente (2002); Goswami (2013).

[12] Beginning a history of Afro-Asian solidarity with 'color-caste', however, can only really offer a precious and blanched history of solidarity below the colour line. The term was offered mostly by well-meaning white sociologists and anthropologists; DuBois and Ambedkar, among others, were never fully convinced that the term was either useful or accurate. On the contrary, DuBois and Ambedkar demanded a considerably more difficult (and pessimistic) vision for Afro-Asian solidarity than the trajectory that 'color-caste' inaugurates. For a celebratory history of the 'color-caste' trajectory, see Slate (2013).

by anthropologists colluding with the colonial State. As Nicholas Dirks has written, British rule in India rigidified caste differences and maintained the purity of Brahmanical rule and untouchable pollution. By removing, or at least minimizing, the relationship between caste and territory, British orientalists and anthropologists tethered caste to religion, thereby removing it from the sphere of secular politics. Consequently, caste was a sign of Hindu backwardness *and* Indian authenticity.[13]

To recall, according to anthropologist Louis Dumont's infamous account of the caste system in *Homo Hierarchicus*,[14] the Indian caste system operates by way of a purity/pollution binary (outside of history), which structures a religious hierarchy outside of the realm of politics. A hierarchical system like caste, for Dumont, is inherently, philosophically, and logically opposed to liberal European models of individuality and equality. Caste in South Asia refers, in its most general sketching, to four positions (*varnas*) which divide members of Hindu society: Brahmin, Kshatriya, Vaishya, and Shudra.

If we are to gain a full sense of the academic-aesthetic range of caste, then, we must account for the widespread collusion of early social sciences, nineteenth-century high philology, and colonialism. The emergence of caste as a rigidified hierarchy thus emerges from the academic professions' collaboration with colonial power such that a distinctly European history of interpretations became a 'social fact'.

To borrow a phrase from Gopal Guru, 'Dalits need theory as a social necessity.'[15] For this reason, we need a greater appreciation of Ambedkar's turn to early twentieth-century sociology at the moment of its 'hesitation' in order to best understand the damning critique made available by reworking the more metaphysical leanings of the conjuncture in the service of a triply anticolonial, anti-caste, and anti-authoritarian social science.

To get at this, as I have mentioned previously, we might foreground a curious term found scattered throughout Ambedkar's writings (but especially important in *Annihilation of Caste* [1936]) and trace its circuitous path through early twentieth-century

---

[13] Dirks (2003).
[14] Dumont (1980).
[15] Guru and Sarukkai (2012: 24).

pragmatism, social psychology, and neo-empiricism that form the promiscuous basis for the sociology that Ambedkar was to inherit, adapt, and, most crucially, render politically potent (pushing it to its edges) in colonial and postcolonial India. As Arun Mukherjee argues, 'Reading [Ambedkar] in isolation, without paying attention to ... an astounding number of other thinkers both contemporary and from the past, does justice neither to the richness and complexity of his thought nor to his belief in the common destiny of humanity.'[16] The term 'endosmosis' was borrowed from biological sciences for use in philosophy, political theory, and psychology by a curious network of thinkers in the American and French academies. Like Mukherjee, I think attention to this term is crucial to understand Ambedkar's argument in *Annihilation of Caste*; I part ways with Mukherjee when she insists this reveals a commitment to democratic proceduralism. My analysis in the following sections begins with her analysis but departs it in favour of an appreciation for Ambedkar as someone who exceeds the trajectory promised by Dewey's use of 'social endosmosis' and, consequently, reveals a longer genealogy of the term. Reading Ambedkar and his use of endosmosis through and by way of the early moment in sociology reveals an outstanding network of thinkers (all of whom were reading each other); for the sake of this chapter, I have focused on the triangulation of three: John Dewey, William James, and Henri Bergson. I move first to Dewey, Ambedkar's advisor at Columbia; and then, in pursuit of the curious biological term, to James and Bergson.

'Prof John Dewey, who was my teacher and to whom I owe so much, has said...'[17]

Ambedkar's *Annihilation of Caste*, self-published in 1936 as an undelivered lecture, is a systematic deconstruction of the caste system and its justifications. It was meant to be a lecture for the Jat-Pat-Todak Mandal, a faction of the Arya Samaj interested in dismantling the caste system as part of a broader project of Hindu reform movements. The lecture that became *Annihilation*

---

[16] Mukherjee (2009: 368).
[17] Rodrigues (2002: 313).

of Caste, however, was deemed too radical for the collective, who insisted that the dismantling of caste come from within the privileged-castes, not from untouchables or Dalits.

Ambedkar insisted that the full title of *Annihilation of Caste* include the subtitle, 'An Undelivered Speech', and it opens with his correspondence with the Jat-Pat-Todak Mandal so that 'the reader will be in a position to lay the blame where it ought properly to belong' in regards to the undelivered condition of Ambedkar's speech.[18] As an 'undelivered speech', therefore, we might consider the production of *Annihilation of Caste* to insist on an unfinished conversation rather than authorial text.

The text moves forward by accomplishing a series of critical moves. It opens with a concern for contemporaneous social movements and an analysis of oppressive anti-Dalit events in Maharashtra and north India. Ambedkar then proceeds to offer a global analysis of demands for justice and national independence, with a particular focus on the ways in which 'religious' and 'social' movements have been seen as particular in opposition to the universality of 'politics'. On the contrary, as Ambedkar shows, these binaries elide many of the intersecting concerns of most revolutionary movements. Consequently, the status of the individual under an oppressive social or religious structure is no less 'political' than that individual's claim to the right of democratic equality. Relatedly, caste—which, by justifying itself as a 'religious' matter has allowed 'politics' to continue on without solving it—is in fact political and economic. 'The caste system is not merely a division of labor,' writes Ambedkar. '*It is also a division of laborers.*'[19] Caste is, therefore, an impediment to political revolution and economic progress. In the next section, Ambedkar systematically disregards the notion that caste is hereditary and that caste purity is a practice of racial improvement over time.

The longest section, however, focuses on the idea that caste has prevented Indians from forming a society, due to a lack of a shared consciousness. Consequently, for Ambedkar, Hindu reliance on caste is anti-social in its essence. To claim, therefore, that a State called 'India' deserves independence as a unity is fundamentally incorrect. 'Caste has killed public spirit,' Ambedkar concludes.

---

[18] Rodrigues (2002: 203).
[19] Rodrigues (2002: 233).

'Virtue has become caste-ridden, and morality has become caste-bound.'[20] The last section describes the possibility for the annihilation of caste, which Ambedkar suggests is best accomplished through inter-caste marriage. Where the Manusmriti allows 'no place for reason to play its part',[21] 'you must give a new doctrinal basis to your religion—a basis that will be in consonance with liberty, equality, and fraternity; in short, with democracy'.[22]

Ambedkar concludes by adding what, at first glance, appears to be a rhetorical flourish: 'I am no authority on this subject,' he adds, noting that he is indebted to John Dewey, his advisor at Columbia University, for his thoughts. Nevertheless, I think this reveals the fundamental orientation of an anti-caste, anti-authorial, and anti-colonial vision, heralded under the disavowal of one's own authorial position.

'So deeply embedded is Dewey's thought in Ambedkar's consciousness that quite often his words flow through Ambedkar's discourse without quotation marks,'[23] notes Arun Mukherjee in her exhaustive essay on the affiliations between Ambedkar and his mentor. 'Unless we understand something of John Dewey,' writes K.N. Kadam, an early biographer of Ambedkar, 'it would be impossible to understand Dr. Ambedkar.'[24] Ambedkar himself insisted on this relationship as well: 'If Dewey died, I could reproduce every lecture verbatim,' he allegedly told a student newspaper.[25] Ambedkar's own comments about Dewey are, I think, different in kind from those by Kadam and Mukherjee, namely, that Ambedkar's own assertion is simultaneously more humble and more transgressive.

Mukherjee's excellent analysis of Ambedkar's endless citation of Dewey is nonetheless insightful, however. She notes that both thinkers share an interest in democracy, social change, communication, education, and individuals as always already social (and socialized) beings. Moreover, she writes, both thinkers share a wariness of teleological thinking, especially of crude versions of Marx and Hegel. She carefully and helpfully illuminates a shared

---

[20] Rodrigues (2002: 259).
[21] Rodrigues (2002: 296).
[22] Rodrigues (2002: 311).
[23] Mukherjee (2009: 247).
[24] Kadam (1997).
[25] Quoted in Mukherjee (2009: 347).

insistence on present- and future-oriented action in contradistinction to an adherence (or worship) of the past. At the same time, the stakes for Ambedkar are rendered much higher than those for Dewey. Unlike Dewey, whose personal views were likely more radical than the ones he published,[26] Ambedkar 'drags Dewey ... to the edge',[27] and offers a more radical pragmatic egalitarianism.

Mukherjee provides an extensive catalogue of Dewey's quotes without formal citation in Ambedkar's *Annihilation of Caste*. In place of repeating her excellent work here, we may notice trends in Ambedkar's usage of Dewey that centre most provocatively around terms like 'communication' and 'consciousness of kind'.

'Consciousness of kind', first introduced by sociologist Henry Giddings, refers to one's recognition of another as a being of like mind. 'Consciousness of kind', a term Giddings developed from Adam Smith's writings on sympathy, is a prerequisite for a society.[28] 'There is no Hindu consciousness of kind,' Ambedkar writes. 'In every Hindu the consciousness that exists is the consciousness of his caste. That is the reason why the Hindus cannot be said to form a society or a nation.'[29] (This quote is often used to argue that Ambedkar was 'improperly' anti-colonial.[30])

'Communication', for both Dewey and Ambedkar, refers not simply to dialogue between humans, but rather to an empathetic structure of feeling that makes dialogue possible. Communication, far from being a rational or procedural element of democracy, is rather the foundational affective condition of its possibility. Quoting Dewey without citing him, Ambedkar writes: 'The only way by which men can come to possess things in common with one another is by being in communion with one another. This is merely another way of saying that society continues to exist by communication—indeed, in communication.'[31]

Mukherjee also attributes Ambedkar's use of 'social efficiency' to Dewey, though the term originates from a British pedagogical theorist, Benjamin Kidd and conservative American sociologist

---

[26] Quoted in Mukherjee (2009: 347).
[27] Mukherjee (2009: 349).
[28] Giddings (1896).
[29] Rodrigues (2002: 242–3).
[30] Shorie (1997).
[31] Rodrigues (2002: 204).

David Snedden.[32] Dewey found 'social efficiency' to be far too linked with social Darwinism to be appropriate in a diverse classroom, and offensive to the democratic project he envisioned. In Ambedkar's hands, 'social efficiency' refers to a practice whereby a man's job would be based on his cultivated skills, not the accident of his birth. On its own, this might stink of social Darwinism, but here it forms the basis of an anti-caste critique rooted less in the individual and more in the 'social' sphere of her emergence.

'Association' is the final term in our current conglomeration. An ideal society, for Ambedkar, has the maximum possible amount 'full and free ... interplay with other forms of associations',[33] in addition to shared consciousness across social groups. Or, alternatively:

> The strength of a society depends upon the presence of points of contact, possibilities of interaction between different groups which exist in it. These are what Carlyle calls 'organic filaments' i.e. the elastic threads which help to bring the disintegrating elements together and to reunite them.[34]

These 'organic filaments', as a mode of association, draw our attention to the biological metaphors of Ambedkar's thought (which is a curious juxtaposition to the biological referents of caste hierarchy).

Rather than acknowledge all the Deweyan terms proffered by Ambedkar as a marker of Ambedkar's indebtedness to his advisor (though that too), we might understand Ambedkar has carefully curating a set of Dewey's terms to correspond more closely with an aesthetic/political vision of anti-caste critique. Taken together, Ambedkar's selection pushes us closer to the curious sociological conglomeration of terms indebted to the study of crowd psychology at the turn of the century. 'Communication' and 'consciousness of kind' might be closer aligned to a multitudinous politics of the crowd, wherein the central tenants of liberalism are called into question.

Approaching the most curious term, 'endosmosis', by this route, then, reveals the term's relationship to discourses of contagion and communion, rather than liberal democratic proceduralism. On

---

[32] Labaree (2010: 163–88).
[33] Rodrigues (2002: 279).
[34] Rodrigues (2002: 285).

the contrary, Ambedkar propels us towards a more radical form of democracy:

> In other words, there must be social endosmosis. This is fraternity, which is only another name for democracy. Democracy is not merely a form of government. It is primarily a mode of associated living, of conjoint communicated experience. It is essentially an attitude of respect.[35]

Rooted in an affective relationship with others ('an attitude of respect'), 'associated living' as the form of democracy suitable for an anti-caste critique is related more closely to a politics of multitudes and crowds than of rational humanism. 'There must be social endosmosis', in Ambedkar's analysis here, stands beyond the full reach of the merely political and yet not outside of its considerations.[36]

As Mukherjee has shown, Ambedkar's use of 'endosmosis' appears as early as 1919, in his report before the Southborough Committee on Franchise. 'Endosmosis among the groups makes possible a resocialization of once socialized attitudes ... [which are] essential for a harmonious life, social or political and, as has just been shown, it depends upon the extent of communication, participation or endosmosis.'[37] Again, even at this earlier point, Ambedkar's use of 'endosmosis' occurs in the social realm but is not fully accountable to social-political democratic practice.

Endosmosis also shows up in Ambedkar's later work, especially in 'What Congress and Gandhi Have Done for the Untouchables' (1946), published shortly before Independence, as well as 'India and the Pre-prerequisites for Communism'. In both cases, 'endosmosis' refers to a practice of social affiliation and disregard for social difference:

> What a free social order endeavours to do is to maintain all channels of social endosmosis. This is possible only when the classes are

---

[35] Rodrigues (2002: 276); Dewey (1997: 97–8, 101–2).

[36] It is important to note here that I am not attempting to reinstate a tired binary of 'religious/social' and 'political' wherein caste is rendered apolitical through a de-historicization of its relationship with Hinduism. See Dirks (2003) and Rao (2009). At the same time, Ambedkar offers us, in the guise of an anti-caste critique, a model of democracy that exceeds the boundaries of mere politics. This position has been championed by many contemporary thinkers in India; see, for example, Mehta (2003).

[37] Ambedkar (1979a: 248–9).

free to share in an extensive number of common interests, undertakings and expenses, have a larger number of values in common, when there is a free play back and forth, when they have an equable opportunity to receive and to take from others. Such social contacts [sic] must and does dissolve custom, makes for an alert and expanding mental life and not only occasion but demand reconstruction of mental attitudes.... Manu goes to the length of interdicting ordinary social intercourse.[38]

Note here, especially, the reassertion of an anti-authorial stance (by way of Manu), dedicated instead to the 'reconstruction' (another term borrowed from Dewey) of a society based on contact, commonness, and the 'free play' of interaction, intersubjectivity, and community.

Mukherjee is correct to trace Ambedkar's use of 'endosmosis' back to Dewey, especially in its longer form, 'social endosmosis'. Dewey uses the term most extensively in *Democracy and Education* (1916), which he would have been working on while Ambedkar was his student. Education, for Dewey, participates in the creation of a democracy-to-come insofar as it brings together people from multiple socio-economic backgrounds, and allows them to forge affiliations and associations across social differences. Even as early as 1916, he recognized that public schools provided one of the last places were social groups might actually meet and forge social affiliations across difference. 'A separation into a privileged and a subject-class prevents social endosmosis,'[39] he noted. Dewey was productively unclear on whether democracy produces social endosmosis or vice versa; democracy, for Dewey, was not a teleological result but rather a process of perpetual practice. 'Social endosmosis,' Dewey writes, 'is blocked because society is divided into "a privileged and a subject-class"', which in turn 'make[s] individuals impervious to the interests of others'. Conversely, a pragmatic social endosmosis allows a properly democratic social imagination to emerge.[40]

Ambedkar's argument that an ideal society was produced by ending the isolation of different social groups extends from Dewey's ideal public school, an institution that (Dewey imagined) fostered

[38] Ambedkar (1979b: 113); Mukherjee (2009: 349).
[39] Dewey (1997: 84).
[40] Dewey (1997: 141).

social endosmosis and a 'mode of associated living' whereby antagonistic social groups came into contact. 'Only in [this vision of public school education] can the centrifugal forces set up by juxtaposition of different groups within one and the same political unit be counteracted,' Dewey explains at the beginning of *Democracy and Education*.[41]

Dewey was especially concerned with the emergence of democracy not as a political system, but rather a social phenomenon with political implications. 'A democracy is more than a form of government; it is primarily a mode of associated living, of conjoint communicated experience.'[42] It is certainly clear that Ambedkar drew extensively on Dewey's conception of education for his own anti-authorial anti-caste critique.

In one of his most moving essays, 'Creative Democracy: The Task Before Us' (1939), Dewey expands on the relationship between the duration of democracy and associated life, communication, and common life. The essay argues for the specificity of democracy as a social *and* political project as the cultivation of a 'commonplace of living'.[43] One can easily find proof of Dewey having read *Annihilation of Caste*: 'For everything which bars freedom and fullness of communication sets up barriers that divide human beings into sets and cliques, into antagonistic sects and factions, and thereby undermines the democratic way of life,' Dewey notes.[44]

When Mukherjee argues that '"endosmosis" is used not as a metaphor for one-to-one communication at the individual level but for communication between groups, and, by extension, between socialized individuals representing their group identities,' she is mostly correct.[45] I think, however, that her attention to practices of representation and individuality fails to account for the full range of Ambedkar's (and Dewey's) imagination. Stopping, as Mukherjee does, at Dewey, only provides a partial account of Ambedkar's imagination, to say nothing of the imaginative reach of early sociology. To this end, we should continue back to William James and Henri Bergson in order to provide a richer account of endosmosis

---

[41] Dewey (1997: 25).
[42] Dewey (1997: 87).
[43] Dewey (1988).
[44] Dewey (1988).
[45] Mukherjee (2009: 355).

as the curious metaphor that unites biology, early sociology, and the literary imagination made available by the complete vibrancy of Ambedkar's anti-caste critique.

James and Bergson

As Bernadette Baker and Jeremy Carrette have written, William James represents an inaugural moment in the institutional history of social science, but an inaugural moment whose promiscuity of thought (occultism, pedagogy, spiritualism, anti-imperialism, psychology, philosophy, sociology, political theory, to name a few) has been foreclosed by the narrowing of disciplines.[46]

James and Dewey were colleagues, and often wrote about reading each other's work. Here, for example, is James's review of Dewey's thought:

> Like Spencer ... Dewey makes biology and psychology continuous. 'Life,' or 'experience,' is the fundamental conception; and whether you take it physically or mentally, it involves an adjustment between terms. Dewey's favorite word is 'situation.' A situation implies at least two factors, each of which is both an independent variable and a function of the other variable .... The situation gets perpetually 'reconstructed,' to use another of Professor Dewey's favorite words, and this reconstruction is the process of which all reality consists.[47]

Here again, we see Dewey's investment in biological metaphors as the root for sociological and philosophical theorizing. James is correct to point out that Dewey's sense of 'biology' and human experience are 'continuous', for example. Precisely because of this continuousness, Dewey's investments are, by way of James, in 'reconstructed' process and duration rather than fixed 'situations'.

These influences, of course, go both directions: James was very influential in Dewey's thought, and vice versa.[48] Taken together, Dewey and James articulated a form of pragmatism and empiricism indebted to a radical egalitarianism of experience and experiential

---

[46] Baker (2013); Carrette (2013).
[47] James (1904: 1–5).
[48] See, for example, Buxton (1984: 451–63).

claims, none of which could take authority over others, and, relatedly, none of which could maintain the author position of an empirical description. As James describes it, 'Reduced to their most pregnant difference, *empiricism means the habit of explaining wholes by parts, and rationalism means the habit of explaining parts by wholes.* Rationalism thus preserves affinities with monism, since wholeness goes with union, while empiricism inclines to pluralistic views.'[49]

In other words, at the nexus of Dewey and James is an insistence on an anti-authoritarian science: 'It is putting off our proud maturity of mind and becoming again as foolish little children in the eyes of reason. But difficult as such a revolution is, there is no other way, I believe, to the possession of reality,' James concluded one of his lectures on Dewey and Bergson.[50] A refusal of maturity, coupled with the 'difficult' (and therefore active and wilful) process of becoming, on the contrary, a novice, provides an orientation for a rather different type of sociology/psychology to emerge. Committed to maintaining 'the richest intimacy' with facts,[51] this emergent science revels in 'world of concrete personal experiences to which the street belongs is multitudinous beyond imagination, tangled, muddy, painful and perplexed'.[52] It is a science indebted to wilful immaturity, unknowing, and communal interpretation, that is, a science invested with the same qualities we have been discussing under the sign of the readerly sensibility.

James's anti-colonialism, relatedly, stands at the foreground of much of his thought. James was a founding member of the Anti-Imperial League, and spent time with Swami Vivekananda in USA and UK from 1902 to 1904. The wide reach of James's thought—from religion to empiricism, from vitalism to middlebrow politics—should become a fundamental part of the genealogy of anti-colonial thought, in both its intersections with Indian anti-colonialism as well as the moment when it seems to mirror the productive promiscuity of its alliances. In Leela Gandhi's brief account, James's radical empiricism is a way of being in the world that forms 'the condition of possibility for the ethical or the political, conjuring a

---

[49] James (1977: 633).
[50] James (2000: 755).
[51] James (2000: 501).
[52] James (2000: 495).

subject whose moral or cognitive agency is a function of her implication in ... the muddy perplexities of desire or relationality.'[53]

Stanley Fish has argued that 'if pragmatism is true it has nothing to say to us; no politics follows from it or is blocked by it; no morality attaches to it or is enjoyed by it.'[54] This seems especially false in the network of thinkers we have been discussing (the same network he claims to analyse). Even in its most minor metaphors, James and Dewey imagined a pragmatic science to envision a world 'more like a federal republic than an empire or kingdom'.[55] While this metaphorical aside might not amount to an anti-colonial manifesto, we may certainly locate it within the realm of James's and Dewey's commitment to anti-imperialism, democracy, and egalitarianism by way of philosophy and science.

One of James's closest (and most long distance) collaborators throughout his life was French philosopher, Henri Bergson. Bergson was James's junior, but James was a champion for his work in USA. At his death, James was still overseeing the translation of Bergson's work into English, and James played a large role in Bergson's visiting professorship at Columbia University in 1913. Kennan Ferguson has argued that James and Bergson share an intellectual trajectory often unacknowledged in American philosophy and less often acknowledged in French philosophy.[56]

One is instantly struck, reading the correspondence between James and Bergson, of their mutually constituted readerly sensibilities in relationship to each other. 'I began to read your *Pragmatism* the moment I received it by post and I have not been able to put it down before finishing it. It is the admirably drawn programme of the philosophy of the future,' Bergson wrote to James in 1907.[57] 'If I had not read Bergson, I should probably still be blackening endless pages of paper privately,' James admitted in his lectures in 1909. 'But open Bergson, and new horizons loom on every page you read. It is like the breath of the morning and the song of birds.'[58]

---

[53] Gandhi (2006: 133).
[54] Fish (1998: 209).
[55] James (1977: 776).
[56] Ferguson (2006).
[57] Henri Bergson to William James, 27 June 1907, quoted in Bergson (2013: 361–2).
[58] James (1977: 752).

John Dewey's own meditation on reading offers an insight into the intellectual relationship between James and Bergson: 'A book or a letter may institute a more intimate association between human beings separated thousands of miles from each other than exists between dwellers under the same roof.'[59]

Here, for example, is Bergson's reply to James's *A Pluralistic Universe*, published from his 1909 lecture series by the same name. Bergson is replying to James's reading of Bergson—in other words, Bergson is reading James reading Bergson:

> Dear Professor James, I must tell you straightaway the great joy I experienced reading you. Never have I been examined, understood, penetrated in such a manner. Never, moreover, have I been so conscious of the sympathy and the sort of 'pre-established harmony' which attunes your thought and mine. Let me tell you, moreover, that you have not limited yourself to analyzing my ideas; you have transfigured them, without ever disfiguring them in any way. In reading your exposition of my theses, I thought of those superb reproductions that the great engraving masters made of sometimes quite ordinary paintings.[60]

Here, Bergson offers us a model for an extra-liberal political relationship: of both being 'understood' and 'penetrated' by the other—who, in this model, is an equal. A circular community emerges, whereby each successive reading *adds* to the text, making the previous author substantially less and less important to its construction: a masterpiece having been read from ordinary paintings. This is, in other words, an astounding model for the communal cultivation necessary for radical democratic critique.

This was not merely a closed loop of professional flattery. For Bergson, reading and re-reading James evoked disagreement as well, namely, about the role of empiricism and the conscious. They ultimately agreed (contra substantialism) that consciousness and empiricism were two sides of a single phenomenon: that existence was 'something between the two, always on the point of becoming

---

[59] Dewey (1997: 5).

[60] Bergson to James, 21 January 1909, quoted in Bergson (2014: 363). There are many more examples of this, collected in their correspondence. 'The lucidity of Bergson's way of putting things is what all readers are first struck by. It seduces you and bribes you in advance to become his disciple,' writes James (1977: 732).

or re-becoming conscious, something intimately mingled with conscious life, *interwoven with it.*'[61]

It is this interwoven quality of consciousness, tentatively agreed upon by James and Bergson, that articulates the beginning of endosmosis as it plays out in both a readerly sensibility and Dewey's social theory. Again, contra substantialism, Bergson offers a definition:

> Thus, within our ego, there is succession without mutual externality; outside the ego, in pure space, mutual externality without succession: mutual externality, since the present oscillation is radically distinct from the previous oscillation, which no longer exists; but no succession, since succession exists solely for a conscious spectator who keeps the past in mind and sets the two oscillations on their symbols side by side in an auxiliary space. Now, between this succession without externality and this externality without succession, a kind of exchange takes place, very similar to what physicists call the phenomenon of endosmosis.[62]

In other words, Bergson's analysis of consciousness and duration relies on a biological/physics metaphor whereby cells freely interchange and are interdependent with one another. Similarly, the relationship between consciousnesses and the seemingly 'external' world is one of interpenetration and oscillation.

Throughout his writings, Bergson clarifies the stakes of this metaphorical description. Endosmosis can explain how 'perception and recollection always penetrate each other, are always exchanging something of their substance',[63] and is 'an intermingling of the purely intensive sensation of the mobility with the extensive representation of the space traversed'.[64] The relationship between perception and recollection involves interpenetration and the exchange of substance.[65] Bergson solves, for James, 'how a lot of separate consciousnesses can at the same time be one collective thing'.[66] Endosmosis, for Bergson and James, thus describes a relationship of shared consciousness and perception, not only with

---

[61] Bergson to James, 15 February 1905, quoted in Bergson (2014: 359).
[62] Bergson (2014: 63).
[63] Bergson (2014).
[64] Bergson (2014: 112).
[65] Bergson (2014: 72).
[66] James (1977: 752).

people (that is to say, 'social endosmosis') but also with objects, perceptions, and consciousnesses.

Equally true, however, for Bergson, is a practice that resembles what Dewey would later identify as 'social endosmosis': 'The members of a civic community hold together like the cells of an organism. Habit, served by intelligence and imagination, introduces among them a discipline resembling, in the interdependence it establishes between separate individuals, the unity of an organism of anastomotic cells,' he writes in one of his few texts on social practice.[67] 'Society, present within each of its members, has claims which, whether great or small, each express the sum-total of its vitality. But let us again repeat that this is only a comparison. A human community is a collectivity of free beings.'[68]

Lawrence Westerby Howe, in his essay on Bergsonian endosmosis, asserts the importance of the Greek root *othein* ('push' or 'impulse') in understanding Bergson's critique. Bergson's understanding of endosmosis (like the biological process) insists on a type of *push* that thus allows liquid to move through a semipermeable membrane. For Bergson, this involved a physical correspondence between mind and world, but also a forceful exchange as a mixture of externality and succession. This mixture is promoted by habit, another trait of endosmosis, which accounts for the *semi*permeability of the 'membrane of consciousness. Endosmosis thus refers to 'a repetitious act of intelligence in which elements borrowed from the external world infiltrate interior states of mind [and] the interior states of mind are juxtaposed to one another and made to coincide with elements of the external world'.[69]

Again, it is worth nothing here once more that early sociology's interest in borrowing metaphors from biology is not merely an accident. Rather, it reveals how relatively unconvinced early sociology was of the autonomy or the exceptionality of the human being as a unit of study. Rather, in its moment of 'hesitation', this early moment of sociology veered philosophical and biological, relinquishing even the seemingly exceptional figure of the human to the murkiness and interdependence of cell biology. Might, then, we recover a strain of *fin de siècle* sociological criticism committed

---

[67] Bergson (2014: 298).
[68] Bergson (2014: 296).
[69] Howe (1987: 35).

to a dismissal of the exceptionality of the human, and, relatedly, a vitalist–pragmatist conjuncture committed to a criticism of liberalism as the model of democratic politics?

These questions become especially clear when the Franco-American philosophical triptych is contrapuntally refracted through the political critique of B.R. Ambedkar. Ambedkar's abandonment of the academic practice of sociology in the late 1910s in favour of legal activism meant that his sociological references, even in the late 1930s and 1940s (when sociology had emerged as a discrete field of social scientific enquiry, largely resembling the empirical science that we know now), were indebted to a much earlier, much messier, and much more humanistic moment of social scientific concern. In other words, in contrapuntal hindsight, this vitalist–pragmatist model of egalitarian critique becomes clear in *Annihilation of Caste* and the concomitant shift from 'untouchable' to 'Dalit'.

The stakes of extending the metaphor of 'endosmosis' to its wider context beyond Dewey might not seem clear or particularly high. But if we understand endosmosis as a matter of *contagion* and *interpenetration* rather than merely as 'social mixing', we recover a considerably more radical strain of political thought made possible by Ambedkar's Dalit critique. Inherent in the biological concept of endosmosis is a fundamental challenge to the autonomy of individual membranes; Bergson's playful borrowing of the concept poses a philosophical challenge to the autonomy of individuals (as well as individuals' experiences, durations, and time). If we are too quick to subsume Ambedkar's insistence on 'social endosmosis' into an anti-caste project with liberal democratic practice as its sole end result, then we have, I think, fundamentally understood Ambedkar's radical approach to political practice. Ambedkar's (and Dewey's) frequent references to endosmosis as 'communication' do not refer to procedural democratic practices, 'communication' here is more indebted to its etymological sense of being-with, with the full implication of something resembling intersubjectivity. Given Bergson's lifelong critique of the alleged difference between space and time, 'endosmosis' is a particularly crucial word for understanding Bergson (even though to date it appears to only have been recognized by Howe). Bergsonian endosmosis, containing both a concept of 'habit' (duration) and the concept of interpenetration of membranes (space), metaphysically unites the seemingly perpendicular axes of human consciousness. In this sense, 'time' is rendered in its spatial form as duration and habit interpenetrate human consciousness. Relatedly, a properly 'social' endosmosis, with contagion and communication as its references, refers to a modern egalitarianism based on a model of politics that requires an imagination beyond the confines of a liberal democracy.[70] Endosmosis should thus alert us to a politics of the crowd—a peculiarly modern sociological unit, dependent on biological metaphors of intersection, interaction, and communicability. When Ambedkar suggests endosmosis as the way to 'annihilate' caste, he is referring to a mass politics of endosmosis, made possible by the social semi-permeability of political subjects.

Under Ambedkar, endosmosis, with contagion and association as its references (rather than individuality and transcendence), refers to a modern egalitarianism based on a model of politics that requires an imagination beyond the limits of a liberal democracy. This in turn reveals forms of extra-political solidarity beyond the confines of nations or recognizable identitarian lines, and certainly well beyond pithy claims to 'cosmopolitanism' that reassert liberal solidarity rather than associative and affective communities.

Drawing on early sociology but exceeding its already expansive imagination, Ambedkar envisioned a world whose commitments were underneath and beyond the boundaries of the colonially forged liberalism of the Global South. Of course, an anti-colonial solidarity rooted in non-empirical nineteenth-century vitalism has a difficult time finding root in imperial demands for national (let alone international) legitimacy and expertise. But to agree to these demands was to implicitly agree with the ethics of liberal imperialism that they undergird. In this sense, the failure that has marked Dalit claims of human rights as well as Afro-Asian solidarity and other forms of heterogenous non-identitarian belonging is not that they could not to live up to expectations, but that they failed to fulfil their own sociological fictions. The goal, it seems to me, is to recover, by way of Ambedkar, this lost practice of political and social endosmosis as a way to re-envision forms of ephemeral and intersubjective solidarity which is, to quote William James, 'multitudinous beyond imagination, tangled, muddy, painful, and perplexed.'[71]

---

[70] It does not preclude, of course, Ambedkar's more pragmatic insistence on inter-dining and inter-marriage.

[71] James (1975: 17–18).

References

Ambedkar, B.R. 1979a. 'Evidence Before the Southborough Committee on Franchise'. In *Dr. Babasaheb Ambedkar's Writings and Speeches*, Volume 1, edited by Vasant Moon. Bombay: Education Dept., Government of Maharashtra.

———. 1979b. 'India and the Pre-prerequisites of Communism'. In *Dr. Babasaheb Ambedkar's Writings and Speeches*, Volume 3, edited by Vasant Moon. Bombay: Education Dept., Government of Maharashtra.

Anderson, Amanda and Joseph Valente (eds). 2002. *Disciplinarity at the Fin de Siècle*. Princeton, NJ: Princeton University Press.

Baker, Bernadette. 2013. *William James, Sciences of the Mind, and Anti-imperial Discourse*. Cambridge: Cambridge University Press.

Bergson, Henri. 2014. *Key Writings*, edited by Keith Pearson. London: Bloomsbury.

Buxton, Michael. 1984. 'The Influence of William James on John Dewey's Early Work'. *Journal of the History of Ideas* 45 (3): 451–63.

Carrette, Jeremy. 2013. *William James's Hidden Religious Imagination: A Universe of Relations*. London: Routledge Press.

Chatterjee, Partha. 2004. *Politics of the Governed*. New York: Columbia University Press.

Dewey, John. 1988. 'Creative Democracy'. In *The Later Works: 1925–1953*. Carbondale, IL: Southern Illinois University Press.

———. 1997. *Democracy and Education*. New York: Free Press.

Dirks, Nicholas. 2003. *Castes of Mind*. Princeton, NJ: Princeton University Press.

Du Bois, W.E.B. 2000. 'Sociology Hesitant'. *boundary 2* 27 (3): 37–44.

Dumont, Louis. 1980. *Homo Hierarchicus*. Chicago: University of Chicago Press.

Ferguson, Kennan. 2006. 'La Philosophie Américaine: James, Bergson, and the Century of Intercontinental Pluralism'. *Theory & Event* 9 (1).

Fish, Stanley. 1998. 'Truth and Toilets: Pragmatism and the Practices of Life'. In *The Revival of Pragmatism*, edited by Morris Dickstein, pp. 418–34. Durham, NC: Duke University Press.

Gandhi, Leela. 2006. *Affective Communities*. Durham, NC: Duke University Press.

Giddings, Franklin Henry. 1896. *The Principles of Sociology*. New York: Macmillan.

Goswami, Manu. 2013. '"Provincializing" Sociology: The Case of a Premature Postcolonial Sociologist'. In *Political Power and Social Theory*, Volume 24, pp. 145–75. Bingley, UK: Emerald Group.

Guru, Gopal and Sundar Sarukkai. 2012. *The Cracked Mirror*. Delhi: Oxford University Press.

Howe, Lawrence Westerby. 1987. 'The Process of Endosmosis in the Bergsonian Critique'. *The Modern Schoolman* LXV: 29–45.
Jaffrelot, Christoph. 2005. *Dr. Ambedkar and Untouchability*. New York: Columbia University Press.
James, Williams. 1904. 'The Chicago School'. *Psychological Bulletin* 1 (1, 15 January): 1–5.
———. 1975. *Pragmatism*. Cambridge, MA: Harvard University Press.
———. 1977. *Pluralistic Universe*. Cambridge, MA: Harvard University Press.
———. 2000. *Pragmatism*. New York: Penguin.
Kadam, K.N. 1997. *The Meaning of the Ambedkarite Conversion to Buddhism*. Bombay: Popular Prakashan.
Labaree, David. 2010. 'How Dewey Lost'. In *Pragmatism and Modernities*, edited by Daniel Tröhler, Thomas Schlag, and Fritz Osterwalder, pp. 163–88. Rotterdam: Sense Publishers.
Mehta, Pratap Bhanu. 2003. *The Burden of Democracy*. Delhi: Penguin.
Mukherjee, Arun. 2009. 'B.R. Ambedkar, John Dewey, and the Meaning of Democracy'. *New Literary History* 40 (2): 345–70.
Rao, Anupama. 2009. *The Caste Question*. Berkeley, CA: University of California Press.
Rodrigues, Valerian (ed.). 2002. *The Essential Writings of B.R. Ambedkar*. Delhi: Oxford University Press.
Shorie, Arun. 1997. *Worshipping False Gods: Ambedkar, and the Facts Which Have Been Erased*. New Delhi: ASA Publications.
Shotwell, James. 1964. *The Faith of an Historian and Other Essays*. New York: Walker and Company.
Skaria, Ajay. 2015. 'Ambedkar, Marx and the Buddhist Question'. *South Asia: Journal of South Asian Studies* 38 (3): 450–65.
Slate, Nico. 2013. *Colored Cosmopolitanism*. Cambridge, MA: Harvard University Press.
Viswanathan, Gauri. 1990. *Outside the Fold*. Princeton, NJ: Princeton University Press.

9

A Constellation of Ideas
*Revisiting Ambedkar and Gandhi**

PUSHPARAJ DESHPANDE

The controversial Ambedkar–Gandhi debate has continued far beyond their lives, animated by jousting, artificial attempts at reconciliation, and deliberate caricaturing of their positions. Furthermore, propaganda parading as scholarship has sought to appropriate the two.[1] These arbitrary fabrications are not just 'historical absurdities'[2] but also insult the complex vitality of their diverse ideologies. Both the 'agents ... (have) disappear(ed) as the(ir) ideas get up to do battle on their own behalf'[3] and history is reduced to 'a pack of tricks we play on the dead'.[4]

In gauging the contributions and legacies of Dr B.R. Ambedkar and M.K. Gandhi, this chapter avoids crafting an artificial synthesis. It attempts to objectively analyse the differences, both ideological and ideational, between these towering figures and the historical circumstances in which they operated. It argues that it is in their very differences that we can re-imagine the sociopolitical culture

---

* The following texts helped me formulate ideas and arguments for this chapter: Dalton (2000), Gooptu (2013), and Nauriya (2006).

[1] Gopal (1991: 339–41); Narayan (2009); Noorani (2014).
[2] Skinner (1969: 3–53).
[3] Skinner (1969: 3–53).
[4] Skinner (1969: 3–53).

of India and find strategies to more effectively address caste inequities and discrimination.

Ambedkar and Gandhi on Caste: Influence and Evolution

The most fundamental difference between Ambedkar and Gandhi was to do with caste. Given that Ambedkar saw it as the basis of untouchability and discrimination, he favoured the annihilation of the caste system. Gandhi, on the other hand, was in favour of abolishing caste-based discriminations, typified for him in untouchability, but not caste itself. This cardinal divergence would define not just their politics, but also the political culture of Independent India.

In 'Who Were the Shudras' (1946) and 'The Untouchables' (1948), Ambedkar posited that untouchability as a sociological reality was a relatively recent phenomenon. He argued that historically, when Indo-Aryan tribes were still nomadic pastoralists, there was no discriminatory stratification between the untouchables, Shudras, and Brahmins. He went on to posit that it was the advent of settled agriculture and later Buddhist opposition to sacrificial Vedic religion that led to a Brahmanical counter reaction. In his view, it was 'the political defect of Buddhism' that led to 'the (subsequent) degradation of the Shudras and the relegation of the beef-eating "broken-men" into untouchability'.[5] Evaluating the empirical basis of his assertion lies beyond the scope of this chapter. What is relevant here is that Ambedkar was not only proposing a historical basis to a state of equality, but placed the 'modern struggle for the abolition of caste … (as) a quest for a return to that primary equality that was the original historical condition of the nation'.[6]

Although they vehemently disagreed on the very notion of caste, it is noteworthy that both Ambedkar and Gandhi posited a utopian state of non-discriminatory classification of communities. Ambedkar saw this utopia in the past, while Gandhi opined it existed in the present. In eventually differentiating between caste

---

[5] Chatterjee (2004).
[6] Chatterjee (2004).

and *varna*,[7] Gandhi would argue that 'the present caste system is the very antithesis of *varnasharama*',[8] which he posited was historically a non-hierarchical and 'universal' occupational classification. Specifically, he argued that 'caste has nothing to do with religion. It is a custom whose origin I do not know ... *varna* (has) nothing to do with castes'.[9] Much earlier he had argued that 'in my conception of *varna*, no one is superior to any other ... a scavenger has the same status of a brahmin'.[10]

In this very limited aspect alone was there convergence between Ambedkar and Gandhi. Both idealized a utopian state of equality between castes, with Gandhi imagining the possibility of its existence in the present (once society cleansed itself and made clinically severed caste from varna) and Ambedkar imagining its creation in the future, drawing legitimacy from an ancient past.

In every other aspect, Ambedkar, who did acknowledge Gandhi's contribution to removing social injustices as unprecedented,[11] found Gandhi's understanding simplistic, confused, and later, regressive. Ambedkar would, over the course of two decades, provide an accurate and incisive critique of Gandhi's views, constantly highlighting numerous ideological and conceptual shortcomings. Although Ambedkar would never see this, his consistent and nuanced engagement effected a radical change in Gandhi's views on caste and varna. It is perhaps because of this nescience that Ambedkar never acknowledged the evolution in Gandhi's views or his role in it.

Three distinct periods have been delineated[12] in this evolution, and in at least two phases, Ambedkar has played a crucial role, so much so that in the last years of his life, Gandhi's views mirrored those of Ambedkar's. This aspect has been (deliberately) obfuscated since it has been exigent to fossilize their engagement as mutually antagonistic and perpetual. This caricaturing has consequently legitimatized the existence of continued rivalries and even divisive politics.

---

[7] Varna refers to the practice of stratification of society into classes as prescribed in certain Hindu texts.
[8] Gandhi (1998–2001, Volume LXII: 121).
[9] Gandhi (1998–2001, Volume LXIII: 135, 153).
[10] Gandhi (1998–2001, Volume XXXV: 260).
[11] Singh Rathore (2013: 11).
[12] Lidley (1999).

In what has been characterized as Phase I (1920s),[13] Gandhi argued in favour of continuing the caste system, stating that it had 'saved Hinduism from disintegration' and that it was 'a natural order of society'.[14] While he conceded that 'it has suffered from excrescences',[15] he continued to 'consider the four divisions (of *varnasharama*) ... to be fundamental, natural and essential'.[16] While he attacked caste discrimination and hierarchical stratification as aberrations (he argued that no one would enjoy superior status merely by virtue of the caste s/he was born in), in what would be lambasted as his most regressive belief, he argued in favour of heredity in occupational choices.

Gandhi would find no objection 'if a person belonging to one *varna* acquires the knowledge or science and art specialised in by persons to other *varnas*', but would argue that 'as far as the way earning his living is concerned, he must follow the occupation of the *varna* to which he belongs'.[17] He further argued that 'the *varna* system is to prevent competition and class struggle and class way ... because it fixes the duties and occupations of persons'.[18] Such an understanding was a stark contrast to Ambedkar's progressive views on the inalienable rights of individuals. It also implicitly endorsed the socio-economic suppression of an entire community by virtue of their birth. By Gandhi's own yardstick of *ahimsa*, such an imposition was violent (since it forced an anachronistic view onto both an individual, as well the entire community). The value of his vehement opposition to and substantial work in eradicating untouchability throughout the 1920s diminishes in light of him conflating the fight against untouchability with the fight against caste.[19] Gandhi's views on caste and varna in the 1920s are therefore simply indefensible.

In contrast, Ambedkar's views are progressive and well developed. Unlike Gandhi, he was clear about the fact that 'the division of labour brought about by the caste system is not a division based

---

[13] Lidley (1999).
[14] Gandhi (1998–2001, Volume XIX: 83).
[15] Gandhi (1998–2001, Volume XIX: 83).
[16] Gandhi (1998–2001, Volume XIX: 83).
[17] Ambedkar (1989c).
[18] Ambedkar (1989c).
[19] Roy (2015).

on choice ... (and hence subordinates) ... man's natural powers and inclinations to the exigencies of social rules'.[20] Unlike Gandhi, he also did not believe that removing untouchability would remove discrimination. He posited that 'inequality (was) inherent in the four-caste system' and hence it was the very caste system that had to be 'rooted out'.[21] He would highlight, with unerring accuracy that the 'real violence of caste was the denial of entitlement: to land, to wealth, to knowledge (and) to equal opportunity'.[22] He argued that since 'religion, social status, and property are all sources of power and authority which (allows) one man ... to control the liberty of another',[23] the caste system must be abolished. Therefore, he radically proposed that 'political revolutions (must be) preceded by social and religious revolutions'.[24]

By Phase II (1930s),[25] influenced by Ambedkar, Gandhi glacially began to modify his views on caste. It is after his meeting with Ambedkar in 1931 that Gandhi, for the first time, makes a distinction between caste and varna. He argued that 'caste, in so far as it connotes distinctions in status, is an evil ... I do however believe in *varna* which is based on hereditary occupations'.[26] Soon after, he conceded flaws in his romanticized version of varnasharma by arguing that 'the *varna* system has just now broken down',[27] and that the '*varnasharama* of the shastras is today nonexistent in practice'.[28]

Interestingly, in an effort to circumvent caste/occupational discrimination, Gandhi also tried to endorse a socialist version of professional equality by arguing that 'everyone should have equal payment, whether a barrister or a Shudra (and that) everyone should dedicate his talent to the service of the community'.[29] In a convoluted attempt to address the issue of choice, he went

---

[20] Roy (2014: 235–6).
[21] Roy (2014: 108).
[22] Roy (2014: 98).
[23] Roy (2014): 230.
[24] Roy (2014): 224.
[25] Lidley (1999).
[26] Gandhi (1998–2001, Volume XLVI: 302).
[27] Gandhi (1998–2001, Volume LI: 199).
[28] Gandhi (1998–2001, Volume LXII: 121).
[29] Gandhi (1998–2001, Volume LIII: 484).

on to argue that 'boys (between nine and 16 years of age) should be taught their parents' vocation in such a way that they will by their own choice obtain their livelihood by practicing the hereditary craft ... (From 16–25) ... every young person should have an education according to his or her wishes and circumstances'.[30] Whether there is any real agency left in the choice an individual makes once they have been thus socialized at a formative age is entirely debatable. Therefore, Gandhi's attempt at resolving the very pertinent question Ambedkar raises is feeble. Moreover, Ambedkar rightly dismissed Gandhi's suggestion that professional equality would eliminate caste discriminations by arguing that 'there will be outcastes as long as there are castes, and nothing can emancipate the outcaste except the destruction of the caste system'.[31]

In reply to Ambedkar's masterly 'Annihilation of Caste' (1936), Gandhi again sought to provide validity for his conceptual differentiation between caste and varna. He argued that 'caste has nothing to do with religion. It is a custom whose origin I do not know ... *varna* (has) nothing to do with castes. The law of *varna* teaches us that we have each one of us to earn our daily bread by following the ancestral calling ... The essence of Hinduism is contained in its enunciation of the one and only God as truth and its bold acceptance of ahimsa as the law of the human family.'[32]

Gandhi was implicitly suggesting that high-caste Hindus should transform their attitudes (by divorcing caste and varna, thereby leaving aside discrimination, and using varna merely as a non-discriminatory vocational organizing principle). He thus seemed to be suggesting that 'a person's varna ought to be decided by their worth and not their birth'.[33] In a devastating counter response to this, Ambedkar argued:

> The Mahatma seems to me to suggest ... that Hindu society can be made tolerable and even happy without any fundamental change in its structure if all high caste Hindus can be persuaded to follow a high standard of morality in their dealings with the low caste Hindus. I am totally opposed to this kind of ideology ... how can

---

[30] Gandhi (1998–2001, Volume L: 233).
[31] Ambedkar (1933), quoted in Wolpert (2001).
[32] Gandhi (1998–2001, Volume LXIII: 135, 153).
[33] Roy (2014: 42).

you expect personal character to make a man loaded with consciousness of caste a good man ... a good Hindu there cannot be. This is not because there is anything wrong with his personal character. In fact, what is wrong is the entire basis of his relationship to his fellows.[34]

In critiquing Gandhi's continued attempts at differentiating between caste and varna, Ambedkar further argued:

> I must admit that the vedic theory of varna as interpreted by Swami Dayanand and some others is a sensible and an inoffensive thing; it did not determine birth as a determining factor in fixing the place of an individual in society. It only recognised worth. The Mahatma's views of varna ... makes nonsense of the vedic varna (and) makes it into an abominable thing. Varna and caste are two very different concepts. Varna is based on the principle of each according to his worth, while caste is based on the principle of each according to his birth. The two are as distinct as chalk from cheese.[35]

Quoting from two of Gandhi's earlier articles, Ambedkar skilfully exposed Gandhi's confusion on caste and varna. Specifically, he argued

> Does he regard varna as the essence of Hinduism? One cannot as yet give a categorical answer. Readers of his article on 'Dr. Ambedkar's Indictment' will answer 'No'. In that article he does not say that the dogma of varna is an essential part of the creed of Hinduism. Far from making varna the creed of Hindusim, he says, 'the essence of Hinduism is contained in its enunciation of the one and only God as truth and its bold acceptance of ahimsa as the law of the human family'. But readers of his (other) article will say 'Yes'. In that article he says, 'I do not know how a person who rejects caste, i.e. varna, can call himself a Hindu...'.
> The real reason why the Mahatma is suffering from this confusion is probably to be traced to two sources. The first is the temperament of the Mahatma. He has almost in everything the simplicity of the child with the child's capacity for self-deception ... The second course of confusion is the double role which the Mahatma wants to play—of a mahatma and a politician. As a mahatma, he may be trying to spiritualise politics ... (but) the reason the mahatma is always

[34] Lidley (1999).
[35] Lidley (1999).

supporting caste and varna because he is afraid that if he opposes them he will lose his place in politics.[36]

Ambedkar was undoubtedly accurate in pinpointing Gandhi's lack of clarity about caste and varna. However, to attribute any malicious intent and tacit support of caste (and that too for personal aggrandizement) to Gandhi was unmerited.

By Phase III (1940s),[37] Gandhi's views had undergone a complete transformation, partly because of Ambedkar's radical influence, and party because of his engagement with high- and low-caste Hindus. In 1946, he would tell one of his colleagues that '[he] should become like Ambedkar. You should work for the removal of untouchability and caste.'[38] It has been rightly argued that Gandhi 'recognising the validity of some of his (Ambedkar's) criticisms ... pursued a more radical approach to caste-reform'.[39] As if in reaction to Ambedkar's criticism that Gandhism stands for the iron law of hereditary professions in respect of the SCs, Gandhi stated in December 1947 that a *bhangi*[40] 'should not be forced to clean laboratories today' and that 'if he can become a barrister, he should not be prevented from doing so'.[41]

It has been counterargued that Gandhi's views were 'loaded with caveats and subtleties', where 'he *simultaneously* speaks of the abhorrence of untouchability, equality of all, the freedom for all to pursue their hobbies or interests whatever their caste and class, and the mandate that a person's livelihood ought *nevertheless* to be dictated by that of his forefathers'. Such a reading obfuscates timelines because while it quotes Gandhi from the 1920s and early 1930s, it overlooks his radically different opinions on the subject from the 1940s. In establishing Gandhi's views on varnashrama as 'one of the principle bedrocks for the irreconcilability of Gandhi and Ambedkar', this reading discounts, and hence calcifies, the evolution of thought in Gandhi.[42]

---

[36] Lidley (1999).

[37] Lidley (1999).

[38] Interview with Arjun Rao, Gora's son-in-law, February 1996, quoted in Lidley (1999).

[39] Pantham (2009).

[40] A sweeper or manual scavenger who was one of the lowest amongst the SCs (Dalits).

[41] Pantham (2009).

[42] Singh Rathore (2013: 21–2).

Gandhi would eventually argue for the retention of only one varna that he characterized as *Ati-shudras* that was to comprise of all Hindus. In his ideal version of society, 'all religions will naturally be held equal ... all quarrels arising out of religion, caste and economic differences will be ended. This is the *swaraj* of my dreams ... I am devoting every breath of my life to that effort'. He went on to extoll his interlocutors to 'discard anything ... (which he had said earlier) which may appear ... incompatible with my views given above'.[43]

Perhaps the most definitive example of this radical transformation in Gandhi's thought was his evolved notion of inter-caste marriage, which Ambedkar himself endorsed as the 'structural anecdote'[44] to the caste system. He posited that 'the real remedy (to ending caste discrimination) is intermarriage. Fusion of blood can alone create the feeling of being kith and kin, and unless this feeling ... becomes paramount, the separatist feeling-the feeling of being aliens-created by caste will not vanish ...'.[45] Influenced by Ambedkar, Gandhi, who had earlier only sanctioned inter-caste marriages, now began to exclusively recommend them as panaceas to segregation. He argued 'if ... castes and sub-castes as we know them disappear—as they should—we should unhesitatingly accord the highest importance to marriages between Ati-Shudras and caste Hindus'.[46]

That Ambedkar was instrumental in changing Gandhi's views on caste has been neatly assigned to the dustbin of history, and both giants have been (deliberately) frozen in perpetual battle. However, there is some merit to the argument that Gandhi's views evolved at a glacial pace.[47] It took him nearly two decades to come over to Ambedkar's position and he has been rightly lambasted for this. Criticisms have ranged from the considerate to the uncharitable. On the considerate end of the spectrum, it has been argued that Gandhi was too preoccupied with other struggles (political and welfare oriented) which were interspersed with long periods of internment.[48] On the uncharitable spectrum, it has been argued

---

[43] Gandhi (1998–2001, Volume LXXX: 222).
[44] Lidley (1999).
[45] Lidley (1999).
[46] Gandhi (1998–2001, Volume LXXX: 77).
[47] Roy (2014).
[48] Palshikar (1996); Krishnan (2011); Nanda (1994); Radhakrishnan (1968).

that he lacked adequate commitment (to eliminating caste inequalities) and that there was malicious intent to keep the Shudras and untouchables in their place within the *varnashrama* (for personal political gain).[49]

Problematizing Gandhi and the Congress

A key variable that is overlooked in such contextual assessments is that Gandhi's control over the Congress Party was extremely tenuous, and he exerted limited influence over its political agents. This greatly stunted his ability to affect any kind of policy shift in the party's agenda, try as much as he did.[50] In arguing that 'we hope to become the representatives of the poorest of the poor, the lowest of the low and the weakest of the weak',[51] he repeatedly tried to induce the Congress to take up more substantive issues and to forge an organic connect with the 'toiling voiceless millions'.[52] However, in this, he met with only limited success and his efforts were repeatedly thwarted.

For instance, Non-cooperation Movement witnessed only a temporary shift of leadership to Gandhi. After the movement's withdrawal and Gandhi's subsequent imprisonment in 1922, the old guard of the Congress systematically dismantled everything Gandhi had attempted to institutionalize. After Chauri Chaura, the movement's withdrawal and the loss of political capital for Gandhi, the followers of Tilak—high-caste Hindus who formed the bulk of the Swaraj Party—made a concerted effort to revert back to the old agenda and actively spurned Gandhi's efforts at forging a new constituency or any involvement in constructive work.[53] Mostly drawn from India's most influential opinion makers, the Swarajists dominated the Congress organization, and any breach would have effectively retarded the national movement.[54] This was a specially sensitive issue given the Congress had already seen

---

[49] Roy (2015); Ambedkar (1945); Sagar (2019); Nanda (1994).
[50] Gandhi (1998–2001, Volume XXIV: 13); Ramagundam (2008: 172, 137, 152); Nanda (2007: 234); Gandhi (1998–2001, Volume XXVIII: 86–8).
[51] Ramagundam (2008): 169.
[52] Ramagundam (2008: 169); Krishnan (2011: 1–39).
[53] Ramagundam (2008: 137, 152); Nanda (2007: 234).
[54] Gandhi (1998–2001, Volume XXV: 352).

two major fragmentations, when Annie Besant and her followers left the Congress because of an ideological disagreement over non-cooperation, and when Pandit Madan Mohan Malviya and Lala Lajpat Rai broke away and founded the Nationalist Party which contested elections against the Congress in the mid-1920s.[55]

Furthermore, at Gandhi's insistence, the Congress Working Committee (CWC) adopted a 'Constructive Programme of Social Amelioration' in February 1922, which resolved 'to organise the Depressed Classes for a better life to improve their social, mental and moral condition, to induce them to send their children to national schools and to provide for them the ordinary facilities which the other citizens enjoyed'.[56] In June 1922, the CWC appointed a committee, under the chairmanship of Swami Shraddhanand and consisting of Sarojini Naidu, I.K. Yagnik, and G.B. Deshpande, to operationalize this resolution. However, Swami Shraddhanand, who Ambedkar hailed as one of the 'most sincere champion of the untouchables' within the Congress, was eased out by the other members of the committee.[57] This was then followed by systematic efforts to undermine the constructive programme, as was highlighted in the correspondence between Vithalbhai Patel and Motilal Nehru, and the general secretaries of the Congress Party.[58] In May 1923, the CWC outsourced the programme in its entirety to the All India Hindu Mahasabha.[59]

Gandhi was thus constantly engaged with avoiding the actual (and perceived) fragmentation of organizational unity. After a 'decade long hegemonic contention'[60] between 'Gandhi's realism and the Congress' exigent pragmatism',[61] Gandhi was forced to cede leadership of the organization to the old guard. 'The Congress ... (which) had witnessed a gradual painful shift ... from being debating bodies to activity centred associations ... (had now) reverted to its earlier status'.[62] By 1928, Gandhi had effectively retired from active

---

[55] Bonney (2004).
[56] Ambedkar, cited in Moon (1990).
[57] Ambedkar, cited in Moon (1990).
[58] Moon (1990).
[59] Moon (1990).
[60] Gandhi (1998–2001, Volume XXIV: 13); Ramagundam (2008: 172).
[61] Gandhi (1998–2001, Volume XXIV: 13); Ramagundam (2008: 172).
[62] Gandhi (1998–2001, Volume XXVIII: 86–8).

politics and distanced himself from the Congress when he confided in Motilal Nehru that 'I know that part of the national work is also useful, but my heart has gone out of it and I become more and more inclined to give my time to what is consciously understood as constructive work'.[63] It is noteworthy that throughout this period, and preceding any engagement with Ambedkar, Gandhi actively undertook constructive work against untouchability.

It is only at the 1929 Lahore Congress (after nearly eight years) that Gandhi regained active (but not absolute) leadership of the Congress. He was incarcerated soon after his first major political activity (Civil Disobedience) and the consequent Round Table Conference. Again, his leadership was severely criticized by no less than Subhas C. Bose and Vithalbhai Patel who argued that 'Mr. Gandhi as a political leader has failed', and called for a 'radical re-organisation of the Congress on a new principle with a new method, for which a new leader is needed'.[64]

Nevertheless, Gandhi could have laboured on his moral crusade without the Congress and even joined hands with Ambedkar. Unfortunately, by the time Gandhi saw merit in Ambedkar's understanding of caste and his solutions for redressing casteism, it was too late.

Resistance With-out and Within

Ambedkar was right in pointing out that Gandhi consciously contextualized the struggle against untouchability within his larger politics and did not really attack the caste system (until the 1940s). Ironically, this is precisely because of how Gandhi conceptualized his politics.

With his deeply ingrained belief of the need to 'spiritualise politics',[65] Gandhi would, throughout his career, base the vocabulary of his political morality in Hinduism.[66] In positioning himself inside mainstream Hinduism (the *sanathan dharma*[67]) and

[63] Gandhi (1998–2001, Volume XXXVII: 318).
[64] Sitaramayya (1935: 768).
[65] Deshpande (2014b).
[66] Brown (1977: 14–15).
[67] Sanatana dharma is used to denote the 'eternal' set of duties or practices incumbent upon all Hindus, regardless of class, caste, or sect.

radically redefining it, Gandhi emphasized the ultimate unity of all life and equated 'moksha' with service of mankind, which could only be achieved through selfless dedication to social and constructive work.[68]

While this undoubtedly transformed the Congress Party into a movement,[69] it also 'Hinduized' the Congress. This 'Hinduis(ation) of the national movement, which Gandhi's leadership promoted and symbolised'[70] attracted numerous Hindus into the Congress's fold, some of whom were conservative and had little sympathy either with his interpretation of Hinduism or the secular principles that the rest of the Congress leadership endorsed. These gradually formed the larger part of the social composition of the Congress organization at the provincial level (and somewhat at the national level),[71] and covertly hindered programmes at reforming Hinduism or aimed at ending caste inequities.

Despite this, driven by his spiritual imperatives and Ambedkar's charges (first at the Round Table Conference and then during the Poona Pact deliberations), Gandhi would engage almost exclusively with Harijan issues after his release from prison in 1933 (he would undertake a first of its kind nationwide 'Harijan Tour' exclusively to abolish untouchability and caste inequalities. Along with that, he started a newsletter titled *Harijan*,[72] whose chief purpose was to propagate the removal of untouchability). He situated the struggle to eliminate caste discriminations within the larger framework of cleansing the self and Hinduism itself. Giving a damning indictment of Hinduism, he argued that

> Socially, they (untouchables) are lepers. Economically, they are worse. Religiously, they are denied entrances to places we miscall houses of God. They are denied the use, on the same terms as Hindus, of public roads, public schools, public hospitals, public wells, public taps, public parks and the like ... they are relegated for their residence to the worst quarters of cities and villages where they get no social services.[73]

[68] Deshpande (2014b).
[69] Deshpande (2014b).
[70] Moon (1968: 276).
[71] Mallick (2013: 96–112); Clarke (2002: 350–1).
[72] Originally started as *Young India*, Gandhi converted it to *Harijan*, as part of his politics after the Poona Pact in 1932.
[73] Tendulkar (1951, Volume 3: 159–245; Volume 4: 14–63).

In the course of his nine-month Harijan tour, he undertook two major fasts (8 May 1933 and 16 August 1933) to convince high-caste Hindus of the urgent need to eliminate caste discriminations. His reasoning was that 'if untouchability is removed, it must result in bringing all Indians together',[74] 'in unbreakable heart unity'.[75] In fact, in separating caste as an 'evil' aberration of the varna system, a universal theme in almost all his speeches and articles during this period, was for the high caste Hindus to do 'penance' and 'make reparations ... for the untold hardships to which we have subject them (untouchables) for centuries'.[76]

Given his unique interpretation of moksha, he imagined that these 'reparations' would be in the form of high-caste Hindus performing *seva* (service) for the untouchables, both to uplift them and to end caste discrimination through attitudinal reformations. He would thus argue that high-caste Hindus must organically shift towards 'a spiritual self-rule that stem(med) from the self-disciplined, self-realised individual, liberated from attitudes of exclusivity, (and) absolved from any particularistic identify'.[77]

This produced a vitriolic opposition by the orthodoxy, spearheaded by the Rashtriya Swayamsevak Sangh (RSS) and the Hindu Mahasabha. He was routinely met with black-flag demonstrations and his prayer meets were disrupted. Inflammatory leaflets denouncing him and his aims were widely circulated, and his portraits/effigies were publicly burnt at mass demonstrations. In June 1934, a car believed to be carrying Gandhi was bombed. Even within the councils, this vehement opposition brought about the defeat of the Temple Entry Bill (August 1934). Gandhi would react by defiantly arguing that 'they [high caste Hindus] must either remove untouchability or remove me from their midst'.[78]

In vain, Gandhi even tried to temper his perceived radicalism to convince the orthodoxy to end caste-based discriminations. Towards the end of his life, Gandhi regretted that 'the tragedy is that those

[74] Tendulkar (1951, Volume 3: 159–245).
[75] Tendulkar (1951, Volume 4: 14–63).
[76] Kher (1976: 142).
[77] Shani (2011).
[78] Mukherjee et al. (2000).

who should have especially devoted themselves to the work of (caste) reform did not put their hearts into it. What wonder that Harijan brethren feel suspicious and show opposition and bitterness'.[79]

It is because of this vehement opposition, both within and with-out, that Gandhi may have abandoned his idealistic plans for transforming Hinduism and conceded Ambedkar's position, namely that the caste system had to go. To ignore the very real pressures that he had to grapple and work with is to ignore not just how radical and unprecedented Gandhi's programme was, but also the tremendous resistance to it at the time. This is not to condone his shortcomings but simply to contextualize the historical and sociological circumstances in which he was operating—something that retrospective analyses tend to overlook.

Ideological Irreconcilabilities

There are at least two other areas of conceptual divergence between Ambedkar and Gandhi that are irreconcilable. The first has to do with their views on the rural and the urban, while the other has to do with the method of effecting a social transformation in India. By studying these fundamental differences, we can critically analyse the nuances of their ideologies and evolve better strategies to address caste inequalities.

Ambedkar admired the urban and dismissed the rural as a 'sink of localism, a den of ignorance, narrow-mindedness, and communalism'.[80] He went on to argue that the village represented 'a kind of colonialism of the Hindus designed to exploit the Untouchables ... (who) have no rights. They are there only to wait, serve and submit. They are there to do or to die. They have no rights because they are outside the village republic and because they are outside the so-called republic ... (and) the Hindu fold'.[81] He thus damningly linked the village to casteism, and argued that 'it (the village) is a ... *cordon sanitaire* putting the impure people inside the barbed wire

---

[79] Singh Rathore (2017).

[80] Volume VII, Document 48, paragraph 232, Constituent Assembly Debates, 4 November 1948. Available at https://www.constitutionofindia.net/constitution_assembly_debates/volume/7/1948-11-04; last accessed 4 April 2020.

[81] Moon (1989a).

into a sort of a cage. Every Hindu village has a ghetto ... (where) the Untouchables live'.[82]

In stark contrast, Gandhi imagined India as a 'confederation of self-governing, self-reliant and self-employed people living in village communities, deriving their right livelihood from the product of their homesteads'.[83] Defining the nation as a *praja* (that he saw as neutral to religion, caste, language, and so on), he imagined the village as an association of families aimed at a higher level of self-sufficiency and human existence. While Gandhi's romanticized ideal of these villages (that he parochially titled *Ram Rajya*) emphasized existence that was equitable and ethical, it is also true that it was mythical. His conceptualization was starkly opposed to what reality in the village was, which Ambedkar assessed accurately. In imagining this utopian village ideal as a programmatic goal for Independent India, he told Nehru in 1945, '[Y]ou must not imagine that I am envisaging our village life as it is today. The village of my dreams is still in my mind'.[84]

It is my contention that Gandhi's idealized 'pre-modern organisation of human society and economy' and Ambedkar's 'pro-enlightenment modernism' cannot be divorced from each other because the two seemingly diagrammatic visions are actually complementary.[85] It can be argued that the urban-industrial vision of modernity, entwined as it is with the concept of the modern Indian State, has subtly reinforced exclusion and discrimination on caste lines.

The effort to 'replace the rural (characterised as unorganised, polluted and deprived of resources) with the urban (characterised as a systemised, uncontaminated mega polis abundant with power and water, among other resources) is deeply flawed ... (because) the poor are either un-favourably included by law, or completely excluded',[86] on many grounds, including caste. The concept of purity (and hence exclusion), which is central to casteism, is equally pervasive in urban spaces. For example, it has been pointed out that middle- and upper-class neighbourhoods

---

[82] Moon (1989b).
[83] Deshpande (2015).
[84] Singh Rathore (2013: 23).
[85] Cited in Singh Rathore (2013: 21–2).
[86] Deshpande (2015).

(that may or may not be upper caste) foster casteist attitudes whilst dealing with various staff and service providers. In fact, most of the city's underclass comprises of low caste migrants, and the contractual employment they find does not dissolve ascriptive caste identities.[87] Similarly, the organization of urban geographies invariably ends up mirroring the ghettoization of untouchables prevalent in the village.

Seen in this light, Ambedkar's faith in the urban space as a panacea to casteism was misplaced. This is not to contend that the village is not 'paradigmatic of the oppressive social system' or that Gandhi's faith in village republics was justified, but that the segregation of and discrimination against Dalits continue in diverse forms within the urban space.[88] This is simply because the set of beliefs that shape the caste system are not diluted because of migration and are, in fact, re-deployed in different ways and contexts. This 're-deployment of caste' continues to limit social, political, and economic opportunities for Dalits.

The reason for this 'redeployment' is largely because caste-based prejudice is learned, proselytized, and propagated and, therefore, continues to shape the dynamics of societal relations. It is in this context that Gandhi's emphasis on self-reformation (to cleanse attitudes and beliefs) needs to be revisited. In advocating the reconfiguring of the 'terms of engagement' between low- and high-caste Hindus, Gandhi consistently downplayed the contention that Dalits were not part of the Hindu fold. Conceding that they were not a part of the Hindu fold would have strained the scripturally sanctioned paternal-filial connection between castes that was socially accepted. In discussing this, no endorsement of the perversity of the obvious paternalism is offered.

In fact, Gandhi consciously played on the belief in this connection to motivate high-caste Hindus to 'cleanse' this bond of attitudinal regressiveness and hence to 'reform' their engagement with the Dalit communities. This is not to argue the merits of his ideology but to draw attention to his argument that without effecting an organic transformation in India's civilizational consciousness, people would instantiate and reinforce existing structures of caste.

---

[87] See Vithayathil and Singh (2012); Sidhwani (2015); Kundu (2011); and Sahoo (2016).

[88] Sahoo (2016). Also see Vithayathil and Singh (2012).

Although Ambedkar held similar views in this respect (he argued that 'if the fundamental rights are opposed by the community, no Law, no Parliament, no Judiciary can guarantee them in the real sense of the word'[89]), he almost exclusively vested his faith in the State and a constitutional revolution. In his view, only a legally sanctioned rule of law (that would replace the religiously sanctioned rule of law) would ensure that Dalits got their due and were treated equitably. While it is true that the State has by and large adhered to Ambedkar's vision, the depth of caste consciousness in India and the stratagems that ensure its resilience have not received adequate 'tactical' attention.

It is in this context that the notion of two separate rules of law is discussed. In India, there exists a 'law of the land', which the Constituent Assembly and, later, various governments spearheaded and implemented with varying degrees of success. Covertly resisting and opposing this supra framework exist various dominant communities (who also dominate the State apparatus responsible for the implementation of the law of the land) who religiously adhere to the 'law in the land', which stands in opposition to the secular norms enshrined in the Constitution of India and draws inspiration from similar scriptures that Ambedkar so vociferously decried.

Given this conceptual friction between the two sets of laws, new forms of caste conditions have emerged, most notably, caste resentment. This resentment originates from prejudices stemming from competition over real and symbolic resources and privileges. Consequently, equality of opportunity and status was and is a norm followed more in the breach. Consider that despite reservation in government services, only 11.5 per cent of the A-class administrative positions in India are occupied by Dalits,[90] while 95 per cent of Dalits are clustered in Classes C and D[91] in what can only be characterized as 'inclusionary exclusion'.[92] Similarly, only 8.4 per cent of the A-grade officers in central public sector enterprises belong to scheduled castes. Because of

---

[89] Ambedkar (1979: 222), quoted in Roy (2014: 21).

[90] Government of India, Ministry of Personnel, Public Grievances and Pensions, Rajya Sabha, Unstarred Question No. 3040, answered on 20 December 2012.

[91] Thorat and Senapati (2007).

[92] Adapted from Deshpande (2014a).

these caste-based glass ceilings, it was estimated that over 113,450 job opportunities were lost by Dalits in the central government over a period of ten years.[93]

Similarly, it has been pointed out that Dalits are routinely excluded from employment in the private sector and that applicants are purposefully scrutinized through the lens of caste (to sift out Dalit candidates). A first of its kind survey on the social profiles of 315 senior decision-makers in 37 newspapers and television channels found that 90 per cent of the decision-makers in the English-language print media and 79 per cent in television were upper caste. Not a single one of these 315 was a Dalit. Perhaps the most telling figure that reveals how caste continues to exclude is that 95 per cent of Dalits and Adivasis are employed in the unorganized sector, which is synonymous with low wages and lack of employment or social security.

Testament to the prevalence of caste within the administrative apparatus, it has also been pointed out that the higher the percentage of village-based Dalits in a district, the lower the level of public services. For instance, Dalits have limited access to basic healthcare services. About 62.1 per cent of Dalit households across India have limited or no access to basic sanitation infrastructure while only 21 per cent of Dalit households have drinking water sources located in or near the houses. With regard to land ownership 'nearly 70% of Dalit households either do not own land or have very small landholdings of less than 0.4 hectare'.[94] Finally, despite a number of laws and policies, incidents of caste discrimination and atrocities have consistently increased.

To reiterate, caste and caste discrimination continue to exist because individuals continue to believe in them and perpetuate them. These individuals are members of numerous regressive associations that seek to uphold the caste structure, and hence prescribe conservative scriptural rules. Consistently influencing and infiltrating governments, these overtly and covertly challenge the sovereign position of the State. The State, which, in the Weberian imagination, can only enforce its authority through violence, has been unable to impose constitutional norms effectively primarily because of this.

---

[93] National Coalition for Strengthening PoA Act (2012: Paragraph 31).
[94] Thorat (2009: 28).

The problem is exacerbated because a large section of society has been socialized to orthodox norms that these associations have consistently proselytized. Seen in this light, Gandhi's insistence on seeking the attitudinal reformation of dominant communities (and hence a change in societal norms) through sociopolitical movements has some validity. His point was that society should be organized on the basis of 'voluntary co-operation', not on the basis of 'compulsory co-operation' (which is what the Weberian State can achieve). In this, Ambedkar (a steadfast constitutionalist) and the Congress Party's faith in the State as the only means of actualizing a social revolution was over-pitched.

There is thus an urgent need for a bottom-up socio-economic and political movement that seeks to socialize India to constitutional norms. In actualizing this movement, it would be expedient to remember that both Ambedkar and Gandhi firmly believed in ahimsa as the fundamental principle of organizing a nation, as well as 'resolving conflicts between nations, peoples and socio-political groups',[95] another area of convergence between the two giants that is often overlooked.

* * *

In the end, it must be acknowledged that for too long have Ambedkar and Gandhi been either 'reduce(d) to a common denominator … (or) pit(ted) in intractable, atomic opposition'.[96] While the discourse that surrounds them, both genuine and instrumental, provides us a rich panorama of strategies for the present, what must be recognized is that it is through the interplay of their very differences that we can re-conceptualize the political culture of India and holistically address caste inequities and discrimination.

Therefore, it has been rightly suggested that 'rather than attempting to reconcile (them) in a move that puts harmony and resolution in the foreground and differences in the background … we must … bring these two great men into a *constellation*'.[97] That is the only way we can both deepen and further the promise of India.

[95] Shepherd ([1999] 2004).
[96] Singh Rathore (2013: 28).
[97] Singh Rathore (2013: 27).

References

Ambedkar, B.R. 1945. *What Congress and Gandhi Have Done to the Untouchables*. Bombay: Thacker and Co.

———. 1948. *The Untouchables, Who Were They and Why They Became Untouchables*. New Delhi: October.

Bonney, Richard (ed.). 2004. Three Giants of South Asia: Gandhi, Ambedkar and Jinnah on Self Determination. Leicester: University of Leicester.

Brown, J.M. 1977. Gandhi and Civil Disobedience: The Mahatma in Indian Politics, 1928–34. Cambridge: Cambridge University Press.

Chatterjee, Partha. 2004. *The Politics of the Governed: Reflections on Popular Politics in Most of the World*. New York: Columbia University Press.

Clarke, Peter. 2002. The Cripps Version: The Life of Sir Stafford Cripps 1899–1952. London: Allen Lane.

Dalton, D. 2000. *Mahatma Gandhi: Non-violent Power in Action*. New York: Columbia University Press.

Deshpande, Pushparaj. 2014a. 'Exclusionary Inclusion'. *Economic and Political Weekly* XLIX (48).

———. 2014b. 'Recreating the Congress Movement'. *Economic & Political Weekly* XLIX (32): 23–5.

———. 2015. 'Ruralisation: Reconceptualising India's Civilisational Basis', *Rajya Sabha Television*, 3 November. Available at http://www.rajyasabhatv.com/ruralisation-reconceptualising-indias-civilisational-basis-2.html, last accessed 7 September 2016.

Gandhi, Mohandas K. 1998–2001. The Collected Works of Mahatma Gandhi, 98 Vols. New Delhi: Publications Division, Government of India.

Gooptu, N. 2013. 'Servile Sentinels of the City: Private Security Guards, Organized Informality, and Labour in Interactive Services in Globalized India'. *International Review of Social History* 58 (1).

Guru, Gopal. 1991. 'Hinduisation of Ambedkar in Maharashtra'. *Economic & Political Weekly* 26 (7): 339–41.

Kher, V.B. (ed.). 1976. 'Social Service, Work & Reform', Ahmedabad: Navjivan Publishing Press. Available athttps://www.mkgandhi.org/ebks/social-service-work-reform-vol-III.pdf; last accessed 3 April 2020.

Kundu, Amitabh. 2011. 'The Trends and Processes of Urbanization in India'. Human Settlements Group International Institute for Environment and Development and United Nations Population Fund. Available at http://pubs.iied.org/pdfs/10597IIED.pdf; last accessed 4 April 2020.

Krishnan, P. 2011. 'Synthesising the Gandhi–Ambedkar–Narayanaguru–Marx Visions for Dalit Liberation'. *Social Change* 41 (1): 1–39.

Available at http://indiaenvironmentportal.org.in/files/Gandhi_1.pdf, last accessed 23 June 2019.

Lidley, Mark. 1999. 'Changes in Mahatma Gandhi's Views on Caste and Intermarriage'. Available at http://www.academia.edu/1184254/Changes_in_Mahatma_Gandhi_s_views_on_caste_and_intermarriage, last accessed 28 September 2015.

Mallick, Ayub. 2013. 'Ideology of the Indian National Congress: Political Economy of Socialism and Socialistic Pattern of Society'. *IOSR Journal Of Humanities And Social Science* 12 (2): 96–112.

Moon, P. 1968. *Gandhi and Modern India*. London: English Universities Press.

Moon, Vasant (ed.). 1989a. 'The Indian Ghetto: The Centre of Untouchability, utside the Fold'. *Dr Babasaheb Ambedkar: Writings and Speeches*, Volume 5. Mumbai: Education Department, Government of Maharashtra. Available at https://www.mea.gov.in/Images/attach/amb/Volume_05.pdf; last accessed 4 April 2020.

———. 1989b. 'Untouchability amongst Hindus'. *Dr Babasaheb Ambedkar Writings and Speeches*, Volume 7. Mumbai: Education Department, Government of Maharashtra. Available at https://www.mea.gov.in/Images/attach/amb/Volume_07.pdf; last accessed 4. April 2020.

———. 1989c. 'What Congress and Gandhi Have Done to the Untouchables'. *Dr Babasaheb Ambedkar: Writings and Speeches*, Volume 9. Mumbai: Education Department, Government of Maharashtra. Available at https://www.mea.gov.in/Images/attach/amb/Volume_09.pdf; last accessed 2 July 2020.

———. 1990. *Dr. Babasaheb Ambedkar Writings and Speeches*, Volume 9, Part I, pp. 240–2. Mumbai: Education Department, Government of Maharashtra.

Mukherjee, Aditya, Bipan Chandra, K.N. Panikkar, Mridula Mukherjee, and Sucheta Mahajan. 2000. *India's Struggle for Independence*. Penguin India.

Nanda, B.R. 1994. *Gandhi and His Critics*. New Delhi: Oxford University Press.

———. 2007. The *Nehrus—Motilal and Jawaharlal*. New Delhi: Oxford University Press.

Narayan, Badri. 2009. Fascinating Hindutva: Saffron Politics and Dalit Mobilisation. New Delhi: Sage.

National Coalition for Strengthening PoA Act. 2012. *Joint Stakeholders Report on Caste Based Discrimination in India*. Submitted at 13th Session of the Universal Periodic Review of the UN Human Rights Council, National Campaign on Dalit Human Rights, India, NCDHR.

Nauriya, Anil. 2006. 'Gandhi's Little-known Critique of Varna'. *Economic and Political Weekly* 1 (19): 1835–8.

Noorani, A.G. 2014. 'Ambedkar & the BJP'. *Frontline*, 5 February. Available at http://www.frontline.in/politics/ambedkar-the-bjp/article5643057.ece, last accessed 28 September 2015.

Palshikar, Suhas. 1996. 'Gandhi–Ambedkar Interface: ... When Shall the Twain Meet?'. *Economic and Political Weekly* 31 (31): 2070–2.

Pantham. 2009. 'Against Untouchability: The Discourses of Gandhi and Ambedkar'. In *Humiliation: Claims and Context*, edited by Gopal Guru, pp. 179–208. New Delhi: Oxford University Press.

Radhakrishnan, S. (ed.). 1968. *Mahatma Gandhi—100 Years*. New Delhi: Gandhi Peace Foundation.

Ramagundam, Rahul. 2008. *Gandhi's Khadi*. New Delhi: Orient Longman, Gandhi Smriti, and Darshan Samiti.

Roy, Arundhati. 2014. 'The Doctor and the Saint' (Introduction). In B.R. Ambedkar, *Annihilation of Caste*. New Delhi: Navayana.

———. 2015. 'All the World's a Half-Built Dam—A Response to Rajmohan Gandhi's "Independence and Social Justice: The Ambedkar-Gandhi Debate"'. *Economic and Political Weekly* 50 (25).

Sagar. 2019. 'Give Us a Statue of Ambedkar, Not Gandhi: Ghana University Professor Ọbádélé Kambon'. *The Caravan*, 13 January. Available at https://caravanmagazine.in/caste/gandhi-must-fall-interview, last accessed 24 June 2019.

Sahoo, Niranjan. 2016. 'A Tale of Three Cities: India's Exclusionary Urbanisation'. Observer Research Foundation Issue Brief, Issue No. 156, September. Available at https://www.orfonline.org/wp-content/uploads/2016/09/ORF_IssueBrief_156.pdf, last accessed 23 June 2019.

Shani, Ornit. 2011. 'Gandhi, Citizenship and the Resilience of Indian Nationhood'. *Citizenship Studies* 15 (6–7): 659–78.

Shepherd, Kancha Ilaiah. [1999] 2004. 'Hindutva and the War-Loving Self'. In *Buffalo Nationalism—A Critique of Spiritual Fascism*, edited by Kancha Ilaiah Shepherd, pp. 54–5. Kolkata: SAMYA.

Sidhwani, Pranav. 2015. 'Spatial Inequalities in Big Indian Cities'. *Economic and Political Weekly* L (22): 55–62.

Singh Rathore, Aakash. 2013 'Gandhi and Ambedkar: Irreconcilable Differences?'. *International Journal of Gandhi Studies* 2.

———. 2017. *Indian Political Theory: Laying the Groundwork for Svaraj*. New York: Routledge.

Sitaramayya, Pattabhi. 1935. *The History of the Indian National Congress 1885–1935*. Mumbai: Padma Publications.

Skinner, Quentin. 1969. 'Meaning and Understanding in the History of Ideas'. *History and Theory* 8 (1): 3–53. Available at http://sydney.edu.au/intellectual-history/documents/skinner-meaning.pdf, last accessed 28 September 2015.

Tendulkar, D.G. 1951. *Mahatma: Life of Mohandas Karamchand Gandhi*. Available at http://www.mkgandhi.org/imp_bks_mahatma.html, last accessed 28 September 2015.

Thorat, S. and C. Senapati. 2007. 'Reservation in Employment, Education and Legislature—Status and Emerging Issue'. Working Paper Series, Volume II, No. 5, Indian Institute of Dalit Studies, New Delhi, India.

Thorat, S.K. 2009. *Dalits in India: Search for a Common Destiny*. New Delhi: Sage.

Vithayathil, Trina and Gayatri Singh. 2012. 'Spaces of Discrimination: Residential Segregation in the Indian Cities'. *Economic and Political Weekly* XLVII (37): 60–6.

Wolpert, Stanley. 2001. *Gandhi's Passion: The Life and Legacy of Mahatma Gandhi*. New York: Oxford University Press.

10

Self-Respect as a Primary Political Ideal

*Ambedkar's Challenge to Political Theory**

SHAUNNA RODRIGUES

Self-respect remains one of the most foundational but elusive concepts of modern political thought. Dominant liberal accounts of self-respect substantively frame the concept through counter-concepts such as (*i*) servility, in which a person subordinates himself to someone else, feels that he does not deserve fair treatment, or does not regard as unjust treatment which is demeaning to himself,[1] or (*ii*) shame, which provides a contrast to self-respect by capturing what a person feels when he fails to achieve the excellences required to attain his conception of 'good'.[2]

However, despite being given importance as 'the most important primary good' for a democratic polity,[3] self-respect is predominantly used in a thin and positive[4] sense in most foundational

---

* The author gratefully acknowledges feedback on different drafts of this chapter from Anupama Rao, Michelle Moody-Adams, Sanjeev Kumar, Sudipta Kaviraj, Aakash Singh Rathore, and the anonymous reviewers.

[1] Hill (1973); Kant (2001).

[2] Rawls (1999).

[3] Rawls (1999).

[4] By positive, one means a usage of self-respect that does not invoke a counter-concept.

political arguments on justice, democracy, or toleration. In this thin and positive sense, self-respect is simply defined as the capacity of people to have a sense of justice and their own conception of the good.[5] Here, the thick, substantive form of theorizing self-respect as a counter-concept to ideas like servility or shame comes to be skimmed over, as does the use of political emotion in the formulation of this primary good. Can political arguments that attempt to orient a political community towards self-respect ignore the counter-concepts in opposition to which self-respect is defined?

This chapter attempts to answer this question by positing B.R. Ambedkar's formulation of self-respect against the dominant Rawlsian formulation of the concept. We use a Rawlsian formulation of self-respect as our comparative point in this chapter because predominant theorizing of self-respect as a primary good for a democratic polity has taken place through the Rawlsian paradigm. We argue that this dominant conception of self-respect signifies a normative understanding of the concept that does not explicitly take the social into account in its conceptualization. In using Rawls as a comparative marker, this chapter tries to demonstrate how the critique of social injustice and explanations of the processes that obscure such injustice, as is evident in Ambedkar's work, essentially contribute to the shaping of self-respect as a primary political good.

In doing so, it develops a framework for examining the concept of self-respect through Ambedkar's writings, first, by broadening the range of counter-concepts to self-respect to capture what Ambedkar theorized as 'indirect liberty' and ideas of the human that were caught up in behaviourism. This chapter demonstrates a methodological mode of reasoning in Ambedkar's writings as well, which was to start from what others have called structures and situations of 'social negativity',[6] so that social and political theory could counterfactually make explicit the normative conditions of self-respect. It is through the emphasis on social negativity as a

---

[5] Krishnamurthy (2013).

[6] This term is employed by Axel Honneth to reconstruct diagnostic social concepts in the tradition of the Frankfurt School of Critical Theory, such as Horkheimer's 'irrational organization', Adorno's 'administrated world', Habermas' 'Colonization of the Lifeworld'. See Honneth (2009: 19–40).

point of departure for theory that Ambedkar was able to bring out normative expectations in political, affective, and legal domains.

Second, this chapter attempts to develop Ambedkar's conception of self-respect based on interlinked concepts of notional recognition, communication and political emotion, self-mastery, and public presence as its nodal points. Ambedkar deploys this framework against a far wider range of conceptions of the good than the Rawlsian framework for self-respect. In doing so, he provides us with a positive, substantive, and more workable political ideal of self-respect, making him one of the most profound theorists of self-respect in the world.

This chapter is divided into four parts. In 'Self-Respect as a Primary Good in Rawlsian Liberal Egalitarianism', we assess the manner in which self-respect is theorized as the most important primary good for a just society within the Rawlsian framework. Treating this as a point of comparison, we move to an analysis of counter-concepts to self-respect in 'Self-Respect's Counter-Concepts' that can capture the forms of social negativity against which self-respect needs to be built as a normative concept. In 'The Fourfold Framework of Self-Respect', we reconstruct the outline in Ambedkar's writings that shapes self-respect as a political and relational concept. In the final section, 'Expanding the Political with Pre-conditions for Self-Respect', we look at how Ambedkar's formulation of self-respect de-parochializes the concept of self-respect from its dominant conceptualization in Transatlantic theory.

Self-Respect as a Primary Good in Rawlsian Liberal Egalitarianism

John Rawls describes self-respect as the most important primary good in and for his framework of justice as fairness. He argues that there are two aspects to understanding self-respect as a primary good: first, a person's conviction that her conception of the good or plans for life itself are worth carrying out; and second, a person's confidence in her ability to fulfil her plans.[7] These two arguments form a thin conception of self-respect and emerge from a Kantian liberal tradition of individuals adhering to a moral law.[8]

[7] Rawls (1999: 386–92).
[8] Rawls (1999: 390–1).

Self-respect is conceptualized by Rawls in a thick sense by contrasting it to a counter-concept, the 'moral' emotion of shame.[9] But before we come to the concept of shame, we must look at the two 'social bases' for attaining self-respect according to Rawls.

Rawls requires two conditions or 'social bases' for the attainment of self-respect. First, it can be gained and sustained when a person formulates a life plan, which does not merely involve identifying the activities which a person finds acceptable and enjoyable for life but also involves marking out the liberties and opportunities, income and wealth, from a maximal set of plans that would be required for the sustained pursuit of the same.[10] Second, self-respect should be one which adheres to an 'Aristotelian principle'. According to this principle, a person's ability to fulfil her life plan comes about when she enjoys the exercise of her realized capacities and achieves greater complexity in these the more she realizes them.[11]

Rawls refers to it as a 'principle of motivation'. It not only motivates a person to improve her 'capacities' but also motivates others who see her do so as well. 'Finding our person and deeds appreciated and confirmed by others who are likewise esteemed and their association enjoyed' makes a person more confident of her 'value'.[12] It is this feeling Rawls refers to that leads to 'a sense of mastery' and gives a person the conditions to respect others too. In this way, their common plans can be 'complementary' allowing them to engage with each other in activities that they appreciate and enjoy.[13]

Given these two conditions, the 'goal' of self-respect is to achieve 'excellences', such as 'imagination and wit, beauty and grace', as well as virtues that make us good citizens.[14] The principle of motivation and excellences can be best developed in an association. An association is a space in which the activities that the self sees as important to one's plan of life are affirmed by others. Membership within the association would guarantee recognition

---

[9] Rawls (1999: 388–90).
[10] Rawls (1999: 348).
[11] Rawls (1999: 374).
[12] Rawls (1999: 387).
[13] Rawls (1999).
[14] Rawls (1999: 388, 390).

as well. According to Rawls, this 'assurance' would be sufficient for the self-esteem required of citizens to make political claims in public life.

While one's life plan, the Aristotelian principle, and excellences are conditions, contingents, circumstances, or goals of self-respect, they do not positively define self-respect. Rather, they stand out as concepts, each having a particular relationship with this primary good of self-respect that is foundational to any society which aims to be a democracy. These conditions circumscribe how self-respect ought to be seen but Rawls argues that they do not succeed in capturing, defining, and giving us the characteristics of what self-respect is. This substantial idea of self-respect comes from using the counter-concept of shame against that of self-respect.

Shame, Rawls contends, is felt when one's life plan does not help a person achieve her excellences.[15] It is also felt when an association does not recognize a person who is its member. Thus, it is the lack of opportunities for pursuing excellence and the lack of recognition which cause shame. Shame can be distinguished into 'general' shame and 'particular' shame. Particular shame, or 'natural' shame, is something that arises from the loss of exclusive goods such as property owned by a person. General shame or moral shame, on the other hand, is something that arises from the loss of an 'excellence' which is a good from everyone's point of view.[16] All this causes a person to lose her sense of self-worth and, therefore, reduces self-respect.

This account of self-respect strongly relies on the idea that an individual's conviction and confidence in carrying out a life plan comes from maintaining a consistent 'rationality' of achieving the same plan in life. Therefore, if a person chooses to pursue a new life plan from her current one, she has to work towards a new conception of the good, and this can cause a blow to her self-respect. More importantly, self-respect in these accounts derives from knowing that one has certain basic guaranteed rights, and that one values those rights. These assumptions are what enable self-respect to be employed in a thin sense in political argument, that is, in its limited sense of being the capacity to have a sense of the good and feeling confident in the apparatus required to follow the

---

[15] Rawls (1999: 388).
[16] Rawls (1999: 388–91).

good in predominant Transatlantic uses of the concept.[17] In the process, the substantive formulation of it that develops the idea of self-respect as a counter-concept to the political formulation of shame is undermined, reducing the necessity of thinking about self-respect in a thick, substantive sense.

Self-Respect's Counter-Concepts

In the predominant Rawlsian formulation of the concept, self-respect involves measuring up to standards provided by a 'rational' life plan, living consistently and congruently with one's own values, and becoming the kind of person one thinks one is worth becoming.[18] As a prior reader of Ambedkar, however, several assumptions in this formulation stand out as limiting to the range of ontological conditions against which self-respect can be formulated.

Diversity and the Counter-Concept of Indirect Liberty

First, the Rawlsian formulation does not bring the concept of self-respect in direct dialogue with the dilemmas of living amidst diversity.[19] This diversity, in the Indian context, exists across a 'convex-multiplanar' range. At its extreme levels, this diversity could be understood as 'horizontal' and 'vertical' forms of diversity.[20] In the first form, 'horizontal' diversity, one encounters incongruent moral, ethical, or epistemological doctrines and, as a consequence, differing dictums existing in the society that one is a part of. Ambedkar's writings on diversity repeatedly make this point. There might be people who adhere to different religions, ideological positions, or different ways of reasoning. Therefore, there is not always one clear, underlying moral law available in a diverse society that an individual in the pursuit of self-respect can be consistently guided by.[21]

---

[17] Krishnamurthy (2013).

[18] Dillon (1997).

[19] Even when there is a lot written on diversity and pluralism by the thinkers who work on self-respect, there is little written on what the dilemmas of diversity do to the concept of self-respect itself.

[20] Bhargava (2008).

[21] Ambedkar (1945).

The other form of diversity—'vertical' diversity—is deeply oppressive[22] by nature. This kind of diversity is one which is fraught by different dimensions of power,[23] where one party has greater societal capacity to influence the other and determine their place in a social structure. In writing about the second form of diversity, Ambedkar begins to employ counter-concepts to describe the dilemmas that vertical diversity introduces into the pursuit of self-respect.

One of the most powerful counter-concepts Ambedkar provides to self-respect is the idea of 'indirect liberty'.[24] Indirect liberty, he argues, is when an individual is confined to a social structure without any guarantees of social cooperation, including guarantees of protection and well-being gained from oppressive relationships. Indirect liberty gains its significance as a concept from the manner in which those who bear it are kept: (*i*) outside the fold of the social/political association that engages in social cooperation; and (*ii*) considered unfit for human association.[25]

The concept gains a definitive context within a society that practices and/or is shaped by a history of untouchability, which, according to him, is different from other forms of inhuman relationships like slavery.[26] He formulates the idea of indirect liberty using a comparative, philosophical argument that distinguishes the condition of an untouchable from that of a slave in response to various upper-caste public figures[27] who argue that 'untouchability is not worse than slavery'.[28] Ambedkar first points out that slavery was an institution that was recognized and practiced throughout Indian history until 1843 when it was abolished by the British

---

[22] The idea of oppression is used here in the way in which it is formulated by Iris Marion Young. See Young (1990).

[23] The notion of dimensions of power is used herein the way in which it is formulated by Steven Lukes. See Lukes (2005).

[24] He develops this concept in 'Untouchables or the Children of India's Ghetto' (Ambedkar 2014a).

[25] Ambedkar (2014a).

[26] However, its implications are not limited to this context alone and consistently apply to those who are relegated to the margins or limits of the political.

[27] Such as Lala Lajpat Rai in his book, *Unhappy India* (1928). See 'Untouchables or the Children of India's Ghetto' (Ambedkar 2014a: 9).

[28] Ambedkar (2014a: 9).

imperial government.[29] However, untouchability is different from slavery, he argues, because an untouchable is constantly subject to forms of 'indirect liberty'.

Observing various cases of slavery, extending from Ancient Roman to Transatlantic slavery, Ambedkar contended that a relationship between the master and the slave was determined by motives of display, gain and/or productivity on behalf of the master.[30] However, 'it was an investment for the owner' to enable his slave to learn more.[31] When he analyses slavery in eighteenth-century USA, he carefully documents how black slaves were used to build the economy of the American South in the face of 'hostile prejudice'.[32] At the same time, he notes, '[S]lave labour was used for all kinds of work and intelligent slaves were trained as artisans to be used and leased. Slave artisans would bring twice as much as an ordinary field hand in the market ... some masters, as the system became more evolved, hired slaves for their slave artisans. Many slave artisans purchased their freedom by the savings allowed to them above the normal labour expected.'[33] This, according to Ambedkar, allowed slaves to explore 'higher forms' of labour, and develop what we have called 'excellences' earlier in this chapter, albeit in a hostile and deeply oppressive environment.

---

[29] There are other writings of Ambedkar where he points out how some provisions in laws across Indian provinces like the United Provinces Municipalities Act II of 1916, The Punjab Municipalities Act of 1911 contain legal provisions which sanction forced labour (especially with regard to sweepers and scavenging) which can amount to slavery. See Ambedkar (2014a: 257).

[30] 'Educated slaves must have been a necessity in the absence of printing. the busy lawyer, the dilettante poet, the philosopher and educated gentleman of literary tastes had need of copyists and readers and secretaries' ('Untouchables or the Children of India's Ghetto' [Ambedkar 2014a: 10]).

[31] 'Untouchables or the Children of India's Ghetto' (Ambedkar 2014a).

[32] Ambedkar quoted Charles C. Johnson's 'The Negro in American Civilization' extensively to demonstrate how different forms of slave labour was used in the Southern states of North Carolina and Georgia (Johnson 1930). He also writes extensively about slavery in Virginia elsewhere in 'Untouchables or the Children of India's Ghetto' (Ambedkar 2014a).

[33] Ambedkar (2014a).

Further, Ambedkar asserts, given that the slave was considered to be valuable property, a prudent master would not expose his valuable possession to ill health. Rather, it was the duty of the master within an ahistorical structuring of slavery to take care of the health and well-being of the slave.[34] He makes this statement in the form of a structural analysis of slavery rather than as a statement of historical analysis. Whenever he engages in historical analysis, he is careful to note the deeply inhuman forms of subordination and oppression that slaves in different contexts had to undergo.[35]

An untouchable, on the other hand, has his plan of life set for him through his caste status. While he emphasized that slavery was not a free social order, Ambedkar argued that untouchables were 'shut out from any of the avenues' available to slaves to improve their productivity and well-being, even those which were only meant to feed and maintain slavery as a system.[36] The upper caste had no motive of increasing the productivity of the untouchable as its influence over the untouchable did not derive from productive relations. Therefore, the untouchable had no access to 'excellences' or modes of developing them. This is central to understanding how untouchables are 'outside the fold' of Hindus, and thus any social and political association required for any form of social cooperation in India.[37]

Further, unlike the slave in theories of master–slave relationships, the untouchable has to suffer the burden (liberty) of being responsible for his own survival. Upper castes, Ambedkar contended, do not care for health or well-being of an untouchable. Moreover, they actively go out of the way to construct the untouchable as unfit for human association by disassociating with them, avoiding their mere

[34] Ambedkar (2014a: 17).
[35] Ambedkar (2014a: 3–17).
[36] Ambedkar (2014a: 16).
[37] Ambedkar was attempting a comparative assessment of caste and slavery by complicating the idea of 'freedom' or 'liberty' against which the former were conceptualized. However, even though he eludes to them in a few places, he did not seriously take up the question of pre-modern or pre-colonial slavery in India, or across the the Indian Ocean. On pre-modern slavery across the Indian Ocean and in India, see Chatterjee (2019) and Mamdani (2018).

presence, and giving priority to norms of caste association rather than extending health care.[38]

Therefore, over and above experiencing forms of servility that serve as counter-concepts to one's self-respect, the untouchable also has to negotiate with other extreme forms of denial of self-respect caused by different forms of 'indirect liberty'. In portraying it as a concept which theorizes the idea of an individual confined to a social structure without any guarantees of social cooperation, Ambedkar tried to capture within indirect liberty 'all the disadvantages of a free social order' when it is located within different structures, especially one that is framed by untouchability and caste.[39]

Caste Hindus were obligated to practice caste norms, and the same norms did not permit the emancipation of untouchables. Despite untouchables observing a 'common creed' with and wishing to assimilate with Hindus and upper castes having no plausible explanation for untouchability, touchable Hindus did not accept that untouchability is a Hindu problem, and thus did not want to take responsibility for the problems of untouchables.[40] Thus, little onus could be placed on caste norms or the system of 'vertical diversity' they upheld to provide a counter to indirect liberty in the form of self-respect.

Responsibility and the Counter-Concept of Behaviourism

Second, the Rawlsian conception of self-respect does not adequately explore the question of responsibility for self-respect. It is often taken for granted that societal responsibility for self-respect will be guaranteed by the political existence of rights. The self that needs to be respected, therefore, is the self that rights define, defend, and enable. In using a right to define the self, the Rawlsian theory of self-respect demarcates domains of self-respect as covered by the domains of a right.[41]

But what about a self in a society that is still constructing, defining, and enforcing its rights? One Rawlsian response to this question would proceed as follows: The lack of self-respect can be

---

[38] Ambedkar (2014a: 27–34).
[39] Ambedkar (2014a: 17).
[40] Ambedkar (2014a: 3–4).
[41] Rawls (1999).

substantiated as a matter of psychology, given that ideas like shame and servility form the counter-concepts against which self-respect has to be built.[42] Thus, self-respect is not completely defined according to the neatly political terms of rights but also reaches into the realm of psychology or political emotion to become a meaningful concept.

This argument, however, still works with an assumption of what it means to be human, which is to primarily view the human as an equal citizen in a constitutional democracy where a modern democratic State guarantees the protection and exercise of each citizen's rights. The range of emotions against which a Transatlantic liberal theorist like Rawls formulates self-respect, therefore, is far smaller than the range of political emotions experienced by those who theorize from a position where the first assumption starts from not being recognized as human. Conceptualizing self-respect as a matter of psychology in the first way poses the problem of its denial on the individual, rather than treating it as an integral part of the social structures through which persons are given or denied respect.

Further, it is less attentive to other forms of critical and influential Transatlantic theorizing on social psychology within the social sciences in USA at the turn of the twentieth century. This branch of social psychology was used in methods of 'new history', social organization, and theories of social evolution that were a large part of Ambedkar's coursework at Columbia University, especially in courses with Franklin Henry Giddings and John Dewey, who both engaged with and taught courses around the question of conduct, association, and behaviour from the standpoint of social psychology.[43]

Dewey, in particular, in response to theories of 'crowd psychology' that upheld behaviourism and biological and psychological determinism, began to develop a social psychology that could justify social reconstruction.[44] The self, according to him, was a social product constituted through others, organizations, institutions, and culture. Valuing human agency over behaviourism, he argued that humans came to be active interpreters of the symbolic meanings of objects and communication through a process of interaction with

---

[42] Rawls (1999).
[43] Shukla (2019).
[44] Dewey (1957).

others and institutions within a historical and cultural context. Using this to argue that human beings were not internally or externally determined but capable of subjectivity and choice, especially through education, he framed a comprehensive justification for the role of others and institutions in enabling in persons the responsibilities that democracy and deliberation entailed.

Ambedkar was heavily influenced by this conception of the self and human conduct, not only for its conceptualization but also as a method to understand human agency under conditions of deep inequality. Like many contemporary theorists who critique the Rawlsian framework of self-respect,[45] Ambedkar used this conception of the human self to demonstrate how multiple experiences of having and losing self-respect could form a rich and thick concept. Capturing these multiple experiences would need an account of responsibility for self-respect and how it is susceptible to internal problems such as self-deception or weakness of will as well as external forces of discrimination enforced by social structures. Given this, one would have to conceptualize self-respect in a way that emphasizes it as a political and relational concept.

The Fourfold Framework of Self-Respect

While Ambedkar does not dedicate any specific piece of writing to self-respect alone, the idea appears as a foundational concept in all his political speeches and systematic reflections. Ambedkar makes it a point to describe the assertions of the Dalit political subject as the work of 'self-respecting Untouchables' in 'Annihilation of Caste'.[46] When he writes about the various resolutions of movements of 'untouchables' against caste injustice in 'The Revolt of

---

[45] Dillon (1997).

[46] Ambedkar (2014b). Ambedkar ends his letter to Har Bhagwan dated 27 April 1936 defending his speech on the annihilation of caste by commenting on the cancellation of his appointment as the president of the Jat-Pat-Todak Mandal: 'What can anyone expect from a relationship so tragic as the relationship between the reforming sect of Caste Hindus and the self-respecting sect of Untouchables, where the former have no desire to alienate their orthodox fellows, and the latter have no alternative but to insist upon reform being carried out?' (Ambedkar 2014b: 35).

the Untouchables', he states that the object of these resolutions, especially those of direct action such as the Mahad Satyagraha, was 'to foster among Untouchables self-respect and self-esteem'.[47] His forceful arguments to abandon Hinduism in 'Away from the Hindus' and study avenues of conversion to other religions are explicitly justified on grounds of self-respect.[48]

In asserting that Muslims cannot be subject to a majority that identifies as Hindu under Swaraj in India in *Pakistan or the Partition of India*, Ambedkar argues that Muslims and other minorities care more for the recognition of their self-respect than mere good deeds by the Congress.[49] Denial of self-respect to the 'ruled classes' becomes the foundational grounds for the critique of the Congress as the party of a 'governing class', and of Gandhi as the leader of the party, in 'What Congress and Gandhi Have Done to the Untouchables'.[50]

What is attempted here is to bring Ambedkar's reflections on this idea, which is replete in his work, into a framework for a substantive conceptualization of self-respect emerging from his body of thought. This conceptualization of self-respect occurred through a fourfold framework of notional recognition, communication, self-mastery, and public presence. While the first two are points of critique essential to a framework of self-respect, the third and fourth criteria act as forms of reconstruction that could produce practices, attitudes, norms, and justifications for self-respect. The framework develops self-respect as an ideal norm, a primary good, and a right to be demanded from a polity, as well as a justificatory concept, that is, a concept on the basis of which justificatory practices for accepting or rejecting social and political norms could be shaped.

As many have demonstrated, the influence of Deweyan pragmatism and theories of associated life on Ambedkar was profound.[51] Ambedkar's framework for self-respect too was reminiscent of the concepts Dewey deployed in his writings on pragmatism. While this chapter attempts to highlight the intellectual genealogy of

---

[47] Ambedkar (2014a: 258).
[48] Ambedkar (2014a: 403).
[49] Ambedkar (2014c).
[50] Ambedkar (2014d).
[51] Mukherjee (2009); Queen (2015); Stroud (2017a).

his ideas in Dewey, the framework outlined here focuses more on Ambedkar's own expansion of these concepts from the social conditions of a caste-based society which did not take for granted much of the assumptions attached to the human in the modern social sciences.

Notional Recognition

Recognition has often been theorized as constitutive of self-respect, simply because the latter is formed through the considerations different persons in a society extend to the self and, in turn, demand for themselves.[52] Ambedkar's body of work provides us with a series of markers for a theory of self-respect that emphasizes forms of recognition on a range varying from explicit modes of communication to what he calls the 'notional sense' of extending consideration to a fellow being.[53] This range of modes of recognition are constituted by social conditions shaped, in particular, by caste and/or the projected majoritarianism of a governing class.

Here, we construct the notional sense of recognition as a distinct part of his framework in order to emphasize its specific relevance to forms of self-respect as compared to other forms of communication in Ambedkar's fourfold framework for self-respect. Notional recognition, as formulated in his writings, functions as a sense of denial of self-respect that emerges from existing ideas and modes of speech that dismiss or undermine the reproduction of relational norms in a society, especially one framed by caste. This notional sense is triggered through the way in which counter-concepts like indirect liberty or the denial of responsibility for the self-respect of others present themselves in ideas, interactions, policies, and larger structures. This notional recognition cannot always be captured by a conception of recognition alone, but when connected with other conceptions like communication, self-mastery, and public association, it becomes a necessary part of the concept of self-respect.

Ambedkar uses this idea of 'notional sense' to identify attitudes that preconceive or prejudge/prejudice the manner in which others

---

[52] Honneth (1996).

[53] Ambedkar's conception of recognition has been extensively explored by Martin Fuchs (2017). Also see Mahanand (2020).

are considered before they have a chance to display or perform what we described as 'excellences'. These attitudes, he argues, come to be performed not merely through speech and/or discursive formulations, but also through the ways in which bodies come to be assessed and marked as in/accessible, as in/capable of laying claim to the public, and as symbols for the enactment of social distinctions. His reflections on the notional sense through which he identifies the manner in which preconceptions of caste operate to the detriment of recognition are exceptionally profound. These preconceptions manifest in different ways, ranging from the manner in which people do not acknowledge the excellences of those considered to be lower caste or minority public figures to be leaders or thinkers for a polity or society as a whole, to pre-empting or assimilating, and thus limiting, various practices of justification and assertion for political and social equality by lower castes/minorities on their own terms.[54]

At one end of the range, these preconceptions are subtle but enable a systematic undermining of the self-respect of minorities in the public. His 'notional sense' of these preconceptions is captured best when Ambedkar writes about himself as a public political figure in India, putting the public recognition of his social self to scrutiny: 'There is another form of discrimination ... which indicates a systematic attempt to lower the dignity and status of a meritorious untouchable—a Hindu leader would be described merely as a great Indian leader ... whereas a leader of untouchables would be considered only to be a leader of the untouchables.'[55] This lack of acknowledgement takes place not just discursively, according to Ambedkar, but also through a non-discursive sidelining or undermining of the relevance of Dalit thought, culture, and literature within Indian society. Notional recognition thus marked the difference between making political choice real or nominal, between the ability to do or refrain from doing things publicly.[56]

The prevalence of such preconceptions, even when caste-based discrimination does not explicitly take place, leaves the self to

---

[54] On Ambedkar's conception of the minority, see Dara (2009), Rao (2009), and Chatterjee (2018).
[55] Ambedkar (2014c: 109).
[56] Ambedkar (2014c: 110).

negotiate with these prejudgements that determine her suitability in social intercourse rather than place the responsibility/burden of judgement on those exercising these preconceptions in their interaction with the self.

Being aware of this notional sense, both in how one extends preconceptions to others and perceives their extensions to oneself, is the first step in a framework that can proceed towards communication in a society that values self-respect. Ambedkar's constitutional framework to increase the public presence and thus critical space for Dalits to assert themselves, was as much a framework to enable society in India to take responsibility for the regulative operation of the preconceptions internalized in their communications due to caste and majoritarian structures, and thus a necessary step to emancipation, than it was to aid emancipatory struggles in India with tools of justice.[57]

At the other end of the range of the notional sense is its operation in a blatant debate on where the onus of responsibility for emancipation of society as a whole and 'untouchables' in particular must lie. In response to Gandhi's position that the emancipatory responsibility of abolishing untouchability rests with upper caste Hindus, Ambedkar strongly asserted that it is important to have faith in oneself in 'the battle of reclamation of human personality'.[58] Ambedkar pointed out that Gandhi's construction of emancipation for untouchables disregarded the operation of notional preconceptions on the Dalit self. Gandhi had constructed Dalits as being externally determined rather than as humans who are capable of worldmaking. In Gandhi's denial of this fundamental basis for self-respect, Ambedkar identified an approach that did not contain notions of recognition but those of paternalism.

Thus, in shaping the range of notional recognition, Ambedkar demonstrated that self-respect is not merely shaped by the recognition gained within an association but also through the denial of social recognition meted out by people who are not part of one's association.[59] This denial of social recognition may not always be absolute but could be withheld constantly.

[57] Kannabiran (2012).
[58] Ambedkar (2014b).
[59] Ambedkar (1945).

Communication and Experiencing Emotion

As John Dewey's student at Columbia University, Ambedkar imbibed and worked into his own thought many conceptual categories and tools that Dewey employed. Communication was a concept that he derived centrally from the Deweyan framework.

Associating with people who have things in common with each other, such as their aims, aspirations, and knowledge, was a necessary condition for developing self-respect in Ambedkar's framework, like it is in the predominant Rawlsian framework. However, Ambedkar argues that this is not a sufficient condition for self-respect. Across his writing, and especially in his most well-read texts like 'Annihilation of Caste' and 'Evidence before the Southborough Committee on Franchise', Ambedkar points out that prior to the act of building associations comes the capacity to note what one has in common with those one wants to associate with.[60] For this, people would have to communicate with and participate in each other's' activities. Communication is foundational to the 'conjoint communicated experience' which leads to associated life.[61]

Impediments to this conjoint communicated experience come from both horizontal and vertical kinds of diversity. Both these kinds of diversity can prevent a person belonging to one community or caste from feeling like she can associate with people. However, caste consciousness subordinates man's natural inclination to the exigencies of communication across caste communities, thus denying people the communication they need in order to work out one's plan for life.[62] It is this caste consciousness that sets the terms of the conversation rather than communication happening on a self's 'own terms'. The emphasis in Ambedkar on developing an argument on 'one's own terms' is foundational to understanding communication as a nodal point in the framework for self-respect.

Further, communication does not take place with finding mere commonalities with others. Rather, it comes about when individuals share and participate in a common activity in a way that arouses the same emotion in people—an emotion that makes the individual

---

[60] Ambedkar (2014b).
[61] Ambedkar (2014b: 248–9).
[62] Ambedkar (2014b: 48).

a 'sharer' in associated activity so that 'he feels its success as his success, its failure as his failure'.[63] This idea, called social endosmosis, was also borrowed from John Dewey. However, Ambedkar reconstructs the idea through the counter-concepts he formulates it against. Caste consciousness as the counter-concept to communication prevents those who are subordinated through this consciousness from experiencing a broader range of feelings such as exhilaration or celebration, the feeling of discovery on gaining knowledge, or even the feeling of smugness gained from winning a political argument. In using this argument on communication in his framework of self-respect, Ambedkar gave us an idea of self-respect that does not merely gain from a man's capacity for practical reason, but also from his capacity to feel a broad range of emotions. The importance of emotions to self-respect was strengthened by Ambedkar's argument of how caste comes to restrict any feeling of 'a sense of mastery' (to use a Rawlsian term) or self-mastery over the range of emotions that one can have in life. Therefore, he radically redefined self-respect to contend that it does not merely gain from the range of opportunities that are available to people, but also in terms of the range of emotions available to them.[64]

Self-Mastery through Reconstruction

The moral self, defined by the capacity to reason between what we morally ought and ought not to do, which is viewed as a central human capacity in the Rawlsian framework, is not a given in Ambedkar's writings.. Further, the moral self, which acts in and through reason, is not a guaranteed realization either. For Ambedkar, acting on social reality could not merely happen through abstract forms of theoretical reason, but required a different anchor. But where was this anchor to be found if dominant traditions in society condemned those it called its own to a caste order?

In developing moral arguments for the self, Ambedkar's initial writings display an adherence to a teleological idea of the march of history leading to self-mastery, attained through modern ideas of justice, equality, and liberty, that defined the social sciences at

---

[63] Ambedkar (2014b: 51).
[64] I am grateful to Sanjeev Kumar for making me think of this shift through the concept of self-mastery. On this, also see Guru (2019).

the time when he was writing. However, this changed in his later writings as he began to place a greater emphasis on assessing the condition of the self on ontological grounds. In doing so, he turned to different traditions of Buddhism in India to provide a way out of the degrading religious practices imposed by a caste order justified by Vedic Hinduism. In turning to Buddhism, Ambedkar shifted his focus from a critique of existing social norms shaped by Hinduism to a justification of self-mastery through the reconstruction of ethical norms and practices of Buddhism and their contemporary relevance to the social and political in India.

As Kanchana Mahadevan points out, for Ambedkar, this reconstruction provided for Dalits both an exit from the oppressive structures of caste as practiced within Hinduism, as well as a route to self-mastery.[65] If one receives no recognition from those who frame the traditions that one is subject to and cannot lay any claim to reconstructing those traditions in a substantive manner, then a route for an exit of the self from these traditions must be available or else the self would constantly be crippled by its traditions rather than transformed by it. Conversion, thus understood, was a move to counter the conditions of indirect liberty. However, any positive argument on exiting one set of traditions had to be substantiated by finding an anchor, in other comprehensive traditions that made themselves available for reform or reconstruction, through which the self could act on and be in the world.

Ambedkar saw Buddhism as one such comprehensive tradition because of its emphasis on the experiences of the self rather than the infallibility of certain rituals and rules. According to Ambedkar, the followers of the Buddha were free to modify or abandon any of his teachings if it was found that, at any given point of time or under any circumstances, the teachings of various traditions of Buddhism did not apply. In reconstructing different tenets of Buddhism as an ethical body of thought that Dalits could embrace and follow, Ambedkar emphasized the Buddha as a human being upholding freedom with compassion or *karuna* at every step. The appeal of this reconstruction to the goal of self-respect was as foundational to his deployment of Buddhism as a moral doctrine that could enable a political community to develop as a fraternity.[66] In a

---

[65] Mahadevan (2008).

[66] Rodrigues (1993).

political act of self-mastery, Ambedkar converted to Buddhism to indicate his own exit from a religion that enforced a stigmatizing caste order.

In using reconstruction as a method of self-mastery, Ambedkar followed an argument of the self in temporality as formulated by Dewey by conceptualizing the self to be someone who lives in the present.[67] Thus, materials of the past could not be posed as 'rivals to the present'. In doing so, some have argued that he was also embracing the Buddha's law of impermanence or *sarvam anityam* and the Eightfold Path that 'focuses on the cultivation of active experience and virtue in the present: right views, aspirations, speech, conduct, livelihood, effort, mindfulness, and concentration'.[68] Others have noted that the rhetorical activity that he employed in the lead-up to the mass religious conversion to Buddhism was to justify a reorientation towards a tradition indigenous to South Asia that contained a body of 'concepts that echoed his early appeals for self-respect among untouchables'.[69]

Reconstruction or/and conversion, therefore, became important acts of self-mastery as these actions would provide a sense of accomplishment and excellence in constituting the moral principles that the self could pursue. Self-mastery, within Ambedkar's framework, therefore, emerges from constituting moral principles from within traditions that question oppression. In using Buddhism as the tradition that could be reconstructed to do so, Ambedkar was not questioning the oppression of only the caste order coming from Vedic Hinduism, but also a uniform, historically situated European modernity that was being imposed on India and elsewhere during this time. This second kind of questioning emerges particularly in his later writings where he begins to assess the self on ontological grounds.

Without this reconstruction, one would have to live at the cost of one's self-respect. Without it, man would become a 'mere cipher'.[70] Developing self-respect as self-mastery, therefore, was not merely a question of gaining excellences as Rawls formulates it, that is, through the Aristotelian principle, but 'a ceaseless struggle' of

---

[67] Dewey (1988).
[68] Queen (2015: 8).
[69] Stroud (2017b).
[70] Keer (1990: 127).

gaining self-mastery through reconstructing traditions from which one derives strength, confidence and recognition to overcome difficulties imposed by a hierarchical and limiting social or caste order.

Public Participation in the Substantive Formulation of Rights

Ambedkar had a peculiar approach towards rights: He treated them as an important end to be achieved but did not want to treat rights as pre-given, especially in a society which had to overcome a lot before being able to guarantee those rights. He was writing at a time when he was attempting to orient a political community towards the idea of rights. Given this, he was starting from an assumption that rights have to be constructed and developed. This implied that self-respect could not merely be attained through the establishment of a right. Rather, the right had to be fought for, developed, and shaped by the self in a polity in a way that would suit the formulation of self-respect by diverse people on their own terms.

If rights are a construction in the process of attaining self-respect, this process ought to manifest in the way in which public discourse takes place in India. The shaping of rights had to be carried out by the right holder in her discovery and public negotiation of the terms through which she lives her life. Rights, therefore, do not come to be a guarantee of the State alone, rather they ought to be designed by a public discourse that targets social relations and modes of dominance which constantly suppress people's moral, emotional, and other capacities.

In its enabling function, a right develops only through articulation with greater strength and presence in public discourse, especially if it is articulated as a right required to overcome the difficulties faced by a caste-based social order. The self has to assert this claim in the public domain. However, the responsibility of ensuring that the self has enough presence in the public domain to do so cannot lie with a particular emancipator or one particular group like the upper castes, but has to lie with the public as a whole and the State that governs it. It was in making claims on institutions and other citizens with an expectation that these claims could be made in one's own terms that self-respect could be accomplished.[71]

---

[71] Ambedkar (2014d).

Ambedkar illustrates this point in his writings on minorities. Granting minorities representation in proportion to their numbers was necessary but not a sufficient condition to creating the space for them to make their claims as citizens in the public domain. What made this representation substantial was the weight that the State and other citizens would give minorities to ensure their representation translates into a genuine public presence needed to secure their best interests.[72]

In thinking about rights in this way, Ambedkar begins to rework frameworks provided by theorists like John Dewey, by informing it with a wider range of experiences, emotions, and systematic reflections shaped by caste and diversity in India. There are some aspects of Kantian republican theory in this argument—Ambedkar often treats self-respect as consisting in an individual becoming aware of her capacity to make a claim, and therefore gaining the strength and presence in the political domain rather than letting the right remain latent and suppressed in a way that holders are not aware they can exercise it.[73] But these similarities need not divert us from the constructive challenges that Ambedkar puts forward to dominant liberal political theory: First, the fundamental considerations that go into building a democratic public and establishing self-respect cannot be overcome through rights alone; and second, although rights are essential as guarantees by the State, they have to be substantiated through the public presence of those claiming rights if they are to guarantee self-respect as a primary political ideal.

Expanding the Political with Pre-conditions for Self-Respect

In building a framework for self-respect in this way, we have shown how Ambedkar foregrounds the assumptions present in political claims for self-respect, consistently links them together, coherently justifies these linkages, and assesses them against the normative claims that the concept proposes. He also buffers these claims against consequences emerging from different situations, pointing out to the manner in which they fit in or clash

---

[72] Dara (2009).
[73] Queen (2015).

with other claims in relevant situations. In doing so, however, he develops self-respect as a concept which could make a claim to be a thin universal while also being conceptually substantiated with a rich, lived-in character of the practices and intuitions with which the Indian political domain can construct and deploy it.

At the start of this chapter, we argued that self-respect, although theorized substantially against its counter-concepts like servility and shame in predominant frames of political theory, continues to be used in political arguments through a thin formulation, that is, as the capacity to have a sense of justice and a notion of the good. But we asked if this was sufficient to orient a political community towards the ideal of self-respect

Even as Ambedkar used and employed several ideas emerging from Transatlantic political philosophy, he profoundly reconstructed the assumptions behind their conceptualization. He became a radical political thinker not just because he used modern liberal ideas in an Indian context where they had transformative consequences, as he has often been interpreted,[74] but because he reconstituted the substantive aspects through which these ideas are conceptualized, particularly the counter-concepts against which they gain meaning. Further, he demarcated innovative ways in which these concepts could be politically deployed. In doing so, Ambedkar provided us with methods of contesting the assumptions of Transatlantic liberal political theory as well.

Why does this chapter call Ambedkar's expanded conceptualization of self-respect a challenge to political theory? The claim that political theory emerging from the Transatlantic world can be 'universal' is, today, a fairly contested one. The contestation of the universality of concepts employed in political theory has emerged from different areas or critical traditions within the discipline.[75] Many of these critiques focus on exposing the

---

[74] Bajpai (2009).

[75] Out of frameworks of critical political theory, the one which most recently has engaged with non-European political thought has been comparative political theory. See Jenco (2007), March (2011), Simon (2017), and Rathore (2017). While comparative political theory reaches into non-European political thought, there has been a lot of work on how political theory emerged from experiences of empire and thus needs to be critiqued as universal political thought. See Arneil (1996), Muthu (2012), Mantena (2010), and Getachew (2019).

deliberately obscured or unacknowledged biases in the discipline towards European or Transatlantic experiences of developing political concepts. In contrast to this parochialism, they argue that political concepts must emerge from a systematic reflection of the effective histories, experiences, and practices of the selves, communities, or polities outside the Transatlantic world.

Babasaheb Ambedkar stands out as an exemplary political thinker who deployed such methods to forge a thin universal of self-respect. Reading a thinker like Ambedkar prior to reading Transatlantic theoretical writing allows a student of political theory to immediately notice the different methods and assumptions that go into how conceptual theory is built and sustained within different political contexts, even though there might be several overlaps between the ends of such conceptualizations. This is why this chapter constructed itself as the encounter with Rawlsian liberal theory of a 'prior reader' of Ambedkar.

Ambedkar provides us with substantial formulations of counter-universals, like self-respect, that could have a significance even outside that of the local or the subcontinental world. He de-parochializes political theory by more than just decentring from or departing from Transatlantic political theory. As a political thinker, he reconstitutes the terms as well as the audience of political theory, reaching out to those who are not merely interested in the workings of the political domain, but also looking for a way to build the preconditions that would enable themselves to enter this domain as self-respecting equals.

References

Ambedkar, B.R. 1945. *Pakistan or the Partition of India*. Bombay: Thacker and Company Limited.
———. 2014a. *Dr. Babasaheb Ambedkar Writings and Speeches*, Volume 5, Reprinted edition. New Delhi: Dr. Ambedkar Foundation.
———. 2014b. *Dr. Babasaheb Ambedkar Writings and Speeches*, Volume 1, Reprinted edition. New Delhi: Dr. Ambedkar Foundation.
———. 2014c. *Dr. Babasaheb Ambedkar: Writings and Speeches*, Volume 8, Reprinted edition. New Delhi: Dr. Ambedkar Foundation.
———. 2014d. *Dr. Babasaheb Ambedkar: Writings and Speeches*, Volume 9, Reprinted edition. New Delhi: Dr. Ambedkar Foundation.
Arneil, Barbara. 1996. *John Locke and America: The Defence of English Colonialism*. Oxford: Oxford University Press.

Bajpai, R. 2009. *Debating Difference: Group Rights and Liberal Democracy in India*. New Delhi: Oxford University Press.

Bhargava, R. 2008. 'Political Secularism'. In *The Oxford Handbook of Political Theory*, edited by John S. Dryzek, Bonnie Honig, and Anne Phillips. Oxford: Oxford University Press. doi: 10.1093/oxfordhb/9780199548439.003.0035.

Chatterjee, Indrani. 2019. 'Theory from the South III: On Slaves and Freedmen in Precolonial South Asia'. *Borderlines*. Available at https://www.borderlines-cssaame.org/posts/2019/10/31/theory-from-the-south-iii-on-slaves-and-freedmen-in-precolonial-south-asia-a-conversation-with-indrani-chatterjee; last accessed 4 January 2020.

Chatterjee, Partha. 2018. 'Ambedkar's Theory of Minority Rights'. In *The Radical Ambedkar: Critical Reflections*. New Delhi: Penguin Random House.

Dara, Krishnaswamy. 2009. *The Idea of Minority in Ambedkar's Thought: Equality and Differential Rights*. Germany: VDM Verlag Publishers.

Dewey, John. 1957. *Human Nature and Conduct: An Introduction to Social Psychology*. New York: Modern Library.

———. 1988. 'Time and Individuality'. In *Later Works of John Dewey*, Volume 14, edited by Jo Ann Boydston. Carbondale and Edwardsville: Southern Illinois University Press.

Dillon, R.S. 1997. 'Self-Respect: Moral, Emotion, Political'. *Ethics* 107 (2): 226–49.

Getachew, Adom. 2019. Worldmaking after Empire: *The Rise and Fall of Self-Determination*. Princeton, NJ: Princeton University Press.

Guru, Gopal. 2019. *Is There a Conception of the Exemplar in Babasaheb Ambedkar: Conversations with Ambedkar*. Delhi: Tulika Books

Fuchs, Martin. 2017. 'Recognition across Difference: Conceptual Considerations against an Indian Background'. In *Transnational Struggles for Recognition: New Perspectives on Civil Society Since the Twentieth Century*, edited by Dieter Gosewinkel and Dieter Rucht, 252–76. New York: Berghahn.

Hill, Jr, T.E. 1973. 'Servility and Self-Respect'. *The Monist* 57 (1): 87–104.

Honneth, Axel. 1996. *The Struggle for Recognition: The Moral Grammar of Social Conflicts*. Cambridge, MA: MIT Press.

———. 2009. 'A Social Pathology of Reason: On the Intellectual Legacy of Critical Theory'. In *Pathologies of Reason: On the Legacy of Critical Theory*, edited by James Hebbeler, Axel Honneth, and James Ingram, pp. 19–42. New York: Columbia University Press.

Jenco, Leigh. 2007. 'What does Heaven Ever Say? A Methods-Centred Approach to Cross-Cultural Engagement'. *American Political Science Review* 101 (4): 741–55.

Johnson, Charles Spurgeon. 1930. *The Negro in American Civilization: A Study of Negro Life and Race Relations in the Light of Social Research*. New York: H. Holt and Company.

Kannabiran, Kalpana. 2012. *Tools of Justice: Non-discrimination and the Indian Constitution*. New Delhi: Routledge 2012.

Kant, I. 2001. *Groundwork for the Metaphysic of Morals*. Indianapolis: Hackett.

Keer, D. 1990. *Dr. Ambedkar Life and Mission*. Mumbai: Popular Prakashan.

Krishnamurthy, M. 2013. 'Completing Rawls' Arguments for Equal Political Liberty and Its Fair Value: The Argument from Self-Respect'. *Canadian Journal of Philosophy* 43 (2): 179–205.

Lukes, S. 2005. *Power: A Radical View*, Second Edition. Basingstoke: Palgrave Macmillan.

Mahadevan, K. 2008. 'Conversion, Recognition and Pluralism: Dr. Ambedkar's Democratic Buddhism'. In *The Philosophy of B.R. Ambedkar*. Pune: Indian Philosophical Quarterly Publication.

Mahanand, Jadumani. 2020. 'Ambedkar's Critique of Recognition'. *Studies in Indian Politics* 8 (1): 22–38. doi: 10.1177/2321023020918055.

Mantena, Karuna. 2010. *Alibis of Empire: Henry Maine and the Ends of Liberalism*. Princeton, NJ: Princeton University Press.

Mamdani, Mahmood. 2018. 'Introduction: Trans-African Slaveries Thinking Historically'. *Comparative Studies of South Asia, Africa and the Middle East* 38 (2): 185–210.

March, Andrew. 2011. *Islam and Liberal Citizenship: The Search for an Overlapping Consensus*. Oxford: Oxford University Press.

Mukherjee, A.P. 2009. 'B. R. Ambedkar, John Dewey, and the Meaning of Democracy'. *New Literary History* 40 (2): 345–70.

Muthu, Sankar (ed.). 2012. *Empire and Modern Political Thought*. Cambridge: Cambridge University Press.

Queen, C. 2015. 'A Pedagogy of the Dhamma: B.R. Ambedkar and John Dewey on Education'. *International Journal of Buddhist Thought and Culture* 24: 7–21.

Rao, Anupama. 2009. *The Caste Question*. Berkeley: University of California Press.

Rathore, Aakash Singh. 2017. *Indian Political Theory, Laying the Groundwork for Svaraj*. New York: Routledge.

Rawls, J. 1999. *A Theory of Justice*, Revised edition. Cambridge, MA: The Belknap Press of Harvard University Press.

Rodrigues, V. 1993. 'Making a Tradition Critical: Ambedkar's Reading of Buddhism'. In *Dalit Movements and the Meanings of Labour in India*, edited by P. Robb, pp. 299–338. Oxford: Oxford University Press.

Shukla, R. 2019. 'Dr. Ambedkar's Courses at Columbia'. South Asia Study Resources Compiled by Frances Pritchett. Available at http://www.columbia.edu/itc/mealac/pritchett/00ambedkar/timeline/1910s.html; last accessed 9 April 2020.

Simon, J. 2017. *The Ideology of the Creole Revolution: Imperialism and Independence in American and Latin American Political Thought.* Cambridge: Cambridge University Press.

Stroud, S.R. 2017a. 'What Did Bhimrao Ambedkar Learn from John Dewey's *Democracy and Education*?' *The Pluralist* 12 (2): 78–103.

———. 2017b. 'The Rhetoric of Conversion as Emancipatory Strategy in India: Bhimrao Ambedkar, Pragmatism, and the Turn to Buddhism'. *Rhetorica* XXXV: 314–45.

Young, Iris Marion. 1990. *Justice and The Politics of Difference*. Princeton, NJ: Princeton University Press.

Index

activists 45, 99, 114, 116, 121, 124, 149, 153; killing of 101
Adivasis 98–9, 115, 237
adult education 61; radical 41–2. *See also* education
affirmation 10, 151
affirmative action 110, 113–15, 117–18, 120–2, 125–8; policies of 110, 113–14, 121, 125, 127–8
agency 10, 32, 119, 121, 150
ahimsa (non-violence) 171, 189–91, 222, 224–5, 238; reconstructing concept of 190
Ambedkar, B.R. 76, 175, 228; adoration of 2; as Babasaheb xxviii–xxix; as Bhim xxv–xxviii; birth of 31; as Bodhisatta xxix–xxxi; caste identity on 3; as Chairperson of Constitution Drafting Committee xxiv; at Columbia University xxvi, 177; and concept of freedom 109; constituency of 90; on Constitution 93; and democracy 77; Dewey, Gramsci, and 52–63; education of xxv, xxvii, 32, 54, 176; educational thoughts of 45; educational work of 44; as faculty of Sydenham College xxvi; and Gandhi on caste 220–8; and Gramsci 31, 33, 47–8, 51, 67–8; intellectual career of 131, 134–8; Kadam on 178; as law minister xxix–xxx; legal practice of xxvii; life story of xxiv, xxiv–xxxii, 178; at London School of Economics (LSE) xxvi; as *marga-data* 3; as member of Legislative Assembly of Bombay Province xxvii–xxviii; as Parsi seeking accommodation xxvi; politics and 149; pragmatism of 176; recognition for framing Indian Constitution 175; as representative of Depressed Classes 109; resigning from Nehru Cabinet xxx; scholarship from Sahu Maharaj of Baroda 196; as sociologist 199, 215; working for Baroda State xxvi; writings of xxxv–xxxvi, 135, 193, 200, 244–5, 260
Ambedkar–Gandhi debate xxxv, 162, 219, 225–8
Ambedkarites xxiv, xxix, 34, 92, 160, 197
American Pragmatism 59, 176–9, 193; Dewey and 176

Annihilation of Caste xxiv, xxviii, 58, 63, 133–9, 153, 157, 161–2, 183–7, 200–4, 208, 254, 259; three principles in xxxiv
antagonism 64, 151
anti-colonialism 154, 199, 210, 216
anti-imperialism 209, 211
assimilation 154, 161
atrocities 2, 102, 116, 172, 237

backward classes 2, 11, 160. *See also* Other Backward Classes (OBCs)
Baldacci, M. 35–9, 41, 60
Bergson, Henri xxxv, 196–8, 201, 208–13, 215
Bergsonian endosmosis, Howe on 214–15
Besant, Annie 229
Bharatiya Janata Party (BJP) 84
Bose, Subhas Chandra 1, 230
Brahmanism 86; hegemony of 155; social order of 172
Brahmins xxx, 1, 6–7, 27, 46, 112, 164–5, 200, 220–1
British rule. *See* colonialism
Broccoli, Angelo 38–9
Buddha 2–3, 18–19, 77, 84–5, 133–4, 144–6, 166, 171, 190, 261; as anti-authoritarian 145; doctrines of 189; teachings of 84, 134, 144, 190
Buddha and His Dhamma, The xxxi, 84, 144–6, 153, 166, 171, 189, 191
'Buddha and Karl Marx' xxiv, 144
Buddhism xxxi, xxxiv, 7, 18, 44, 84, 86, 112, 132–4, 143–6, 150, 166–7, 182, 190–3, 261–2; as alternative to Hinduism xxxi; Ambedkar and 54; Charvaka school of 112; conversion to xxxi; as ideal religion 134; *maitri* in 145, 147, 167; as 'truly egalitarian' 18

Buddhist 83, 85–6, 91, 132–4, 140, 144, 147, 149, 163, 166, 192; sanghas 86, 91
Buttigieg, Joseph 41–2

capitalism 44, 104
caste xxxvi, 3–6, 8, 27–9, 44–5, 58, 111–12, 117–19, 136–9, 151, 161–2, 164–5, 169–70, 182–3, 186, 199–201, 220–7, 232–5, 237, 256–61; Charvaka school attack on 112; as 'closed corporations' 4; consciousness 18, 225, 236, 259–60; in democracy 44; Dirks on 117; Gandhi on 223–4; hierarchies in 4, 112, 118, 126, 164, 172, 205; injustice 184; movements 161; reform 226; 'rigidification' of 165; segregation of 169; separation 185; structure 104, 159, 237
caste Hindus 4, 7–8, 11, 14–15, 17, 25–7, 58, 115–16, 227, 252; untouchabiity and 8
caste system 3–4, 6, 8, 16, 18, 26–7, 55–8, 88, 109, 111–12, 155–8, 164–6, 181–3, 200–2, 222–4; compartmentalization in 23; eradication of 28; exclusionary 111; Gandhi and 221–2; inequality in 223; six features of 4–5
casteism 3, 164, 233–5
Chatterjee, Partha 64, 155, 198
civil: disobedience 96, 230; liberties 138; rights 113, 151, 197; society 115, 124
class struggles 13, 44, 126, 151, 154, 170, 222, 226; as 'struggle of hegemonies' 37
collective: action 114, 117, 158; freedom 160; solidarity 2, 17; thinkers 33, 43, 50–2, 63, 68

colonial: domination of 151, 162, 171; injustice by 150, 152, 158–9, 172; State 158–9, 200
colonialism 53, 56–7, 67, 88, 99, 109, 149, 155–61, 172, 200, 233
Columbia University xxvi, 175–7, 196–7, 199, 203, 211, 253, 259
Communal Award xxviii, 14–15
communication xxxvii, 55, 176, 181, 203–4, 206, 215, 245, 253, 255–6, 259; and advocacy 192; Ambedkar and 258–60; Dewey and 183, 208; as educative 55; endosmosis as 215–16; and experiencing emotion 259–60; liberalism and 205; for 'notional sense' 256; and political emotion xxxvii, 245; for social change 192
communism 179, 206
communists 27, 81, 100–1
companion, concept of 118–19, 123–4. *See also* 'fellow feeling'
compensation 88, 121–2, 125–6, 159–60
compensatory discrimination 121; Galanter and 118
conceptualization 109, 125, 158, 234, 244, 254–5, 265–6
Congress xxiv, xxvii, xxx, 15, 27, 64, 90, 97, 228–31, 238, 255; Hindus and 231
consciousness xxxii, 5, 32, 34, 80, 162, 204–5, 212–14, 216, 260; Bergson on 213; and materialism 132
Constituent Assembly 15, 22, 78, 90–2, 95, 97, 103, 141–2, 149, 168, 236; State socialism and 89
Constitution of India xxviii–xxx, 19, 21, 76, 87–9, 91–9, 101, 103–4, 113–15, 117–18, 121–3, 126–8, 131–2, 156–7, 160–1, 175, 236–8; and Ambedkar 91–3; Chairman of Drafting Committee of xxiv, 90–1, 198; Preamble to 21

constitutional: equality 126; law 87–9, 103; morality 94
constitutionalism 157, 161
conversion 15–18, 29, 58, 66, 150, 163, 169, 255, 261–2; to Buddhism 150
customs 10, 58, 165, 188

Dalit/Dalits 2–3, 9–12, 14, 23, 25–7, 33–4, 44–5, 48, 50–1, 65–6, 68–9, 98–9, 102, 110–16, 127–8, 153–5, 171–2, 175–6, 179, 235–7; activism 69; basic amenities and households of 237; biographies 114; burning of women and children of 102; education and 32; and entrepreneurship 115; gaining prominence xxvii; in government services 236; intellectuals 114; and Kilvenmeni incident 102; labelling as 175; leaders 3, 153–4, 158, 162; liberation 2; literary works 115; literature 23, 34; massacre of 102; middle class 114; mobilization of 117; movement 114, 116, 148; and political power (*sattaa*) 47; politics 23, 154; in private sector 237; public services and 237; rape victims 102; self and society 52; as 'Slaves of slaves' 65; stoning at bridegroom of 116; struggle 153; students 116, 185; subjectivity 150–2, 154, 157; Swaraj 66, 68; three-fold injustice on 111; women 33, 43–5, 48, 50, 52; women writers 33; women's education and 44, 48, 50–1, 69, 156, 243
degradation 7, 9, 96, 171, 220, 261
democracy xxiii–xxiv, 12, 32–4, 42–3, 60–1, 76–88, 93–8, 100–1, 103–5, 118, 122, 142, 161, 168, 180–4, 191–3, 196, 203–4, 206–8;

Index

bourgeois 103, 155; concept of 56, 60, 76–7, 80, 87, 103, 182; deliberative 86; denial of 100; economic 81, 87–8, 90, 96, 98, 103; educating to 34–43; egalitarian 126; elections in 85; of ethical code 86; as 'good society' 77; Gramsci and 60; as ideal 135; interrogating of 98–9; parliamentary 78, 81–2, 89, 91; political 22, 45, 48, 81–2, 87, 96–8, 104, 141, 143; social 45, 79, 81, 88, 95–6, 103–4, 143; for successful 93–5; Urbani on Gramsci's 37
Democracy and Education 53–4, 57–8, 180–7, 207–8
democratic: government 78–9; intellectual 32, 50–1, 63; polity xxxvi, 12, 154, 164, 243–4; process 32; republic 77, 99–100; right to participate in process of 51; socialism in 97; society 170
democratization xxix, 155; of water, Ambedkar as father of xxix
depressed classes xxviii, xxxi, 17, 95, 109, 151, 156, 159–60, 164, 166, 169
Dewey, John xxvi, 46, 52–63, 176–7, 179–80, 183–4, 196–7, 201, 203, 215, 253, 255, 259–60, 262, 264; conception of education 208; 'democratic ideal' of 58, 183; democracy and 61; and 'method of democracy' 60; philosophy and 83; pragmatism of 62, 83; Ambedkar and pragmatism of 179; and James 210; writings of 180; Siegfried on 62
Dewey–Gramsci connection 52–63
dhamma (justice) xxxi, 18, 84, 140, 144–7, 153, 166, 171, 189, 191
dictatorship 36, 89, 96
dignity 10, 34, 112, 116, 150, 156, 257

Directive Principles of State Policy 91, 97–8
Dirks, Nicholas 117, 200
disadvantaged 48, 110, 118, 125–7, 157, 171
discrimination 112, 117, 127, 150–2, 159–60, 220, 222–4, 234–5, 237–8, 254, 257; Bhakti movement against caste-based 112; by caste 69, 112, 117, 153–7, 159, 220, 224, 227, 231–2, 237, 257; Gandhi and caste-based 220; institutionalized social 111
dissenting, decimation of 99–101
diversity 163, 248–9, 259, 264
dominant groups 21, 65, 158
domination 7, 10, 23, 37, 69, 97, 158–9; principle of 149
drinking water xxv, xxix; denial of xxix
Du Bois, W.E.B. xxxv, 199
Dussel, Enrique 68–9

economic: deprivation 111; democracy 87–90; equality 19, 24, 79, 139; inequalities xxxi, 81–2, 91, 104; power 7, 19
economy, planned 19
education xxv, xxvii, 34–5, 41–8, 50–1, 53–4, 56–8, 60–2, 64, 68–9, 118–19, 155–6, 176–7, 181–7, 207; access to 155; of Buddhism xxxi; of Dalits 34; Dewey and 56; formal xxvii, 58, 62; free and compulsory primary 19; Gandhi on 224; Gramsci and power of 34–43; policies 33; punishment for seeking 46; role of 53; as task for Dalits 69; as tool 32; traditional places for 56; of weaker sections 33; women/girls xxx, 33
education to democracy 43–52
educational relationship, and fundamental power to think 35, 38

educational system 33; Buttigieg on Gramsci and 42
educational thought 45; of Ambedkar 49; Gramsci and pedagogic- 41
egalitarianism 122, 126, 154, 187, 211; modern 216; radical 155, 209
electoral politics 98, 115; system 104, 171
elite 22, 28, 35, 52, 154; Brahmanical 154; middle-class 154
emancipation 9, 17, 39, 46, 51, 53, 55, 95, 252, 258; strategy for 27
Emerson, R.W. 92, 167
empiricism xxxv, 199, 209–10, 212
endosmosis xxxv, 196–8, 201, 205–8, 213–16; to 'annihilate' caste 216
enlightenment 55, 146, 172; values 87
equality 19–24, 77–81, 93–4, 96, 103, 113–15, 118–20, 122–6, 128, 131–4, 136–9, 141–2, 144–5, 147, 151, 155–6, 159–61, 169, 178–9, 192–3; Ambedkar on 156; concept of 78, 118, 122–3, 156; formal 118, 121, 157; Gandhi on 226; liberal 155–6; of opportunity 156; principle of 138, 159; violation of right to 123
ethical: agents 152, 163, 167; code 85–6; presuppositions 163
Eurocentrism 66, 149
exclusion xxv, 19, 32, 69, 103, 112, 161, 165, 171, 175, 234
exploitation 33, 99, 138, 158

'fellow feeling' 8, 12, 17, 20, 23–4, 137, 142, 145
Foucault 46, 48, 60
fraternity 19–22, 24, 28–9, 77–80, 84, 86, 96, 103, 105, 132–4, 136–7, 141–5, 147, 169, 178–9
free social order 137, 141, 251–2

freedom 63, 66, 81, 109–10, 138, 151, 159–60, 165, 167, 171, 179; of speech 99, 145–6; of thinking 145
French Revolution xxxiv, 19, 77, 133–4, 178
fundamental rights 91, 98, 114, 139, 160, 236

Gandhi xxviii, xxx, xxxv–xxxvi, 1, 3, 11, 14–17, 25–6, 45, 47, 63–5, 90–1, 99–100, 137–9, 162, 137–9, 171, 219–35, 238, 255, 258; and Ambedkar, feud between 63–5, 91, 226; on Ati-shudras 227; campaign against untouchability 26, 64, 230–1; caste-based discriminations 220; on caste system and Hinduism 222, 224; and Congress 64, 228–30; and Dewey, re-education 63–9; fast unto death by 65; 'Harijan Tour' of 231–2; and Hinduism 230, 233; influence of Ambedkar on 223, 226–7; and inter-caste marriages 227; at Lahore Congress 230; orthodox Hindus and 17; Quit India Movement by 100
Giddings, Franklin Henry 204, 253
Good Society 163–73
goodwill 14, 78, 110
governance 86–7, 92–3, 158, 160
Gramsci, Antonio 32, 38, 47, 50; and Ambedkar as collective thinkers 33–4, 47, 52–63, 68; birth of 31; and Dewey 59–61; and education 41, 47; 'Italian experience' of 42; pedagogy and 36, 42; on power of State 37; *Prison Notebooks* of 34, 39, 59; on schooling and education 34–5; Thomas on texts of 40

Harijan tour 231–2
Hegelian 59, 61

hegemony 35–9, 41, 153; concept of 36–8, 41; emergency of 38; intellectuals and 39; relationship in 37–8; struggle for 34–43
Hegemony and Pedagogy 35–6
high-caste Hindus 156, 185, 224, 228, 232, 235
Hindu Mahasabha xxx, 232
The Hindu Social Order 6, 11, 134, 136–41
Hindu *svaraj* 64, 66
Hinduism xxviii, xxxi, 17–18, 55, 57, 132, 136–7, 154, 157–8, 161–2, 169, 171, 224–5, 230–1, 261; and absence of modern political beliefs 161; essentials for 137; Gandhi on 222, 224, 231–2; purification of 155; structural violence in 171; wholesale construction of 154
Hindus 4, 6–8, 11, 13–15, 17, 25–7, 56, 58, 115–16, 168, 224, 226–8, 231–3, 235, 251–2; definition of 6; as majority 12, 15, 25; myths of 154; reformist phase of 132; religion of 26, 28, 143, 157, 165, 189; as society 2–3, 5–6, 8–9, 11–12, 16–18, 22, 26–7, 151, 155, 159, 164; tradition of 54, 182, 188
human beings 8, 116, 120, 123, 125, 128, 138–9, 141, 164–5, 169–70, 172, 212, 214; as creative agent 87; moral equality as characteristic of 139
human dignity 87; untouchability against 26
human personality 43, 140–1, 258
human rights 97, 216; Žižek on 64
humiliation xxv, 69, 117, 125, 166, 171

identities 8, 29, 150, 161, 163; caste 150; communitarian 154; as group 153

imperialism 88. *See also* colonialism
impurity 46, 112
inclusionary exclusion 236
independence 2, 53, 84, 97, 100, 102, 159, 202, 206
Independent India 19, 45, 68, 98, 110, 113, 116–17, 127, 197, 220, 234
Independent Labour Party xxviii–xxix, 11, 19; bill on 'birth control' by xxix
Indian National Congress (INC) 149, 158, 160
Indian Political Theory 63, 66, 172
'indirect liberty' 244, 249–50, 252, 256, 261
individualism 61, 83, 137, 173; moral 149
inequality 3–5, 18–19, 21–4, 62, 81–2, 96, 113, 117–18, 123, 158, 160, 231, 233; abolition of privileges as 78; inherent in four-caste system 223; struggle against xxxi
injustice 24, 110, 110–13, 116–18, 128, 158–9, 165, 187, 244; historical 109–11, 117, 123–8, 151, 159, 172; neo-colonial 172; social 33, 54, 187, 244; untouchability as historical 113
intellectuals 32–4, 39–40, 42, 51, 56, 69
inter-caste marriage xxx, 203, 227
intra-caste inequality 121
isolation of caste 25, 125, 186, 201, 207

Jaffrelot, Christophe 198
'Jai Bhim!', cry of xxix
James, William xxxv, 177, 197–8, 201, 208–13, 216; and anti-colonialism 210; radical empiricism of 210

Jat-Pat-Todak Mandal, Ambedkar at 161, 201–2
Jaykar, M.R. 1, 90
Jodhka, Surinder S. 112
justice xxiv–xxv, xxxi–xxxii, xxxvi–xxxvii, 24, 27, 118, 136, 155–6, 159–60, 170, 172, 201–2, 244–5, 258, 260; concept of xxiii, xxxii, 118

Kabir, Sharada. *See* Savita Ambedkar
Kadam, K.N. 77, 203
Kantian: liberal tradition 245; republican theory 264
karma doctrine 8–9
Kashmiri students, on sedition charges 99
Khalid, Omar 100
King Jr, Martin Luther 2–3
knowledge, exclusion of Dalits from 46
Kumar, Kanhaiya 100

labour rights xxviii–xxix
law 20–1, 24, 86, 88–9, 94, 98–9, 101–2, 113, 115–17, 124, 127, 192, 224–5, 234, 236–7; exploitation of 102
Lenin 36, 38
liberal democracy 216
liberalism 44, 87, 150, 160, 205, 215
liberation xxxi, 11–12, 15, 27, 50, 155
liberty 19–22, 77–9, 81, 89, 96, 98–9, 128, 131–4, 136–8, 141–2, 145–7, 169, 178–9, 192–3; classification of 138; concept of 78, 138, 145; denial of 77, 99, 128; equal 139, 142; political 138; as right to life 138
Lincoln, Abraham 76, 78; and 'Negroes question' 63

lower castes 4, 116, 154–5, 164, 171, 257; atrocities on 116; representations of 171; rights of 154; violence against 164

Mahad public tank well, arrest for drinking from xxix
Mahadevan, Kanchana 261
Mahars xxv, xxix, 1, 148
majority 12–16, 28–9, 83, 85, 88–9, 93, 95, 103, 192, 255; as communal 88; principle of rule of 12; seats in legislature 13
Malviya, Madan Mohan 229
Manusmriti xxx, 136, 189, 203; burning of xxvii, 17
Maoists 99–100; labelling as 99
marginalization 151–2, 159
Marxism xxviii, 11, 24, 36, 58–9, 64, 80, 84, 119, 123, 146; communist model and 86; and Pragmatism, Liguori on 59; 'species being' of 79
mass: conversions 18; movements 155
Milind College, Aurangabad 180
Mill, John Stuart 20
minorities xxiv, xxxi, 12–15, 20–1, 39, 85, 88, 95, 128, 257, 264; resistance of 13
mobilization: civil society for 115; political 113, 124, 127
modernity, colonial 151–3, 157–62, 166, 234
moral: equality 139; idealism 87; imagination, collective creation of 25; norms 113, 148, 150
morality 18, 140, 145, 149, 158, 162, 189, 203, 211, 224
Mountbatten, invalidating Ambedkar for Constituent Assembly 90

Mukherjee, Arun 185, 201, 203–4, 206–8
Muslims 14, 29, 98, 255; population of 13

Nagappa, Sardar 15–16
Naidu, Sarojini 229
national movement 151, 153, 228, 231; Hinduization of 231
nationalism 20, 151, 153, 160; political 155
nationalists 153–4, 160
nationalization 19, 88–9
nationhood 20, 23–5
Nehru, Jawaharlal xxx, 1, 3, 90, 92, 175, 234
Nehru, Motilal 229–30
Non-cooperation Movement 96, 228–9

Objective Resolution 89–90
On the Margins of History 32, 49
'one man, one value' 19, 22, 96
'one vote, one value' 13
oppressed groups 5, 11. *See also* subaltern classes/groups
oppression 21–2, 58, 62, 98, 100, 122, 185–6, 188–9, 251, 262; caste 58, 185–6, 189
Other Backward Classes (OBCs) 2, 18, 160
outcaste 111, 115, 224

Paik, Shailaja 45–51, 69; on Gramsci's concept of 'praxis' 47; and Gramsci's education 45
Patel, Vallabhbhai 92
Patel, Vithalbhai 229–30
pedagogy 35–6, 40, 42, 54, 209; relationship in 37–40
Peirce, Charles S. 83, 177
peoples' movements, suppression of 101
perfectionism 152, 163, 167–8, 170

Periyar 166
phases 124, 132–3, 221–2; Buddhist 132–4, 140, 144, 147; reformist 133; of transition 132
Philosophy of Hinduism 136–8, 140–1, 167
Phule, Jotirao xxv, 46–8, 50, 162, 166; opening schools for Dalits and women 46
political: absolutism 157; communities xxiii, 40; consensus 123, 125–8; emotions xxxvii, 244–5, 253; institutions 124, 161, 163, 171; intervention 124; philosophy 34, 86, 149, 161, 172, 177, 183, 265; power xxiii, 9, 11–12, 19, 40, 47, 65, 95, 103, 109–10, 157; reforms 104, 159, 172; revolutions 11, 80, 202, 223
political theory xxxv, 3, 66, 123, 125, 154, 163, 199, 201, 209, 265–6; contemporary 111; Indian 66, 172; Kantian 245; liberal 24, 170, 264; transatlantic 64, 265–6
pollution 4, 6, 18, 111–12, 120. *See also* impurity
Poona Pact 65, 231
population policy xxix
poverty xxix, 44, 62, 69, 138
power xxiii, 7, 9–14, 19, 28, 34–7, 47, 50–1, 65, 80, 92, 94–6, 103, 109–10, 157–8; informal configurations of 153–7; seizure of 80; sharing of 12–13
pragmatism xxxv, 59, 62, 83, 92, 193, 197, 199, 201, 209, 211; Fish on 211
prejudices 13, 84
protection 21, 186, 249, 253
public: association 256; conscience 8, 20, 95, 114; presence xxxvii, 245, 255, 258, 264

Public Participation in the Substantive Formulation of Rights 263–4

Queen, Christopher 53–4, 180

racism 60–3, 67, 120
Rai, Lala Lajpat 229
Rajagopalachari, C. 1
Ramabai, Pandita xxv, 166
Rashtriya Swayamsevak Sangh (RSS) 232
Rathore, Aakash Singh 33, 63–7, 69
rationalism xxxi, 210
rationality 82–7, 247
Rawls, John xxxvi, 64, 244–7, 253, 262; and framework for self-respect xxxvi, 244–5, 252, 254, 260
reasoning 67–8, 123–4, 232, 244, 248. *See also* rationality
recognition 10, 51, 53, 113, 115–16, 118–20, 122, 124, 126–8, 171–2, 175, 245–7, 255–8, 261, 263; denial of 116, 124, 126; ideas of xxxvii; lack of 247; need for 172; notional sense of 256; political 63; right to 128; social and political 53, 110
reconstruction 52, 54, 56–7, 180, 182, 184–6, 191, 193, 207, 209, 253, 255, 260–2; of world 45
redistributive justice 113–20, 122–6, 128; conceptualization of 125; equality and 120–7
reductionism 140, 142
reformers xxv, 153, 155, 185; liberal 153
religion 17–19, 26, 44, 55–6, 77, 103–4, 118–19, 132–3, 136, 140, 143, 147, 157, 164, 168–9, 187–9, 193, 223–4, 227; criteria for criticism of 136; discrimination by 181; as ideal 133–5, 140, 143, 147

'Religion of Principle' 187–93
'religion of rules' 189; for abolition of 163
representation 13–14, 27, 65, 104, 119, 151, 158–9, 171, 208, 213, 264
representatives 14–16, 64, 77, 88, 97, 171, 228
Republican Party of India xxx, 11, 19
resentment 14, 128, 167, 236
reservations 27, 113, 127, 160, 173, 236; social policy of 12, 27, 160
resolutions 90, 92, 155, 229, 238, 254–5
revolution 80–1, 89, 96, 144, 210
Riddles in Hinduism xxx, 141, 143–5
rights xxviii, xxx, 19, 97, 99, 110, 125–6, 145, 148, 154–5, 159–61, 233, 252–3, 263; Dalit women and 50; equality of 19, 118, 179, 182; formulation of 263–4; of lower castes 154; vs national security 99; to women xxx; of workers 19
riots, caste-based 115
Robinson, James Harvey xxvi, 176, 196
Rodrigues, Valerian 196
Round Table Conference (RTC) xxiv, xxviii, 1, 15, 65, 109, 230–1; representing depressed classes at xxviii; separate electorate issues at 14
Roy, Arundhati 114
Rule of Law 101–3, 236
Russell, Bertrand 59

salvation 65, 157, 166
satyagrahas xxvii, 64, 92, 96–7; march to Mahad (1927) xxvii
Savarkar, V. xxx
Savita Ambedkar xxvi, xxx, 176
Scheduled Castes (SCs) 2, 11, 13–14, 16, 33, 98, 118, 160, 226, 236
Scheduled Tribes (STs) 33, 98, 160

schooling 42; Ambedkar on 45, 47, 149; Gramsci on 34–6, 47. *See also* education; pedagogy
sedition charges 99–100
self-consciousness 4, 23, 38–9, 61
self-mastery xxxvii, 245, 255–6, 260–2
self-reliance 43–52, 83
self-respect xxxvi–xxxvii, 9–10, 17, 24, 43, 51–2, 120, 150, 243–9, 252–66; denial of 256; of minorities 257; and notional recognition 245, 255–8; Rawls and 244–8
Seligman, Edwin xxvi, 176, 196
separate electorate xxviii, 14–16, 25, 27, 29, 65–6; Gandhi against 14
servility xxxvi, 243–4, 252, 265
sexism 62, 67
shame xxxvi, 26, 167, 243–4, 246–8, 253, 265; Rawls on 247
shared: collective identity 24; common sense 82, 84
Shastras 45–6, 170, 185, 223
Shotwell, James xxvi, 176, 196–7
Shudras 45–6, 200, 220, 223, 228; degradation of 220
Siddharth College, Mumbai 179–80, 192
Sikhism 18, 112
slavery 9, 117, 170, 249–51; perpetual 157
social 87–90; change 122, 154, 159, 171, 184, 192, 203; conformism 37; contacts 18, 207; Darwinism 205; efficiency 204–5; endosmosis 169, 196, 201, 206–8, 214–16, 260; equality 17, 19, 24, 138, 257; ethics 18, 85; groups 4, 39, 49, 157, 161, 164, 183, 205, 207–8; injustices and Gandhi 221; life 80, 145–6, 158, 168; justice 33, 109–10, 150–2, 154, 160–1, 170, 172–3, 178–9, 192–3;

mobility 156; movements 122, 124, 128, 202; negativity 244–5; philosophy 19, 25, 77, 133–4; positions 7, 150; psychology xxxv, 3, 5, 201, 253; reform movements 112; reformers xxv, 155; reforms xxviii, 104, 170, 192; revolution 9, 238; transformation xxxvi, 28, 80–2, 132, 168, 233
social order 5–6, 87, 162; Brahmanical 172; Hindu 6, 11, 134, 136–41; injustice embedded in 111; sacredness of 170; trio of principles and 143
socialism 19, 27, 44, 80–1, 89, 91, 97–8
society as ideal xxxiv, 134–6, 169, 182, 205, 207
Southborough Committee xxiv, xxvii, 181, 206, 259
State 65, 89; emancipatory role of 28; and society 22, 28
State Socialism 19, 88–9, 97, 103; proposal of Ambedkar for 97
States and Minorities xxiv, 88
Stroud, Scott 53–4, 175
'struggle of hegemonies' 37, 50, 58
subaltern classes/groups 32–5, 36–7, 39–41, 45, 47–9, 56, 65, 67–9, 158; collective will of 43; democratic emancipation of 40; education and 46; Gramsci on 49; position of 158; refiguring the 40; subjectivity of 34
subordinate groups 160; Gramsci on 65
subordination 39, 54, 65, 159, 251; culture of 55
Swaraj 63–6, 154, 171, 227, 255

temple-entry campaigns 46, 56, 115–16, 232; Kalaram Temple satyagraha xxvii; satyagrahas as 16–17

terrorists 100; labeling as 98
three principles, interrelation among 140–3; justification of 139–40
Tilak, Bal Gangadhar xxvii, 47, 228
Togliatti 36; Palmiro, proposal for 'Leninist Gramsci' 36
trio of principles 141–2, 147; analysis of 142; in Buddhism 143–4; theorization of 133
Tufts, James H. 187–8, 190

Uber, Roberto 58–9
underprivileged 79
unequal societies 4, 97, 123
untouchability xxxvi, 3–16, 22–3, 25–7, 32–3, 53, 62, 111–17, 157–9, 220, 222–3, 226, 230–2, 249–50, 252; analysis of 9; eradicating 27, 222; eradication of 23, 27–8, 222; evidence of 116; Gandhi and 16, 64, 226; justification of 7; origins of 6–7
untouchable xxiv–xxv, xxviii, 5–10, 12, 14–18, 25–7, 55, 58, 64, 175–6, 228–9, 231–5, 249–52, 254–5, 257–8; plight of xxviii; separate electorates for xxviii; and votes 15
upper castes 27, 56, 58, 110, 112, 116, 125, 153–4, 235, 237, 251–2, 258, 263
urban spaces 159, 234–5
Urbani, Giovanni 36–9

Valmiki, Omprakash 115
varna system 162, 221–7, 232; Gandhi on 221–2, 227; vedic theory of 225

varnashrama 221–3, 228; Gandhi on 226
Vedic Hinduism 261–2
Velaskar, Padma 44–5
Vemula, Rohith 69
vested interests 29, 89, 97
victimhood 23, 126
victims 24, 93, 121, 125; and condition of social position 7; degradation on 24; and false consciousness 27; and fellow feeling 24; law and protection against 21; social construction of 121; 'social death' for slavery 117
village 7, 28, 115–16, 149, 231, 233–5; access to wells in 115; Ambedkar on 233, 235; as colonialism of Hindus 233–4; Gandhi on 234–5; panchayats 91
violation 99, 113, 123, 126
violence 11, 81, 96, 164, 170–1; against Dalits 65, 171–2; Ambedkar and 164, 171; and colonial injustice 152; on Hindu religion, lower castes and 164; on subordinate groups 160; Weberian State and 237

West, Cornel 58–9
Who Were the Shudras 220
Wolff, Jonathan 119
women: empowerment of xxx; Phule for upliftment of 48; rights to xxx

Young, Iris Marion 111, 128

Zelliot, Eleanor 155, 176

Editor and Contributors

Editor

Aakash Singh Rathore is the author of *Ambedkar's Preamble: A Secret History of the Constitution of India* (2020) and a regular contributor to the *Indian Express* and *Outlook* magazine. Rathore has taught at Jawaharlal Nehru University (JNU), University of Delhi, and Jindal Global University, India; Rutgers University and University of Pennsylvania, USA; University of Toronto, Canada; Humboldt University of Berlin, Germany; and Libera Università Internazionale degli Studi Sociali (LUISS) Guido Carli, Italy.

His twenty previous books range in theme from political philosophy, law, and religion to literature, sports, and wine. These include *Hegel's India: A Reinterpretation, with Texts* (2017) and *B.R. Ambedkar's The Buddha and His Dhamma: A Critical Edition* (2011). He is also the author of the forthcoming book, *B.R. Ambedkar: A Biography*.

Contributors

Neera Chandhoke is a professor (Retd.) of political science at the University of Delhi, India. She is also the author of *Democracy and Revolutionary Politics* (2015), *Contested Secessions: Democracy, Rights, Self-Determination and Kashmir* (2012), *The Conceits of Civil Society* (2003), *Beyond Secularism: The Rights of Religious Minorities* (1999), and *State and Civil Society: Explorations in Political Theory* (1995).

Pushparaj Deshpande is the managing trustee and director of Samruddha Bharat Foundation, New Delhi, India. He has worked on legislation and policy with various legislators and with the Rajiv Gandhi Foundation. He has also worked alongside a political consultancy, Rajya Sabha TV, and a national political party. He also writes columns for diverse publications. He has attended Wolfson College, Oxford University, UK, and St. Stephen's College, University of Delhi, India.

J. Daniel Elam is an assistant professor in the Department of Comparative Literature at the University of Hong Kong, China. He has written extensively about South Asian anti-colonial thought. He is the co-editor, with Kama Maclean and Chris Moffat, of two volumes on revolutionary anti-colonialism, *Revolutionary Lives in South Asia* (2014) and *Writing Revolution* (2017). He is also the author of *World Literature for the Wretched of the Earth* (forthcoming).

Pradeep Gokhale is an adjunct professor in the Department of Pali at Savitribai Phule Pune University, India. He was also a professor in the Department of Philosophy at Savitribai Phule Pune University, India. He is the author of *Inference and Fallacies Discussed in Ancient Indian Logic* (1992), *Vadanyaya of Dharmakirti: The Logic of Debate* (1993), *Hetubindu of Dharmakirti: A Point on Probans* (1997), *Lokayata/Carvaka: A Philosophical Inquiry* (2015) and *The Yogasutra of Patanjali: A New Introduction to the Buddhist Roots of the Yoga System* (2020). He has also co-authored *Recollection, Recognition and Reasoning: A Study in the Jaina Theory of Paroksha Pramana* (2011) with S.S. Antarkar and Meenal Katarnikar; edited *The Philosophy of Dr. B.R. Ambedkar* (2008); and co-edited *Studies in Indian Moral Philosophy: Problems, Concepts and Perspectives* (2002) with S.E. Bhelke and *Buddhist Texts and Traditions* (2015) with Mahesh Deokar and Lata Deokar.

Bhikhu Parekh is a fellow of the Royal Society of Arts, London, UK, and of the Academy of the Learned Societies for Social Sciences, London, UK, and professor of political philosophy at the University of Westminster, London, UK. Parekh is the awardee of the Sir Isaiah Berlin Prize (2002), the Distinguished Global Thinker Award (2006), the Interdependence Prize from the Campaign for Democracy (2006), and the Padma Bhushan (2007). He has authored *Rethinking Multiculturalism: Cultural Diversity and Political Theory* (2000), *Gandhi* (2001), *Colonialism, Tradition and Reform* (1999), *Gandhi's Political Philosophy* (1989), *Contemporary Political Thinkers* (1982), *Karl Marx's Theory of Ideology* (1981), and *Hannah Arendt and the Search for a New Political Philosophy* (1981).

Shaunna Rodrigues is a doctoral candidate and teaching fellow at the Department of Middle Eastern, South Asian and African Studies at Columbia University, New York, USA. She holds an MA and MPhil in political studies from JNU, New Delhi, India, and a BA (Hons) in economics from St. Stephens College, University of Delhi, India. Her work examines Islamic justifications of liberal constitutionalism, intersections between Muslim and Dalit political thought in India, and processes of public formation in the Global South. Prior to graduate school, she worked in Manipur and Tripura in Northeast India and has co-authored *Growing Up in a Conflict Zone: Children Surviving Conflict in Tripura* (2016) with Melvil Pereira.

Scott Stroud is an associate professor of communication studies at the University of Texas, Austin, USA. He works in the areas of philosophy and communication, and is the author of the books *John Dewey and the Artful Life* (2011) and *Kant and the Promise of Rhetoric* (2014). He is the program director of media ethics at the Center for Media Engagement at the University of Texas, Austin, USA.

Anand Teltumbde is a civil rights activist and political analyst. He has authored many books (translated widely in most Indian languages) on peoples' movements with particular emphasis on the left and Dalit issues. His books include *Dalits: Past, Present and Future* (2016), *The Persistence of Caste: The Khairlanji Murders and India's Hidden Apartheid* (2010), *Scripting the Change: Selected Writings of Anuradha Ghandy* (2012), *Ambedkar in and for the Post-Ambedkar Dalit Movement* (1997), and *Hindutva and Dalits: Perspectives for Understanding Communal Praxis* (2005). He is a regular contributor to *Outlook India*, *Tehelka*, *Mainstream*, *Seminar*, *Frontier*, and *Economic & Political Weekly* in which he writes a regular column, 'Margin Speak'.

Vidhu Verma is professor at the Centre for Political Studies, School of Social Sciences, JNU, New Delhi, India. Her areas of research include comparative political theory, feminist political theory, State and civil society, affirmative action policies, and social justice in India. She has recently edited *Secularism, Religion, and Democracy in Southeast Asia* (2019), *State in India: Ideas, Norms and Politics* (2018), and *Unequal Worlds* (2015). She has also co-edited and contributed to the volume *Empire of Disgust* (2018). She is the author of three books, including *Non-discrimination and Equality in India: Contesting Boundaries of Social Justice* (2012), besides articles in several journals.

Cosimo Zene is professor emeritus of study of religions and world philosophies at SOAS, University of London, UK. He is the author of *The Rishi of Bangladesh* (2002) and several articles on the political philosophies of Antonio Gramsci and B.R. Ambedkar. He has also published on the interdisciplinary nature of the study of religions, on the anthropology and philosophy of 'Gift and Givenness' (ethnographic film: *The Vow* [2014]) and on inter-philosophical dialogue as foundational for world philosophies. He is currently working on two forthcoming volumes, *Gramsci on Religion* and *World Philosophies in Dialogue*, and a monograph, *Itinerary of the Gift*.